SOCIOLOGY
IN THE
PHILIPPINE SETTING

By

CHESTER L. HUNT
RICHARD W. COLLER
SOCORRO C. ESPIRITU
JOHN E. DE YOUNG
SEVERINO F. CORPUS

DEPARTMENT OF SOCIOLOGY
UNIVERSITY OF THE PHILIPPINES

ALEMAR'S
749 Rizal Avenue, Manila

ALL RIGHTS RESERVED
COPYRIGHTED 1954
BY CHESTER L. HUNT

PRINTED IN THE PHILIPPINES

FOREWORD

In 1937, Professor H. O. Beyer and Mr. Francisco Ponce, faculty members of the Department of Sociology and Anthropology at that time, had their students fill out a questionnaire to find out the students' comparative interest in the study of sociology based on Philippine or American materials. The answers of the students showed conclusively that the students appreciate and can understand better the principles of sociology when they are illustrated with Philippine rather than American materials. The title of the book, "Sociology in the Philippine Setting" is appropriate and the contents should prove interesting for they are within the experience of the students.

Like any beginner in the field of the social sciences, "Sociology in the Philippine Setting" may have its shortcomings, but its merits should not be overlooked. The collaboration among the authors, three Westerners and two Filipinos is a good team for the selection of materials for comparative purposes. The cosmopolitan character of the authorship should prove valuable also in the development of proper attitudes regarding many of the controversial points on social relations.

"Sociology in the Philippine Setting" contains a greater variety of principles of sociology than is ordinarily given to beginning students in sociology. It includes topics which are new in the development of the study of sociology. Experienced teaching and proper guidance of students in the study of this volume should make the course a good introduction for students in the field of the social sciences.

SERAFIN E. MACARAIG

Manila
April 3, 1954

PREFACE

This book has been written by sociologists in the University of the Philippines in an effort to produce a text for elementary students which would describe sociological principles in a cultural setting familiar to Filipino students. It is based on the premise that, although sociological principles have a universal application, they are best comprehended in terms of the individual's own environment. The text does not attempt to give an exhaustive analysis of Philippine social institutions, but has used materials from the local scene which illustrate the operation of social processes. Similarly, it is not a book on social problems, although certain aspects of social pathology are related to the general frame of reference. The aim of the book is to help the student begin to see his own society as part of a general social structure, in the belief that this orientation will assist him to better understand his society and to participate more effectively in social movements which are compatible with the student's values and ideals.

In the belief that many of the present tensions of society are explainable by the drift from primary to secondary groupings, we have made extensive use of the concepts of *gemeinschaft* and *gesellschaft* developed by Ferdinand Tonnies. Seeking for local equivalents of these terms, we have used for the former, the Tagalog expression *damay*, but have retained the German term *gesellschaft* as we were unable to find another local expression with a similar connotation.

Another theme which runs throughout the text is that of cultural history and cross cultural comparison. This is a method of helping the student to understand the roots of present institutions and his indebtedness to the rest of the world. It is also a technique by which the student may be assisted to analyze the nature of social differences and uniformities. While the value judgments of the authors inevitably influence their writings, no attempt has been made at special pleading in behalf of any particular cultural system. As far as humanly possible, contemporary social institutions are described objectively; leaving to the student the decision as to the type of changes, if any, which may be desirable.

The arrangement of the chapters was made with a view to the needs of the beginning student. The first three chapters attempt to furnish him with the rudiments of the concepts and vocabulary which are developed more fully in latter parts of the text. Chapters four to fifteen consider specific phases of social life, while chapter sixteen deals with an approach to social amelioration. The discussion as to the nature and role of sociology is left to the final chapter on the theory that the student is not capable of assimilating this type of discussion at an earlier stage. The authors are aware that such a text is necessarily incomplete and have provided at the end of each chapter a list of references, questions and projects designed to stimulate further study. The alert teacher will, of course, be continually adding his own study aids to those suggested.

While we have tried to write in clear and simple language, no effort has been made to avoid the usage of standard sociological terms. The acquisition of a specialized vocabulary is an important part of a student's education and we have provided a glossary to help him cope with the less familiar expressions.

The text has the strengths and weaknesses which accompany any joint endeavor, and discerning readers will notice some variation in style and emphasis in different chapters. Professor Coller is responsible for chapters 5, 6, 11 and 12. Professor de Young is the author of chapter 1 and Professor Espiritu of chapter 2. Professor Hunt has the major responsibility for chapters 3, 4, 7, 8, 9, 10, 13, 14, 16 and wrote chapters 15 and 17 in collaboration with Professor Corpus. The various authors come from both American and Filipino backgrounds and represent a variety of religious beliefs and social viewpoints. They are united by their common interest in the scientific study of society.

In addition to the authors listed, other persons have helped in the production of this text. Professor Maureen Nelson of the University of the Philippines Social Welfare Section and Professor Honesta Guiang of the College of Education gave valuable suggestions for the chapters dealing with Social Work and Rural Communities respectively. Needless to say, they should not be held responsible for the viewpoints expressed. Professor David Wico of the University History Department checked the entire manuscript and made many helpful comments. Dr. Benecio Catapusan, executive secretary of the Association of Christian Schools and Colleges and professorial lecturer in Sociology, discussed the general plan of the book and has contributed a great deal to the authors' understanding of Philippine social life. Mrs. Maria Kalaw Katigbak contributed much of the material used in the chapter on the Family, and while she does not bear responsibility for its final form, she should receive the major credit for its application to the local scene. Other parts of the manuscript were read and criticized by Professor Ricardo R. Pascual and Mr. Thomas McHale who likewise gave valuable assistance but are not to be held responsible for opinions or style of treatment. Mr. Cayetano Santiago Jr. and Miss Belen Tan Gatue were helpful in checking source material. Professor Enrique Fernando of the University College of Law gave valuable suggestions for the chapter dealing with Social Factors in Industry; like the other consultants he should not be held responsible for the opinions expressed.

Students of sociology in the Philippines will detect the influence of Professor Marcelo P. Tangco and Dr. Serafin E. Macaraig. Professor Tangco taught sociology courses for many years in addition to his work in the field of anthropology. He also collaborated with Dr. Macaraig in the 1948 revision of the latter's book. Dr. Macaraig was for many years the major professor of Sociology in this institution, and through his teaching and publishing activities has made a major contribution to the advancement of social science. The present text refers frequently to his volume, *Sociology*, which was first published in 1938. Our text was largely inspired by Macaraig's work which was the initial systematic presentation of sociological principles in a Philippine setting.

This text would not have been possible without the encouragement and support of Dr. Tomas S. Fonacier, Dean of the College of Liberal Arts of the University of the Philippines. The preparation of the manuscript for publication represents careful hours of labor by Mr. Jose P. Cruz. Finally, as is usually the case, the work of completing the book could not have been accomplished without the help of my wife who read proof, assisted in the typing and put up with a dislocation of household routine during the process.

CHESTER L. HUNT

15 May 1954
University of the Philippines.

AIDS FOR STUDENTS AND TEACHERS

The questions, projects and suggested readings at the end of the chapters and the glossary at the end of the book have been designed for the convenience of students and teachers. They are not exhaustive, but are designed to facilitate the use of the textbook. The questions are included to help the student find out whether or not he has grasped the meaning of the material covered in various chapters. If, after finishing the assigned reading, he can answer these questions, then he probably has a fair understanding of the chapter; otherwise, he should reread the chapter and then, if still in doubt, should ask the help of the instructor. The instructor may find it advisable to use these questions as the basis for the formulation of examination questions.

The projects are supplementary assignments which may be given to students. They are only suggestive and the teacher will doubtless have additional assignments which may be more pertinent in a particular area.

Students should be encouraged to use the glossary in conjunction with the reading of each chapter. In this fashion, they will gradually build up a vocabulary which will enable them to understand sociological literature.

The suggested readings are included for the guidance of both instructors and students. They may be used as additional assignments and they will help to broaden the understanding of particular types of subject matter. Most of the references included are still currently available and should be a part of any college library.

CONTENTS

I SOCIOLOGICAL FOUNDATIONS

CHAPTER 1
The Nature of Culture 1

CHAPTER 2
Nature and Role of Group Behavior 19

CHAPTER 3
Social Causation of Personality Variation 36

II THE BASIC SOCIAL INSTITUTION

CHAPTER 4
The Family 61

III COLLECTIVE BEHAVIOR

CHAPTER 5
Crowds and Publics 95

CHAPTER 6
Public Opinion, Propaganda, and Mass Interaction .. 107

CHAPTER 7
Social Class Structure 130

CHAPTER 8
Relationship of Ethnic Groups 163

CHAPTER 9
Religion and Society 204

IV COMMUNITY LIFE

CHAPTER 10
Rural Communities 234

CHAPTER 11
The Urban Community 261

V SOCIAL ASPECTS OF POPULATION

CHAPTER 12
Population Growth and Distribution 291

VI INSTITUTIONAL CHANGE AND SOCIAL WELFARE

CHAPTER 13
Social Aspects of Industrialization 326

CHAPTER 14
Agrarian Conflict 353

CHAPTER 15
Education in its Social Setting 379

CHAPTER 16
Social Work 412

VII THE FUNCTION OF SOCIOLOGY AS A SCIENCE

CHAPTER 17
The Role and Scope of Sociology 436
GLOSSARY 449

APPENDIX
Summary of the Hardie Report 465
Note on Minority Peoples in the Philippines 467
The Scope of Sociology and Fields of Specialization 470
Types of Agencies Which Employ Sociology and Social Work Majors 472

NAME INDEX 477

SUBJECT INDEX 479

CHAPTER ONE

THE NATURE OF CULTURE

"The life history of the individual is first and foremost an accommodation to the patterns and standards traditionally handed down in his community. From the moment of his birth the customs into which he is born shape his experience and behavior. By the time he can talk, he is the little creature of his culture, and by the time he is grown and able to take part in its activities, its habits are his habits, its beliefs his beliefs, its impossibilities his impossibilities."

— Ruth Benedict, *Patterns of Culture*, New York, Houghton Mifflin Co., p. 2.

The Study of Sociology

Sociology is primarily concerned with studying man in his social relationships. Two of the most important factors in social relationships are the interaction with others which takes place within the group and the culture which is transmitted by the group. The first two chapters in this book concern the nature and influence of culture and of group interaction. The third chapter considers in detail some of the variations in human conduct which develop as a result of cultural differences and group interaction. The rest of the book is devoted mainly to a further analysis of these basic themes in different institutional settings.

What is culture?

The term "culture" like many of our words has different shades of meaning depending largely on the person who is using it. In a popular sense, it is generally thought of in terms of refinement. A person who likes symphonic music, the arts, the classics, is often referred to as a person with culture. The biologist, on the other hand, may think of it in the sense of a culture as a medium in which a colony of bacteria may be grown. These are limited meanings and to the sociologist and to the student of sociology the term 'culture' carries a much broader and significant meaning.

Some sociologists, striving for a term that is not burdened with so many diverse connotations, have used the phrase "social heritage" as a synonym for culture. Culture can be defined as the sum total of the complex social heritage of a group which is created and transmitted from one generation to another. As such, culture includes non-material as well as material elements, its content ranging from the moral and religious values of a group to the physical objects which man uses to survive.

E. B. Tylor, an eminent English scholar and one of the great pioneers in the field of anthropology, first defined culture as "that complex whole which includes knowledge, belief, art, morals, law, custom, and any other capabilities and habits acquired by man as a member of society." [1]

Modern anthropologists and sociologists have rephrased and paraphrased Tylor's definition thousands of times, but all agree that the essential point of a definition of culture lies in the ability of the cultural patterns to be transmitted from one group to another.

Culture distinguishes man from animals.

In man, the family and the group are all important in preserving the life of the young and in preparing the individual for existence within his society. The young of some species of animals can fend for themselves at an early age. Left to themselves, they will survive and through instinct as well as a process of trial and error may learn the techniques necessary for existence of their kind. The young of man cannot survive if abandoned. If by some rare chance, a human infant could be kept alive in a state

---

[1] E. B. Tylor, *Primitive Culture*, Seventh edition, New York, Brentano's 1924, p. 1.

CHAPTER I. THE NATURE OF CULTURE

of nature, he could develop only into a biological human without any of the socialized attributes of his group.

Man has certain outstanding physical and mental advantages over the lower animals. Language development is the key factor in man's success in creating and preserving culture; for without language the ability to convey ideas and traditions is impossible.[2] Through language, knowledge may be perpetuated and passed on from one generation to the next. In the realm of language achievement, the animal world cannot compete. The great apes may at times make use of a rudimentary tool, which in a sense is a cultural element, but their crude communication system prevents the transmission of the idea of using the tool. Hence, every ape that does learn to use a stick as a tool, must do so through a process of individual trial and error.

The origin and development of culture depended primarily upon man's higher brain development. It is this brain development which enabled man to use tools in a meaningful way. A material culture, no matter what the degree of complexity, cannot come into being without the making and using of tools. The use of language and tool making are the two main prerequisites with which man created his culture.

Culture is learned.

Culture is the outgrowth of human society. Certain species of animals live in groups, but group living without the above characteristics does not result in culture. The behavior pattern of an animal group is largely instinctive, and any learning of social behavior can result only from imitation. Man's behavior patterns, on the other hand, are not the result of instinctive patterns, but are composed of the social habits that each new individual begins to acquire soon after birth from the other members of his group. In this respect all culture is learned. Man

---

[2] William F. Ogburn & Meyer F. Nimkoff, *Sociology* 2nd Ed., 1950. Houghton Mifflin Co., New York, p. 36.

alone is capable of passing on acquired behavior patterns to his offspring.

All peoples have culture.

A common error into which many of us fall is to think of our particular group as possessing culture or "being cultured" and others as being "uncultured". Thus we tend to look down upon peoples whose culture patterns are simpler than ours and to dismiss them as being inferior. This is a fallacious idea, for man in all societies has evolved a satisfactory social way of life. A Negrito group in the jungles of Zambales who live in a simple food-gathering and hunting pattern has "culture" in this respect just as much as does a group living in the highly industrialized urban area of Manila. The only essential difference between the culture of such a simple food-gathering people and that of a group of city dwellers lies in degree of complexity and attainment of material ways. The Australian aborigine may be able to put all his material belongings in a string net, a basket or two, which the women of his family will transport from one camp site to the next. By the standards of our complex material culture, this is a very meager type of material culture pattern. Yet in the realm of kinship organization and in mythology, the Australian aborigine reaches heights of complexity and elaborateness that makes comparable patterns in our society seem meager and undeveloped. It is very dangerous to assume, then, that degree of development of material culture also assumes limited development in other phases for the very reverse may be the case.

Culture content may vary tremendously from one group to another, but no group can exist without an intricate cultural web to hold it together.

Culture is a group product.

If an individual cannot exist outside of the group, culture, likewise, is a group product and is never produced in any society by the work of a single individual. Man

CHAPTER I.   THE NATURE OF CULTURE   5

is born into a group whose cultural patterns have been shaped over a thousand generations. Many of the patterns change or die away with time, but culture grows through accumulation and a strong pattern of continuity runs from one generation to the next.

Difference between society and culture.

Another mistake is that of confusing culture and society. In reality, each is a separate though related phenomena.

A society is a group of people bound together in a more or less permanent association who are organized for collective activity and who feel they belong together. A society is made up of individuals who are interacting to each other in a shared pattern of customs, beliefs, values, and traditions. The common pattern to which they are reacting is the culture of the society. One writer striving to put this in simple words summed up culture or shared pattern "as the cement which binds the members of the group into a living organism." [3]

Folkways.

If culture is the cement binding the society together, the behavior patterns of the group are the basic ingredients of this cement. The sociologist has devised special terms for these behavior patterns. Those types of behavior that are organized and repetitive are known to the sociologist as the "folkways" of a society. These are the group way of doing things and commonly are called 'customs'. The term 'folkways' has been given these customs from the title of a famous book on customs published in 1906 by the pioneer American sociologist, Sumner. This classic book, *Folkways*, shattered many of the popular ideas about customs and culture patterns. Sumner brought forcefully to the attention of the students of his day the important

---

[3] Stuart Chase, *The Proper Study of Mankind*. 1948, p. 61. Harper & Bros. N.Y.

fact that an infinite variety of customs exist and that these customs have a strong compulsive nature.

Any single culture has such a variety of customs or 'folkways' that simply to list them would be a monumental task. It would also be an unending task for, as we shall see later, new folkways arise, old ones may change or even die. The folkways of a group are the behavior patterns of its everyday life. The reason the sociologist adopted the use of the term 'folkway' rather than keeping the older term 'custom' was to emphasize that they were the accepted behavior way of the folk or group. Folkways involve the way we eat, how we dress, and a myriad of behavior patterns that we follow because they have been impressed upon us from the time we are born. They have been called the habits of the group and have developed through the many centuries of a group's history to meet its daily problems. Changes and additions gradually are made, for folkways adapt themselves to the conditions of life of each generation. Many of the folkways that govern you today will be quite different from those that will govern the behavior of your children. To observe changes in the folkways, all one has to do is to contrast the patterns of behavior that were followed by your parents with those that you follow at the present time. A generation ago, the folkway which involved the segregation of girls in middle class families was still strong enough to prevent many families from sending their daughters to the co-educational schools and colleges which were then just starting in the Philippines. Today co-education is an accepted folkway among many Filipinos.

As a member of a group you follow these folkways because, as the result of trial and error adjustments of the past, they are the practical solutions of daily needs. Pressures both direct and indirect operate on the individual to make him conform to these group habits. You follow customary practices so as not to be too different from the rest of your group and thus invite disapproval or ridicule. At times the social pressure that makes one conform to the folkways is so powerful that even laws will be violated if it is necessary to do so to follow the folkway.

Mores.

Certain of the customary behavior patterns or folkways fall in a special category because they have taken on a moralistic value. These special folkways which involve moral or ethical values are termed the "mores" of a society and involve respect for authority, marriage and sex behavior patterns, religious rituals, and other basic codes of human behavior. They are considered essential to the group's existence and accordingly the group demands that they be followed without question. To the group, the mores delineate the "right or proper" way to behave and behavior contrary to this right way cannot be permitted. While the term, "mores" (sing. *mos*) is simply the Latin word for custom, the sociologist has designated it as a special word for the type of folkway which is all compulsive.

A member of a group who violates the mores is antisocial. In a sense, he is an enemy of the group for he is attacking its moral and ethical foundation. Hence he must be punished and punished severely as a warning to others that such behavior will not be tolerated.

The strength of the mores is illustrated in the customary practises of certain societies which may require physical discomfort, pain, or even torture to be borne in order to carry out the mores. The scarification and teeth filing practises of primitive groups demonstrate that physical comfort is secondary to obeying the accepted customary practise. In a tribe where teeth filing practises may be found, not only will every boy and girl have to undergo this painful procedure, but they will be expected to comply without showing fear or revealing the pain they may suffer. Nor should the student think that mores of this nature operate so strongly only among primitive groups. A highly complex civilization such as that of classical Chinese society required an exceedingly painful foot binding custom to be followed with respect to girls of the upper classes. The result of tight binding of the foot from early childhood was to create a small, hoofshaped deformed foot. Through the centuries the deformed foot had come to be regarded as a sign of status as well as an element of beauty. In short, the custom had come to be regarded as the "proper" way and was followed without question and without regard for the physical pain that the small girl suffered during the years that her feet were tightly bound.

The manner in which mores can make anything seem right is seen by comparing certain moral values in a society at different periods of its history as well as comparing different societies. In most societies incest is strongly abhorred and a prohibition against this behavior exists in the mores. Breaking of the incest rule is severely punished, often by death in some simpler societies. Yet under certain circumstances and at special times the mores might operate to make incest the proper way. The required marriage of brother and sister of the royal family in such places as ancient Peru, Egypt and classical Siam illustrates the power of the mores to determine the apparent rightness of a form of conduct.

Mores, like ordinary folkways, are subject to change, although it might be said that changes in the mores generally occur more slowly than changes in the folkways. But they do change, and what may be considered right and proper at one time may be considered wrong at a later period in the same society. A common example used to illustrate this is to show how slavery at certain times in a people's history may have been considered proper and right. In the early 19th century when slavery was still legal, even the Bible was quoted to show that slavery was not only proper but was the will of God. Later the mores surrounding the slavery pattern were completely reversed so that slavery came to be considered immoral and wrong.

CHAPTER I. THE NATURE OF CULTURE 9

Mores then are extremely powerful. The important thing is that, to the members of a group following them, they are all compulsive at the time they are operative.

Mores and laws.

In certain societies many of the mores are formalized in the shape of laws. Not all laws are necessarily mores, nor are all mores part of the legal code. Ordinarily though, the laws of a nation are simply the legalizing in the form of codes or formal statutes of the ethical and moral values embodied in the mores of the group. At times in our modern society, this legal formalization of certain mores brings about a type of cultural lag. Mores tend to change and many of our modern societies have found themselves with outmoded laws which people no longer follow. At an earlier period these may have been mores and were legalized in the statutes to intensify the conformance of the group to them. As the times change, so did the mores, resulting in an outmoded law. Often these outmoded laws tend to be forgotten and may remain on the statute books for a generation or more without being repealed. Many are of a restrictive nature such as laws that forbid entertainment on Sunday, the selling of food on the Sabbath, and the like. Because of this restrictive character, these old forgotten and outmoded laws sometimes are called "blue laws". Their main significance to a student of sociology is in their eloquent testimony of how mores change over a period of time within the same society.

If the law and the mores should come in conflict, the mores prove to be the stronger. Not infrequently, we have instances where legal regulations of a group are broken without hesitation if the mores demand a different way of behavior. In the United States, a law to prohibit the sale of liquor failed to work because the use of liquor was sanctioned by the mores of a large part of the population. Another example of the inability of law to counteract the mores is seen in the failure of the Spanish attempt to force a group of the mountain people to wear trousers instead of the G-string.

Institutions.

When the folkways and mores become so integrated that activities are formalized on a unit basis, they become the institutions of a group. The family, the church, the state, and other of our institutional units result. The institutional patterns of Filipino society will be treated fully in later chapters.

Culture and the Group.

It is through the possession of a common culture that the members of a society acquire the feeling of unity which enables them to live and work together as a functioning entity. The functions that culture plays for the group have been well summarized by the Gillens who point out that culture performs several important functions in group life.[4]

1. It sets up a series of patterns for meeting the *biological demands* (primary drives) of the group members for sustenance, shelter, reproduction and protection.

2. It provides rules that enables the individual members of a group to adjust to their environmental situation. This enables the group to act as a unit whenever the situation so demands.

3. Through the common culture, the members are provided channels of interaction which help prevent conflict. It outlines for the individual the acquired needs of his group and provides for their satisfaction. The culture thus not only provides a pattern for the development of the individual but also allows a way in which the group can adjust to its basic needs.

---
[4] J. L. Gillen and J. P. Gillen, *Cultural Sociology*, New York, The MacMillan Co., 1948, p. 149.

CHAPTER I. THE NATURE OF CULTURE 11

Culture and the individual.

As pointed out in a previous paragraph, the culture provides the individual with a large number of ready made adjustments which he has only to learn. Thus the individual in most of his ordinary ways of behaving does not have to waste time in trial and error methods nor does he have to analyze and solve daily problems.

By providing a set of *"familiar stimuli* to the individual to which he has only to respond in a familiar way," a great deal of confusion in the life of the individual is prevented.[5] Ordinarily, we do not realize how significant this familiar type of response has become to our behavior. You have only to be plunged into a different culture to realize how much of your life is channelled in ready set ways. A Manila driver suddenly set down in Hongkong where the traffic is on the left side of the road, would be plunged into an unfamiliar situation and would react in a confused manner. A Filipino student attempting to board a bus in San Francisco or New York City by the center door of the bus not only would find himself in a state of confusion since the center door is used as the exit, but his action would throw the other passengers momentarily into an unfamiliar situation. Confusion and excitement would result. Our daily life flows smoothly because our culture has mapped out channels of behavior for us.

The Organization of Culture

Culture traits and culture complex.

While the culture of a group is an integrated network of folkways, mores, systems of beliefs and institutional patterns, we can break this larger total system into simple units or elements called cultural traits.[6] A culture trait, either of a material or non-material nature, represents a

---
[5] Ibid, p. 150.
[6] Linton, Ralph. *The Study of Man.* Appleton-Century, N. Y. 1936, p. 33.

single element or a combination of elements relating to a specific situation. It is a cultural element which cannot be broken down into any smaller segments. Examples of cultural traits from lowland Filipino culture would include such practices as the wearing of wooden clogs, kissing the hand of the elders after Sunday mass and the Angelus, the use of a bolo by the farmer, and countless other single acts or objects. Yet simply to list the separate traits existing in a culture would result only in an inventory which would not give an integrated picture of how the culture operates. Cultural traits do not exist as separate, unrelated entities but operate meaningfully only in relationship to others. Clusters of culture traits are known as culture complexes which in turn group together to form a culture pattern.

Cultural patterns.

The cluster of related traits that are involved in wet-rice agriculture in the Philippines is an example of a culture pattern. This wet-rice pattern represents a complex of many cultural traits, invloving the use of the carabao or water buffalo, a certain type of plow and harrow, a flooded field, a special species of rice, special methods of planting and transplanting, and a host of other traits. All these complexes of traits form an integrated pattern which results eventually in a crop of rice.

Universal or basic cultural patterns.

Although culture may vary tremendously from place to place as to its content, there are certain basic patterns common to all cultures. These uniformities are called the universal patterns of culture. Since satisfaction of the wants of men everywhere is basically the same, certain common denominators of behavior result. Man, in all societies, faces fundamental needs relating to sustenance, to procreation and to the protection of his group. Around these fundamental needs, man everywhere has built up parallel patterns of behavior. Wissler, an American an-

CHAPTER I. THE NATURE OF CULTURE

thropologist who first used the phrase the universal culture pattern, classified them into these categories.[7]

1. Speech and Language
2. Material Traits
   a. Food habits
   b. Shelter
   c. Transportation
   d. Dress
   e. Utensils, tools, etc.
   f. Weapons
   g. Occupation and industries
3. Art
4. Mythology and Scientific Knowledge
5. Religious Practises
6. Family and Social systems
7. Property
8. Government
9. War

Anthropologists have demonstrated over and over that regardless of complexity of detail, all cultures tend to conform to this fundamental plan.

Culture area.

The anthropologist has also pointed out that peoples within contiguous geographic areas or within the same general geographic area tend to possess a fairly homogeneous cultural pattern. Such a region is known as a culture area. In the culture area there may be a considerable number of independent societies but the dominant cultural pattern will always be the same. Distinct cultural areas can be depicted for the various regions of the world. The Philippines, for example, lies within a Malayan cultural area which has in common a basic wet-rice type of agriculture, the same general pattern of house type, a similar foundation of spirit worship, similar birth practises, similar

---

[7] Robert S. Park: editor, *An Outline of the Principles of Sociology*. Barnes & Noble, New York, 1946, pp. 196, 197.

ceremonies and rites devoted to rice cultivation, and a number of other similar trait complexes.

Within a culture area it may be possible to distinguish many local and national cultures, each of which may occupy a definite area of distribution. Hence the culture area does not necessarily coincide with either the geographical or dialect boundaries of a people. The Philippines and the neighboring region to the South is an excellent example of how groups with a variety of different dialects and languages can fall within one large culture area.

Within each culture area, a culture center can also be delineated. This is the part of the area where the distinctive culture patterns are the most typical and dominant, and where many of the traits and complexes first originate and from which they spread. The cultural center need not coincide with the geographical center of the area. In the Philippines, for example, it might be said that Manila and its surrounding metropolitan region could be called the culture center for the entire country. Cebu would be the culture center for the Visayan sub-area.

Culture change.

A culture is always growing, for new ideas, new techniques are added and old ways constantly are being modified or discarded. This is as true for the most isolated and simple society in the world as it is for a highly complex society. The degree of change and the rate of change may vary enormously. Change is slow in a primitive isolated society and rapid in a contemporary industrialized society. But nowhere will the culture of a group remain static. The universality of culture change is echoed in the nostalgic utterances of the elders of non-literate, remote societies who cry.

"When we were young" runs the widespread, oft-repeated plaint, "things were different. Our generation respected their elders, and knew how

Chapter I. THE NATURE OF CULTURE

to worship the gods. Today everything is changed, the young are unwilling to learn and follow."[8]

In our modern machine age civilization, the rapid changes that occur from one generation to the next are even more outstanding. Changes in a culture can be brought about by new cultural ideas either being introduced from within or from without. Those changes that occur within a society are the result of discoveries or inventions; while those from outside are brought about through the medium of culture borrowing.

All culture traits result originally from invention. A distinction sometimes is made between discovery and invention. Some writers hold that discovery is the initial perception or recognition of previously unnoticed relations between aspects of nature and their significance for human life.[9] An example of an initial discovery would be the perception of a completely new idea such as the fact that copper ore melted in a fire creates a new substance. An invention, on the other hand, is the putting together of already known elements to create a new relationship.

A number of factors exert influence on the number and type of inventions any society will produce. Since every invention involves a combination of existing culture elements, the degree of elaboration of a culture is significant. The societies with a large and complex store of culture traits obviously will have the greatest number of new inventions.

Ox drawn motorized rice mill is combination of old and new cultural traits.

Culture also grows by the spread of traits from individual to individual and from one group to another. The spread of a new cultural trait is called diffusion.

---
[8] Herskovits, M. J. "The Process of Cultural Change, p. 143. In *The Science of Man in the World Crisis.* Ed. R. Linton. Columbia University Press, N. Y. 1948.
[9] Gillen & Gillen *Op. Cit.*, p. 176.

Diffusion taking place within the group, that is from individual to individual, is sometimes called primary diffusion. Inter-group or inter-society diffusion is the passing of new traits from one society to another. The term "borrowing" is used for the group that receives the new element.

Diffusion is the principal source of culture change. Most cultures are built up through an accumulation of borrowed traits.

The borrowed trait must be adapted or fitted into the culture of the group taking it on. Those new traits which are the most readily modifiable or which meet an existing need adapt themselves quickly to the new culture. Most borrowed traits tend to undergo some modification as they are adapted into the new culture pattern. At times, though, a new trait may be taken over completely without adaptation. Present day Filipino culture is the result of the borrowing of diverse culture elements and fitting them together to form a workable unit.

Summary

Culture is that complex set of behavior patterns impressed upon the individual by his group and passed down from generation to generation through the process of interaction. All culture is learned in this sense. It includes all the material traits of a people as well as the non-material elements.

Every society has culture. Culture may differ in degree of complexity of detail but not in meeting the group's basic needs. Since man's basic needs everywhere are similar, a basic pattern of culture common to all societies has resulted. This is called the universal pattern of culture.

No single individual is ever responsible for the culture of his group. The cultural pattern in which he develops is the result of a thousand generations. Neither the individual nor the group can exist without one another.

Acting as the adhesive factor in holding the group together is the pattern of customary behavior known as the folkways and the mores. These folkways are of infinite variety and have a strong compulsive nature.

Nowhere will the culture of a society remain static. It is constantly shifting and changing to meet the demands of each generation. Culture change is adaptive so that culture in any group always tends to form a consistent and integrated whole. All the basic needs of man are satisfied by his culture.

QUESTIONS

1. In what way does culture distinguish the behavior of man from that of animals? Do animals have culture?
2. How does the culture of technologically advanced people differ from that of primitive people? Is the culture of primitive people ever complex in nature?
3. Distinguish between folkways and mores.
4. What is the relationship of law to the mores?
5. What role does culture play in the life of the group?
6. Describe what is meant by culture area. What sub-areas are present in the Philippines?

PROJECTS

1. Describe the changes in the folkways which have taken place in your home town over a period of the last fifty years. Include such matters as dress, dietary habits, relation between parents and children and patterns of education.
2. List and describe the folkways you find on the college or university campus which were not present in other communities.

SUGGESTED READINGS

All of the books suggested here are basic works which deal with the topic of culture. If this list is used for supplementary reading, the teacher should indicate which sections of the books he wishes the student to read.

Gillen J. L. and Gillen J. P. *Cultural Sociology*. MacMillan Co. N. Y. 1948.

Linton, Ralph. *The Study of Man*. Appleton-Century, N. Y. 1936.

Linton, Ralph, editor, *The Science of Man in the World Crisis.* Columbia University, N. Y. 1945.

Ogburn, William F. and Nimkoff, Meyer F. *Sociology*, 2nd Ed. 1950, Houghton Mifflin Co., N. Y.

Obrien, R. W., Schrag, C. C. and Martin W. T., *Readings in General Sociology,* Houghton Mifflin Co., N. Y. 1951.

Park, Robert E., editor. *An Outline of the Principles of Sociology.* Barnes & Noble, N. Y. 1939.

Young, Kimball. *An Introductory Sociology.* American Book Co. N. Y. 1934.

CHAPTER TWO

NATURE AND ROLE OF GROUP BEHAVIOR

It is a commonplace that we all live in social groups. Each of us is a member of from one to a hundred—family, gang, neighborhood, community, religious denomination, political party, trade union, professional association, civic league, social club, nationality; any or all of these and many others. It is equally true, though perhaps a little less obvious, that our individual happiness and success are bound up with the functioning of these groups. They give us companionship, affection, security, prestige, and financial gain. They make demands upon us for loyalty, enthusiasm, time, energy, money, and sometimes life itself. Thus it is almost impossible to conceive ourselves as working, playing, loving, fighting, hoping, and fearing, except as members of social groups.

— Stuart A. Queen, W. B. Bodenhafer, and E. B. Harper, *Social Organization and Disorganization*. New York: The Thomas Y. Crowell Co., 1935, p. 1.

The Individual and the Group

Group life is indispensable to the individual. If it were not for the protection, care and attention that an infant receives from his group, it is doubtful if he could survive. When a child is born he is physically, psychologically and socially helpless. He is completely dependent upon other human beings for his physical needs and organic wants. As he grows older and develops physically and socially, he plays with other children in the neighborhood. He begins to realize that more and more pleasures are possible only in groups. A child cannot play hide and seek by himself; a boy cannot play baseball alone, nor can he indulge in other competitive games by himself. He has to belong to a team in order to enjoy certain types of fun. Many satisfactions in life are thus enjoyed only through human associations and group life.

An individual likes to be with others; he feels lonely and uneasy when deprived of the association of other human beings for any length of time. How shall we account for man's apparent gregariousness? There is no instinctive urge in man which makes him seek the company of his fellows. The basis of this desire for association can be found in the needs and habits of the individual. It is said that when a baby is born, his craving is not for human beings, but for the satisfaction of his organic needs. He has no recognition of parents, so that anyone who feeds him will gain his affection. Since the needs of the child, in the ordinary course of events, are supplied by older human beings, the child becomes dependent on them. Thus human group life becomes indispensable to him.

An individual finds himself belonging to a complex of social groups. He belongs to a family group, the play group of children, and the neighborhood group. When he goes to school, he joins the school group, clubs, athletic societies, debating teams, and social and religious organizations. As he matures, he joins groups in which he works for a living for himself and his dependents. He becomes a member of church groups in order to satisfy his need for religious guidance and inspiration; he fraternizes with other members of his group for the pleasure of social interaction.

The group is viewed as a "number of persons who have common interests, who are stimulating to each other, who have common loyalty and who participate in common activities."[1] A group is not a mere collection of individuals, but an aggregate of personalities acting and interacting with one another in the process of living. Interaction takes place whenever human beings are in contact with one another. To be a member of the group, one must participate in the common life and activities of the group.

---

[1] Emory S. Bogarus, *Sociology*. The MacMillan Co., New York, 1949, p. 4.

CHAPTER II. NATURE AND ROLE OF GROUP BEHAVIOR 21

Kinds of Group Life

Human social groups may be classified in numerous ways. Many attempts have been made to do this, and the most common basis of differentiation has been according to function and structure. Social groups may be voluntary or involuntary, social or anti-social, permanent or impermanent, public or private, sanctioned or unsanctioned. However, all groups, regardless of the basis of their classification, may be considered as under the heading of primary or secondary.

The Primary Group

Primary groups are small "face-to-face" groups in which contacts are direct, personal and immediate. They are characterized by a strong "we feeling". The term "primary groups" was popularized in sociological literature by Charles Cooley, who called them the "nursery of human nature." He describes them as:

> . . . Those characterized by intimate face-to-face association and cooperation. They are primary in several senses, but chiefly in that they are fundamental in forming the social nature and ideals of the individual. The result of intimate association, psychologically, is a certain fusion of individualities in a common whole, so that one's very self, for many purposes at least, is the common life and purpose of the group. Perhaps the simplest way of describing this wholeness is by saying that it is a "we"; it involves the sort of sympathy and mutual identification for which "we" is the natural expression. One lives in the feeling of the whole and finds the chief aims of his will in that feeling.[2]

These groups become very effective because they are personal in nature; they have the element of intimacy. Although such direct contact as "face-to-face" relationship is generally present, it is not absolutely indispensable.

---

[2] Charles H. Cooley, *Social Organization*, Charles Scribner's Sons, New York, 1909, p. 27.

What is indispensable is the intimacy and fusion of personalities. It is possible that two persons may carry on a correspondence, as between pen pals, having all the elements of a primary relationship even when they have not met. The relationship involves identification and subordination of one's wishes and ambitions to the good of the group.

The primary groups, because of their intimate contacts, exercise a tremendous influence on the individual members. They exert a direct and lasting influence upon the origin and growth of a person's basic ideals in life. The family, the neighborhood group, the work group, the school group and the play group of children are examples of primary groups. The family, the play group and the school group exercise the most significant and profound influence upon the social behavior of individuals.

C. A. Ellwood [3] emphasizes three ways in which the primary groups influence social behavior. First, they socialize the individual; second, they transmit the culture of the group; and third, they are the source of primary social ideals.

The primary groups socialize the individual.

The family provides companionship and fellowship. Its members acquire the "we" feeling; their contacts are intimate, personal and "face-to-face." In the family, the members learn to cooperate with one another and to recognize the feeling of responsibility and duty to the group.

A child is born into the group as a helpless being, devoid of knowledge of the social world. He is born with certain potentialities, impulses, tendencies, muscular coordination and reflex mechanisms. His close and intimate associations with his parents and those immediately around him develop his feelings, attitudes, and habits. As the child acts, those around him react by showering him with

---

[3] C. A. Ellwood, *The Psychology of Human Society*, D. Appleton and Company, New York, 1925.

encouragement, approval and praise when he is good; but will also rebuke, frown, blame and even punish him when he is bad. Through the process of reward and disapproval, the child learns early in life the patterns of behavior expected of him by his primary group.

It has been pointed out earlier in the chapter that gregariousness or sociability is not an internal drive with which a human being is endowed from birth, rather it is the result of learning and habit. The gradual awakening of a child's social consciousness takes place in the primary groups when he realizes that group life is essential not only to supply his needs, but to satisfy his craving for human association. It is in the primary groups that the individual emerges as a social personality.

Primary groups are sources of fundamental social ideals.

We have mentioned that groups consist of a number of interacting personalities. Interaction consists of cooperation or conflict. In the life of an individual, there are clashes of interests, wishes, values, or attitudes. At the same time, there is cooperation; through processes of adjustment, the fundamental human values emerge in the personality of the individual. This situation occurs constantly within the primary groups. In the quarrels of childhood, the individual obtains his first lessons in tolerance, understanding, sympathy, cooperation, mutual regard and respect for one another. Within the family group, the child learns the fundamental and basic patterns connected with sex, parenthood, and kinship. The ideals of service, freedom, justice, toleration are formed largely in the experiences of neighborhood life.

Secondary Group

Secondary groups are those which do not necessarily involve "face-to-face" association or intimate and personal relations. The members are aware of them and take cognizance of them, but they do not feel that their lives are bound up in them, except in time of social crisis. The members may be separated from one another by distance or by lack of personal physical contact. Their contact may be through correspondence, through the press, through the radio, telephone and other means.

The essential characteristic of secondary groups is their casualness in contact. Relationships within the secondary groups lack the intimacy and that "we feeling" so conspicuous within the primary groups, but the "face-to-face" contact may not be excluded. For instance, a student in a very large class sees and hears the lecturer, but he may never get to know him. Many teachers and businessmen are members of professional organizations, but their participation in the groups has not extended beyond paying the annual fees.

Secondary groups may be governmental units, political parties, religious organizations, athletic and social clubs, and business corporations. The possibilities are varied and numerous; society is full of different types of groups. The primary groups existed from primitive times, and for a considerable number of years, they were the only forms of human association. The secondary groups are a later development and did not emerge until civilization was far advanced.

The impersonal nature of secondary group behavior is brought out by Vidal A. Tan in his rather whimsical account of his impressions of New York City.

> . . . In New York, people seem so busy and so deeply concerned with their own affairs that they no longer know how to smile. Some of them seem to wear masks, like "guys and dolls" who conceal their inner world from the busy chatter outside. They walk hurriedly—tack! tack! tack! —on the sidewalk like robots, unfeeling and unconcerned.[4]

The man who emphasized the importance of the distinction between primary and secondary groups was a

---

[4] *The Sunday Times Magazine*, Manila, Dec. 28, 1952.

German sociologist named Ferdinand Tonnies. He used the German terms *gemeinschaft* and *gesellschaft* and these terms have become a part of the vocabulary of sociologists in all countries. These classifications are applied to entire social groups to designate whether their social life is characterized by the primary or the secondary type of interaction. In looking for a local equivalent of these terms, we selected the Tagalog term *damay* which indicates a situation in which primary group contacts were dominant. *Damay* has the meaning of mutual helpfulness and implies the existence of a small, intimate group. Since there seemed to be no Filipino word which could be used to indicate secondary groupings, we have retained the German term *gesellschaft*. Most social groups include both types of social interaction, but usually the barrio is characterized by a *damay* type of society and the large city has the fullest development of the *gesellschaft*. These terms will be used frequently throughout the text.

Sacred and Secular Societies

Another distinction often made in sociological discussions is that between a "sacred" and a "secular" type of society. In the sociological sense, these terms do not necessarily have a religious connotation. A "sacred" society is one which has a strong traditional, unified type of culture which subjects most of the populace to a common set of mores and folk ways. This kind of society has a general agreement on what is right and wrong and produces stable, well integrated types of personalities. It is inclined to keep the old patterns and is resistant to rapid change. The "secular" society lacks a common cultural basis and has divergent folkways and mores. It is apt to be characterized by variation, tolerance and confusion. Individuals in such a society are less stable but more adaptable. The society itself has less respect for tradition and a greater willingness to accept change. The mores of such a society may be in conflict with each other, and individuals may feel the lack of certainty as they decide on matters of daily conduct.

Both of these types of societies have their strong and weak points and are cited here to indicate extreme variations in the cultural setting of human groups. Hawaii, with its many different nationality groups could probably only exist as a "secular" society in which no one group was able to dominate the culture. The feudal territories ruled by the nobles of medieval Europe represent an approximation of a "sacred" type of society.

General Character of Groups

The "in-group" and "out-group" feeling.

During the Japanese occupation of the Philippines, guerilla units were formed everywhere. One such unit was organized in Polo, Bulacan, which is not far from the city of Manila. Nearness to the city and the fact that Polo is a town directly in the path to the central provinces, attracted many strangers who were either evacuees or just passersby. Whenever any of these persons were in town, the first thing the townsfolk did was to find out who the stranger was, what was his purpose, and how long was he staying. Any outsider from the group was considered a prospective Japanese spy and therefore, an enemy. He belonged to the "out-group" and the "in-group" would not accept him until he could prove his motive and identify himself completely with the "in-group".

The out-group and in-group relationships exist whenever there is a feeling of strangeness or enmity between groups. Toward the members of the out-group, we feel suspicious, antagonistic, and scornful, but to anyone in the in-group, we are predisposed to be understanding and sympathetic. In the American culture, this feeling is manifested in the connotation attached to the word, "nigger", "dirty foreigner", "blasted Jew" and the like. In Filipino culture, we use the word "mestizo" not only to identify a person of mixed racial parentage, but someone acts the

CHAPTER II. NATURE AND ROLE OF GROUP BEHAVIOR

way he does because he is a "mestizo" and is therefore excusable for his conduct as belonging to a group different from ours—an out-group.

The out-group and in-group feeling cuts across the classification of groups into primary and secondary. This feeling can be found in either type of group. In modern society, we find that individuals belong to so many groups that they may have a number of both in-group and out-group relationships which overlap. One may be a member of a senior class to which a freshman will be considered as belonging to an out-group; yet the same senior and freshman may both be members of an athletic team, in which case, they have an in-group relationship to each other. Thus we find that in modern social groups, the in-group and out-group relationship does not have the same meaning and intensity as it would in a more simple society.

Ethnocentrism is the extreme preferential feeling which individuals have for the customs of their own group. It is the idea that one's group is more important than any other. It is an expression of group solidarity combined with antagonism toward outside groups.

Under the Nazi government of Germany, the Germans were taught that they belonged to the "master race", superior to all others. The Japanese before World War II, believed that they were the "chosen people" to lead all Asiatic races in a co-prosperity sphere. The Americans think of the United States as the most democratic country in the world today. The Filipinos believe that they have the highest standard of living among the Oriental peoples. It is interesting to note that every country has something equally outstanding of which to boast. Even the primitive tribes are inclined to regard themselves as better than other groups. In fact, the more limited the contacts with the rest of the world, the greater is the degree of ethnocentric feeling. Ethnocentrism is important to the group because it serves to develop and reinforce the solidarity of the group and strngthen the "we feeling." On the other hand, ethnocentrism may prevent members of the group from appreciating genuine values in other cultures.

The group exerts pressure on the activities of the individuals.

Group life may be stimulating or monotonous depending on the kind and amount of stimuli present. Life in the group is satisfying, but at other times, it may be frustrating. Individuals in the group are generally sensitive to one another's opinions; they seek group approval and avoid group disapproval. Hence, the group can and does exert pressure on the activities of individuals. The individual in the group is not completely free to choose any course of conduct that he desires. Whenever he deviates from the group opinion, his activities are restrained through disapproval and punishment. This group pressure may be direct or indirect, but it is always present.

When the interests of the individual conflict with those of the group, he has four alternatives. He may submit to the mores of the group and stifle his own ideas; he may work within the group to change some of its ideas and so become a reformer; he may become a revolutionist and seek to change the nature of the group by force; and finally, he may leave the group and seek fellowship with another which is more to his liking. In the *damay* type of society, it is very difficult for the individual to resist group pressure; in the *gesellschaft*, group pressure is still strong but it is easier for the individual to change his group relationships.

Group pressure often operates on the unconscious and unorganized level. The folkways, mores, and group ideals are the forces involved, and they are made effective by public opinion and gossip. Unorganized and informal forms of social control are found to be more effective than laws and regulations. Human beings have a strong desire for acceptance and approval, and this feeling is the basis of social control through informal methods.

Human groups are always agents of social control. In every society, certain beliefs are approved and others are condemned. Conformity to the ideals and beliefs of the group is regarded as essential; deviation may have unfortunate consequences. Galileo was persecuted because his beliefs deviated too much from the approved types. In modern society, deviation from the average is tolerated provided it follows certain approved directions. In competitive games involving athletic ability, to deviate and be a champion is approved and is lauded by the group. Inventors and men of science like Einstein who are extreme deviates in approved channels, become heroes and idols of the group.

Deviation and variation vary from group to group. There are certain personalities who are condemned in one group and accepted and honored in another. In our society, psychopathic personalities who go into trances and maintain supposed communication with the Unknown will be sent to the Psychopathic Hospital for treatment. Yet there are other societies and groups in which these personalities will be highly honored and appreciated. In some primitive societies, such a person would be accepted and revered and might become a medicine man who would eventually gain influence and wealth.

Social pressure functions to bring into conformity the actions of variants and to induce and preserve that group solidarity which will insure the survival of the group. Social pressure is a process of strengthening approved social behavior and habit systems while eradicating or discouraging those disapproved.

Groups and Personality

Groups determine to a large extent, the personality of the individual. The type of personality an individual acquires will depend upon the extent and kind of his experiences in the different groups of which he is a member. Groups are composed of individuals acting and interacting upon one another; thus a continuous process of adaptation and adjustment takes place. Personality emerges out of this process of interaction and adjustment in the group.

In the study of personality, two important factors should be considered—the factors of heredity and environment.

The hereditary factors of personality.

Heredity does not develop human nature by itself without assistance, but it furnishes the raw materials out of which experience will shape and mold personality. Each individual is born with certain biological structures inherited from his parents, who in turn, inherited them from their ancestors. These biological structures include the nervous system, the ductless glands, the organic drives and the general and specific capacities for mental behavior. Heredity furnishes the mechanisms, but experience determines the way they will be used. Although intelligence is a hereditary mechanism, a degree of mental alertness can be acquired. Hunger is a native and innate drive, but the different attitudes and habits built around it are a result of conditioning and experience.

Environmental factors in personality.

Personality develops through contacts resulting from the varied interactions and adaptations of different individuals in their collective efforts to satisfy their human needs and wants. These interactions are learned behavior which is commonly found in all cultures and in all ages. In any group life there is leading, following teaching, imitating, fighting, praising, blaming and ostracizing. These processes furnish the social experience necessary for the formation of personality.

Specific events and circumstances in the environment influence the development of personality. These are social situations characteristic of group life. The individual finds himself in a series of social situations to which he must

Chapter II. Nature and Role of Group Behavior

react. For example, the child in his early infancy must learn to control his physiological tensions and visceral tensions in accordance with approved usages of his family and social group. When he is hungry and he cries, he is not fed until it is time to feed him. He must learn to control his contractions of the muscles of his stomach and put up with his hunger feelings and endure the intervals between feeding times. The child must learn to manage and control his bladder and bowel movements to conform to the requirements of the group. Even his emotional reactions must be controlled and trained. His energies must be directed towards socially approved channels. His ways of feeling, thinking and behaving are patterned after those of his own group. Thus, the experiences of early childhood are of the greatest significance in the development of personality.

Mechanisms of Social Interaction

We have learned that individuals are born into established groups and receive stimuli to which they react, and so develop their personalities. We have learned the significance of the process of interaction and the value of group experiences in affecting personality. Whether an individual becomes a leader or follower, a bully, or a liar; whether he feels superior or inferior, whether he is selfish or unselfish depends upon how he meets the challenge of social experience.

The development of social attitudes which affect the growth and development of personality depends upon how an individual makes use of certain fundamental behavior mechanisms. These are imitation, suggestion, sympathy and identification.

Imitation is both an unconscious or conscious reaction. The blundering and groping ways of an infant in learning motor reactions, like closing and opening the hands and articulating sounds in his first attempts at learning speech are illustrative of unconscious imitation.

Imitation means copying the object or action. Conscious imitation involves setting up a model or pattern. This implies selection and deliberation. However, imitation is possible only if one already possesses the behavior patterns necessary to imitate a particular behavior. A child cannot take on the mother's manner of speaking if he has not yet acquired the ability to speak. Likewise, one has to have previous lessons in music if he wants to imitate the techniques of the masters.

Suggestion and imitation in many cases overlap, but they are actually independent of one another. The main difference between suggestion and imitation is that in suggestion, the tendency to react is already present and can be directed in any situation almost automatically; while in imitation, the tendency towards action has to be motivated and aroused. In ordinary life, someone may suggest some course of action and almost unconsciously the suggestion is carried out, especially if the initiative comes from a respected or beloved person. In a child, the response is mostly automatic. A tone of voice, a look, or a word is enough to convey to the child what an adult in authority wants him to do.

A child's response to suggestion is not always positive. Sometimes, resentment and defiance are shown against a person in authority, his response is negative and aggressive. There is a tendency to thwart every suggestion coming from a disagreeable source.

Sympathy is the ability to put one's self in the place of another and to fell as he would if confronted by the same circumstance. When he watches a game he identifies himself with the pitcher or the catcher and he responds to what he sees. In watching a movie, the audience gets vicarious experiences through living in imagination the life of the hero or heroine. Sometimes, we actually experience physical participation as when a car leaps through the air.

Imagination plays an important role in arousing sympathy, although it is difficult to imagine what one has not actually experienced. We shudder when a person falls because we have gone through the experience of falling and suffering. The degree and intensity of our sympathy depend upon our past experience in a similar situation.

Identification is closely akin to sympathy. It is the ability not only to place one's self in the position of another but actually to feel that he is the other. In our sympathy with the misfortune of another we are not satisfied in the thought that we also have suffered as he is suffering, but we feel that his pains are also ours. The late Pedro Abad Santos was a rich landowner in Pampanga. Because he sympathized with the lot of the small tenants, he became their leader and their disputes and problems with the other landlords became his. He devoted his life to the amelioration of the common "tao" and became a Socialist leader. In his fashion he sought to "identify" himself with the tenant group.

Summary

Every human being enters the world as a member of a social group. Group life is indispensable to the individual and is necessary for the satisfaction of human needs and wants. Groups may be primary or secondary. The primary groups are characterized by "face-to-face" contacts which are direct, personal and intimate. Primary groups socialize the individual, transmit the culture of the group and they are sources of fundamental social ideals. Because the primary groups have the first chance in the molding and shaping of the personality of the individual, they exercise the most significant and lasting influence upon social behavior. Primary groups have existed from primitive times, while the secondary groups are a later development.

Social groups are characterized by "in-group" and "out-group" feeling which exists whenever there is a feeling of enmity or strangeness between members of groups. Extreme forms of "in-group" feeling may result in ethnocentrism. Ethnocentrism is the idea that one's group is the best and no other group is superior to it.

Group pressure is always present to bring about conformity to approved social behavior. It may be conscious or unconscious, but it is a recognized force to perpetuate solidarity and the "we-feeling".

Personality develops through contacts resulting from the various interactions of different individuals in their collective effort to satisfy their human needs and wants. The development of social attitudes depends upon how an individual makes use of certain fundamental behavior mechanisms. These are imitation, suggestion, sympathy and identification.

QUESTIONS

1. What are the different ways by which social groups influence social behavior? Explain.

2. Why are the early years of a child's life vital for the development of personality?

3. What do we mean by "physiological tensions"? Why is it necessary to control them?

4. How is the development of the "self" dependent upon the opinions of others?

5. What is the process of interaction? How does it affect the socialization and personality of the individual?

6. Define and contrast the processes of imitation and suggestion, sympathy and identification. Give examples of each.

7. Define *damay* and *gesellschaft*, "sacred" and "secular" society.

PROJECTS

1. Make a list of the different social groups to which you belong. Classify them into primary and secondary groups. What are the characteristics of each group?

2. What is ethnocentrism? Make a study of different claims of superiority of the Filipino people as found in Philippine history textbooks and textbooks on Philippine social life. Which of them can be substantiated by facts and which of them are mere ethnocentric manifestations?

3. Prepare a list of different character traits possessed by individuals whom you admire. Which of these traits are developed in

CHAPTER II. NATURE AND ROLE OF GROUP BEHAVIOR   35

childhood? In adolescence? In adulthood? Can you separate the effects of heredity from those of environment? If so, how? If not, why not?

SUGGESTED READINGS

Linton, Ralph, *The Cultural Background of Personality*, New York and London, New York, 1945.
  Five essays which attempt to bring together anthropology and psychology in the study of personality by providing a common terminology and frame of reference.

Young, Kimball, *Social Psychology*, Alfred A. Knopf, New York, 1930.
  See Parts III and IV for an account of the role of the group in shaping personality.

Park, Robert E. and Burgess, Ernest W., *Introduction to the Science of Sociology*.
  Chapter 2 on "Human Nature" and Chapter 6 on "Social Interaction" are essentially concerned with the influence of the group.

Cooley, Charles H., *Social Organization*, Charles Scribner's Sons, 1909, New York.
  Especially Chapter III. This is one of the earliest discussions of the concept of the primary group.

Osborn, Loran David and Neumeyer, Martin H., *The Community and Society*, American Book Company, New York, 1933.
  Chapter 19 on "Group Experience: Social Interaction" deals with group interaction. It begins with the individual social units and continued to a discussion of the various media of communication.
  Chapter 26 on "Human Personality" is a very good reference for the study of social processes. It deals with the social processes and their products beginning with human wants, which constitute the drives to action, and following through to human personality.

CHAPTER THREE

SOCIAL CAUSATION OF PERSONALITY VARIATION

Just as the typical height of the Japanese people is different from that of the American people, etc., so the behaviors that are typical of the Japanese differ from those that are typical of Americans. Japanese and Americans have, in other words, different human natures. Earlier students endeavored to find norms of behavior that would hold true for all of mankind throughout all of human history. But no specific pattern of action that has any such universality has as yet been discovered. When we get beyond broad generalizations, such as that human beings eat and that they take care of their offspring, there is nothing that can be said of mankind as a whole. What people eat, when they eat, and how much they eat have varied from place to place and from time to time. Who takes care of infants, how they are taken care of, etc., also vary from time to time. The similarities that exist among the members of a given society cannot, therefore, be traced to something inherent in the nature of man. They are a result of the fact that the majority of the members of a given society have had much the same set of social experiences.

— Richard T. LaPiere and Paul R. Farnsworth, *Social Psychology*, New York, McGraw-Hill, 1942, p. 148.

Why People Are Different

One of the most obvious paradoxes of human life is that while all people have the same basic physical nature, their social behavior takes an infinite variety of patterns. Every branch of science has attempt to account for these

Chapter III. PERSONALITY VARIATION

differences and all of them have a contribution to make. The three types cited here are examples of the different approaches to the problem.

The *geneticists* emphasize the fact that all men are not really the same in their hereditary equipment. Some are tall, others are short; some have blue eyes and others brown; some have the type of central nervous system which favors high mental achievement, others are less favored in this respect.

The *physiologist* is likely to emphasize that, whether the cause is hereditary or environment, there is a great deal of difference in the way in which the physical organism functions in different individuals. The most dramatic indication of this is the way in which glandular function influences the energy of different individuals. The man who appears too lazy may be suffering from glandular deficiency, while he who is credited with a driving ambition may be simply manifesting the effect of an overactive thyroid.

The *psychologist* is likely to explain human behavior by the individual reaction to a wide variety of possible personal experiences. Frequently, the difference between the happy, contented person and the bitter, suspicious malcontent is traced to childhood experiences which may run the range of patterns between loving care and tenderness or indifference and rejection.

All of these explanations and a great many others are valuable in helping us to explain variation within a particular group. The question which they leave unanswered is why variations also occur, not only between individuals, but also between different groups of people. Within any division of humanity, one will find wide variations in heredity, physiological functioning and psychological experiences. The theories we have suggested will help to explain, for instance, why all Tagalogs are not the same, but they do not explain why Tagalogs as a group seem to be sharply different from Moros, Chinese, Americans, Ifugaos, Negritos, etc. As students of sociology, we are mainly interested in the factors which influence group behavior, and this means we are trying to understand the nature of the variations in conduct which we find between the many recognized divisions of mankind. To follow this inquiry, we must look at factors which seem to affect various groups differently and thus might explain the variations in their behavior. Two common explanations of this type are the biological and the geographic.

Biological Explanations of Human Variation
Racial groups.

The hereditary influences which most obviously affect large groups of people are those involved in determining race and sex. Racial divisions are most frequently based on differences in color and thus men are divided into black, brown, yellow or white groups. While the alleged races include a great variety of fine shades of color, yet large numbers can be grouped together on this basis. Other physical differences also used as racial criteria include: height, shape and size of head, width of nose and lips, texture of hair and color of eyes. All of the racial groups include individuals varying from the usual pattern in one or more ways and no exact definition of race is possible but the persistence of similar traits is strong enough for us to separate many large groups of people on this basis. The point, however, is not whether there are physical differences between peoples, but whether these physical differences also determine differences in temperament, character and intelligence.

This question has not been finally answered, but the evidence thus far indicates that there is no necessary relationship between racial traits and social behavior. The present differences between racial groups reflect differences in educational opportunity and cultural background. When these factors are kept constant, there seems to be no

Chapter III. PERSONALITY VARIATION

relationship between racial traits and the factors which determine social behavior.[1]

Sexual Differentiation.

Just as the earlier belief that social behavior was determined by race has fallen into question, so men have begun to question the extent to which difference in sex involves a difference in behavior. In fact, one even finds that the movement to end slavery based on racial inferiority occurred at about the same time as the movement for women's suffrage and female emancipation. In the nineteenth and twentieth centuries, the racial groups which were held as slaves gained their freedom and legal rights and, at the same time, women began to gain the right to vote, to control property and to engage in hitherto masculine occupations.

In many areas, the arguments in favor of slavery were based on the supposed inferiority of the slaves, who were thought unfit for anything except unskilled tasks. Women were not considered exactly inferior, but rather

---

[1] A striking confirmation of this viewpoint is found in the intelligence tests administered by the American Army during World War I. In these tests, the *overall* score of Negroes was considerably lower than the overall score of the white groups. This test was widely cited as evidence that the popular notion of colored inferiority had a scientific basis. When the test results were broken down by states, an entirely different pattern emerged. Here, a comparison of Negro soldiers in northern states with white soldiers in southern states showed the Negroes to be superior.

The explanation seemed to be that the Negro IQ score reflected the fact that Negroes in general suffered from limited educational facilities, economic discrimination and cultural backwardness. The comparatively few Negroes who lived in the northern states (where educational facilities and the general cultural background were more advanced) actually had better opportunities than the majority of southern whites. In other words, the poor average score of Negroes on this test was related to the fact that all Negroes suffered from an unequal chance in society and that most of the Negroes lived in the South where cultural opportunities for both white and Negro were limited. When a comparison was made in which the situation was reversed and the Negroes had better opportunities than the whites, their intelligence score also excelled that of white soldiers. Klineberg, Otto: *Race Differences*. Harper and Bros., New York, 1935, pp. 182-183.

"different". While viewed as sensitive and emotional, they were thought to be devoid of logical faculties and to lack some types of manual skills and therefore, had no need for formal education and were unable to fathom the complex questions involved in government. Their role is expressed in the German saying: *"Kuche, Kinder and Kirche"* (kitchen, children and church). In the church, they were the most faithful worshippers, but were considered unfit to be clergy.

The studies of the anthropologists indicate that variation in the role of women is not altogether a modern affair and show that while most cultures consider that women should have a unique status and should develop "feminine" rather than "masculine" qualities, there is considerable variation in the definition of what constitutes "feminine" or "masculine" qualities. In this respect, it is interesting to note that, although in modern times the tabu against women serving as clergymen has held fairly strong in most religious groups; in the Philippines, at least, this tabu itself is a fairly recent development. Thus in pre-Spanish days, the most important religious leaders in certain areas of the Philippines were priestesses, and officiating at the religious services was usually a feminine task.[2]

Margaret Mead has made a number of studies under the heading of *Sex and Temperament*[3] and finds that there is no consistent pattern. In one culture, the woman will be shy, modest and retiring; while in another culture, the situation will be reversed and the men will be found to have personality traits which we consider womanly. One rather objective type of evidence indicating variations in the concept of women's roles is found in the following table giving division of labor in various societies.

---

[2] Mendoza-Guazon, Maria Paz: *The Development and Progress of the Filipino Women*, Kiko Press, Manila, 1951, p. 12.

[3] Mead, Margaret: *Sex and Temperament in Primitive Societies*. Morrow, New York, 1935. (Also, a more recent book, *Male and Female*, Morrow, New York, 1949).

CHAPTER III. PERSONALITY VARIATION 41

Table I
Sex Specialization in Occupations *

	Males Exclusively	Males Predominantly	Males or Females	Females Predominantly	Females Exclusively
Pursuit of sea mammals	34	1	0	0	0
Hunting	166	13	0	0	0
Trapping	128	13	4	1	2
Fishing	98	34	19	3	4
Gathering shellfish	9	4	8	7	25
Gathering fruits, berries, nuts	12	3	15	13	63
Preservation of meat and fish	8	2	10	14	74
Gathering herbs, roots, and seeds	8	1	11	7	74
Cooking	5	1	9	28	158

* George P. Murdock, "Comparative Data on Division of Labor by Sex," *Journal of Social Forces*, 15: 551, May, 1937.

Similar differences in the sexual division of labor may be found in more advanced societies. In comparing the Philippines and the United States, one finds that, in the Philippines, pharmacy is largely a women's work; while in North America, feminine pharmacists are almost unknown. Filipino women work in the fields at labor which Americans would consider too heavy for women and are more likely to be shopkeepers than are American women. On the other hand, the male secretary is predominant on the Filipino scene and is a *rara avis* in the United States. Housework is carried on predominantly by women in both countries, but the American husband may assist in some of the household chores. In both countries, women comprise the bulk of nurses and elementary teachers, while the most highly skilled restaurant cooks tend to be male.

All modern nations have seen a tremendous change in the role considered proper for women and it is now generally agreed that any intellectual and most manual pursuits can be performed by either men or women. During the period of World War II, the list of occupations open to women expanded to include such tasks as auxiliary soldiers, welders, factory workers, riveters and bus drivers. On the other hand, men have been known to become skillful in knitting, household tasks and the care of the children. Likewise many social customs associated with an earlier period such as the strict chaperonage of women and the restriction of their legal rights have also fallen into discard.

The discussion as to the proper spheres for men and women, however, still goes on and indicates a strong feeling that, although we are no longer so sure of the exact pattern, there are still distinct masculine and feminine spheres. The specialization of the childbearing function is an undeniable fact which has consequences in the life attitudes of women and men, in their training in the home, in their sense of values and in their conception of what is a "manly man" or a "womanly woman". While we find in all societies, distinctions in the roles of men and women; we also find that these distinction are not the same and vary from one culture to another. Evidently, the mere existence of different sexes explains only a portion of the difference in roles which society has established. Biology establishes the basis for differentiation, but the majority of the specific patterns are socially determined.

Geographic factors in differentiation.

Geographic factors, including the type of natural resources, climate and topography of an area, play a powerful role in influencing cultural development. Where these are least favorable, as in the extremely cold regions, humans do not live at all and where climatic conditions are difficult, but not impossible, as in the desert and some of the Arctic regions, population is scarce and cultural development limited. Similarly, clothes tend to be adapted to the climate; while industry and agriculture develop according to the resources available. Housing, too, tends to follow the needs of the climate. The nipa hut of the Filipino farmer obviously appears to be adapted to a tropical island; while the Eskimo's igloo of snow blocks seems an equally natural adaptation to the conditions of the far north. Even the rise of civilizations seems to rest on the basis of peculiar natural environments. Certainly, the position of England as an industrial leader is related to its vast supplies of coal and its place as the head of the world's largest colonial domain seems a natural result of its location as an island close enough to Europe for easy trade, but still protected by water from foreign invasion. Likewise, the more recent rise of the United States is related to the fact that the North American continent contains a large share of the world's fertile agricultural lands and mineral resources.

On closer examination, however, one finds several loopholes in any absolute theory of geographic determinism. The resources of the United States could give rise to a large industrial civilization, but for hundreds of years, the inhabitants of North America were less advanced than those in areas of the world where natural resources were more limited. At a time when Europe, Asia and Africa boasted flourishing civilizations, the region which is now the United States was thinly populated by people who were largely dependent upon hunting and food gathering. Evidently the natural resources of North America made possible an advanced civilization, but did not force an advanced technology to develop. Similarly, Japan occupies somewhat the same position in reference to the rest of the Orient that England occupies in relation to the European continent. Recent history in which Japan has become an important industrial and military nation would seem to bear out the influence of geographic location. If geography is responsible for the rise of Twentieth Century Japan as a world power: then the question arises: what was responsible for the period of several hundred years in which Japan was completely isolated from the rest of the world? Japan had the geographic base which could be utilized by either a static isolated island or a dynamic world power, but its actual development was evidently determined by something more than geography.

The matter of housing, which was cited earlier as an example of geographic influence, also affords some contradictions to this idea. If the snow igloos of the Eskimos are explained by the climate then how does one explain the fact that the Lapps, living under similar climatic conditions, live in tents made from the skins of arctic animals? Apparently, natural resources did not absolutely dictate the type of housing used by either of these societies.

In the Philippines and most other areas, we have been accustomed to recognize especially the differences between men living in the mountains and those whose home is in the lowlands. In fact, we frequently use the phrase "mountain tribes" to indicate an entirely different type of culture. It is true that the type of life in the hills is different from that of the plains, but it by no means follows that nature has dictated any specific pattern of life for the mountaineers. In the mountain areas, one will find the Negritos who look to the mountains as a source of some game and wild fruits, the Ifugaos who have developed the world famed rice terraces, and also the highly skilled and educated mining engineers who consider the mountains primarily as a source of mineral wealth. These three groups live in a common geographic environment, but their ways of living are far apart.

Human life is based on geographic considerations and must be adapted to the possibilities offered by the natural environment. Those possibilities are not exhausted by any one pattern of life, but offer an almost infinite variety of possible choice. The range of human alternatives is set by the natural environment, but the actual choice of specific patterns is apparently subject to other factors.

Cultural Origins of Individual Difference
Effect of Occupational Differences.

If the natural factors of biology and geography exercise only a minimum of influence on personality, then we

Chapter III. PERSONALITY VARIATION

must turn to the social factors which we designate by the term culture. Here, perhaps, the most obvious influences are those which seem apparent in every geographic area, such as the effect of engaging in different occupations or of living in a rural or urban habitat.

Occupational differentiation has long been recognized even to the extent of deliberately trying to mold personality to fit a specific occupation. The man who becomes a soldier undergoes a long period of training, not only to learn military techniques, but also to assimilate the frame of mind appropriate to a soldier. As a civilian, he has been encouraged to exercise independent judgment, preserve his own safety at all costs, and insist upon his democratic rights as a sovereign individual. The soldier has to learn to accept the commands of authority even if he thinks them mistaken, to submerge his own personality to that of the military unit and to expose himself to obvious danger whenever this aids military plans. The process of learning to "feel" like a soldier is a difficult one. A major aim of the elaborate period of military training is expressed in the phrase, "You are in the army now."

Personality changes of equal or greater magnitude occur when one is trained to be a clergyman, lawyer, physician, secretary or engineer. Each of these occupations and many others require a long period of formal training in which the process of adjusting the personality to the demands of the occupation is equally important as technical training. Occupations which do not require as much formal training also leave their stamp on the personality of the worker. Thus, the stevedore on the docks, the machinist in a factory, the pedler on the corner and the government clerk in an office not only do different kinds of work, but the requirements of their jobs encourage different personality traits.

Perhaps the farmer should be discussed separately from other occupations because not only does he do a specific kind of work, but he is under the influence of a different type of culture. The city man thinks of time in terms of clock hours; the farmer, in the working period from sunrise to sunset. The urban dweller measures land in metric terms, the *tao* in terms of crops planted or harvested. The city man governs his life in terms of a cash profit and loss economy which enables him to get money to buy groceries and pay the rent. The *tao* sees little money, builds his own *nipa* hut and raises most of his food. The city man has been trained to conform to the time card, the assembly line, the cash ledger and the bus schedule; the *tao* moves with the rhythm of the seasons and the mores of an ancient tradition. In general, the farmer lives in the informal *damay* society while the urban dweller finds himself in an impersonal *gesellschaft* setting.

Regional differences.

Within any given area, differences of occupation, education and habitat mold personalities in different patterns, but the difference between regional or national groups maybe even more striking. These groups expose their members to a variety of experience, but they also tend to develop certain distinct patterns which distinguish them as a group. Osias has attempted to describe some patterns of Philippine behavior in a book entitled *The Filipino Way of Life*. In showing the need of such a book, he points out that such a study is essential to foreigners so they may better understand Filipinos and to Filipinos so they may come to understand their culture and thus better realize their strengths and weakness.[4] J. C. Laya, dealt with the same theme in a work of fiction in which the theme of the story revolves about an Americanized Filipino who fails in the effort to change the culture of his home village.[5] Both of these books emphasize the dominant traits of Filipino character and the way in which they differ from the traits of other nationalities.

---

[4] Osias, Camilo: *The Filipino Way of Life*, Ginn and Co.. Boston, 1940, p. 122.

[5] Laya, J. C.: *His Native Soil*, University Publishing Co., Manila, 1941.

Chapter III. PERSONALITY VARIATION

Some of the items on which groups differ would include the respect (or lack of it) for manual labor, thrift or extravagance, cooperation or aggression, contentment or restless ambition, modesty or boldness, enterprise or caution and industriousness or indolence. Usually, a consideration of national traits leads to a consideration of what is good or bad in the nation's life. Two traits frequently associated with Filipinos may serve to illustrate this thesis. One is the modesty and politeness which help people to move without friction among their fellows and which are usually regarded as part of the contribution of Roman Catholicism. On the debit side of the ledger, there is the accusation that Filipinos are over sensitive and "poor sports."[6] Macaraig believes that due to cultural change this defect is rapidly being eliminated.[7] In this case, the cultural change is the participation in competitive sports which supposedly teaches the athlete that he can lose a game without "losing face." Similarly, if he learns to accept gracefully a harsh decision from the umpire, he may be less apt to wield a bolo when his pride is wounded in non-athletic encounters. Seen in this light, the importance of athletics may perhaps lie as much in their effect on the national character as in their contribution to recreation or physical development.

One of the noteworthy attempts to relate a national trait to social conditions is found in Rizal's treatment of the charge that Filipinos were indolent and hence incapable of assuming responsibility. Rizal does not deny the charge, but analyzes the social conditions which might support indolence and lead to a feeling that faithful labor was fruitless.

> A fatal combination of circumstances—some independent of the will in spite of men's efforts, others springing from stupidity and ignorance,

---

[6] See discussion in Kalaw, Maximo M.: *Introduction to Philippine Social Science*, Manila, Philippine Education Co., 1938, pp. 173-210.

[7] Macaraig, Serafin E.: *Introduction to Sociology*, Manila, University of the Philippines, 1948, p. 59.

others inevitably concomitant with false principles and still others resulting from more or less base passions—has induced the decline of labor, an evil which, instead of being remedied by prudence, mature reflection, and recognition of the error made, through a lamentable policy, through regrettable bigotry and contumacy, has gone from bad to worse until it has reached the condition in which we now see it...

The pernicious example of the invaders in surrounding themselves with servants and in despising manual or corporal labor as a thing unbecoming the nobility and chivalrous pride of the heroes of so many centuries, those lordly airs, which the native have translated into *tila ka castila* (just like a Spaniard!); and the desire of the dominated to be the equal of the dominators, if not essentially, at least in their manners; all this hauteur had naturally produced aversion to activity and fear or hatred of work...

Along with gambling—which breeds dislike for steady and difficult toil by its promise of sudden wealth and its appeal to the emotions—with the lotteries, with the prodigality and hospitality of the Filipinos went also, to swell this flood of misfortunes, the religious functions, the great number of fiestas, the long masses for the women to spend their mornings and the novenaries to spend their afternoons, and the night for the processions and rosaries... It is well, undoubtedly, to trust greatly in God; but it is better to do what we can do and not trouble the Creator every moment, even when these appeals redound to the benefit of His ministers. We have noticed that the countries which believe most in miracles are the laziest, just as spoiled children are the most ill-mannered. Whether they believe in miracles to palliate their laziness or they are lazy because they believe in miracles, we cannot say; but the fact is that Filipinos were much less lazy before the word miracle was introduced into their language...

The very limited training in the home, the arbitrary and barren system of education in the few centers of learning, that blind subordination of the youth to persons of greater age, influence

CHAPTER III. PERSONALITY VARIATION 49

the mind so that a man may not aspire to excell those who preceded him, but must merely be content to go along with or march behind them. Stagnation forcibly results from this tradition; as he who devotes himself merely to copying divests himself of other qualities suited to his own nature, he naturally becomes unproductive,—hence, decadent. Indolence is a corollary derived from the lack of stimulus and of vitality.

What (the Filipino) lacks is, in the first place, liberty to allow expansion to his adventure-some spirit; and secondly, good examples, beautiful prospects for the future.[8]...

Studies of small groups whose developments have proceeded on different lines than that of technologically advanced countries, gives even sharper evidence of the extent to which attitudes, now taken for granted, may be socially determined. Goldman cites the Ifugaos as an example of a group whose culture may influence men to develop intensely competitive acquisitive attitudes.

The male Ifugao is motivated by the drive for wealth in property and the power and prestige that go with it. To attain this end he must be aggressive and valorous, but above all shrewd. "One of the fine points in buying consists of an insidious hospitality on the part of the purchaser which gets the seller and his kin drunk so that they forget some of their prerequisites. In their economy of a fixed and limited supply the Ifugao honor those who can accumulate the most even at the expense of their neighbors. The man of wealth, the *kadangyang*, may take two or even three wives and be envied, though monogamy is the cultural pattern. A lesser man would be hounded to death for daring such a thing. On the other hand, the man of wealth must not be stingy. If he is to maintain his status as a *kadangyang* he must continually redistribute some of his wealth in a series of elaborate and costly feasts to the populace. Along with and fitting

---

[8] Rizal, Jose: *The Indolence of the Filipino*, in Craig, Austin, *Rizal's Life and Minor Writings*, 1927. Manila, Philippine Education Co., pp. 265-304.

into the economic framework of desire for wealth is the Ifugao emphasis on pride. The man who is slow to avenge a kinsman's death is stung into action by his sister's giving him her skirt to wear. It is pride as well as business necessity that drives an Ifugao to bear down on his debtor or to resist a creditor. What the Ifugao fears most is loss of face...

The emphasis upon property and upon wealth and the competitive forms associated with that emphasis run consistently through every aspect of Ifugao social relations. In religion, the favors of the gods must be bought with bribes, and the wealthy as exhibiting the greatest supernatural blessings are the most effective priests. In law, most of the disputes center about property or the collecting of loans. Marriage is but another phase of the economic struggle, serving as a means for joining two parcels of valuable rice land..." [9]

Perhaps even more entrenched in our thinking than the notion that men are inherently competitive, is the idea of man as possessing limitless wants which he strives constantly and unsuccessfully to satiate. This notion is based on the easily observable fact that a rise in income never seems to be sufficient to keep pace with our expenditures. The man making 1,000 pesos per year looks on the man making ten thousand as one who should certainly be able to satisfy all his needs. The 10,000 peso man finds trouble living within his means, but regards the millionaire as beyond concern for material needs. The millionaire, however, struggles to get more millions to provide more investments, more yachts, more mansions and, above all, more security.

The Ifugaos were cited as an example of a preliterate culture which developed on competitive lines in the struggle for wants which were never satisfied. The migratory Negrito groups illustrate exactly the opposite trend among

---

[9] Mead, Margaret, editor, *Cooperation and Competition Among Primitive Peoples;* Goldman, Irving, "The Ifugao of the Philippine Islands," McGraw-Hill Book Company, Inc. New York, 1937, pp. 174-175. Reproduced by permission of McGraw-Hill.

CHAPTER III. PERSONALITY VARIATION 51

another preliterate group. The following report of a conversation between an American visitor and a Negrito chief is a case in point.

> The last day we were with the Negritos we asked Baraca (a chief), "What shall we bring you next time we come?" He looked at his inadequate clout—the only clothing he wore—"You need not bring me a clout for I have one." Then he looked into his bare house, at his silk hat hanging on a crooked stick at his silver headed cane stuck in the roof, at his watch dangling from his clout. He sighed, "I have everything." [10]

Cultural conflict.

Culture in small groups with a common way of life presents relatively few complications and may lead to rather definite forms of social adjustment. In more complex society, one is apt to be influenced by a number of contrasting influences. Sometimes this comes about by geographical movement from one area to another. The man reared on the farm may move to the city and find his traditional ideas challenged by urban concepts or the migrant may leave his native land entirely and go to a country with a different language, government and social life.

While migration is almost certain to lead to cultural confusion; remaining in the same area will not guarantee stability. Take, for instance, the example of a German born in 1890. His youth would have been spent under the government of the Kaiser, his early life under the Republic, his period of middle-age under Hitler's dictatorship and his later years in a country controlled by an occupation army. Such a man would have found that, just as he was adjusting to one governmental regime, it was succeeded by another which appealed to entirely different values. It is no wonder that under such rapid change, many people develop insecurity and uncertainty.

---
[10] Cole, Mabel Cook: *Savage Gentlemen*, D. Von Nostrand, New York, 1924, p. 169.

Even under a stable government, the change in industrial methods, popular style and current beliefs may result in the same confusion of ideals and conflict of values. This conflict may be based on fundamental principles or it may be reflected in such matters as style of clothing. For some

Picture taken at a Malacañang ball, showing present Filipino formal attire. Reading from the left are President Ramon Magsaysay, Mrs. Magsaysay and Speaker Jose B. Laurel, Jr. Photo by courtesy of the Philippines Free Press.

time, western fashions were considered a badge of modernization, but Filipinos are now realizing that indigenous styles may have a special value. The *barong tagalog* (male dress shirt) and the mestiza dress (formal feminine attire) are often worn by the most sophisticated members of metropolitan society and are beginning to be adopted by resident foreigners.

Marginal Man.

Sociologists have used the term "marginal man" to describe one who is torn between two or more cultures. He is considered marginal because he is on the edge of several cultures, but is not entirely controlled by any. Thus, he is unable either to cling to the old viewpoint or to scrap it and accept the new. He suffers from the lack of certainty and moral stability which such a condition produces, but he profits from developing an insight which is sharpened by the need to analyze and appraise the various types of social life he has encountered. Such individuals sometimes become demoralized and drift into criminal behavior. On the other hand, they may become able business men who see opportunities neglected by the local inhabitants or brilliant writers who can analyze factors which others have taken for granted.

In our discussion of the role of modern woman, we said that the idea of what constituted "feminine" behavior had greatly altered in recent years. One observer suggests that in the case of the Filipino woman so many changes have taken place in a short space of time that perhaps she occupies a "marginal" role. This observation would apply best to the upper class society woman and to a much lesser degree to her barrio sister who is further removed from the rapid changes of the current scene.

Whether the marginal position is good or bad is debatable; some would prefer the quiet certainty built on traditional behavior and others would call for the complete surrender to whatever is new. The in-between position is not necessarily a happy one, but it seems destined to become increasingly common in the years ahead. Let us now take a brief look at the portrait of the "marginal woman" as described in a witty and somewhat imaginative manner.

Our knowledge of the pre-Spanish Filipina is necessarily limited to the uncertain testimony—

characteristically tongue-tied about women—of the ancient Chinese chronicles. Women then seemed to enjoy an easy equality with men which was based not on condescension, but on genuine respect...

By 1521, a date associated with "the coming of the white men" or "the discovery of the islands", depending on what history book one reads, the Filipino woman was a forthright, hedonistic little pagan, and the Spaniards, even while he cast lewd eyes on her brown and perfumed body, determined to save her soul...

But here a knife-sharp line must be drawn. For more than 300 years after Magellan, the Spanish friar and the *encomendero* took the Filipina in hand—a tutelage which was to produce the shy, diffident, puritanical, tear-stained little women of the late nineteenth century...

As a young girl, she was trained to obey her father and the Señor Cura, to cast her eyes down, to pray the rosary, to be pure, to hide her emotions, to look up on all men as "the devil incarnate". He set the *dueña* to watch over her, and locked her up in *colegios* where she languished for years, learning to read a missal, to write enough to sign her name but not enough to communicate with her sweetheart, to embroider a little, to faint at the mention of a beloved name, to sit on a pillow by a shuttered window, to look forward to the joys of the just in Heaven. Anything beyond rudimentary schooling was denied her. A young Filipina of the Spanish era could take the veil, drift into spinsterhood (*"Para vestir santos"* was the Spanish phrase for it) or she could marry, after a long and extremely circumspect courtship, the young man who least offended her parents' sensibilities, and thereafter stay at home in a state of chronic pregnancy...

The God-inspired imperialism of the American president in 1899 found the Filipino woman "imitative... appreciative... glad to be educated... ambitious to learn." The new man in the Filipina's life, the *Americano*, with his bold and brash democracy, was a Pygmalion of another persuasion. He told the Filipina, sympathetically, that

Chapter III. PERSONALITY VARIATION

she was repressed, that she was wasting her talents in the kitchen, that she was too pretty to hide under so much dry goods. He opened the schools to her, encouraged her to speak her mind, and told her that even greater than virtue was "independence of character". He tantalized her with the ideals of equality and freedom and showed her that life was meant to be "fun"...

Any part-time psychoanalyst will be able to tell, at this point, that the matter with the Filipino woman is a split personality. Part of her has remained the innocent, poetic, vulnerable homebody that she was at the close of the Spanish era; the other part tries hard to catch up with the modern American woman who can drive a car, have an affair and bear children only when she wants to.

Without actually discarding her traditional Filipina dress, she has made it into a costume-ball travesty, to be worn only to some dances and Rotarian parties. By throwing away the overskirt, the shawl and most of the bodice, acquiring a new figure with imported whalebone and fashioning the conventional butterfly sleeves of Swiss material, she has given the national dress the hybrid character of her own person. She goes to church in the morning, and gives her opinions on free love to the Philippines Free Press in the afternoon: she secretly yearns for the libertine codes of Hollywood movie stars, but refuses to let her *novio* kiss her. She has learned to blow cigarette smoke into her eyes and to hold an eight-hour job in Manila's downtown, but she has to be home before dusk or Mama will spank. She wears a chemise under her daring sunback dress, and a large towel over her bathing suit. She goes to ball games and prize fights, but faints in the excitement. She drinks ginger ale at nightclubs, so everyone will think it is a Scotch highball, but is indignant if anyone gossips about her drinking. She is always talking about birth control, but she has an average of five children to prove that all she does is talk. She still has not decided which is more fearful, hellfire or social disgrace, and neither is she sure whom to follow, Emily Post or the catechism...

For the Filipina is a woman with a past—a long, unburied, polychromatic, delicious past which is forever returning to color her days. There have been three men in her life; her Asiatic ancestor, the Spanish Friar, and the Americano, and like Chekov's *Darling*, she echoes all of them in her person...

Perhaps, in a few more generations, the Filipina will crystalize into a clear, pure, internally calm, symmetrical personality with definite facets in the predictable planes. Perhaps, in time, the different strains which now war within her in mongrel contradictions will have been assimilated into a thoroughbred homogeneity. But when that happens the Filipino woman will have lost the infinite unexpectedness, the abrupt contrariness, the plural unpredictability which now make her both so womanly and so Filipino.[11]

Variation within the group.

This viewpoint of the cultural determination of social behavior has been challenged on various grounds. Some would feel it gives inadequate consideration to hereditary influences, others note the tremendous variation in personal tastes and aptitudes to be found in any society and insist that the explanation of differences must be on an individual rather than a group basis. Much of this opposition is based on the failure to recognize that society and the individual are not separate entities, but different aspects of the same reality. Society is made up of individuals and has no reality apart from the people who comprise it, but individuals find their only possible expression in terms of the society of which they are a part. Ruth Benedict expresses the situation in these words:

> Every private interest of every man and woman is served by the enrichment of the traditional stores of his civilization. The richest musical sensitivity can operate only within the equipment

---

[11] Carmen Guerrero-Nakpil: "The Filipino Woman," *The Philippine Quarterly*, March, 1952, Manila, pp. 8-17.

and standards of its tradition. It will add, perhaps importantly, to that tradition, but its achievement remains in proportion to the instruments and musical theory which the culture has provided. In the same fashion a talent for observation expends itself in some Melanesian tribe upon the negligible borders of the magico-religious field. For a realization of its potentialities it is dependent upon the development of scientific methodology, and it has no fruition unless the culture has elaborated the necessary concepts and tools.[12]

Another aspect of the situation is the case of the individual who seems to defy cultural norms. Society chooses from the tremendous variety of human behavior those patterns it wishes to stress and those it wishes to minimize. For the most part, human behavior does follow the societal norm; but there are occasional individuals whose behavior does not agree with the practices of society. These individuals may have peculiar physical traits or they may have developed a general attitude or specific interest which society does not encourage. In a society which emphasizes commercial values, some men may strive for the self denial of the hermit; and in a monastic society, some of the brothers may develop a greed which the Order condemns.

What this means is not that society is without influence, but that in any given society some individuals are found whose potentialities do not coincide with the type of behavior desired by the society. In a rigidly authoritarian group, such individuals are condemned and isolated; in a democratic society, they may be tolerated and have some chance to influence the values of the group. They may become great inventors and social innovators, frustrated abnormals, or persecuted victims of the urge for conformity. In any event, the principle of determinism has to be based on the idea of probability rather than absolute certainty. Human nature is plastic enough that, given certain social pressures, a specified type

---

[12] Ruth Benedict, *Patterns of Culture*, Mentor Books, New American Library, 1950, pp. 222-283.

of personality is *apt* to develop. Both human nature and society are complex enough that absolute uniformity is never achieved.

An example of the relation of social norms to individual variation is found in the social provision for the expression of bereavement at funeral services. Some societies, such as that of the Plains Indians in the United States, encourage an extravagant outward expression of grief; while highly rational religious groups like the Unitarians, discourage what they consider excessive weeping and wailing. In either society, are found individuals who may have to force an expression of mourning or to check a strong impulse to emotional expression. Such individuals find that their culture produces frustration, but they do not disprove the effect of the culture on the majority of the group. An even more striking example is afforded by the efforts of the military authorities to produce soldierly attitudes. Through army training, the regimentation needed for army life is produced in a majority of recruits. In every army, some do not respond to this conditioning and become deserters or slackers, but the contrast between soldiers and civilians still remains. The presence of these exceptions indicates the limits and complexity of cultural conditioning, but it does not refute the statement that the majority of people respond to whatever values the culture emphasizes.

Summary

The presence of individual variation has been explained on the basis of physical heredity, physiological functioning and psychological experiences. These explanations offer light on differences within the group but do not adequately explain differences between entire groups. To explain this type of group difference we must turn to a factor which could be expected to affect many people in the same way. The biological traits of race and sex have been examined as possible explanations and found inadequate. In the case of racial groups we find no proof that the physical

Chapter III. PERSONALITY VARIATION

characteristics which determine race are related to social behavior. With sexual differentiation we find that the varying roles of the sexes in different societies disprove the idea that sex inherently sets definite behavior patterns.

Another variable which affects large groups of men is the range of geographic conditions. This variation in the natural environment of human groups places limits upon the choices which a group can make and still survive, but it does not restrict the group to any specific adjustment. The natural environment is a limiting factor in human adjustment, but by itself it cannot be considered responsible for the actual variation we find in human societies.

In seeking for an explanation of group differences, we turn next to cultural variation. Here we find that various groups have developed strikingly different cultures and that these cultures in turn influence individual behavior. Examples were given of the relation of specific cultures to the encouragement of traits of character. Such traits of character, although encouraged by the culture are not held to the same degree by all members of society. This indicates the presence of rifts within the cultural pattern itself as well as the variety of human response to any specific stimulus. The general proposition that variations in the culture patterns of a society produce variations in the behavior of its members is based on probability rather than absolute uniformity and hence is not vitiated by these exceptions.

QUESTIONS

1. Does race determine intelligence?
2. Granting that inherited characteristics influence intelligence and temperament, is heredity the cause of differences between large social groups?
3. Should women's activities be confined to the home?
4. Do you agree that the urban Filipina is in a "marginal" group? Is this also true of the rural Filipina?
5. With the aid of illustrations from your own experience, indicate the nature and importance of personality differentials associated with.

(a) occupation
(b) social class
(c) sex
(d) national or regional group

6. Do competitive athletics change the personalities of the participants?

7. Is indolence still a Filipino trait? What other contributing factors would you mention beside those discussed by Rizal?

PROJECTS

1. Compare two of your relatives with regards to group influences in their development and point out the differences in attitudes due to these influences.

2. Compare two groups in your home town and list the contrasting ways in which they affect interests, ideals and patterns of living of their members.

3. In one of Rizal's novels trace the relationship between group influences and personal attitudes of the main characters.

SUGGESTED READINGS

Benedict, Ruth: *Patterns of Culture*, New American Library of World Literature, 245 Fifth Avenue, New York, 16, N.Y., 1934 edition with 1950 reprinting. Available in 35¢ edition.
An account of culture patterns in four primitive societies, Excellent general discussion of the relationship of culture and personality.

Mead, Margaret: *Male and Female*, Morrow, New York, 1949. Discussion of the influence of culture on sexual roles in various cultures.

Faris, Ellsworth: *The Nature of Human Nature*, McGraw-Hill Co., New York, 1937. The first part of this volume deals with the group forces which make the individual a person.

Laya, J. C.: *His Native Soil*, Manila, University Publishing Co., 1941. Fictional account of conflict between Filipino and American cultural patterns.

Osias, Camilo: *The Filipino Way of Life*, Ginn and Co., Boston, 1940. Discussion of cultural influences which have shaped Filipino personality.

Kalaw, Maximo M.: *Introduction to Philippine Social Science*, Manila, Philippine Education Co., 1938. Pages 173 to 210 contain a discussion of cultural traits in reference to personality.

CHAPTER FOUR

THE FAMILY

A great many people today speak as if the family were in some special sort of danger in our times. We hear a great deal about "saving the family" and about "preserving the home." Authors and lecturers describe how the family is threatened by divorce, or by mothers who work outside of the home, or by unemployment, or by lack of religious training of children. Each of them, depending on his experience in his own home and on his observations in the families he knows, selects something which he thinks should be changed—or should be preserved—and says that if this or that were done, the family would be "saved."

To an anthropologist such phrasings are dangerously misleading. He has studied the family among naked savages and in contemporary civilizations and he knows that it has survived in all human societies known in the record of mankind. Just as surely he knows that the family takes all kinds of different forms.... The ethics of marriage, the specific close emotional ties for the child, the nature of the dependency of the children upon the parents, even the personnel which makes up the family—all these differ even in Western civilized nations. The anthropologist knows that the changes taking place in the home in any decade in any country do not mean that the family is now about to disintegrate under our eyes unless we do something about it. The problem as he states it is quite different; how do legal and customary arrangements in the family tally with the arrangements and premises of the whole way of life which is valued in any tribe or nation?

— Ruth Benedict, "Chapter IX" in *The Family: Its Function and Destiny*, by Ruth Nanda Anshen, editor, Harper and Brothers Publishers: New York, 1949, p. 159.

Three Types of Contemporary Families

A Bontoc highland family.

Agnep and her husband Bog Bog live in a one room house with a stone walled pig pen immediately adjacent. Agnep is twenty-nine, has been married twice and has given birth to six children of whom four are living. Her first pregnancy occurred when she was a girl of sixteen living at the *oolag* (girl's dormitory). The man wanted to marry her and sent presents to her family who were agreeable to the match. However, when the omens were cast the bile of the chicken was bad so marriage was impossible. The evidence of pregnancy only increased her desirability and soon she had another suitor. This time the omens were favorable, the wedding feast was held and they set up housekeeping in a house vacated by her husband's father. After four years when no further children had come Agnep asked her husband for a divorce. He agreed and with the consent of the old men of the village they divided their property and separated. A few months later Bog Bog proposed to her and they set up housekeeping in her mother's home which Agnep as the eldest daughter had inherited.

Agnep goes to the fields everyday during the planting and harvesting season while her husband remains behind and watches the youngest children. The two oldest children, a daughter of twelve and a boy of seven stay in the *oolag* and the boy's dormitory, but help during the day in the work in the rice terraces. The father hunts, gathers fruit and one time worked for a few months in the gold mines near Baguio to get money to buy an iron roof. The basis of their livelihood is land, consisting of three fields which Agnep inherited from her mother and three fields which Bog Bog received from his father at the time of his marriage. Although the land is worked as a unit, the couple are aware of their separate holdings, and it is expected that girls will receive land belonging to the mother and boys will inherit from the father. Children are seldom disciplined but usually grow up to accept their role in the family without much difficulty. Some of the children have attended school in the nearby mission, but Agnep had no schooling herself and shares the fear of the old men that formal schooling would make the girls unwilling to work in the fields and lure the boys away from their home district. The diet consists of rice, fish, camotes and a variety of fruit, all of which are produced in the neighborhood. Agnep and her husband seldom sell rice and may handle only forty or fifty pesos in the course of an entire year—most of which is spent for a few simple items of clothing. Bog Bog wears only a G string, his wife at first wore only a *tapis* (skirt) but now adds a blouse on trips to Bontoc. Years ago Agnep's mother used to weave clothes and blankets but Agnep now finds it easier to buy these items.

Middle class Manila family.

Consuelo Capunan was married to her husband Jose when she was twenty-four and he twenty-seven. She had graduated from the University of the Philippines when she was twenty-one and had been a teacher for three years. She and her husband had been closely chaperoned before marriage but on one occasion they arranged a clandestine meeting in a motion picture house. This was their only "date" of this type and gave them both a feeling of being quite "modern" in their conduct. When they were married they went to live in the house of the groom's parents where they remained for fifteen years until both of his parents died. They then sold the house and bought a new one in the San Juan district.

In addition to five children, the household consists of an unemployed uncle, a cousin who is going to school, and a widowed sister of Consuelo. Consuelo returned to teaching when her oldest child was eight years old. The housework is taken care of by three servants; maid, *lavandera* and houseboy, while her sister looks after the children.

Jose is a government official with a salary of four-hundred pesos a month, and makes an extra hundred teaching night classes in a private college. Consuelo earns two hundred a month as a public school teacher and they clear about a thousand pesos a year from ten hectares of land which they own in Zambales. Consuelo handles the money with her husband keeping ninety pesos a month for personal expenses. Their diet is mainly rice and fish with meat twice a week and milk for the younger children. In the first years of marriage, they kept a pig under the house; in their new home the pig has a separate pen in the backyard.

Once in a while Consuelo and her husband go to a movie or visit some of their relatives, but usually she remains at home while her husband is out with some of his male friends. Her husband's nocturnal activities are rather a mystery to Consuelo as he always seems to be going to some kind of meeting or party. She knows that some of her friends' husbands are maintaining *queridas* (mistresses) and occasionally she wonders about Jose, but assumes that he could not do this without spending more money. Consuelo once joined the League of Women Voters, found it hard to get to meetings and has become inactive. She is a faithful Catholic and seldom misses Sunday Mass or a day of obligation but feels that more than this is too much for one who is a working woman. Consuelo and Jose are both fond of their children and always try to be on hand to tell them goodnight. The children seem to be a little spoiled but are always affectionate and make good grades in school.

Chicago family.

John Green and his wife Dorothy were married when he was twenty-five and she was twenty-three. They met on a blind date arranged by John's roommate and were married six months later. Dorothy was a graduate of Illinois University and worked for one year as an assistant editor for a woman's magazine. She had dated several men and "necking" had been rather a routine feature of

Chapter IV. THE FAMILY

her high-school and college experience. It was common talk around college that many of the girls had sexual relationships but this was not true of Dorothy or most of the girls she knew personally. She was not altogether sure that virginity was really a virtue but it seemed the safest policy.

After marriage the couple moved into a three room apartment and Dorothy continued working for three years until her first child was born. They have now been married fifteen years, have two children and have moved into a small house in the suburbs. John is the manager of an insurance office making about eight thousand dollars a year. They draw up a budget for family expenses but John handles the money and gives Dorothy an allowance of two hundred dollars a month for groceries and personal expenses. They keep a balance of about five hundred dollars in a checking account and own a thousand dollars worth of stocks. They also own the house and are making monthly payments on the mortgage.

No relatives live with them and they have no servants. Household equipment includes refrigerator, electric stove, electric mixer, frozen food locker, vacuum cleaner, electric washing machine and dryer. Their car is a two year old Chevrolet sedan. Their diet runs heavily to meat, potatoes, and salads with much use of packaged frozen foods. They consume three quarts (approximately three liters) of milk daily. After the birth of the first child, Dorothy was forced to spend most of her time at home, and only when the children were both of school age was she able to resume her activities with the women's group of the Presbyterian Church, The Association of University Women, The League of Women Voters and a Friday afternoon bridge club. John is an active member of the Masons, Kiwanis and Chamber of Commerce. During the fall of every year he spends a good deal of time in drives to collect money for the Community Chest. He helps take care of the children, often acting as baby sitter while his wife is attending meetings; occasionally he washes the dishes, helps with the meals, tends the yard, and does other odd jobs about the house.

In their second year of marriage, Dorothy suspected that John was having an affair with an old girl friend. She was furious and threatened divorce, only yielding when John promised to avoid all such relationships in the future. Dorothy feels that only a weak willed wife would allow her husband to carry on with another woman. John and Dorothy occasionally go to plays or concerts alone, and once every two weeks John plays poker with a group of male friends. Usually most of their social life is spent together. They are both members of the local Presbyterian Church and attend services about twice a month. Their children are independent youngsters, and Dorothy occasionally thinks that they lack respect for their parents. Sometimes she and John think they would like a large family, but they have decided that two children are all they can afford. Dorothy often thinks she is wasting her talents and ought to go back to work, but she is afraid that a maid would cost more than she could make. John's father is dead and his mother lives in an old ladies home; they had invited her to live with them but she was afraid she would not fit into the household and wanted to keep her independence. Dorothy's parents live in Florida and they try to visit them every two or three years.

Family patterns.

The description of these three families gives some idea of the variety of family patterns although it is far from exhausting the list. Families may be polygamous (multiple husbands or wives); they may stress the importance of the mother (matriarchal) or of the father (patriarchical) or may even be centered about some non-parental grouping giving dominant authority to the mother's brother. Families may have an endogamous character requiring marriage within a specific group or they may have an extreme exogamous emphasis which taboos marriage within the tribe or clan. Even within the same culture, family patterns vary greatly between urban and rural sections, and reflect

Chapter IV. THE FAMILY

such differences as religious affiliation, nationality background and class structure. A mere listing of different patterns would require many pages, and volumes have been written describing the various family systems.

For the purposes of this chapter we shall devote most of our attention to the middle or upper class Filipino family and its effect on society. Our reason for this treatment is that most college students come from this type of family even though a majority of the total population live in rural areas where family patterns hold more rigidly to a traditional form. While the urban middle class family is not typical of the majority family pattern it does exercise a major influence in society and probably indicates the way in which the rural family is apt to develop in the future. However, the middle class urban family cannot be treated as an entity complete in itself. It has roots in the family systems of the primitives and it is being drawn toward a drastically different type of pattern which is prevalent in the west. Hence, to understand this type of Filipino family we must know something of other family systems as well. Keeping in mind that any attempt to generalize over wide areas tends to oversimplify the picture, we might now profitably look at a list of major differences between certain family systems.

PRIMITIVE OR FOLK	FILIPINO	WESTERN
Very strong trend to either Paternal or Maternal dominance.	Paternal dominance with modification.	Trend toward complete equality between husband and wife.
Economic basis of family as holder of property and source of labor.	Important in property holding, less effective as labor unit.	Economic role greatly diminished except as a unit of consumption.
Little discipline of children who are regimented by social and environmental pressure.	Combination of discipline and indulgence in treatment of children.	Trend toward equality in parent child relationship.

PRIMITIVE OR FOLK	FILIPINO	WESTERN
Romantic love secondary to economic and kinship considerations in marriage choice.	Romantic love exalted but subordinate to parental approval.	Romantic love all important with parental approval playing minor role.
Relatively free relationship with opposite sex before marriage.	Pre-marital associations heavily chaperoned.	Little chaperonage but tabus restrict pre-marital conduct.
Society tends to approve fairly wide range of sex activity, in both pre-marital and post-marital status No commercialized vice or prostitution.	Double standard with much latitude for men but little for respectable women. *Queridas*, consensual marriage and prostitution increase opportunities for sexual activity.	Tendency to a single standard for both sexes with fewer tabus for both. Prostitution plays minor role and mistresses are rare. Common law marriage usually confined to lowest socio-economic group.
Divorce easy to obtain on many grounds. Usually no financial hardship on either party since land and property are merely divided.	No divorce. Legal separation without right of remarriage.	Divorce obtainable on many grounds but subject to legal restriction and financially burdensome.
Large family group including collateral relatives although older children often live in separate dormitory. High birth rate and high infant mortality.	Large family group often including three generations and collateral relatives in same house. High birth rate. Infant mortality between Primitive and Western.	Small family includes only two generations and no collateral relatives. Low birth rate and low infant mortality.

CHAPTER IV. THE FAMILY

PRIMITIVE OR FOLK	FILIPINO	WESTERN
Family is a means to economic gain and social status with consciousness of individual property even after marriage.	Integrated and prosperous family a major goal for all family members.	Happy family is important but the value of family is seen primarily in its contribution to the individual happiness of family members.

Filipino Family

Courtship.

Courtship, mating, and divorce among the ancient Filipinos revolved around the "dowry".[1] The "dowry" was a gift turned over by the groom to the bride's parents practically in exchange for his bride. The terms of a "dowry" were discussed with great tact and diplomacy by elderly representatives of both parties. Some historians, like Alip,[2] have described such protracted conclaves as "sort of business-like," except that the Filipinos of those days were loquacious in language and refined in speech, unlike some businessmen of today.

It was customary for the wise parent to turn over the "dowry" to her daughter as part of her paraphernal property brought into the marriage; but, if it was kept by the parents, it was returned to the groom in case of divorce. The disposition of the "dowry" as decided upon by the elders showed upon whom lay the fault of the divorce. The wife could keep it if her husband was to blame.

This system of preparing a "dowry" for the bride still has its vestiges in the wedding customs of the Philippines. In Filipino weddings, the bridegroom assumes all respon-

---

[1] Dowry ordinarily refers to the custom in many European societies of the bride's parents giving a substantial present to the husband. Here it has the opposite meaning of a gift by the groom's parents to those of the bride. This is sometimes known as "bride purchase" although it is seldom a market type of transaction.

[2] Eufronio M. Alip, *Political and Cultural History of the Philippines*, Manila: Alip and Brion, 1950, pp. 60, 61.

sibility for the preparations including the wedding dress and the celebration. This contrasts with the practice in western societies where this type of expense is cared for by the parents of the bride. In western areas, some brides would feel socially disgraced to have the groom assume any wedding expense except the purchase of the marriage license and the fee of the clergyman or judge who officiates at the ceremony; in the Philippines, some brides would be shocked at the suggestion that they share in the cost of the wedding.

In many rural areas, indirect courtship with gifts for the bride's family and negotiations by intermediaries is still the customary procedure. Sometimes, indeed, the young swain may consult the *teniente del barrio* who in turn will approach the parents and arrange for a meeting between the parents of the young man and the parents of his potential bride. If the grandparents are living they too must be consulted. Marriage is an alliance of families not just individuals, and before final sanction can be given all of the relatives have a chance to voice their feelings.

The individualistic trend of *gesesllschaft* society has begun to manifest itself in urban areas. Here, the family influence is still important, but the young people are given a greater chance to manifest their own choice. In some circles, the chaperone has been replaced by group dating on the theory that this is less burdensome on the parents, and that the presence of a group will prevent infractions of the mores governing pre-marital behavior. In still other circles, engaged couples may be allowed to go to social affairs without being a member of a group or under the eye of a chaperone, but this is still regarded in many groups as a rather questionable practice. Free association of the young is thought to threaten both the concept of pre-marital chastity and the influence of the family over the marital choice.

In Filipino society, the chastity of the bride is regarded as the greatest virtue, and individual romantic impulses are considered less important than the judgment

CHAPTER IV. THE FAMILY

of the family group on the suitability of the marriage partner. Concern over chastity goes beyond the limits of technical virginity, and it is often thought that any kind of association with the opposite sex beyond the most formal type makes the bride less desirable to the future husband. This situation is moderated somewhat in the *damay* setting of rural society in which girls are heavily chaperoned but may associate with a large circle of men inside the family group. Usually they will also have some informal association with other men in the barrio activities and in agricultural work.

Usually one of the features of a family system which stresses family control of courtship and marriage is the early marriage of the young woman, since this solves the problem of controlling romantic impulses. In some cultures this even extends to marriage arranged before puberty. The Philippines has seen a considerable emphasis on the desirability of later marriages but the earlier pattern still survives. The census reports for the period between January and June 1952 showed that of a total of 58,177 reported marriages, 525 brides were under 15 and 1,595 were fifteen years old; thus nearly four percent of these marriages involved girls under sixteen years of age.[3]

Authority in the family.

The question of who is the boss in the Philippine family revolves around the usual patriarchal control of the father as contrasted with the wife's role as family treasurer. Although the father is the acknowledged head of the family, the position of the Filipino woman is also high and respected. In fact, this elevated regard for her status in the family is considered unique in the Far East, where woman has generally been taken as the inferior of man.

Even in the ancient Philippines, says Dra. Encarnacion Alzona, the Filipino woman had high status.

---

[3] *Journal of the Philippine Statistics*, Volume V, No. 9, September, 1952, Table 3, Bureau of the Census, Manila.

"upon marriage a woman passed to the control of her husband, although she retained certain rights which enhanced the dignity and importance of her position in the family. She was treated by her husband as an equal; she retained her maiden name, shared his honors, and disposed freely of the property she had brought into the marriage. She was consulted by her husband about his affairs, and he would not ordinarily enter into contracts or agreements without her knowledge and approval." [4]

It was really the Spaniard with his Code of Roman Laws who relegated the Filipino woman to the position of inferiority where the Americans found her. These laws aimed to confine woman inside the home by forbidding her the right to transact business without the legal sanction of her husband, and removed from her the right to dispose of her own paraphernal property.

Today, however, the Filipino woman has regained most of her traditional rights. The New Civil Code now allows her to hold property in her own name, to dispose freely of her paraphernal goods, and to transact business without the prior consent of her husband. She has the same suffrage rights and educational privileges as any man. This high position of the Filipino woman is important in assaying the conservative character of the Filipino family. Through her influence in it, the family has remained traditional in form and character. It can be said, therefore, that although the Filipino family is patriarchal in authority, the most influential member in it is the Filipino woman.

Authority in the family is determined not only by sex, but also by age, with the grandparents playing an influential role. Indeed, the Revised Civil Code specifically states, "Grandparents should be consulted by all members of the family on important family questions." [5]

To this day, children still feel the compulsion to inform their elders about important events in their lives and

---

[4] Encarnacion Alzona: *The Filipino Woman*, Manila, 1934, pp. 15-16.
[5] Title XI, Article 312, p. 66. *Civil Code, op. cit.*

CHAPTER IV. THE FAMILY

to make some gesture of consulting them. On the eve of going abroad, for example, they make the rounds of the relatives; after the honeymoon, the newlyweds always make the rounds again, on both sides, to introduce the new member of the family. If they have built a new home, it is expected to be seen first by the elders before they will feel free to give gay parties in it for outsiders.

The children are also responsible for honoring the dead. It is part of their loyalty to the kin group. A grave without a candle or a wreath of flowers on it on All Souls' Day is a disgrace. The last wishes of a dearly departed are taken with great seriousness, as are his desires while in life regarding the plans for the family.

For example, a dead father can still impose a ban against a son's marriage with an undesirable woman. In fact, it can sometimes be said that the dead have greater power than the living. There is a chance of arguing with the living and changing their minds. In the Visayas, the force supporting this power of the elders and the dead over the children is called the *gaba* or curse that is supposed to descend upon those that dare to go against the tradition of obedience. Of the *gaba*, there is less and less now, but the ancient tradition still has a lingering influence on behavior.

Authority in the Filipino family goes vertically downwards on the basis of age. After the parents, the oldest child exercises authority over the rest, and the principle holds true down the line. Any older brother or sister has authority over the younger and cannot be talked to disrespectfully. In cases of death or absence, it is taken for granted that the eldest sibling takes over the responsibilities of the parents.

This deference to the authority of age is so strongly defined that it has obtained definite terminology of address. To this day, when speaking in the dialects, children address their parents in the third person. For example, they say *kayo*, not *ikaw* for "you". Following the same principle, eldest brother is called *Kuya* or *Manong*, and the eldest sister *Ate* or *Manang*. The second eldest sister is called *Ditse*, and so on. This pattern of family authority has accordingly led to a great cultural emphasis on obedience. One indication of this pattern is that about 80% of the juvenile delinquents in the Welfareville training center have been charged with disobedience. This stems from the cultural interpretation of misbehavior.

It should be pointed out here that this authoritative position of seniority is taken very seriously by those concerned because it is one with a great deal of responsibility attached to it. An elder brother takes over in cases of death or incapacity of the father. He may sometimes even supersede his widowed mother in authority because he is "the man" in the family. He will feel that it is his duty not only to feed his younger brothers but also to give them education, which, somehow, is the height of ambition for all families, whether rich or poor.

It is not unusual for such elder brothers to postpone their own marriages until the last youngster has gone through school, or to build their mothers and the young ones a small cottage before they will build themselves a comfortable home. Neither is it unusual to find the youngest in any family with less character and independence of mind because they have been indulged in their slightest wish on the theory that they had received less of their parents' "strong" years.

Size of family.

The Filipino family is consanguinal in that it revolves around the principle of kinship. It recognizes relationships with cousins far removed and takes them into the household as family members if called upon to do so. Thus, the Filipino family, like the Chinese, can be very large indeed.

A large family is respected, and perhaps, also feared in the community. The tradition of unity can make it very powerful and influential. It is rare for a family member to go against the general stand of his family, whether this be in politics, business or religion. To marry into a large family, therefore, can help many a young man further his ambitions. He is usually pointed out as a "lucky" boy, and he will occasionally mention his marriage in cases where he will need to boost himself in the group.

The size of the family is not dependent altogether on the birth rate but is extended by the *Compadre* system.[6] The *compadre* or *comadre* becomes known to the child as *Ninong* or *Nino;* their children are *Kapatid sa binyag* to the baptized child. This means that through the religious rite of baptism the *compadre* becomes somewhat of a brother to the parents of the child, and assumes a modified type of parental relationship to the child, while the *kapatid sa binyag* move into somewhat of a fraternal relationship to the child. Thus the *compadre* relationship extends the line of family influence beyond that set even by broad consanguinal lines, and throughout life one has certain privileges and responsibilities to those with whom he is connected by the ties of the *compadre* system.

Religion in the family.

One receives a general impression that religious interest in the Filipino family is almost more family-centered than church-centered. At the least, one could say that the strong familistic tendency found in the traditional Filipino family system also has a noticeable influence on religious life. There are several patterns of behavior which seem to support this view. The first pattern is that whenever some big family event is occurring in the parish church, such as the wedding, baptism, or burial of a relative, even the most anti-clerical members of the kinship group are generally present for the church ceremonies. This would seem to indicate, therefore, that they will go to church for *family* reasons, though ordinarily they would not attend religious services.

Another pattern of a different nature, but which also indicates the familistic attitude, is the widespread incidence of family shrines in Filipino homes. Thus, one may find

---
[6] *Compadre* is the godfather of a child in baptism. The godmother is called either *comare* or *comadre*.

that a family has so set aside a part of their house that they have a veritable little chapel in the house. Certain family members will pray regularly at these home shrines and tend them with great care, though they may rarely go to church. Again, therefore, one would say that this shows a family-centered religious attitude. Interestingly enough, these family shrines are far fewer among American Catholics than among Filipino Catholics. Moreover, those Catholics in the United States who do possess these shrines often have a much less elaborate type.

On the other hand, the families of China and Japan very frequently have family shrines which are analogous to those found in the Philippines. Yet the peoples of Japan and China are predominantly non-Christian. This would all seem to indicate that the presence of family shrines is more related to the type of family system which exists in any culture than to the religion of the people. The families of both China and Japan have shrines just as do the Filipino families. Both China and Japan have an emphasis on families, just as does the Philippine culture.

Still another type of behavior which seems to support these views is the importance placed on the All Saints Day ceremonies. The tremendous flocking of people to the cemeteries on this day seems to show that family relations are considered to be of prime importance even after death. This attitude is, of course, consistent with a familistic culture pattern. Here again, it should be observed that in China and other countries which are predominantly non-Christian, the same sort of ceremonies for the dead are found. In fact, many of the most enthusiastic devotees of this custom in the Philippines are the non-Christian Chinese residing in the community. The point here also is that this type of behavior is apparently more related to the sort of family system which prevails in a society than to its specific religious beliefs.

In summary then, it can be said that certain things seem to indicate that religion in the Filipino family shows a strong tendency towards a family-centered orientation.

Chapter IV. THE FAMILY

Although it is undeniably true that religious beliefs exert a tremendously powerful influence on a society, the interaction is by no means one-way. We also find that the family system of a society, together influence on the particular forms of religious behavior.

Family Pathology.

No human institution works perfectly and the family too has its share of difficulties. The difficulties of the family are based on the fact that intimate association with the resultant sharing of responsibility demands a mature attitude which many people fail to develop. The stability of the family is likewise limited by the fact that the process of social change may bring together as husband and wife people with different ideals about family life. All of the various types of family patterns experience some difficulty, but this pathology (illness) expresses itself differently in different cultures. This is brought out in the regional classification of families by Folsom.[8]

> The Northern family type in Europe has "sex equality, non-seclusion and moderate physical labor for women; some acceptance of chivalry; a single standard of sex behavior, whether on a strict or libertarian level; divorce in preference to toleration of extra-marital relations; late marriage; secular control of marriage and divorce; scientific infant care and rigorous child discipline."
>
> The Southern type of family Folsom describes as with "sex inequality or patriarchy and some seclusion of women from activities; moderate physical labor for women; male jealousy and possessiveness with less chivalry in the attitude towards women; a rather frank double standard of sex behavior for married people as well as unmarried; early marriage; church control of marriage and divorce; unscientific infant care and less austere child discipline." [8]

[7] Joseph K. Folsom, *The Family*. John Wiley & Sons. New York: 1943, p. 97.
[8] *Ibid.*, p. 98.

Some of the features of the "southern type of family" are often ascribed to Catholic influence but this is undoubtedly an over-simplification. This pattern of family behavior is prevalent throughout the Orient and also in some rural areas of countries in which Protestants are the dominant religious group. It is a pattern which tends to develop in well established agrarian type of societies and to break down with the extension of industrialization and the expansion of formal education.

Another example of the differential treatment of family pathology may be seen in the attitude toward prostitution, defined as extending sexual favors to more than one person in return for a specific cash payment. Prostitution exists in all civilized societies, and attitudes vary between suppression and segregation. Those who would tolerate but segregate the practice in restricted districts argue that it can never be entirely eliminated and that segregation and regulation permit medical supervision which minimizes the effect of this type of vice. Those who attempt to suppress prostitution admit that they may not be completely successful, but feel that attempts at suppression will at least reduce the total amount of prostitution and minimize the attractiveness of the practice. They claim that toleration gives legal sanction to undesirable behavior and encourages people to consider it an accepted part of society. They also argue that regulation is never complete and that effective medical supervision is impossible since a prostitute may be infected within a few minutes after she has passed a medical inspection.

Catholic countries in the past have usually inclined to a policy of regulation and segregation and it is even possible to cite statements of the church fathers defending this position. Thomas Aquinas quotes with approval a statement by Augustine in which the latter regards toleration of prostitution as the price paid for the defence of virtue in respectable women. To quote Augustine: "If you do away with harlots the world will be convulsed with lust."[9]

---

[9] *Summa Theologica*, II-II, Q 10 A 11. See discussion in Jacques Leclerq, *Marriage and the Family*, New York, Pustet & Co., 1949, pp. 345-346.

Chapter IV. THE FAMILY

It should be added, however, that we have no empirical proof that the presence of commercialized vice leads to a higher standard of morality in the rest of the female population.

In most European and South American countries a policy of segregation has been followed: sometimes explicitly recognized by the law and sometimes encouraged by the police in spite of legal prohibitions. In the Philippines, segregation was the rule until the abolition of the segregated district in Manila in 1917. Since that time, prostitution has been illegal but is frequently tolerated by the police on the basis of the usual arguments in favor of a policy of segregation. In the United States, the usual policy, with occasional exceptions, has been to attempt suppression in line with the Puritan tradition which is unwilling to accept the visible presence of deviant behavior. This attitude has been reinforced by the experience of the armed forces in World War II when it was found that vigorous attempts at suppression seemed to lower the incidence of venereal disease.

Evidence of family pathology in the Philippines would include the maintenance of a *querida* system among the well to do and of consensual unions (not sanctioned by lawful marriage) among the lower classes. The presence of prostitution has been widespread enough in urban areas to warrant alarm about the practices of "sex gangs" in recruiting inmates of brothels. Likewise the evidence of illegitimacy indicates that the emphasis on chastity is not completely successful. The most recent figures, those for the period January to June, 1952, indicate that 2,535 births out of 92,535 were registered as having occurred outside of wedlock.[10] This is a figure comparable to about three percent of the total births and undoubtedly underestimates the total since mothers strive to avoid the labeling of a child as illegitimate. No figures on the extent of desertion are available, but social agencies find this is a continuing problem.

---

[10] *Journal of Philippine Statistics*, Volume V, No. 9, Table 4.

In many countries, extreme family difficulties end in divorce, but postwar legislation outlaws this practice in the Philippines, although a few of the wealthy resort to foreign divorce and a mutual agreement not to file bigamy charges in the case of remarriage. Divorce was virtually non-existent during the Spanish period; allowed for adultery only during the time of American rule; made relatively easy under the Japanese, and completely abolished after World War II. The ground for abolishing divorce was partly religious and partly a feeling that divorce was so evil in its effect on both children and parents that it should not be allowed.

Abolishing divorce however, means only that we have suppressed some of the symptoms of family distress rather than effecting a cure. Divorce is undoubtedly a measure which brings suffering as well as relief. Thus it is extremely difficult to say which is more undesirable; an intact but loveless household where affection has been replaced by hate, or a broken household which requires many painful readjustments. Indeed, it might be argued that legal divorce is less objectionable than the maintenance of *queridas* or irregular consensual marriages which exist without legal protection or supervision.

In any event, the abolition of divorce is less important than is attention to the basic causes of family disatisfaction. These causes seem to lie in two directions: personal psychological differences and sharp cultural conflict. All of our studies of marital adjustment show that the egotistical, self-centered type of individual has a difficult time adjusting to the give and take of married life; also people whose temperaments are sharply different, the extrovert and the introvert, the cheerful and the depressed, the gay and the serious, seldom see life in the same way and find living together difficult.

Cultural conflict is probably inherent to some degree in a rapidly changing world, but usually we find that the sharper the conflict the greater is the strain on marriage ties. For this reason intermarriage between those of different ethnic, religious, or social backgrounds is fraught with danger because they bring together men and women who do not have a common definition of the basic values and ideals they consider important. In the throes of romance it may seem that love will conquer all, but in day to day living the couple who do not eat the same kind of food, go to the same church, enjoy the same recreation and have similar ambitions for their children find the influences which pull them apart steadily increasing while the bonds of affection become constantly weakened.

No certain cure exists for marriage troubles because the essential limitations of human nature make perfection impossible in any relationship. One of the arguments for allowing divorce is the feeling that mistakes in choosing marriage partners are bound to occur and hence society should allow changes to be made without forcing the individuals involved to legal subterfuge or actual violation of the law's commands. On the other hand, it is argued that family stability is so important that the law should not countenance the breakup of a family.

To strengthen the marriage bonds we seek to disseminate through school courses, articles in the press, and other media of communication, an understanding about the nature of the privileges and responsibilities of married life. We hope that young people will understand the need for a serious consideration of the life partner from the standpoint of a life long companionship. Further, we strive to increase the number of people qualified to act as marriage counselors who may be able to interpret to those in marital difficulties the source of their difficulties. Those in emotional turmoil seldom see themselves clearly, and a skillful adviser may help them to an understanding of both the other party and themselves. Finally, family stability is simply one aspect of social stability and all the factors which work for mental health and a smoothly functioning social order also work for better family adjustment.

In one sense, the presence of divorce in the western world is a manifestation of the spirit of individualism which demands that marriage favor personal happiness and is unwilling to tolerate a situation in which the husband and wife sacrifice their own happiness in behalf of the supposed good of the family group. The older patriarchical pattern sacrificed individual happiness in behalf of family life. The newer individualism may err equally by sacrificing the stability of a permanent relationship in search of an unreachable romantic goal. The development of a family pattern which neither binds the individual slavishly to an institution nor wrecks the family group by individual caprice is regarded by many as a major task of our day.

One must remember that this discussion uses "pathology" to indicate the deviation from the "ideal family life" as viewed in the Philippine mores. If the discussion were centered on family life in a culture whose mores differed greatly from those of the Philippines, the definition of "pathological" behavior would also differ. A further point is that these deviations from the culturally-influenced standards may be condemned publicly but tolerated, if not given actual approval, in private. This raises the question as to which set of standards is really representative of the culture—the private or the public one.

An additional view on this topic, expressed by Kingsley Davis,[11] is that deviations from the cultural ideals, such as prostitution, serve a functional purpose and so may actually contribute to family and social stability, much in the same vein of thought as the preceding quotation from St. Augustine.

Family conflict.

While family conflict may be a source of pathological development, it is important to recognize that a normal amount of disagreement is to be expected between the members of any human group, and it is a part of the process which may lead to ultimate improvement.

---

[11] Kingsley Davis, "The Sociology of Prostitution," *American Sociological Review*, Vol. II, No. 5, October, 1937.

CHAPTER IV. THE FAMILY 83

Much family conflict in the Philippines may be interpreted as the result of the gradual westernization of the urban family which casts doubt on the validity of ancient patterns and is in direct conflict with the practices in rural communities. It is thus a part of the conflict which comes about in the transition from a *damay* society with fixed norms to the more loosely structured folkways of the *gesellschaft*.

In the rural family, the pattern is still the traditional one of over a century ago. It has hardly altered since then. The authority of the elders is as strong as ever, so that the young are made to stay close to them on the farm, even though there may be over-crowding in the locality. The rice is cooked in the same red clay pot placed on the traditional iron tripod and heated by five pieces of kindling cut by the eldest son after his hours of school. The English that the children have learned in the barrio school is seldom heard within the nipa walls. Nor are the words of the cleanliness song always carried out in practice in the *batalan* where the water in the large water jar has come from the river a mile away.

The rural family is still frankly communal; there is so little to divide, anyway. This communal feeling has led to a lack of ambition among the family members. If one raises a flock of chickens to improve his lot, his less ambitious neighbors will soon be asking them from him one by one, as festive occasions arise. In the end, no one has any chickens in the neighborhood, nor cares to raise any.

There are no newspapers to be had. Even if there were, with no cash in its hands, the rural family could not buy any. There is no electricity, and hence no radio. There is no desire for change or improvement. Whatever ferment there is has come from outside the family, in the form of a labor recruiter, perhaps, or a rich relative. The inertia of centuries is too deeply seated to be easily changed.

In great contrast is the urban Filipino family. It is a world apart from the rural family. It has been influenced tremendously by the West through the medium of books, the movies, the foreign residents, the schools, the radio. It is active and ambitious. It usually knows English. The mother has a job, and all the children go to school as far as their income will let them. The prosperous Filipino urban family is much like its counterpart in New York or Madrid.

Although to all external appearances, this urban family is no longer what it used to be, still the traditional pattern of Filipino family life remains under its seemingly strange exterior. The vertical authority of the father and the eldest children is still recognized, although its field of influence has become more limited. The high position of the woman is still recognized and respected, even more so, because of the modernization of the laws referring to women. There is practically no more communal feeling about the family property, most of which has been acquired through individual effort and not through inheritance or endowment from ancestors. There is a decided democratic atmosphere in the urban Filipino family which was not apparent before. The children have closer ties with their parents, and the parents have more things in common.

The children of urban families, and probably eventually of rural families, too, are in a state of confusion—torn between the newer pattern of western life and the traditional practices and unable to find their place in either setting. Thus, the family status of the urban child places him somewhat in the position of the typical "marginal man."

Parents feel inadequate before the confusion of changing generations. Some of them simply move with the tide while others take up a futile defense of the "good old days" when standards of proper conduct were understood by all. Husbands and wives often find that the role of the married woman today who works in an office and participates in community activity is hard to reconcile with the simple "Maria Clara" ideal of the past. The wife who is educated and alert is seldom content with a situation in which propriety demands that the married woman remains at home while her husband is free to go as he pleases. The husband, on the other hand, finds it difficult to reconcile the freedom demanded by the modern woman with the notion of male dominance which has been a part of his upbringing. Children likewise are torn between notions of family loyalty and the newer individualism which demands the right to work out one's own life plans.

The present day is a time when the older customs are being destroyed and newer ways of behavior are not yet accepted by all parts of the community. In the past, family adjustments were made in accordance with the *mores* or traditions of the family group. The *mores* controlled personal behavior. Allowances were sometimes made for incompatibility with the family standards, but these allowances were circumscribed and limited within a certain boundary.

Conflicts within the family have arisen on account of both psychological and cultural causes brought about nearly always by the changing times. Families differ widely in the amount and intensity of their conflicts, depending on the amount and intensity of the outside influences that come in to contradict the family *mores*, or traditions. Usually, in an isolated family in the rural regions, the conflicts are more psychological in character, whereas the urban families undergo conflicts along cultural lines.

Conflicts in the family are not only inevitable in view of the modern age we are now in, but they can be healthy for the family, and have their definite functional value. It is through conflicts and their solutions that families may set up and achieve new goals, that division of labor and cooperative action between the members is developed, that individuals come to subordinate their interests to the general family welfare. Without conflicts, families would remain stagnant.

Social Role of the Filipino Family

Security.

The power and stability of the Filipino family make it in every sense a major source of social security. The family takes care of its members in case of need and provides the individual with the sense of social solidarity acquired from membership in a strong primary group. It is through the family that the individual finds his place in the community and establishes his status with other men. While the economic role of the family in case of financial disaster is well known it should not be forgotten that the psychological security provided by a closely knit family structure is equally important. The family gives one an island of security in a world of chaos. If the family system of the Philippines has weaknesses then these shortcomings are largely the defects of its virtues.

Authoritarianism.

If we assume that the family is the nucleus of the larger society in which individuals develop the ideals and attitudes which are to influence them in later life, then we also assume that it is difficult to have one type of relationship inside the family and an entirely different type of relationship outside of the family group. For this reason, we have begun to raise the question as to whether a democratic culture can be nourished in an authoritarian family. In other words, if the child in the family is taught to accept without question the advice of the elder, can he learn in later life to think for himself? If family life is characterized by a chain-of-command method of reaching decisions, can he function in groups in which decision is reached by democratic discussion?

The vertical lines of authority by which a fairly rigid discipline is established hardly seem to be compatible with a democratic state which attempts to encourage the equal participation of all its citizens. One may well ask how the child develops the skill of democratic participation in political life when his home life is based on the unquestioning acceptance of authority. In this sense, a family system which seems to operate smoothly may still be of doubtful value as preparation for life in the larger community.

Conservatism.

When all important decisions have to be made by the entire family group with the elders having the most influence, the effect is inevitably to discourage initiative and to slow down new developments. When the family softens the blow of disaster and, at the same time, takes from the more fortunate members the fruits of their success it simultaneously penalizes the ambitious and rewards the lethargic. It is certainly arguable that strong family control has militated against the pioneering and the risktaking demanded by modern business enterprise and technological advance.

This somewhat critical discussion of the role of authoritarianism and conservatism in the Filipino family is based on the premise that the direction of social change is toward an urbanized *gesellschaft* type of society. If this premise is accepted, then family traits may be evaluated on the basis of whether or not they are in harmony with the demands of a rapidly changing society. It should be remembered, however, that authoritarianism and conservatism contribute to stability in the social order and a sense of security in the individual. A more loosely knit and less authoritarian family may facilitate the acceptance of change, but it may also lead to a greater degree of social unrest and personal disorganization. No existing family pattern is either completely good or altogether bad, and the future trend in family relationships is related to the type of changes which may take place in the total culture.

Community spirit and civic participation.

When one grows up in a system which stresses the loyalty to a large family group, it is easy to give this family loyalty greater stress than the loyalty to the nation or to abstract ideals of justice. Nepotism (the favoring of relatives) is to be expected when it is taken for granted that members of the family always pull together. Both private business and public life suffer from a persistent feeling that individual capacity is less important than the obligation to help the members of one's family.

Similarly, the failure of welfare institutions to gain effective support either from private contribution or governmental appropriation is at least partly related to the demands of the family group. In *Philippine Social Trends* it is estimated that the 3,300,000 normal families in the Philippines carry an extra load of some 4,000,000 dependent relatives.[11] This "family burden" may well incline the individual to believe that when he has taken care of his needy relatives he has met his charitable obligations and thus blind him to the plight of those whose needs are not met within the family system.

The Filipino family *does* participate in community activities, contrary to prevailing impressions. The trouble lies in the fact that its participation is still carried on through channels laid out generations ago.

For example, all families join in celebrating the town or barrio fiesta. Together with everyone else, they consider the day theirs, decorate their houses accordingly, prepare sumptuous feasts for outsiders, and help their neighbors put up the welcome arches at the street corner. The whole affair is a community endeavor carried out in the traditional pattern of *barangay* feasting. Even the menus for such occasions have hardly suffered a change.

The Filipino family also joins the community in helping out a neighbor who has had a death in the family or an accident. It helps in his wedding preparations, which are often too much for a single family to afford, in building his house, in moving it out to another place. The harvesting and the planting of rice is a group endeavor.

In fact, it is not education in community cooperative work that the Filipino family lacks but a new channeling of this traditional training. With new and more utilitarian avenues for community work, much can be done in improving the welfare of Philippine society.

---

[11] The President's Action Committee on Social Amelioration assisted by United Nations Consultants, *Philippine Social Trends*, Manila, 1950, p. 24.

Economic influence.

The effect of the family influence on economic activity is to minimize individual initiative and cause business decisions to be made upon a group basis. It has the effect also of causing business relationships to parallel closely the family structure. The result of this may be seen in the presence of enterprises in which management, labor and capital all come from one family group. Such an enterprise has difficulty raising money for expansion of business activities, and its employment policies are dictated by lines of family authority and obligation. It tends to be conservative for the more aggressive individuals may be held back by the conservative influence of the total family group.

This Filipino family pattern is in direct contrast with a society in which the young are encouraged to strike out on their own, and in which the employment of relatives is viewed with suspicion. It is related to the reluctance of Filipino investors to place their money in enterprises beyond the control of the immediate family and is a partial explanation of the indifference to join stock enterprises and even to commercial banking. Supposedly, a capitalistic economy is governed only by profit and loss considerations, but family dominance insists that the preferential position of relatives is at least as important as mere business efficiency. In this sense, family values may be viewed as antagonistic to the values of individual enterprise and probably retard business development.

On the other hand, when the entire culture is pervaded by a willingness to accept the need of change in economic activity, family solidarity may strengthen the enterprising individual. The Ilocanos, the most migratory group in the Philippines, are characterized by a family cooperation in which the entire family finances the pioneer in new fields, and later moves as a unit when conditions warrant. Similarly, the Chinese family in the Philippines functions as a school in which the skills and attitudes essential to business success are learned in the home

Even in these cases, however, the tendency is to restrict enterprise to the family group and to limit the individual to the role which the family feels is acceptable. Thus, the value of family cooperation and support must be balanced against the restraint on individual initiative and the difficulty of establishing working relationships beyond the family group.

Supervision of marital choice.

The basis of the chaperonage of the young is partly a desire for maintenance of family control and partly a desire that young women remain chaste at all times. The assumption is that free association will inevitably lead to relaxation of virtue. Such a system, in practice, often gives rise to a group of restricted women while the men are free of moral blame when they associate with women outside the pale of respectable society. It denies the opportunity of acquaintance before marriage, and means that young people go into marriage without the type of understanding which develops from friendly association. Western students of family life often point to the desirability of acquaintance with several of the opposite sex before choosing a marriage partner; a situation impossible in a society which forbids casual friendships between men and women.

Chastity is not dependent upon any specific type of chaperonage system. On the one hand, ideals of chastity may be so firmly inbedded that they constitute an effective guide for conduct when no third party is present. On the other hand, the existence of illegitimate children in societies with a chaperonage system indicates that this system is no iron clad guaranty of sexual purity.

The present uncertainty about the merits of a chaperonage system is related to the clash between the patriarchal and the companionate concept of the marriage relationship. In surrounding countries of the Orient and in South America parental control is emphasized and it is not expected that wife and husband will be perfect companions; rather, each has a separate sphere of activity which is well defined. Under these circumstances, a chaperonage system is in harmony with the culture and no important discontent arises.

When the emphasis in marriages is on companionship and individual happiness then a freer type of courtship assumes importance. If the husband and wife are to be companions, sharing their social life and making joint decisions on family problems then individual compatability is paramount. Logically, if husband and wife are to be companions after marriage then the unmarried should select suitable companions through acquaintance before marriage. Debate on the necessity of chaperonage in the Philippines is one aspect of a society which is attracted to the individualistic emphasis of the *gesellschaft* society, but which still clings to the more rigid social controls of the *damay* community.

Summary

The Filipino family system grew out of the family structure of the primitives, took shape under the influence of Hispano Catholic ideals and is presently challenged by the impact of American individualistic emphasis. The family structure is being modified by the growth of *gesellschaft* type concepts which challenge the rigid social structure of a *damay* society. The resultant cultural clash produces confusion and uncertainty although the basic family structure seems highly resistant to change. Specific issues include the acceptance of the vertical lines of family authority, the prohibition of divorce, agitation for revision of courtship customs and the merits of the small versus the large family group.

The type of family structure has far reaching influence and affects political, economic and social life as people carry into these spheres habits and attitudes learned in the family. In general, the prevailing system emphasizes loyalty, stability, obedience and kinship obligations while minimizing individual initiative and community responsibility.

Family pathology is manifested by marital dissatisfaction, the *querida* system, consensual marriage and prostitution. The attitude toward family pathology is affected by the widespread acceptance of a double standard of morality which assumes nearly opposite ideals for masculine and feminine conduct along with the existence of a group of women beyond the pale of respectability.

Indications of possible change are seen in the gradual breaking up of large and powerful family groups and in the increased mobility which scatters both families and individuals. The effect of increased marriages between social classes and across ethnic lines is to further decrease the power of the authoritarian pattern. This infusion of new blood and contrasting ideals may help to bring about a synthesis of the older patriarchial family of the Spanish period and the companionate type of family pattern prevalent in the American sphere.

QUESTIONS

1. What are the chief differences between the three families describe in this chapter? What are the most important strengths and weaknesses of each family patterns?

2. What are the good and bad points of the abolition of divorce? Do you feel that the abolition of divorce is consistent with other trends in family life?

3. Even when no religious opposition is present birth control has aroused little interest in countries whose family pattern is similar to the Philippines. How would you account for this?

4. Describe the effect of family life in politics, social welfare and business. Do you feel that family influence should be modified in these areas? How?

5. What is meant by family pathology? How would you deal with this problem?

6. Do you see any conflict between the employment of women in the modern day and their position in the family? Describe.

7. How does the double standard of morality affect the family pattern? What type of family system do you feel is most congenial to the perpetuation of the double moral standard? What type is most hostile to this standard? Why?

8. What is meant by the distinction between cultural and psychological causes of family conflict?

9. Why do you feel that the chaperonage system caused less controversy seventy years ago than it does today?

10. Is coeducation compatible with the traditional family pattern? Defend your answer.

CHAPTER IV. THE FAMILY 93

PROJECTS

1. Write a paper describing the structure and activity of your own family. Indicate the personnel, division of labor, lines of authority and common activities. Indicate the similarities and differences with the patterns described in this chapter.

2. Read and report on one of the references in the bibliography.

3. Describe the type of courtship system prevalent in your locality. Describe changes, if any, which seem to have come about in the last twenty years. Is the system uniform or are there groups in the community which follow another pattern?

4. Analyze the economic activities of your family or other families with which you may be familiar. If you have worked in a government office or a fair-sized private company describe the evidence of family control apparent in this setting.

SUGGESTED READINGS

Anshen, Ruth Nanda — *The Family: Its Function and Destiny.* Harpers, New York, 1949. — Series of provocative and easily read essays on various phases of family life: Specific chapters make good student assignments.

Burgess, Ernest W., Lock, Harvey J. — *The Family.* American Book Co., New York, 1945. — A basic text by two of the foremost American authorities on the family.

Goodsell, Willystine — *Problem of the Family.* D. Appleton-Century Co., New York, 1936. — Good historical approach coupled with social problem orientation.

Leclerq, Jacques — *Marriage and the Family.* Pustet & Co., New York City, 1949. — An authoritative work on the social philosophy of the family written from the Catholic viewpoint.

Macaraig, Serafin E. — *Sociology.* University of the Philippines, 1948, pp. 74-111. — Social aspects of Filipino family life.

Mihanovich, Schnepp — *Marriage and the Family.* Brun Publishing Co. Milwaukee, 1952 — A treatment of the Family from the Catholic viewpoint. Includes a presentation of evidence from empirical studies about family trends.

Mendoza-Guazon, Maria Paz — *The Development and Progress of the Philippine Woman.* Kiko Press, Manila, 1951. — Feminine progress in the Philippines.

Queen, Stuart A. and Adams John B. — *The Family in Various Cultures.* J. B. Lippincott Co., 1952 — Comparative study of family patterns in different cultures.

Stern, Bernard J. — *The Family Past and Present.* A cross cultural approach to the family with special attention to current cultures.

COLLECTIVE BEHAVIOR

Introduction.

We now come to one of the parts of sociology which has received added attention in recent years. The interest in collective behavior has grown with the development of social psychology. Undr this topic are considered those group ways of acting where the ordinary folkways and mores do not apply. Thus collective behavior is viewed as a special kind of human group experience.

In the sections on culture and primary group life we noted that many of the things which we do are simply a following of the culture patterns which are learned in primary group contacts. However, in collective behavior the ordinary patterns of conduct are often cast aside so that new and surprising or shocking group behavior appears. This special way of group acting is given particular attention by sociologists for two main reasons:

1. The new ways of acting may be accepted by the society and become part of the culture.
2. In our present society, the shift from the *damay* type of close neighborly relationship to the *gesellschaft* type of society makes many more people susceptible to collective behavior. Moreover, in such a situation, collective behavior may bring some order into the lives of people who feel a lack of their former *damay* patterns of life.

In our modern world, all forms of collective behavior tend to have a great influence. Collective behavior follows certain definite patterns which the student of sociology should strive to understand.

CHAPTER FIVE

CROWDS AND PUBLICS

The conclusion to be drawn from what precedes is that the crowd is always intellectually inferior to the isolated individual, but that, from the point of view of feelings and of the acts these feelings provoke, the crowd may, according to circumstances, be better or worse than the individual. All depends on the nature of the suggestion to which the crowd is exposed. This is the point that has been completely misunderstood by writers who have only studied crowds from the criminal point of view. Doubtless, a crowd is often criminal, but also it is often heroic. It is crowds rather than isolated individuals that may be induced to run the risk of death to secure the triumph of a creed or an idea, that may be fired with enthusiasm for glory and honor, that are led on—almost without bread and without arms, as in the age of the Crusades—to deliver the tomb of Christ from the infidel,... Such heroism is without doubt somewhat unconscious, but it is of such heroism that history is made. Were peoples only to be credited with the great actions performed in cold blood, the annals of the world would register but few of them.

— Gustave Le Bon, *The Crowd: A study of the Popular Mind.* London, T. F. Unwin, 1897, pp. 13-14.

Types of crowds.

The crowd is one of the most popular subjects of study in the field of collective behavior, perhaps because crowd behavior is often dramatic. When we use the term "crowd" in sociology we attach a special meaning to the word. Just as in so many other cases, the definition of a word by sociologists is not the same as the definitions used by other people.

In sociology the word "crowd" refers to a group of people assembled at a particular time who have a common center of attention, influence each other emotionally, and share a common experience. The individuals who comprise the crowd are in close physical contact—some writers call it a "shoulder-to-shoulder" situation. The temporary nature of the crowd is one of its most prominent traits. A crowd only exists at one particular place at one given time. If the same people meet at anothr place and time and form a crowd, it would be regarded as a completely different crowd situation. The emotional inter-relationships in a crowd are a basic part of the group. If there is only a collection of people in one place and there is no emotional influencing of each other, we would not call it a crowd. This emotion can grow so strong that the individual crowd members may "forget themselves" and just follow the actions of the group in an impulsive manner.

There are four major types of crowds according to some sociologists. These four are:[1]

1. The casual crowd
2. The conventional crowd
3. The acting crowd
4. The expressive crowd

The *casual crowd* is the sort of grouping which can be seen every day in the centers of large cities. An example in Manila would be the gathering of people around a sidewalk musician in Quiapo. Another case would be the clustering of people which forms around a traffic accident or a street fight. As the word "casual" suggests, this sort of crowd has little unity. The individuals are just attracted to something for a very short time. Some of the people may only pause for a minute to see what the group is watching, while others may stay for a much longer time. There is always some trace of emotional feeling, however. The center of interest may stir up the

---

[1] This classification and the subsequent exposition are adapted from Herbert Blumer, "Collective Behavior" in *New Outline of the Principles of Sociology*. Alfred M. Lee, Editor, 1946, pp. 178-179

Chapter V. Crowds and Publics

beginnings of curiosity, fear, anger, amusement, and so on, but these emotions never grow very strong in this type of crowd. Casual crowds merely form, become interested in something for a moment, and then drift apart.

The *conventional crowd* has a much more definite nature than the casual type. The members of a conventional crowd assemble for a regular or "conventional" reason. The examples which come most quickly to mind are the athletic contests between the various colleges and universities such as one sees in the stadium in Manila. In such a contest as a basketball game, we have the crowd assembling at a given time and place which was selected and announced well in advance. The group also follows certain regular patterns in such things as seating, cheering, and intermissions. However, we must emphasize that *an audience is not a conventional crowd*. In the theater, for example we find the audience, which is different from the crowd in one important point. The members of an audience do not have a direct emotional influence on each other. For example, in an exciting basketball game one can cheer loudly to encourage the players and also encourage others to cheer. But in a concert or debate if one were to cheer during the program it would be considered improper. This difference exists because the members of a crowd can and do influence each others emotions, while the members of an audience expect to concentrate on the program and so do not like any disturbance. However, it should be added that an audience may be changed into a crowd in some cases.

The *acting crowd* is usually the most interesting type to students of sociology because of its well-known behavior. In the acting crowd, the emotion of the group becomes intense, and the crowd then performs collective action towards an object. Another and popular name for this type of crowd is the term "mob." Thus we frequently read in our newspapers of mob behavior. There are some famous examples of acting crowds in Philippine history. Macaraig cites the riot against the Amoy Chinese in

October, 1924 during which several acting crowds damaged property and attacked people.[2] Another case was the attack on foreigners which occurred in Manila in 1820. At that time, some French scientists had arrived in Manila to collect specimens for research. Unfortunately, a terrible epidemic broke out in Manila shortly after the arrival of these scientists were causing the disease through magic. Accordingly, a crowd of about 3,000 gathered and embarked on a program of killing and looting which lasted for several days. As the activity of the crowd intensified, the feelings became generalized against all foreigners, so that a total of 100 non-Filipinos were killed before the fury of the crowd subsided.[3]

The fourth and last type of crowd in this classification is the *expressive crowd*. In this case, the crowd becomes greatly excited but lacks a specific object of attention. Since there is no specific object of interest, the crowd excitement then begins to "express" itself in a pattern of *rhythm*. This rhythm is the special mark of the expressive crowd. It may take the form of vigorous singing, hand clapping, stamping, swaying, or a special kind of dance. This rhythmic behavior continues to grow until the crowd excitement reaches a peak—sometimes called the "ecstacy" of the expressive crowd. The emotional feeling of the group then gradually subsides as the members return to their ordinary emotional condition. This particular kind of behavior has led to this crowd also being called the "dancing crowd."

Such a type of crowd is sometimes seen at certain celebrations such as a victory bonfire where students may form a "conga-line" or "snake-dance." Some American Indian tribes had similar dances either as a preparation for warfare or a celebrtion of conquest. An extreme form of "jam session" where addicts of the so called "hot

---

[2] Macaraig, *Introduction to Sociology*, Revised Edition, 1948, pp. 226-227.

[3] Calip, Resurrección, "Massacre in Binondo," *Sunday Times Magazine*, July 10, 1949, pp. 42-43.

Chapter V. CROWDS AND PUBLICS

music" gather is another example. Before shifting our attention, however, it should be mentioned that a single group may change from one type of crowd to another. Thus a casual crowd may become an acting crowd or a conventional crowd may become the expressive type. We now turn to the general characteristics of crowd behavior which are common to all of the four types.

The first and most important feature of crowd behavior is "circular interaction." This trait refers to the particularly emotional nature of crowd behavior. For example, let us say that one individual called "A" becomes excited. Perhaps "A" has seen a traffic accident. Then if "A" has a companion "B", "B" may also get excited because of the influence of his friend. But the excitement of "B" will then go back and stimulate "A" who according gets more excited. Thus it begins to go between them, with each one making the other person more excited. In such a case, we say that there is circular interaction because the emotional interaction of the two persons is going in a circle. Now if we add some more people to the situation, the interaction will naturally become more complex and the excitement can also develop more rapidly. This is a basic process in the formation of any crowd and its later behavior.

The excitement of the different crowds is naturally not the same. The casual crowd is the least stirred up while the acting and expressive crowds are the most excited. In accompaniment to this rise of crowd excitement and emotion comes the loss of "self-consciousness," that is, the more that one joins in the feeling of the group, the less will he be conscious of his own "self" and his own ideas. So the self-consciousness becomes replaced by a "group-consciousness"—thinking more in terms of what "we" will do, instead of what "I" will do.

"Milling" is another general trait of all crowds. This term refers to the physical movement of the crowd members within the group. As a crowd aseembles one may notice that some of the individuals will push forward, others will step backward, while still others may go from side to side. Part of this behavior is a result of the interest in the object of attention—people in the crowd want to see and hear what is happening. Another part of the milling comes from the growing excitement. The crowd members are expressing their emotional state by their restless movement. And yet, this milling also serves to increase the crowd excitement.

The rise of suggestibility is an especially prominent feature of crowd experience. As the circular interaction goes on and the excitement grows, the crowd members are more willing to follow the suggestions of the leaders in the group. This means that there is actually a great decrease in critical thinking. If it goes far enough, the individual is ready to act on impulse, not reason; and he is ready to act immediately. This explains the unpredictable and often startling nature of the acting type of crowd. Along with the rise of suggestibility also usually comes a sense of power and righteousness to that an acting crowd believes that it *can* and *should* do what it desires.

Why do people engage in crowd behavior? This question is often asked, and these are some of the answers given.[4] Novelty is one explanation. That is, people are attracted by something which is unusual. So it is that people will gather to see an accident or a fighter or a basketball game. Another reason given is that since we human beings have a combination of reason and emotion in our make-up we are always attracted by the emotional mood or tone of a crowd. This is especially true if we are already feeling some emotion which needs release. Also, it is observed that individuals who have an unstable emotional life are often more attracted to crowds.

Then there is the factor of social tensions and unrest. It has been noticed that crowds are much more likely to

---

[4] These factors in crowd behavior are largely drawn from Sutherland and Woodward, *Introduction to Sociology*, Second Revised Edition. 1940, pp. 318-322.

CHAPTER V. CROWDS AND PUBLICS 101

form when people are restless and uneasy about something. An example of this is the amount of crowd behavior found in countries when there is an economic depression. In Manila during 1946 there was a great deal of unrest among the American soldiers who were waiting to go home. This situation led to crowd behavior by these "G.I.'s" in the form of demonstrations. So we say that the cultural background has a great influence on the origin of crowd behavior. Other reasons have also been given as explanations for the rise of crowds, but these seem to be the most direct and important causes.

The relationship between crowds and the culture of their members is found in more than just their sources. It has also been observed that the center of interest which attracts a crowd varies according to the values of the culture. For example, in the early days of the American Western settlement a horse thief was regarded as one of the worst criminals and so was often lynched by an acting crowd. This was related to the culture of that time in which horses were absolutely essential. The attention of an acting crowd in the Philippines, however, is much more likely to focus on something else, since horse stealing is not generally regarded as a major problem in the culture.

Crowds are also linked to their culture in their way of expressing themselves. The following is an incident which shows this fact in regard to a conventional crowd. A famous singer went to another country to perform. After her program the crowd showed great excitement and began to whistle loudly. The artist then burst into tears because she believed that the whistling meant disapproval. However, the actual case was that the crowd was hailing her and asking for an encore!

The differences in acting crowd behavior which are related to culture are quite commonly recognized. For instance, in the Bible we read that the Jews of that time would gather into a crowd and stone some offender to death. In the Philippines, on the other hand, we often hear or read of a crowd using bolos or the *sundang* on a person who offends them. The use of tar and feathers is a particular sort of punishment formerly used by crowds in some parts of the United States. The offender was thickly coated with tar and then a layer of feathers was applied, making the person look like some grotesque sort of bird. All of these examples show that the behavior of a crowd often follows certain *general* culture patterns of its society. The exact details of the crowd's action are of course unpredictable, but these general trends can be recognized. Now we leave the crowd and turn to another major form of collective behavior—the public.

The Public

The term "public" as it is used in sociology designates a group of people who are interested in an issue, have different ideas about the issue, discuss the issue, and try to form a group opinion. Probably the most common and clear-cut example of the public is found during an election in a democratic country. In an election we have the choice of candidates as the issue, and the various groups of interested voters as members of the election "public." During the campaign period there is usually a great amount of discussion over the candidates, and lastly the formed group opinion is expressed through the means of voting.

From the preceding, statements, one can see that the sociologist has a special use for the term "public" which again differs from the usage of others. Thus, a sociologist would say that a public is *not* a "following." A following would be those people who are interested in some special topic but who do not discuss the topic or from an opinion. A "fan-club" composed of those who admire a certain actor or actress would be called a "following." Other followings would be groups of sports enthusiasts, hobby clubs, racing fans, or the general radio audience. None of these are considered as public because they lack discussion and the growth of an opinion.

Chapter V. CROWDS AND PUBLICS

The public, as has been stated, includes all of those people who are interested in an issue. Thus, depending on the issue, the public may be very large or rather small. For example, the members of a public may be only a few hundred people, or it may include most of the residents of a city, a province, a nation, or possibly even the world. Now some of these members of the group will have one view of the issue while other members will think otherwise. We call these various divisions of the public by the name "interest groups." Naturally, there will be one interest group for each "side" or view of the issue. However, we also find some people in the public who are interested in the issue but who have not yet decided which "side" or view they will follow. This group within the public is called the neutral or "listening" part of the public. We will mention more about them in the next chapter. It is important to realize that the membership of the public and its interests groups changes according to changes in the issue. Also, it should be noted that one person may belong to several publics at the same time, if he is interested in several issues simultaneously.

The greatest difference between a public and a crowd is the matter of emotion. The public emphasizes rational discussion. Therefore, the members of a public try to "see through" any expressions of emotion so that they can look at the issue more critically and objectively. The crowd, on the other hand, is based a great deal on emotion, so that the members of a crowd often oppose attempts at rational discussion and critical thinking. In popular words, we would say that the public uses its head, while the crowd uses its heart.

Since rational discussion is an essential part of the public, the question of communication is extremely important. This is true because the very organization and functioning of a public depends on people first hearing about the issue and then being able to communicate with each other for discussion. If there is no communication the public can not exist. Today the modern means of communication have enabled the growth of huge publics. In former times when there were no daily newspapers, radio sets and stations, motion pictures, and television facilities, the problems of communication set a limit on the size of publics. Now, however, it is quite possible to have a world-wide public discussing a certain issue. This development of communication also means that the members of a public may not even see each other, since the interaction of the discussion is often indirect. This indirect contact in the public is another great difference from the crowd, since the crowd depends on direct personal contact for its growth. Hence, crowds are always local while publics may be local or extremely far-flung, depending on the issue and the communication facilities.

Ogburn and Nimkoff have also pointed out that in a small primitive society where the culture is relatively stable and the *damay* type of neighborly relationship prevails, the publics are also of a particular kind. So we find that in a *damay* sort of community "... the number of interest groups will be small and the number of social issues that arise will be few, because conditions remain relatively unchanged over long periods of time and because such problems as arise can often be dealt with in terms of the prevailing folkways." [5] However, in the modern type of *gesellschaft* society which especially exists in the larger cities of the world, including Manila, we find that the issues and the interest groups are more numerous and varied, and that communication draws many more members into the group of the public. Thus *gesellschaft* society means an increase of issues, interest groups, discussion, and members. So we find that the public is becoming of more importance in our modern *gesellschaft* society.

Summary

In sociology, the crowd refers to a grouping that is local, temporary, focused on a particular interest, and united by emotion. The crowd is often classified into four major types: casual, conventional, acting, and expressive. Each

---

[5] Ogburn and Nimkoff. *Sociology*, Second Edition, 1950, p. 123.

Chapter V. CROWDS AND PUBLICS

type has its own particular characteristics in structure and function.

All crowds possess certain common traits. Circular interaction is the most important factor in the rise and spread of crowd behavior. Milling serves as an expression of the group restlessness and also serves to intensify the emotional atmosphere. As the crowd excitement rises, especially in the last two types, the loss of self-consciousness occurs plus the rise of a feeling of power and righteousness. The crowd is also rendered more suggestible and so is ready to act impulsively.

The principal bases of crowd behavior are related to human nature and society. The wish for novelty is given as one possible factor. Human emotion and the tensions present in a culture are viewed as other sources. Crowd behavior is related to culture in both origin and expression. The culture sets the possible range and indicates certain general favored patterns for action.

The public is analyzed as a special group apart from a following. The most essential elements of a public are an issue and the rational discussion of it by interest groups. In addition to interest groups the public also includes a neutral group of interested but undecided members. As issues and events change so does the composition of the public vary. In our present society with the shift from the *damay* relationship to the *gesellschaft* situation we find larger publics with more issues, interest groups, and discussion than before.

QUESTIONS

1. How can you show that crowd behavior is a natural part of group life?
2. What is suggestibility? Are individuals in a crowd more suggestible than when alone? Why?
3. Are educated people less suggestible than those who are not educated? Why?
4. How is crowd behavior influenced by the culture?
5. What are the basic differences between the four types of crowds?

6. How does a public differ from a crowd?
7. Can people from different traditions participate in the same crowd?
8. What is the role of the "neutral" part of the public?

PROBLEMS

1. Make a scientific analysis of some crowd in action. How was it formed? What attracted it? How was it finally scattered? Why?
2. Make a scientific analysis of an issue and the public which forms around it. What are the various interest groups? Did they change as time passed? Did new interest groups appear? What means of communication were used for discussion?

SUGGESTED READINGS

Blumer, Herbert: "Collective Behavior," *New Outline of the Principles of Sociology*, Part IV, Alfred M. Lee, editor, 1946. Barnes & Noble. — A near classic statement of theory on crowds and the public by one of the great authorities in this field.

Britt, Stewart H.: *Social Psychology of Modern Life*, New York. Rinehart and Company, Inc., 1941. Chapter 12. — An extremely readable, cleverly illustrated book which presents some rather unusual material on crowds and the audience.

Piere, Richard T. and Paul R. Farnsworth: *Social Psychology*, New York, McGraw-Hill Book Company, Inc., 1942. Chapter 21. — Contains excellent material on the expressive crowd ("audience *fanatique*") and the acting crowd.

Sutherland, R. L. and Woodward, J. L.: *Introductory Sociology*, Chapter 12, Second Revised Edition, 1940. — A clear and fairly detailed analysis of crowds and the mechanisms behind crowd behavior by two of the leading sociological authorities.

Young, Kimball: *Social Psychology*, Second Edition, New York. F. S. Crofts & Co., 1947. Chapter 16 contains one of the most comprehensive sections available on the psychology of the crowd and audience.

CHAPTER SIX

PUBLIC OPINION, PROPAGANDA, AND MASS INTERACTION

We ordinarily think of public opinion as a sort of social weather. At certain times, and under certain circumstances, we observe strong, steady currents of opinion, moving apparently in a definite direction and toward a definite goal. At other times, however, we note flurries and eddies and countercurrents in this movement. Every now and then there are storms, shifts, or dead calms. These sudden shifts in public opinion, when expressed in terms of votes, are referred to by the politicians as "landslides."

— Robert E. Park and Ernest F. Burgess, *Introduction to the Science of Sociology*, Chicago, University of Chicago Press, 1921.

In the preceding chapter, public opinion was mentioned as the outgrowth of the discussion process within the public grouping. One can therefore view public opinion as a product of social interaction. Just as certain substances will crystallize under the proper conditions, so is the formation of public opinion related to certain conditions. It has been noted that the quality of public opinion is directly related to the facilities for communication and the amount of available information.[1] Thus extremely limited communication would also limit the amount of participation in the discussion. Also, such a situation would reduce the membership of the public, since news of the issue could not travel far. For example, gossip was the most common device for discussion in the Philippines before modern inventions were brought in. As a result discussion was centered on local issues and did not cover a

---

[1] Macaraig, *Op. cit.*, pp. 63-64 and 67-69.

wide area. A lack of adequate discussion thereby naturally lowers the quality of the resulting opinion.

The relationship between the available information and the formation of public opinion is also quite plain. Since the public emphasizes rational discussion, it is especially interested in facts. Now if the facts are not available, or if they are not correct, the discussion will accordingly suffer. Public opinion which rests on incomplete or erroneous facts is like the proverbial house built on sand. Since facts are often hard to obtain in a complex *gesellschaft* society this situation assumes greater interest today. Moreover, since we regard the opinions of intelligent well-informed citizens as fundamental in democratic government, these influences on public opinion should receive our careful attention.

Communication Facilities

One of the most important aspects in the formation of public opinion is the availability of communication facilities. These facilities make it possible for people to keep in touch with the rapidly changing interests of *gesellschaft* society. Their absence limits public opinion to a dependence on gossip and other sporadic and unreliable avenues of communication. At the turn of the century the Philippines had extremely limited communication facilities but their expansion has been rapid in the last fifty years.

The school are one of the most important means of communication and their expansion has been spectacular. In 1900, the Philippines had only 6,900 elementary pupils in the public schools and no public secondary system existed.[2] In the school year 1951-1952 there were 4,018,476 pupils in the public schools with an additional 772,850 in the private institutions.[3] These figures give convincing evidence of the extent to which this medium of communication has increased.

---

[2] Macaraig, *op. cit.*, pp. 63-64.
[3] *Journal of Philippine Statistics*, Vol. V, No. 10, pp. 62, 63; Vol. VI, Nos. 1-3, pp. 55-64.

CHAPTER VI. PUBLIC OPINION

Turning again to the early years of this country we find that there were about 41 newspapers in 1903, the majority of which were in Spanish and had a limited circulation. In 1938 there were 262 newspapers with a total circulation of 1,500,000 according to the records of Macaraig.[4] Apparently the shift since 1935 has been towards a decreasing number of newspapers with an increasing circulation. According to the 1952 figures, there was a total of 527 publications in the Philippines that were issued more than twice a year. The estimated total circulation of these various publications was somewhat over three million.[5] However, according to certain unofficial estimates,[6] the actual number of newspapers represented in this total may have been about 50, and probably half of this number were located in Manila. When one considers the fact that the mortality rate of publications of all sorts has been extremely high in the Philippines since World War II, this drop in the number of newspapers is not particularly surprising.

In regard to circulation it is unofficially estimated that the newspapers of Manila probably have a circulation of somewhere between 300,000 and 350,000. The official figures are considerably higher, but for various reasons the actual circulation is estimated to be as noted above. About 35% of the circulation of Manila newspapers is in Manila and the remainder is in the provinces.

The balance of the total circulation of three million as given for all publications in 1952 would then be accounted for in the sales of magazines, journals, bulletins, and provincial newspapers. For example, there are at least six comic books which are published fortnightly in Manila which have a combined circulation of at least 300,000. There is also a group of ten magazines published

---

[4] Macaraig, *op. cit.*, pp. 63-64.
[5] *Journal of Philippine Statistics*, Vol. V, No. 10, Oct. 1, 1952, Table 21, p. 59.
[6] The circulation of periodicals is often a closely guarded trade secret and the published figures are not always reliable. The figures used in this discussion were obtained from personal interviews with representatives of advertising agencies who regularly check periodical circulation.

weekly in various dialects in Manila and elsewhere which have a combined circulation of at least 450,000. Thus although the figure of three million may be excessive, we are fairly certain that the bulk of the printed matter which reaches the Philippine population is generally in the form of magazines, bulletins, journals, and the like.

Turning to the language usage found in Philippine publications, several distinctive patterns are evident. Of the six fortnightly comic books, all are printed in Tagalog. In the weekly magazine field one finds that eight out of the total of 18 are in English, three are in Tagalog, two in Ilongo, two in Cebuano, and one each in Chinese, Bikolano, and Ilocano. However, of the eight magazines in English six of them are published as supplements to daily newspapers. This means that there are only two separate English language magazines which are published on a weekly basis and which have a combined circulation of about 100,000. The total circulation of the non-English weekly magazines is estimated at about 410,000. This is considerably greater than that of the newspapers or even of the comic books.

In regard to daily newspapers, one finds a different pattern. Out of the fourteen leading newspapers printed in Manila, seven or exactly one-half are printed in English. The others are distributed as follows: four Chinese, two Spanish, and one Tagalog. The combined circulation of the English language daily papers printed in Manila equals approximately 260,000 while the non-English papers have a total circulation of about 41,000.

An examination of the regular monthly magazines and the one fortnightly magazine reveals another pattern of interest. In this category which has a total of nine publications, all are printed in English except for two which are bi-lingual (English and Tagalog). The two bi-lingual magazines have a total circulation of about 80,000, while the other seven magazines in English have a combined circulation of 855,000. This would seem to indicate that in the magazine field those publications in the dialects or in a bi-lingual form reach a wide audience. A somewhat different pattern is found when one turns to the trade journals and special interest or policy publications.

The first and most striking feature of this group is that every single publication in it is in English. From medical journals through labor papers to industrial news sheets there is a uniform adherence to English. However, as might be expected, these special interest publications have only a limited circulation. The twenty-one trade magazines reach a combined circulation of 49,314, while nineteen special policy publications have a total circulation of 80,500.

From the standpoint of language usage, English is predominant in newspapers, trade magazines and special policy publications. Tagalog is favored by the comic magazines and a wide variety of languages are utilized by the various weekly magazines. This would seem to indicate that English is the most effective language for reaching an intellectual type of audience. On the other hand, magazines which specialize in popular fiction have been able to tap an extensive market by utilizing the local vernaculars.

Motion picture houses are found in most places which have electricity and reach a large number of people. English language movies are predominant in the larger cities but a flourishing local industry has developed in the production of films in Tagalog and, to a lesser extent, in other Philippine languages. Unfortunately, we were not able to obtain reliable estimates as to the number of people viewing films although one may assume that a large proportion of the population is reached by this medium.

Turning to other forms of communication one also finds a notable development in the Philippines. The roads in 1909 totaled only 209 kilometers whereas in 1935 there were 15,990 kilometers of roads. This was paralleled by a jump in the registered motor vehicles from 7,372 in 1918 to 44,362 in 1935.[7] Compare the foregoing figures to those for 1935. As of June, 1953 there were 29,218 kilometers

---

[7] Macaraig, *op. cit.*, pp. 63-64.

of roads in the nation—almost double that of 1935—and a total of 106,944 registered vehicles. These vehicles included 49,997 automobiles, 55,267 trucks, buses, and trailers, and 1,680 motorcycles. In addition, there were also 68 air ports and 112 registered aircrafts in the Philippines.[8]

The growth in communication with foreign lands is partly demonstrated by the rise of maritime activity. In **1905 only 558 foreign vessels entered Manila, whereas 1,232** were recorded for 1934.[9] Compare this to the figure for all Philippine ports in 1953 which reached a total of 21,107 vessels cleared.[10]

In regard to radio the increase is also quite marked. In 1935 there were 89 radio stations,[11] whereas in 1953 there were 186.[12] Telegraph stations, however, showed a much lower rate of increase. In 1935 there were 435 telegraph offices,[13] but by 1953 this had only risen to 464.[14] However, the use of telephones in the Philippines is still only in its infancy. The Government Bureau of Telecommunications reported a total of 3,016 telephones for 1953 and the Philippine Long Distance Telephone Co. reported 31,640 subscribers.[15] Although this is a rise from previous decades it has been observed that "...as of January, 1952 the U.S. had 29.3 telephones per 100 population, Japan 2.4, Puerto Rico 1.8, Malaya 0.5, while the Philippines had only 0.1." [16]

The foregoing discussion provides a clear demonstration of the growth of some of the chief agencies of communication in the Philippines. This has several important

---

[8] Report of Phil. government agencies as collected in The National Economic Council, *The 1953 Economic Development Program*, Part I, "The 1948 and 1950 Economic Development Programs and Their Implementation, Manila, December 24, 1953 pp. 177-180 and Appendix 10-17.
[9] Macaraig, *op. cit.*, p. 64.
[10] Nat'l. Econ. Council, *op. cit.*, Appendix 10-10.
[11] Macaraig, *op. cit.*
[12] Natl. Econ. Council, *op. cit.*, p. 184.
[13] Macaraig, *op. cit.*, p. 64.
[14] Natl. Econ. Council, *op. cit.*, p. 184.
[15] *Ibid.*, pp. 184-185.
[16] *Electrical Communications*, June, 1953.

CHAPTER VI. PUBLIC OPINION

effects on public opinion. For one thing, these various media increase the influence of *gesellschaft* ways of thinking on the development of public opinion. Thus the factor of tradition carries less weight in the formation of opinions. Another effect would be an extension of the range of opinion formation, that is, the greater facilities for communication now mean that more people can participate in the discussion of issues. This further means that a greater variety of ideas on an issue are expressed as more varied groups of people join in the discussion.

With the exception of the schools, most of this growth of communication facilities has taken place in the larger centers which have a fairly reliable source of electricity. Only a small number of periodicals reach the rural sections, and many barrios have neither radios nor movies due to lack of electricity. Modern means of communication have expanded fairly rapidly in the cities but in rural areas their growth has been much slower.[17]

It must be clearly recognized, that public opinion is almost never unanimous. There are always some members of the public who maintain a "minority" opinion. Thus public opinion is actually a combination of several shades of opinion rather than the unanimous judgment of a whole group. Therefore, one can say that public opinion is already formed when there is a clear majority who share a common view of the issue.

As new issues are met, discussed, and resolved by the public the mores may be affected. For example, the issue of whether it was good to abolish slavery or not was discussed in many parts of the world, including the Philippines. Today, now that the issue has been settled, people would feel that a return to slavery would violate the mores. Anti-slavery feeling has thus risen out of the group's decision and become a part of the culture.

At the present time there is a great interest in public opinion because of its crucial role in democratic society.

---

[17] For a more extended discussion of this point see chapter ten, *Rural Communities*.

114 SOCIOLOGY IN THE PHILIPPINE SETTING

As a result, the measurement of public opinion has become a special field of activity. There are now organizations whose only task is to measure public opinion and publish their findings. Leaders in democratic government systems have the regular elections as a formal expression of public opinion, but they also wish to know the attitudes on other subjects such as taxation, appropriations, and foreign affairs to serve as a guide to action. Businessmen make use of public opinion measurement to learn of the wishes of consumers and their opinions toward possible commercial developments. Social scientists measure public

Picture shows a public opinion research team getting consumer reactions. Both business and government are finding that it is important to sample the opinion of the people they serve. Photo by courtesy of the Manila Times.

CHAPTER VI. PUBLIC OPINION

opinion as a means of analyzing human social behavior. Other groups are also interested in public opinion such as schools, churches and reform organizations but those mentioned first are the most prominent groups.

The formation of public opinion shows certain differences in the *damay* situation as compared to the *gesellschaft* pattern of social relationships.[18] In the *damay* type of community the range of the issues and the resulting opinions are fairly limited. People are not greatly interested in discussing matters outside of their own local group. Moreover, the facts are ordinarily easy to discover and verify, for it is almost impossible to conceal anything in such an intimate community atmosphere. Since the members of the *damay* group generally have similar attitudes and beliefs, public opinion is usually formed easily and serves as an immediate guide.

On the other hand, the formation of public opinion in a *gesellschaft* society is often markedly different. In the first place, the greater amount of communication increases the number and variety of issues. Therefore, members of a public are involved in much more discussion and it covers a wider range. The individuals in a *gesellschaft* setting frequently discuss complex international issues for example. Also, the facts are often more difficult to obtain and verify. Thus the discussion may be based on information which is not wholly reliable. And then lastly, since there is less unity of interests and values in a *gesellschaft* community, it is correspondingly more difficult to produce a clear-cut opinion in a reasonable length of time. Thus both the formation and characteristics of public opinion are greatly influenced by the culture from which it rises.

Propaganda

It is perhaps easiest to remember the definition of propaganda as a deliberate attempt to lead people to ac-

---

[18] This analysis is drawn from Kimball Young, *Social Psychology*. Second Edition, 1947, pp. 434-437.

cept a certain idea or belief and so influence their opinions and behavior. One can readily see from this definition that there is a close relationship between propaganda and public opinion. Thus in the public grouping we find that the neutral or listening part of the public is the target of all the propaganda which each interest group sets forth. In fact, one of the greatest factors in the formation of public opinion today in the *gesellschaft* setting is propaganda. Therefore, we now turn our attention to this important social force.

Today the word "propaganda" has an unfavorable air, so that people often condemn a printed or spoken production by calling it "propaganda." However, in its origin the world is really a neutral term. Its root is related to "propagate" which means to multiply or spread. Thus in 1633 the Roman Catholic Church established the "Congregation of Propaganda" which was merely an agency to foster the growth of the church and the Catholic religion.[19] In sociology today, the word "propaganda" is used in the original neutral sense, so that here it means all attempts to change people's thinking, whether for better or worse.

There are some well-known devices which are used in propaganda to make it effective. Perhaps not all of these techniques or devices are used in one single piece of propaganda, but it is almost certain that at least two will be found. Since modern advertising is the most common form of propaganda today, some of the best examples of these devices are found in advertisements. The devices and their descriptions are as follows:[20]

> 1. *Repetition* — In this case an idea is presented time and time again until it is virtually "burned" into our consciousness by the constant stimulation. A good illustration of this technique is found in modern radio "commercials" where the same words, phrases and even tunes are repeated day and night with tiresome regularity.

---
[19] Young, *Social Psychology.* Second Edition, 1947, p. 502.
[20] The following description is largely drawn from the Institute for Propaganda Analysis, *The Fine Art of Propaganda*, New York, 1939, pp. 23-24.

Chapter VI. PUBLIC OPINION

2. *Name-calling* — The propaganda here tries to give us a "shorthand" sort of stimulus by summarizing an idea in one word which has a special meaning. It applies a label. Thus a political candidate may be described as a "hero" or a "savior" while his opponent may be termed a "war-monger" or a "radical."

3. *Glittering Generality* — This means the use of a word which has a purposely vague meaning. For instance something may be praised as being "progressive" or be condemned as being "subversive." However, in both cases the words actually have no specific meaning, so that they appeal more to emotion than reason.

4. *Testimonial* — This technique consists of having respected people endorse or support the propaganda and its aims. The advertising which features the stars of radio, stage, and screen recommending certain soaps, cigarettes, and beverages is a common example of this device. Its effectiveness rests on the general human attitude that such prominent people surely must know what is good.

5. *Plain Folks* — This refers to an attempt to relate the propaganda to the so-called "common man." This appeal would naturally have the most effect in a culture where the "common man" is regarded with favor. Candidates for election, for example often try to gain votes by showing that they are just "ordinary citizens" and belong to the people. So we find that candidates will don overalls and a straw hat when they talk to farmers. Or, on the other hand, certain companies will deliberately emphasize that their product is used by the ordinary person. The effectiveness of this device rests upon the human trait of often identifying oneself with the common man, so that what "Mr. Average" does we believe should also suit us.

6. *Card-stacking* — This term comes from gambling. A dishonest card player would sometimes arrange the playing cards in a deck so that the whole game would be planned in advance. Here the term designates the use of carefully selected bits of information which present only one side of the topic and do it as forcefully as

possible. It is not telling untruths, but rather telling only partial truths.

7. *Band Wagon* — In the earlier days of American history the musicians of a street parade frequently rode in a wagon. The little children then tried to jump on the band wagon and ride in the parade. The application of this behavior to propaganda is quite direct. An item of propaganda will frequently mention that everyone else is believing this or doing that so why don't you "jump on the band wagon" and join the others. It is linked to the popular notion that the majority is always right. Thus we see advertisements claiming that 9 out of 10 people are using a certain product, and so urging us to do the same.

After reading the above list of propaganda devices one may begin to think that propaganda is all-powerful and make us do its every command. However, that is not the actual case. There are some definite limits to the influence of propaganda. The first and perhaps most effective limit comes from knowledge. If one knows the truth about something he or she is much less affected by propaganda. Thus if we know that a candidate for public office is really a complete rascal we would probably be little swayed by his propaganda.

Another limitation on propaganda comes from the folkways and mores of a culture. It is virtually impossible to convince people to do something which is against their mores. And it is even difficult to lead people to change or go against their folkways. For instance, it would probably have little effect today if someone were to crusade for polyandry in the Philippines because it is against the mores. This limit to propaganda explains the difficulties of such programs as public health education, for as Macaraig emphasizes, it is often a matter of trying to change the customs of a culture.[21]

Counter-propaganda also checks the effectiveness of propaganda. Although neither party may be telling the truth, the opposing groups might caused each other's in-

---

[21] Macaraig, *Op. Cit.*, pp. 36-37.

Chapter VI. PUBLIC OPINION

fluence. As a result, the subject of the propaganda is probably not convinced by either side, although he still does not know the truth. Then lastly there is always the technique of restricting the effects of propaganda by censorship.

Censorship has been viewed as a negative method of limiting the influence of propaganda since it merely prevents its expression without offering any alternative. That is why a truly effective censorship is usually coupled to a program of counter-propaganda. So while propaganda tries to shape public opinion, censorship tries to reduce the amount of propaganda and general information which the public receives. Censorship is therefore selecting what materials may be transmitted and what information should be prohibited from distribution. The degrees of censorship vary, so that in a dictatorship, censoring is often extremely strict while elsewhere it may be much less. However, it has been pointed out that even in a democracy, there is always a certain amount of informal, private censorship.[22]

The significance of propaganda in our present life is great. For one thing, much of modern business depends on the use of advertising as a special kind of propaganda. In a *damay* situation, buying and selling is ordinarily done on a direct and personal basis, especially if the society has a handicraft economy. Thus one can personally judge things on their own merits.

However, in the modern, industrialized *gesellschaft* society, much of the commerce is impersonal and indirect and so we put more faith in advertising. A product now may be popular only because of the propaganda which the advertising agencies use to promote it. For example, in the beverage and tobacco fields, there is very little difference between products of the same class. Therefore, the huge sale of one cigarette or one soft drink is probably due more to advertising than to the special merits of that one product.

---

[22] Sutherland and Woodward, *Introductory Sociology*, J. B. Lippincott Co., Chicago, 1940, pp. 779-781.

We should also notice that in our modern cities with their highly developed systems of communication, propaganda of all kinds is usually more effective. Since it is often hard to get the facts in such a situation, people tend to rely more on the information contained in propaganda. Then they are greatly influenced by the propaganda itself because it is presented so well and in so many ways. This matter should be of particular concern to us today, for in a democracy we traditionally emphasize the importance of citizens who are well-informed with the correct facts. Hence in a modern democratic society there is a special problem of "seeing through" the greater amount of propaganda which is now also much more influential than ever before.

Stereotypes

In the preceding passages, it was noted that name-calling was one important propaganda device. The effectiveness of this technique depends a great deal on the use of "stereotypes" which are a special variety of names or words. A stereotype can be defined as a false idea or belief which regards all members of a group as having identical traits. The word originally came from a printing process in which a number of identical castings are made from one mold. In a social stereotype we think that the members of a group all have identical characteristics, as if they were all castings made from one mold.

A stereotype is always at least partially false. This is because a stereotype always says that *all* members of a group have certain identical traits. Thus the stereotype that "*All* Turks are cruel" is automatically false because it says *all*. In every human group there is a great variety of persons so that there are always many exceptions to every stereotype. Some writers accordingly describe stereotypes as false "pictures in our heads" since they never correspond to reality.

Another important feature of stereotypes is that they are almost always linked to a strong emotion. This gives

Chapter VI. PUBLIC OPINION

a great deal of force to stereotype since they appeal to emotion rather than reason, and will almost never be changed by any logical argument, for emotions are not rational. Therefore one can present all of the available scientific evidence against a stereotype and yet, after the presentation, those who hold the false belief will generally remain unchanged. When a person's stereotype notions *do* change it is usually because of some emotional experience, for example, forming new friendships.

It should be emphasized that stereotypes may be favorable or unfavorable. In either case they would naturally be just as inexact. Thus a stereotype that "all postmen are cheerful" would have no more validity than one which states that "all mechanics are deceitful." They both again have the error of viewing all of the group members as having identical traits.

Some of the more common stereotypes are often summarized in words which are called "epithets." An epithet tries to characterize or describe its subject, frequently in a single word. The easiest epithets to remember and describe are the unfavorable ones. So for example we find that the word "Hun" was used in World War I to depict a stereotyped idea of savage brutal Germans. The word "Chink" has also been associated with an unfavorable view of Chinese. A contrast between unfavorable and favorable epithets might be illustrated in the words "Rookie" and "Regulars" as used in the army. "Regulars" not only classified some of the group as different but also was associated with a certain favorable stereotype. However, this example is not perfect because it does not always apply.

Because of their emotional connections we often find stereotypes and epithets in propaganda. They serve to excite people and sway their thinking by an appeal to their feelings rather than to reason. Moreover, the stereotype or epithet is able to convey a whole idea or description of a group in just a few words. Thus a propagandist gets the double effect of increasing the power of his appeal and also saving effort by using stereotypes and epithets.

In regard to our present culture, we find that stereotypes are just like the other parts of collective behavior, for they are also becoming of greater importance. As our culture becomes more complex, there is a greater growth of stereotypes. This is a natural human reaction. One wants to simplify things so that they are easier to understand and to manage. Therefore as the *damay* type of personal relationships grow fewer we are dealing more with *groups* rather than persons. In an effort to simplify this changed situation we then try to characterize the groups and so develop stereotypes. Therefore one finds more relations based on stereotypes in the *gesellschaft* city situation where the impersonal contacts between groups prevail. Lastly, it should also be noted that stereotypes can have a disorganizing effect on human relationships. For one thing, they often lead to misunderstandings and tensions between groups since each group has a false idea of the other. Stereotypes can also have a great influence on our personal relationships. One may, for example, be prevented from enjoying a certain friendship because one has a stereotyped view of another person.

Mass Interaction

In this section we shall examine the special behavior of the group called a "mass" by certain sociologists. Again, it must be emphasized that both the name and the group are given some very special meanings which are different from those used by others. According to some sociologists the "mass" is a human grouping whose membership cuts across such lines as status, vocation, education, and wealth; and which acts individually but in a uniform way.[23] A detailed description of the specific traits of the mass will help to make this definition clear. In the first place, we find that the mass usually includes all kinds of people. Thus it may have rich and poor, ignorant and educated, employers and jobless, and the crim-

---

[23] This definition and the following discussion are based on Blumer, "Collective Behavior." *New Outline of the Principles of Sociology*, Part IV. Alfred M. Lee, editor, 1946.

Chapter VI. PUBLIC OPINION

inal with the law-abiding citizen. In this case the mass is similar to the public, for they both may contain all types of people. Secondly, however, the mass is described as anonymous. That is to say that the individual members in the mass are seldom known to each other. This is very different from the public and the crowd.

Another special trait of the mass is that communication and interaction are at a minimum. Thus, in the mass, communication is usually only of the "news" type in which information is merely passed around. So that we see no debate, discussion, or circular interaction in the mass. Again this is a great contrast to the public and the crowd. This also means that the mass is not emotional.

Then, as mentioned in the definition, the members of the mass act in a uniform way but as individuals. There is accordingly no general group action or unity. Rather, it is merely a loose grouping of people who all happen to be doing the same thing. Thus mass behavior actually consists of the *total* of separate individual decisions and actions. So we find that the ordinary traits of a society are absent in the mass. There are no folkways or mores nor is there any kind of cultural pattern. The only prominent feature of the mass is the particular set of actions which is performed by the separate individuals. Now we will turn to some actual cases of mass behavior which display these characteristics quite plainly.

One of the most commonly cited examples of mass behavior is the gold rush. In 1849 the news of a gold discovery in California set off a great rush to the location. All kinds of people dropped their work and made individual decisions to join the rush. There was no milling, circular interaction, or discussion. The individuals alone just decided to go after they heard the news. Also, there was no particular group unity. Each individual was trying to take care of his own claim first and get ahead of the others. It was "every man for himself." And then lastly, the separate members of that gold rush were not only unknown to each other, but also to outsiders. Thus the group was fully anonymous.

Photograph shows crowd of people gathered outside of Baclaran Church. This is considered an example of mass behavior in which many people assemble together but crowd interaction is limited. Photo by courtesy of the Manila Times.

An observer can notice many instances of mass behavior in the Philippines. Because of certain cultural emphases, some of the best examples are found in the field of religion. Thus some writers have commented on the popular "rushes" to places where miracles are said to occur. Probably the most outstanding example in the immediate post-World War II era was the Lipa case.[24]

In 1948 it was announced that the Blessed Virgin Mary had let fall a shower of rose petals in Lipa, Batangas. Accordingly, thousands who heard of this report began to flock to Lipa. The numbers of people became so great that the transportation companies were running special busses to accomodate the throngs. Just as in the California gold rush, the news travelled far, so that accounts also appeared in other countries. This rush to Lipa

---

[24] A brief mention of this and other post-war miracles is found in "Another 'Miracle' Makes its Bow in Bulacan." *Sunday Times Magazine*, Sept. 21, 1952, pp. 12-15.

CHAPTER VI. PUBLIC OPINION 125

continued until the Catholic authorities officially declared that the miracle was not genuine.

Another instance of mass behavior in the Post-World War II period of Philippine history centers on a suburb of Manila. This is the novena to Our Lady of Perpetual Help which is held in the town of Baclaran. Again there is found the general flocking of people to the favored spot. It is estimated that about 70,000 people visit the shrine at Baclaran every Wednesday.[25] Again the individualistic role of the members in the mass is clearly evident. Thus the parish priest writes that "Each person making up those thousands remains an individual, praying alone." [26]

Crazes, fads and fashions.

There are some special variations of mass behavior which are listed as crazes, fads, and fashions.[27] They usually are described as being more temporary but less rational than ordinary mass behavior. The *craze*, as the name suggests, is the most irrational of these three variations. In 1939, for example, there rose a widely publicized craze among college boys in the U.S. which consisted of a contest in swallowing *live* goldfish. These crazes are also sometimes called "rages" or "social epidemics."

The word "fad" is applied to behavior which is similar to that of a craze but not so extreme. The "yo-yo" fad or the jig-saw puzzle fad are good illustrations. People play with these devises for a while and then their interest dies out. Moreover, they are not limited to any one place or time. Thus the writer has seen these fads in both the United States and the Philippines at various times and places. Fads may also appear in a verbal form. In the immediate post-World War II period in Manila we had the rise and spread of the "Siga-Siga" expression. It

---

[25] This account is drawn from L. A. O'Leary C. SS. R. "New Baclaran Church" *Sunday Times Magazine.* February 24, 1952, pp. 14-16.
[26] *Op. Cit., Sunday Times Magazine,* p. 16.
[27] A considerable part of this section is drawn from Stewart H. Britt *Social Psychology of Modern Life,* 1941, pp. 247-250.

was given a whole variety of meanings and was applied in very different situations.

Fashions usually have a longer life than fads or crazes. . In addition, they have other special differences. For one thing, fashions generally have a direct relationship to prestige. Hence, if one has the clothes, house furnishings, and type of automobile which fit the fashions of the time, one can gain prestige. Other forms of mass behavior do not usually have such a close relationship to group approval. This also means that a fashion follows a special pattern of growth and spread. Thus it has been obsedved that fashions tend to spread from the upper levels of a society downward.

Fashions also usually are spread through more deliberate effort than crazes or fads. So we see special magazines devoted to clothing fashions, while the latest designs of vehicles or buildings are also usually well advertised. Fashion therefore is more related to careful planning than fads or crazes. Some observers also believe that there are certain cycles or rhythms in fashion trends which appear through the years. However, it should be added that both crazes and fads may become more stable and so change into fashions.

Viewing mass interaction as a whole, certain implications seem particularly significant. The first is that mass interaction can have a tremendous effect on a society. For example, cigarette smoking began as a fad. Then it became a type of mass behavior, and has now entered the folkways. In the Philippines, it has brought the establishment of new kinds of tobacco farms and factories. At the same time, the demand for Philippine cigars abroad has evidently lessened. Thus the whole nation felt the effect of the change to cigarette smoking.

Secondly, as mentioned above, the patterns of mass interaction may add to the body of folkways and mores. In addition to cigarette smoking, one may list the use of certain cosmetics and the wearing of wristwatches as other cases. Thus part of culture change springs from mass interaction. Then lastly, this sort of group behavior is now becoming of greater importance. Today more people are transferring from the *damay* situations to the *gesellschaft* type of community life. This means that they are now more likely to join mass interaction since they are more easily influenced by its attractions. Thus greater numbers of people are involved and so the total effect of their individual actions is now also greater.

Summary

Public opinion is the product of discussion within the public grouping. Its quality is directly related to the amount of communication and reliable facts. Public opinion is never a unanimous agreement but rather a collective majority opinion. The measurement of public opinion is now a specialized field of analysis which is utilized by many different leaders and researchers.

Propaganda is a word that actually is neutral in meanin. In the field of propoganda there are certain general devices which are used to influence public opinion. However, the effect of propaganda and its special techniques is limited by knowledge, the culture, counter-propaganda, and censorship. Today propaganda has a greater influence in the *gesellschaft* setting and so is of increased importance.

Stereotype represent false ideas about groups and are of great significance in public opinion and propaganda. Since they are emotional in nature, stereotypes do not yield to logic. Epithets are common abbreviations for stereotypes, and are especially used in propaganda. The relationships between groups and individuals, particularly in the *gesellschaft* setting, are strongly influenced by stereotypes.

Mass interaction refers to the special type of individual actions which are done anonymously and yet have the total effect of group behavior. The mass is a special type of group which has traits very different from either the crowd or public. Crazes, fads, and fashions represent variations of mass behavior. They are usually more temporary and less rational. However, they have certain special traits also, particularly fashion. These variations may change and become regular examples of mass behavior, in some cases. The effect of mass interaction is often much greater today, especially in the *gesellschaft* situation.

QUESTIONS

1. What are the influences which shape public opinion?
2. How can we best protect ourselves against the effects of propaganda?
3. Under what conditions is propaganda most effective; least effective?
4. What are the differences between the public, the mass, and the crowd?
5. Why do stereotypes exist?

PROJECTS

1. Visit a dozen homes and find the publications they read and the radio programs to which they listen. Write a report indicating the type of communications to which these homes are exposed.
2. Make a comparison of two American movies and two Tagalog movies. Analyze the differences between them and explain in ttrms of cultural background.
3. Clip from publications examples of the propaganda techniques mentioned in this chapter. Explain the way in which each clipping utilizes the technique you have indicated.

SUGGESTED READINGS

Blumer, Herbert: "Collective Behavior," *New Outline of the Principles of Sociology*, Part IV, Alfred M. Lee, editor, Barnes & Noble, New York, 1946.
   A near classic statement of theory on public opinion and mass interaction by one of the great authorities in this field.

Britt, Stewart H.: *Social Psychology of Modern Life*, Chapter 12, Rinehart and Company, New York, 1941.
   Contains an excellent though brief section on crazes, fads, and fashions.

Chapter VI. PUBLIC OPINION

Lee Alfred M.: *How to Understand Propaganda*, Rinehart and Co., New York, 1952.
This book offers an excellent analysis of propaganda in a semi-popular form by one of the experts in the field.

Macaraig, Serafin E.: *Introduction to Sociology*, Chapter 5, 1948.
This chapter contains a full discussion of public opinion formation in the Philippines both in the past and present and its relationship to the means of communication.

Salumbides, Vincente: *Motion Pictures in the Philippines*, Manila. Published by the author, 1952.
A historical description of the development of motion pictures in the Philippines with special reference to the Tagalog movies.

Young Kimball: *Social Psychology*, Chapters 9, 17, 18, 19 and 20, Second Edition, F. S. Crofts & Co., New York, 1947.
These chapters offer a technical analysis in great detail of stereotypes, fashion, public opinion and propaganda.

CHAPTER SEVEN

SOCIAL CLASS STRUCTURE

Although our democratic heritage makes us disapprove, our class order helps control a number of important functions. It unequally divides the highly and lowly valued things of our society among the several classes according to their rank. Our marriage rules conform to the rules of class, for the majority of marriages are between people of the same class. No class system, however, is so rigid that it completely prohibits marriages above and below one's own class. Furthermore, an open class system such as ours permits a person during his lifetime to move up or down from the level into which he was born. Vertical social mobility for individuals or families is characteristic of all class systems. The principal form of mobility in this country are through the use of money, education, occupation, talent, skill, philanthropy, sex, and marriage.

Class varies from community to community... Yet systematic studies from coast to coast, in cities large and small and of many economic types, indicate that, despite the variations and diversity, class levels do exist and that they conform to a particular pattern of organization.

— W. Lloyd Warner, Marchita Meeker, Kenneth Eells, *Social Class in America: A Manual of Procedure for the Measurement of Social Status*, (Chicago: Science Research Associates, 1949), pp. 23-24.

Nature of social classes.

We are all familiar with the division of the University into various classes such as freshman, sophomore, junior and senior. This gives us not only a measure of the student's academic progress, but is also a method of

Chapter VII. SOCIAL CLASS STRUCTURE

placing large groups of students in relation to other groups of students. In addition, we have learned to expect somewhat different types of behavior from the various classes. The freshman is new in the university environment, is frequently confused in his new surroundings and is likely to be touched by periodic waves of homesickness. He is not altogether sure of the proper behavior for college students and is occasionally reminded by upper classmen of his inferior position. The senior is usually quite sure of himself in the college setting, has high prestige on the campus in relation to underclassmen and feels that by his success in college he has begun to "make good." Juniors and sophomores tend to fluctuate between the uncertainty of the freshman and the overwhelming assurance of the senior.

The term *social class* is simply the expression of a tendency to define relationships between large groups of people in the total society. We speak of people is upper class, middle class or lower class and we associate certain behavior traits with the various social classes. Since the society outside the campus is much more complex than the college world, the basis for social groupings is less definite and is determined by a greater number of factors. Some of the items used to distinguish social classes include: income, ownership of land, prestige of family, occupation, type and amount of education, size and location of homes and the type of friends with whom one associates on an equal basis. The emphasis on these factors varies in different societies. One society may emphasize the ownership of land; in others, it may be the prestige of the individual's family which determines his own classification; while in some societies, the amount of income may be the most important criterion. All societies seem to use a combination of several of these traits although they usually do not give equal importance to them.

In addition to these factors, which may be considered to be of a rather basic type, there are certain types of behavior frequently related to class standing. Usually, the various social classes will wear different kinds of clothing, prefer different types of recreation, develop a distinctive type of speech and cultivate a distinctive etiquette manifested not only in table manners, but in most social relationships. These subsidiary distinctions act as a badge by which one can easily determine the social class of an individual even without knowledge of the factors mentioned in the preceding paragraph.

This distinctive behavior is a part of the individual's culture and, while it may be changed, the process is far from easy. George Bernard Shaw's play, *Pygmalion*, deals with the attempt to change the behavior of a young servant girl in such a way that she will be accepted as an upper class lady. In the process, she not only acquired a new wardrobe, but painfully altered her entire personality. The term "new rich" is frequently applied to those who have acquired the finances associated with upper class status, but have not yet become at ease with upper class behavior patterns.

Varieties of Class Structure in Different Parts of the World

Since the Philippines has been affected by influences from Oriental, Spanish and American sources, it seems worth-while to look at the variety of class structure which is found in these societies. All of them have affected the Filipino idea of social class to some extent.

The Philippines is usually regarded as a part of Southeast Asia. This region has developed a class system largely based on a combination of hereditary family prestige and the ownership of land. It consists of a very small upper class group of large land owners who form a hereditary aristocracy and a large lower class group of farm laborers. The great majority of the society are poor, uneducated and landless. Between them and the top group is a small group who operates estates, hold minor governmental offices and manage the flow of commerce. In the Twentieth century, two new elements entered the picture: the European

Chapter VII. SOCIAL CLASS STRUCTURE

capitalists who developed large plantations and the Chinese or Indian migrants who were either laborers or small scale capitalists. The latter group made rapid progress and have some of the characteristics of middle class groups as these have developed in Europe and the United States. As yet, the total numbers in this category are small and they are not completely accepted by the native populations.

In the traditional Asiatic society there is no pretense of equality and people take it for granted that fate has placed them in the position they occupy. The upper class stresses an avoidance of manual labor and emphasizes its position by long fingernails which must be shielded from toil and by wearing clothes which would be a hindrance to physical labor. The society has a very small upper class, a small and subordinate middle class and a very large lower class. The differences between the classes in terms of wealth, education and even legal rights are very great.

The traditional Spanish pattern is similar to the Oriental with the difference that income variation between the classes may not be quite as great and that commerce, manufacturing and the professions are better developed. Also, governmental and religious institutions are more elaborate and the top clergymen, governmental officials and army officers form an important part of the upper class. Like the Oriental societies, it is characterized by a small and powerful upper class, a slightly larger middle class with little power and a great mass of people on the bottom rung of the social ladder.

The American society is characterized by a proportionately large middle class which sets the tone for the entire society. This middle class is based on a wide distribution of landholdings, universal education and an advanced technological development. Extremes between rich and poor are not so large as in other areas and it is fashionable to attempt to ignore differences which do exists. There is a feeling that men are fundamentally equal and that it is the expected thing for an individual to improve his class status. The income of the rich has been limited by taxes which rise as high as 90% on the top incomes. Likewise, the income of the poor is increased by minimum wage laws and free government services.

The United States does have wide variations in wealth and social position, but is noted for its lack of "class consciousness" and rich and poor alike tend to consider themselves middle class. In a frequently quoted survey in Fortune magazine, the following table was used to express American attitudes on social class.[1]

Upper class	7.3%
Middle class	70.4%
Lower class	22.3%

Other variations from the Oriental and European patterns include a tendency for children of all classes to attend the same school system and for upper classes to give at least lip service to their respect for manual labor. Thus, it is socially proper for even the very rich to **occasionally** do their own household chores and to boast of their experience as manual workers. There are no honorific social titles and the rich pride themselves on their "democratic" manners.

A different appraisal of the American class system which strives to estimate the *actual* distribution of population in the United States by social class was made in 1950. This work, done by Carson McGuire, appears below:[2]

Upper	3%
Upper Middle	9%
Lower Middle	36%
Upper Lower	35%
Lower Lower	17%

As one can observe, there are great differences between the table based upon "class consciousness" and th one based on actual estimates of socio-economic standing.

---
[1] *Fortune Magazine*, February 1940, p. 14.
[2] Carson McGuire, "Social Stratification and Mobility Patterns" *American Sociological Review*, Vol. 15, 1950, p. 200.

CHAPTER VII. SOCIAL CLASS STRUCTURE

Class differences are reflected in different types of environment so that there may be more differences between classes within a nation than between members of the same class living in different nations. Photograph shows a wealthy Manila home contrasted with a Manila slum. Photograph used by courtesy of the Manila Times.

Class structure in Philippine society.

On a comparative basis, the Philippine class system appears to have the same economic foundation as that of other Oriental countries. Economically, the system is based primarily on relationship to the land with a powerful group of large land owners and a very large number of *taos* who either have no land or an amount insufficient for a decent living. The middle class is very small, but education is more widespread than in any other oriental country except Japan. The relationship between distate for manual work and upper class status follows the pattern common in both the Orient and Europe.

From a standpoint of attitudes and symbolic behavior, the class system shows a strong European influence. This can be seen if one looks at the differences in education and possessions associated with various social strata.

Ogburn and Nimkoff observe that, "The upper class in America is not unified by common ideals and standards of behavior." [3] In the Philippines, there is a definite effort to give members of the upper class a common cultural viewpoint. It appears that upper class position is associated with a certain Spanish-European pattern which makes for a separate sort of "we-group" feeling or a "consciousness of kind." One writer has observed that Spanish is termed "the language of the aristocracy" in the Philippines.[4]

This pattern is perpetuated by the differences in the schools. The upper class children often attend schools which are partially or wholly staffed by Europeans and so receive a particular sort of training. This is similar to the European system, especially the "public" schools of England and their function in preserving a distinctive upper class culture.[5] A lower class person, on the other hand, is very likely to be entirely a product of the government school

---

[3] Ogburn-Nimkoff: *Sociology*, Second Edition, Houghton Mifflin Company, Chicago, p. 156.
[4] Dionisio K. Yorro, "500 Years of Spanish Heritage in the Philippines," *The Fookien Times Yearbook*, 1952.
[5] The English "public" schools are aristocratic privately owned schools. The bulk of the population attend government operated schools.

CHAPTER VII. SOCIAL CLASS STRUCTURE

system which has a Fil-American atmosphere. In this fashion, two different types of education give distinguishing characteristics to those of different class levels.

The marks and organization of class structure also parallel the European situation in material possessions. In both Europe and the Philippines, the ownership of an automobile and a home with modern appliances reflects a sharp difference between classes. In the United States, there is a difference in quality and price of automobiles and home appliances, but ownership itself is widespread. Thus it seems that in school and possession, the class system is more similar to Europe than to the United States. On the other hand, the American stress on social mobility (the prospect of rising from a lower to a higher status) has greatly influenced the younger generation of educated Filipinos.

Distinction between class and caste.

While most societies have some form of social differentiation, there is a great difference in the extent to which the individual is able to change from the position occupied by his family. The term, "open class" refers to a system in which the classification is made entirely on the basis of individual ability. In this situation, the individual's status will depend entirely on his own efforts and his own efforts and his position in society may be strikingly different from that of his parents. The term "closed class" designates a system in which it is very difficult for the individual to achieve a social position different from that of his parents. The extreme example of a closed class society is found in the caste system and has been most fully developed in the sections of India dominated by Hindu influence.

In the caste system, social position is entirely determined by heredity and since intermarriage between castes is strictly prohibited, the individual is practically helpless to change either his status or that of his children. The barriers between castes are rigid and include not only intermarriage, but type of occupation, place of worship, use of separate roads for travel and separation to the greatest possible degree in all social relationships. The Brahmin in the upper caste group is more likely to be a person of wealth and education but even if he is bankrupt and illiterate he still retains his caste status. The untouchable, whose position is so low that he is outside the framework of the caste system, cannot change his status by individual accomplishments. Even if he is able to overcome his handicaps and acquire wealth and fame he still retains his lowly social status in the eyes of the members of the regular castes. Recent legislation has attacked caste discrimination but it is deeply rooted in the mores and difficult to change. The system is sanctioned by Hindu religious belief and regarded as the will of God by members of both the higher and the lower castes. The only escape mechanisms are a very limited possibility of changing caste through adoption and the hope that in a reincarnation the individual may have a more favorable status. The Hindu believes in a prolonged round of rebirths and if he is unfortunate in this cycle he may be more favored in the next.

Other patterns which approximate a caste system include Negro-White relationships in the United States and the status system of the Ifugaos in Central Luzon.

The position of the American Negros is sometimes regarded as an example of the caste system since, although it is not religiously sanctioned, his position is determined by his racial classification. Even the Negro who is well educated and successful in a profession or business will still be regarded as one of inferior status by many less distinguished whites. The Ifugaos' stress on heredity in determining one's claim to be of top rank, a *kadangyang*, is also sometimes regarded as approaching a caste system.

In actual practice, no society is absolutely open or completely closed. Even in societies such as the United States which lay the greatest stress on individual initiative, the family position plays a great role, since it prevents men from having the type of equal start which would seem to be an essential part of a completely open society. The

Chapter VII. SOCIAL CLASS STRUCTURE

children of the most successful will inherit not only some of their parent's prestige, but also a better chance to acquire a good education and to begin their working life with a fair supply of capital. The children of the poor have to "live down" their parent's lowly status, have more trouble in acquiring a good education and will have great difficulty in obtaining the capital essential for business success. Unlike the untouchable of India, however, if they can overcome these obstacles, they then will be able to rise in status.

The closed class type is likewise never completely achieved. Always, there will be found a few individuals of exceptional ability who are able to break through even the most rigid of caste lines. Aside from the case of the exceptional individual, no society is entirely satisfied with the caste concept. In the United States, the position of the Negro is gradually losing its castelike character and there is a growing tendency to judge members of racial minorities on an individual basis. The Ifugaos find that the aproach of westernization is breaking down the old restrictions and that the young are beginning to marry across caste lines, thus weakening the most essential part of the system. In India, the government has challenged the idea of caste and although caste lines remain important, they have lost some of their former power.

The value of the class versus caste concept does not lie in its absolute character, but in its use as a measuring stick to determine the freedom of movement in different societies. No group carries out either extreme, but some are much more open than others. If a society has many individuals who came from lowly homes and rose to high positions and also other individuals who fell from a high status established by the family then we say there is a high degree of social mobility and that this group approximates the open class category. A group in which only an insignificant minority changes from the paternal standing is near the caste system.

The Americans stress social mobility, but the society contains many obstacles to lower class progress. The

English have a high degree of class consciousness which is somewhat offset by increasing educational opportunities for the lower class. Spain is a country with a strong aristocratic tradition and limited commercial development. India is the classic example of the caste system which is beginning to change toward greater individual opportunity. The Philippines combine wide educational opportunity with great inequalities of wealth, limited commercial development and a strong emphasis on hereditary class distinctions. Plotting various societies on a continuum we would probably obtain a result something like this:

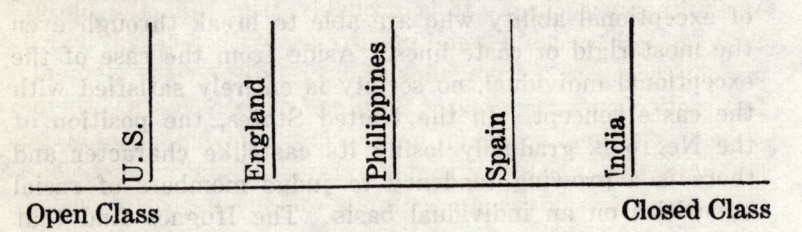

U.S.	England	Philippines	Spain	India

Open Class   Closed Class

Categories of social class in the Philippines.

The complexity of social class structure varies both with the nature of the society and the attitude of the observer. Usually, a modern industrialized society lends itself to numerous group formations which may be considered separate classes, while a strictly agricultural society is somewhat simpler in structure. In the United States, Warner and his associates[6] distinguish nine categories by dividing each of the three main categories into a lower, middle and upper group. In this fashion, they refer to upper-upper, middle-upper, lower-upper, etc. In the Philippines, on the other hand, LeRoy believes that there are only two really important divisions: upper and lower[7] Macaraig insists on the reality of a Philippine middle

---
[6] Lloyd Warner, Marchia Meeker, and Kenneth Eells: *The Measurement of Social Status*, Chicago, Science Research Associates, 1951.
[7] James A. LeRoy, *Philippine Life in Town and Country*, New York, Putnam, 1905.

CHAPTER VII. SOCIAL CLASS STRUCTURE

class, but feels that it has become subordinate to the upper class.[8]

It is impossible to make a classification which will satisfy everyone as observers disagree on how sharp class distinction should be and on the minimum number of people which is needed to constitute a separate category. The situation in the Philippines is further complicated by the absence of detailed studies which would give the type of information needed to make a sound analysis of class divisions.

At the present time it seems necessary to recognize at least four categories of social class in the basic structure of Philippine society. It is probably true that the major cleavage is between a small upper class with a closely allied middle class and a tremendously large lower class element. In practice, however, many Filipinos do not classify themselves as either upper or lower class and this should be recognized in an attempt to understand social divisions. The following table gives an estimate of income distribution which is one factor in social stratification.

Table 1 — Percentage of Filipino Population in Various Income Categories.*

Income	Percentage of Population Receiving
Under ₱600	39.4
₱600 — ₱1080	32.7
₱1080 — ₱1800	17.3
₱1800 — ₱3600	1.2
₱6000 — ₱14000	0.4
₱14000 — plus	(2,000 recipients)

* *National Income and its Distribution Technical Assistance Administration* United Nations, New York, 1952. We do not have adequate data on Philippine incomes but this estimate is regarded as one of the best available. It was prepared by UN experts in 1948 on the basis of the 1948 census and Central Bank data.

While income is a major method of distinguishing social class it is not the only criterion. The following schedule is the author's estimate of the manner in which income and occupation would vary in different social strata:

---

[8] Serafin Macaraig: *Introduction to Sociology*, Manila, University of the Philippines, 1948, p. 281.

Table 2 — Philippine Social Class Differentials *

Percentage Estimate	Class	Description
1%	Upper Class	Large land owners, highly successful professionals, big business men, top government officials. Income Estimate ₱15,000 upwards.
9%	Middle Class	Minor government officials, some teachers, most business men, owners of medium sized farms. Income Estimate ₱2,500-₱15,000.
20%	Upper-Lower Class	Skilled laborers, government clerks, most teachers, some sari-sari owners, owners of small farms, store clerks, some tenant farmers, most office workers. Income Estimate ₱1,100-₱2,500.
70%	Lower-Lower Class	Unskilled laborers, farm owners with less than 2 hectares of land, most tenant farmers, landless farm laborers, most of the physically handicapped, most household servants. Income Estimate ... Under ₱1,100.

* The percentage estimates are open to challenge since they cannot be substantiated by statistical data. The upper income categories are more generous than indicated by the UN study on the theory that the reports to official sources underestimate the income actually received.

Historical basis of Philippine class system.

From a historical viewpoint, the remarkable aspect of Filipino class structure is the small amount of basic change over a period of several hundred years. Before the Spaniards arrived in the Philippines, the typical system included three classes: the chiefs who owned large amounts of land, a number of free men of lesser rank than the

Chapter VII. SOCIAL CLASS STRUCTURE

chiefs, and a considerable number of slaves. When the Spaniards came, they abolished slavery and appropriated much of the land themselves, but left most of the system uunchanged. This may be explained by the fact that usually colonial powers have found it more convenient to govern by some variation of the system of indirect rule. This system placed the Spaniards in control of most of the country's wealth and utilized the chiefs, who came to be known as *caciques,* as middlemen to direct the work of other Filipinos.

Pelzer describes the situation in this manner:

> The *encomienda* system went out of existence at the beginning of the seventeenth century, and the country was then governed by colonial government officials who, in the political sphere, took the place of the *datus* of pre-Spanish days. The Spaniards were careful, however, not to disturb the social structure of the villages or the social and economic position of the *datus*. The *datus* became known as *cabezas de barangays*. Several barangays made up a *pueblo* or municipality, headed by the *gobernadorcillo*, who originally was elected by all the household heads of a municipality, but later, in the nineteenth century, by the *cabezas de barangay*. Their families constituted the aristocracy and enjoyed special political and social privileges. The Spaniards introduced the term *cacique*, or chief, into the Philippines from Haiti and applied it to the *datus*, or *cabezas de barangay*, and the other leading families of a community. By recognizing them, the Spaniards helped the *caciques* to preserve their power over the people and gave them the opportunity of getting more and more land into their hands, of making more and more people financially dependent upon them (inasmuch as they were the tax-collectors), and of reducing freeholders to the status of tenants. Thus many of the leading families of pre-Spanish days kept their favorable social and economic position, and often strengthened it by inter-marriage with the Spaniards.[9]

---

[9] Karl J. Pelzer: *Pioneer Settlement In The Asiatic Tropics,* American Geographical Society, Special Publication No. 29, p. 89. Used by permission of the publishers.

The American found the *caciques* system repugnant to democratic ideals but, like the Spaniards, soon discovered that it was difficult to root it out. The reliance on the caciques extended even to such apparently remote fields as public health. Victor Heiser, who for many years was commissioner of public health, tells of his reliance on the *caciques*:

> In the health service, we had to recognize the power of the cacique; usually an intelligent person, his opposition could have nullified our efforts. But as soon as he realized that he could get no graft from us, and that, on the contrary, we might bring him added income by making his subject taos more productive, he ranged himself on our side. The *tao* who was as unprogressive as he was gentle, often offered passive resistance to Westernizing, but at a threatening word from his *cacique*, he would prove amenable.[10]

When complete independence came in 1946, the Philippines were still an agricultural country with a few great landholders and large groups of landless *taos*. The *cacique* group had been influential in the independence movement, even as they had been useful to the colonial powers, and they retained their important role in society.

The closest approximation to a change in the class structure in the last five hundred years is the development of a small middle class group. This development is usually minimized by western observers because the composition of the Filipino middle class is different from that in the United States and Western Europe. In these areas, the most powerful middle class element was a rising group of business men. The Filipino middle class consisted of government officials, school teachers and such professionals as lawyers and physicians. This group is numerically small, has less economic independence and is less influential than the middle class of the western hemisphere.

---

[10] Victor Heiser: *An American Doctor's Odyssey*, New York, S. W. Norton, 1936. p. 46.

CHAPTER VII. SOCIAL CLASS STRUCTURE 145

The European middle class emerged from the ranks of the skilled craftsmen of the guilds and gained considerable wealth by their role in the expansion of manufacturing and commerce. This development meant that the power of the old upper class, a landholding feudal nobility, was challenged by the rise of a middle class, the *bourgeoisie* whose wealth came from trade and industry. Since the older patterns of government gave power to the nobility, the *bourgeoisie* felt that a democratic system would give them a greater chance for influence. In their efforts to establish democratic government, they became political opponents of the nobility.

In the Philippines, the middle class group concentrated on the advantages to be gained from education and manifested little interest in commerce. They became spokesmen for the *caciques* and this alliance was strengthened by intermarriage between the two groups. The form of government was determined by the American authorities; the *caciques* and the *intelligentias* acted together to minimize the influence of the *tao* and see that government continued to serve the interests of the landholding group.[11]

Class structure of unassimilated minorities.

The term *unassimilated minorities* is used to designate the groups which are different from the majority because they have been less affected by western influence. They constitute about six per cent of the population and their whole social system is strikingly different from that which prevails in the rest of the country. For purpose of this discussion, we will confine our comments to three groups: the **Ifugaos, Negritos** and **Moros**.

The simplest class structure is found in the Negrito tribes where, although certain individuals are known as chiefs, there is little variation either in social standing or in wealth. The explanation for this situation seems to lie in the primitive nature of their economic life. The

---

[11] See discussion in Macaraig: *op. cit.*, pp. 280-284. Also Hayden, Joseph Ralston: *The Philippines*, MacMillan, New York, 1942, pp. 376-401.

Negritos exist by gathering food in the forest, *kaingin* agriculture, hunting and occasional work as harvesters. They move frequently from place to place; do not accumulate an appreciable amount of property. Under these circumstances, there is little basis for economic differentiation and status is determined by a combination of family position and personal qualities.

The Ifugaos have reached a high state of agricultural development and their famous rice terraces constitute one of the world's greatest engineering achievements. In contrast to the Negritos, they have developed permanent villages and an extremely complicated system of land tenure. Ifugao societies place great stress on the ownership of rice fields and class standing is related to the number of fields which one can claim. The sale of land is hampered by an elaborate system of family claims and the profit from large landholding is reduced by the obligation to share the produce with less fortunate relatives. The disparity in size of landholdings is less than among the lowland Filipinos and the upper class group has not been able to escape from the task of actually working on the soil.

The economic basis of Moro class divisions is similar to that of Christian Filipinos, but the form is somewhat different. This is due to the fact that those in control of the Philippine government (whether Spaniards, Americans or Christian Filipinos) have tolerated the Islamic social system and allowed the Moro leaders to exercise an unusual amount of local control. The main element in the upper class are the *datus* whose income from the land is augmented by the payment of fees for their services as administrators of Mohammedan lanw. This society is also affected by the occasional practice of polygamy and the fact that slavery persisted in this area for a longer period of time than in other parts of the Philippines.

Effect of class status on behavior.

To the sociologist, the major significance of the class system is the difference which may be observed in the

CHAPTER VII. SOCIAL CLASS STRUCTURE   147

overt behavior and the underlying attitudes of the different social classes. Any analysis of these differences in the Philippines will reveal that large groups of people have an environment which is strikingly different from that of the more favored groups and which affects their life in many ways. The late President Quezon has summarized in eloquent language the extent to which the **tao** has remained unaffected by the social changes of the last fifty years.

> ... The poor still have to drink the same polluted water that his ancestors have drunk for ages. Malaria, dysentery and tuberculosis still threaten him and his family at every turn. His children cannot all go to school, or if they do, they cannot even finish the whole primary instruction for one reason or another.
>
> Roads from his barrio or his little farm to the town there are none. Only trails are within reach of his bare feet. As he works from sunrise to sundown, his employer gets richer, while he remains poor. He is the easy prey of the heartless usurer because usury is still rampant everywhere despite legislative enactments intended to suppress it.
>
> That is, concisely speaking, the lot of the common man in our midst after America's long endeavor to give to all fair opportunity in the pursuit of happiness and enjoyment of life.[12]

That this is no isolated viewpoint issued for political consumption may be seen by comparing it with a similar statement by Dr. Joseph Ralston Hayden, an American political scientist and former vice-governor, who spent many years in the Philippines.

> ... who as tenant farmers, renters or virtually landless workers eke out a miserable living from the rich Philippine soil. These people constitute a depressed minority which has been largely left

---

[12] From the "Message on Improvement of Philippine Conditions, Philippine Independence and Relations with the American High Commissioner," *Messages of the President, III,* Part I, Manila, 1938, pp. 211 ff., 223.

behind in the march of Philippine progress. Astonishingly ignorant, for the most part unable to use effectively any language save their local dialects, and economically helpless, it is they who are the most complete victims of the local *cacique,* the remorseless usurer and the exploiting political or religious charlatan.[13]

The most obvious class differences are those of income and wealth and closely related to these are matters of health, education and living standards. The lower classes not only have less money, they also have less chance for education, little opportunity to share in the advance in living standards made possible by modern technology and because of inadequate diet, improper sanitation and insufficient medical care, actually have less chance for life itself. We do not yet have available studies which can adequately document these statements in the Philippines, but in countries where such studies have been made, the conclusions are inescapable.

By way of example, let us take a look at one of the most famous American studies—one made of infant mortality in different income groups in 1936. This study showed that the effect of class differentials begin with birth and that whether a specific infant lives or dies is largely determined by the class status of his parents. The following chart shows the number of deaths per 1,000 of infants under one year of age by income group.[14]

Infant Mortality and Income

Under $ 450	167
450-459	106
550-649	117
650-849	108
850-1049	83
1050-1249	64
1250-and over	59

---

[13] Hayden: *op. cit.,* p. 378.
[14] Woodbury, Robert, "Infant Mortality in the United States," *Annals of the American Academy of Political and Social Science,* Vol. 188:102-04, November, 1936.

CHAPTER VII. SOCIAL CLASS STRUCTURE 149

Less tangible than the effects on health and living standards is the development of divergent attitudes toward the governmental, religious and economic institutions of society. Thus the preceding table dealing with infant mortality and income is not just a simple effect of economic conditions. The data also reflect the varying class attitudes towards modern health practices and medical treatment. Thrift and ambition are vital to economic development, but are attitudes difficult to develop in a group which has little hope for advancement and which feels that society has no concern for their welfare. Government, along with other duties, is the protector of property rights; but this function is likely to arouse little enthusiasm in the hearts of those who have no property to protect. Religion, too, is likely to make a different type of appeal to the poor and ignorant than to the well fed and sophisticated. One general feature of this variation in class attitudes which seems to color all of the other attitudes is that the lower classes usually have more of the *damay* outlook and less of the *gesellschaft* ideas of rational planning and business-like behavior. The following chart is offered as an attempt to summarize the attitudes most frequently associated with class status.

Attitude Toward Governmental Institutions

Upper Class — Appreciate effect of government on own affairs, know leading officials and are interested in politics. Majority will regard governmental regime as basic to their own security and will resist any type of drastic change. Minority will take their own security for granted and work energetically for "efficient" or "humanitarian" regime.

Middle Class — Conscious of duty to be "good citizens." Responsive to appeals for "clean" or "honest" government, but for the most part will resist major change.

Lower Class — (1) May be completely indifferent to government which seems remote and evidently has little effect on them.

(2) May view it as the dispenser of petty favors such as minor jobs and possible payments for votes.
(3) May be whipped up to fanatical fervor by skillful propagandists who appeal to nationalistic, religious or racial prejudice.
(4) May be consciously discontented with status and work for a revolutionary change which promises them greater benefits.

Attitudes Toward Religious Institutions

Upper Class — (1) Take positions of leadership in lay movements and like to be considered "patrons" of the church.
(2) Critical in regard to dogma, but manifest an interest in aesthetic aspects of religion.
(3) May feel above the need for religion and manifest little interest except when custom demands their attendance on special occasions.

Middle Class — Apt to be responsive to appeals on a moral or intellectual basis. Somewhat uncertain about attitude toward traditional church dogmas. Highly critical of religious practices which seem to be excessively emotional.

Lower Class — (1) Responsive to emotional services and religious pageantry. Accept dogma uncritically but frequently fail to carry moral injunctions into practice. Readily accept reports of miracles.
(2) May feel that the church is an upper class institution and be either indifferent or openly hostile.

Attitudes Toward Economic Institutions

Upper Class — (1) Takes superior position and high standard of living for granted. Believes existing economic system is the best possible arrangement. Bolsters self esteem by conspicuously luxurious living.
(2) Morally uneasy because of special pri-

Chapter VII. SOCIAL CLASS STRUCTURE

vileges and seeks to compensate by charity or civic service. Small minority may worry about injustice of society and seek change.

Middle Class — Lauds virtues of thrift, ambition and "decent" living. Torn between desire to improve status by saving money and need to prove their importance by expensive living. Tends to accept prevailing system, but hopes to rise in status.

Lower Class — (1) Take inferior position for granted. Has no realistic hope of improvement. Little chance for thrift and occasional windfalls are used for immediate consumption.
(2) Resent inferior position and hope for change through revolution and different type of economic structure.
(3) May have acquired middle class aspirations and seek rise in status through thrift and increased educational attainments.

The above chart is not exhaustive, but does indicate some of the alternatives which the members of various classes regard as being acceptable to them in institutional relationships.

Perhaps even more basic than institutional attitudes is the reaction of the various classes to the conventional social mores. These are most rigidly observed by the middle class, tend to be lightly treated by the upper class and ignored by the lower class. This is most clearly seen in the areas of sexual conduct and physical aggression. The middle class which, above all else stresses respectability, tends to emphasize peaceful conduct and sexual conventionality. The lower class is apt to wield the bolo rather freely when provoked and to live in "consensual" marriages outside of the legal framework. The upper class often has become somewhat critical of current morality and does not feel that its status is dependent on conventional behavior. Members of this group work off physical aggression in night club brawls and maintain a "querida" system to alleviate the rigors of monogamy.

152   SOCIOLOGY IN THE PHILIPPINE SETTING

THE BROWS	OCCUPATIONS	CLOTHES	READINGS
HIGH BROW	stock quotations and a name	cut along simple lines	leans on the heavy stu
MIDDLE BROW	usually a white-collar	matching ties and socks	Maugham, Sunday Times m
LOW BROW	hand-to-mouth existence	ready-made and loud	comics in the vernacu

The above chart indicates one view of variation in behavior by social classes. It app which appeared earlier in Harper's magazine. These distinction are matters of taste education, constitutes the majority of the lowbrows. Their preferences are usually trad of the educated public while the high brow is a rare species who comprises only a s

Here again, our observations of Filipino society are somewhat impressionistic, but these impressions agree with considerable material which has been obtained on the American scene. Davis made an elaborate study of school room situations and found a major difficulty was the conflict between the middle class morality of the teachers

---
[15] Allison Davis: *Social Factors in Learning*, Cambridge, Harvard University Press, 1949.

CHAPTER VI. SOCIAL CLASS STRUCTURE 153

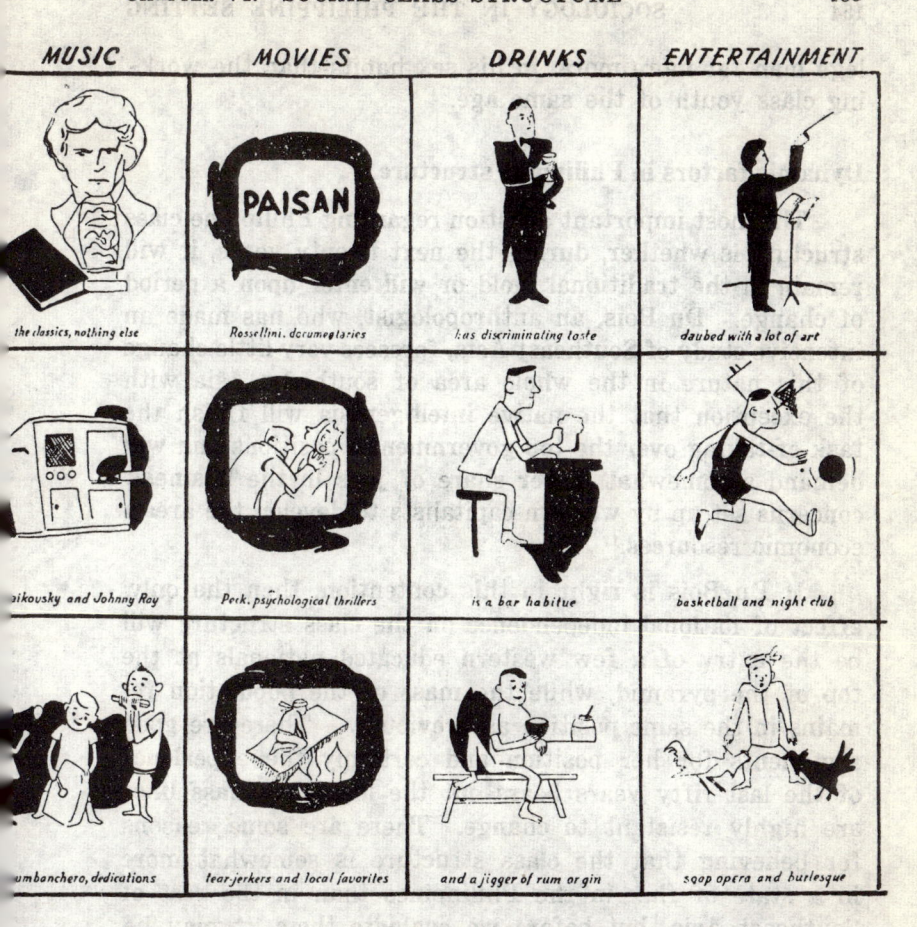

MUSIC	MOVIES	DRINKS	ENTERTAINMENT
the classics, nothing else	Rossellini, documentaries	has discriminating taste	daubed with a lot of art
Tchaikovsky and Johnny Ray	Peck, psychological thrillers	is a bar habitue	basketball and night club
rumbanchero, dedications	tear-jerkers and local favorites	and a jigger of rum or gin	soap opera and burlesque

in the Saturday Mirror Magazine for February 14, 1953 and is adapted from a chart based on background and education. The poorer class, which generally has little and reflect antipathy toward imported patterns. The middle brows include the majority of the population.

and the lower class morality of the students.[15] Kinsey, in his monumental study of the sex habits of American males, found that adherence to conventional conduct was the rule in the middle class male and the exception in the lower class.[16] Contrary to the usual notion he found the col-

---

[16] Alfred Kinsey: *Sexual Behavior of the Human Male*, Saunders, Philadelphia, 1948.

lege man far more moral in his sex habits than the working class youth of the same age.

Dynamic factors in Philippine structure.

The most important question regarding Philippine class structure is whether, during the next twenty years, it will remain in the traditional mold or will enter upon a period of change. Du Bois, an anthropologist, who has made an intensive study of Southeast Asia, foresees very little change of this nature in the whole area of southeast Asia with the exception that the native intelligentsia will finish the task of taking over the top governmental positions and will demand a somewhat larger share of jobs in the business concerns set up by western capitalists to develop the area's economic resources.[17]

If Du Bois is right in this contention, then the only effect of national independence on the class structure will be the entry of a few western educated nationals at the top of the pyramid, while the mass of the population remains in the same position as previously. There are good arguments for her position and certainly the experience of the last fifty years bears out the idea that class lines are highly resistant to change. There are some reasons for believing that the class structure is somewhat more in a state of flux in the Philippines than in the rest of Southeast Asia, but before we evaluate them, it may be best to look at some of the factors associated with the rate of change in class lines.

Static Society	Changing Society
Great inequalities of wealth and income	Limited extremes of wealth and poverty
Cautious capitalist seeking security above all	Venture capital willing to take some risk for big gains

[17] Cora Du Bois: *Social Forces in Southeast Asia*, Minneapolis, University of Minnesota Press, 1949, pp. 25-52.

CHAPTER VII. SOCIAL CLASS STRUCTURE

Static Socitty	Changing Society
Fully occupied areas subject to population pressure	Frontier development
Education restricted to small group	Education open to all with needed ability
Hereditary aristocracy	Minimizing of social difference
Agricultural basis	Rapid industrialization
Marriage along lines approved by family	Romantic love crossing class lines
Permanent residence	Geographic mobility
Racial or religious prejudice limiting occupational choice and business opportunities	Occupational choice based on individual qualifications. No restrictions on any groups

At first glance, Filipino society seems to be rather definitely slanted toward the factors which make for a static society, but a closer analysis reveals some tendency for the more dynamic factors to be increasing in their influence. We shall take up these factors individually.

Great inequalities of wealth. This condition tends to produce a situation in which the rich are satisfied with the security of inherited property and the poor have neither the ability nor the motivation to improve their lot. It is now being challenged through the imposition of relatively modest income taxes on the wealthy and the protection of the poor through minimum wage laws and legislation to protect the rights of tenants. The major question is whether or not such legislation can be enforced in a government dominated by the wealthy groups.

Population pressure. While the Philippines as a whole is under populated, yet population increase in such areas as Central Luzon leads to a constant decrease in economic opportunity and the division of farms into areas too small to support those who work on them. Such a situation means that the farmer is unable to maintain his land, and the end result is that the **hacendero** takes over his land and inequalities are further increased.

Education. While about fifty per cent of the population is illiterate, yet the facilities for education are the greatest of any country in Southeast Asia and appear to be increasing.

Family influence. The prestige of wealthy families is enormous and marriages are usually arranged by family consultation which prevents them from crossing class lines. On the other hand, the younger generation has been greatly influenced by the notion of romantic love and individual choice. If this trend continues, there will be increasing occasions when a lower class person rises in social status through marriage.

Geographic mobility. Here, the picture is contradictory. Millions of Filipinos are so bound by family loyalty and traditional attachments that it is very difficult for them to move to areas of greater opportunity. Conversely, the disruption of the war years weakened local ties and internal migration has greatly increased.

Outside influences. One of the factors which has allowed some to rise in status is the receipt of money from sources not normally a part of the Philippine economy. Prominent in this classification are savings made by migrants who return to the Philippines after spending some time in Guam, Hawaii or the mainland of the United States. This type of work has given some men a chance to accumulate money to finance a business, buy a farm or complete their education. In post war years, the disbursements of the U. S. Veteran's Administration also gave to many a better financial standing than they previously enjoyed. Such receipts can hardly be considered a permanent part of the economy, but the effect has been to enable several thousand Filipinos to accumulate capital and improve their economic standing.

Industrial growth. This has been hindered partly by trade policies which encourage Filipinos to raise farm products and import their manufactured goods and by the reluctance of the wealthy class to assume the risks involved in long term industrial investment. The import control laws have tended to encourage local industry and a small number of industrial developments have taken place as a result. The outlook for the greater capital investment needed to increase the number and size of factories is less encouraging. The government has entered various fields, but governmental revenues are too limited to provide the amounts of capital needed for major industrialization. Foreigners are afraid that rising nationalism will lead to the confiscation of their investments, and native Filipinos are still reluctant to invest in large scale business enterprise. Strenuous efforts are being made to change the situation, and encourage business investment. Without heavy capital investment, business enterprises fail to grow and there is little chance for one to improve his lot by entering new fields of business opportunity.

In Europe and the United States increasing industrialization led to a rapid growth in the size of the middle class and we may assume a similar relationship in the Philippines. Industrialization increases the demands for business executives, engineers and many types of related professional service. It also gives rise to auxiliary opportunities for both retail stores and the suppliers of raw materials. The principal reason for the small size of the Filipino middle class is apparently the comparatively slow rate industrial development.

Ethnic prejudice. This factor operates against a dynamic society by limiting the ability of individuals in certain groups to make the best use of their abilities and money. Since the nation is dependent upon separate efforts of individuals, any attitudes which limit the economic activity of any group of individuals also limit the economic progress of the entire country.

Two attitudes hostile to an expanding economy operate in the Philippines. One affects the Chinese and the other, the native Filipinos. In the case of the Filipino, his historic culture has inculcated attitudes which discourage thrift, inhibit initiative and minimize the value of business activity while placing undue stress on agriculture, government service and the profession. The result is that Filipinos, as a group, have not had outstanding success in business activity. The Chinese in the Philippines have many of the characteristics which mark a rising commercial middle class and their culture seems to be well adapted to business enterprise. Their contribution to the growth of business activity is discouraged, however, by restrictive laws limiting their business expansion.

Frontier settlement. The frontier is a new area in which men are largely dependent upon their own abilities and former class distinctions tend to be minimized. Much of the equalitarian character of American society is attributed to the fact that for hundreds of years one dissatisfied with his lot could move to newly developed areas and make a new start.

The influence which seems most certain to modify existing class relationships is the very rapid settlement which has taken place since World War II in such areas at Mindanao and the Cagayan Valley. Rapid frontier settlement should lead to a situation in which individual opportunity is much greater and class lines are crossed with greater frequency.

Trends. Class structure has shown relatively little change from pre-Spanish days to the present time. An attempt to predict the future discloses conflicting trends and it is difficult to evaluate their relative importance. Social legislation, the spread of education, the decrease in family control of marriage, the growth of industry and the rapid settlement of the frontier are all conducive to a change in class lines. These influences are at least partially blocked by the existence of extremes of wealth and poverty, population pressure, Filipino antipathy to business enterprise, and nationalistic feelings which limit the economic contributions of foreign businessmen. A factor which may tip the scales in favor of a different type of class system is government awareness of the importance of

Chapter VII. SOCIAL CLASS STRUCTURE

economic development and its efforts to encourage business activity.

Is there a class struggle?

Karl Marx, the intellectual father of world communism, predicted that the development of industrial civilization would bring about a sharp struggle between social classes. This struggle would intensify as economic development gradually wiped out the middle class leaving only the lower class, which he called the proletariat, and the owners of business, known as the capitalists. Since the proletariat outnumbered the capitalists, they would eventually win power, take over the ownership of business themselves and inaugurate a classless society. In his judgment, the communist business, and world communism was the inevitable outcome of industrialized society.

His predictions, issued in the *Communist Manifesto* in 1848, have given members of the communist parties a sense of inevitable victory and bolstered their morale at times when the odds against them appeared overwhelming. In practice, communism seems to have made the greatest appeal, not to advanced industrial countries, but to industrially backward areas. Communism has never triumphed in an industrialized country except through Russian intervention. It has made its greatest appeal in Russia and China, both primarily agricultural areas, and today, appears to be stronger in Asia than in Western Europe.

Contrary to the prediction of Marx, industrialization did not wipe out the middle class, but increased its strength while, at the same time, greatly improving the living standards of the lower classes. Also, contrary to predictions Communism has developed a tremendous appeal in the industrially undeveloped countries where the class structure is static and the lower classes see little hope of bettering their condition in the existing society. The United States has a rather definite class structure, but class feeling is low; both because the condition of the bottom group has been improving and because even the lowest classes feel that they have a chance to attain middle class status.

The intensity of class feeling seems to be rather definitely related to culture change in the society. If the bottom group feel they have no chance for a better living, yet feel that they deserve some improvements, they become critical of church, state and business and are ripe for a revolutionary attempt. If they feel that there is hope for peaceful improvement, then they too have a stake in society, are interested in the preservation of its institutions, and hostile to revolutionary change.

Looking at the Philippines, one can find ample evidence of bitter class struggle between the *taos* and the *hacenderos*. Unrest of this type has flared into violence on many occasions.[18] This would include the *Colorum* uprising in 1923, the outbreak at Tayug in 1931, the *Sakdal* revolt in 1935 and the *Hukbalahap* movement, which at this writing, still keeps sections of the country in turmoil. The specific circumstances, the administration in power, and the leaders of the revolts varied; but the underlying theme is the same.

An interpretation of these incidents in terms of class attitudes would stress the deep gulf between the rich and the poor, the unchanging nature of class lines, and the feeling by many of the lower class that the government existed only to exploit the *taos* and to protect the landowners. Whether or not these attitudes can be changed depends upon whether the Philippines can develop a dynamic economy with a growing middle class group and increasing opportunity for all its people.

Summary

Social classes appear in every society and serve the function of determining the relative status of large groups of people. Class is defined by wealth, income, education, heredity, standard of living, circle of friends, pattern of

---

[18] See discussion in Hayden, *op. cit.*, pp. 376-401.

Chapter VII. SOCIAL CLASS STRUCTURE

etiquette and occupation. Philippine society may be divided in four strata: upper, middle, upper lower and lower. Class alignments may change rapidly or persist for long periods. A society in which one may move with relative ease from one class to another is known as open class. A group in which it is extremely difficult to change one's status is known as a closed class society. The extreme example of closed class society is found in the caste system. Philippine society occupies an intermediate position between these two types, but its basic structure has been comparatively unchanging for many years. Indications for the future of class alignments are conflicting, but disclose some hope for the development of a large middle class group. Attitudes and patterns of behavior are closely related to class status and these may result in class conflict. Class struggle does not follow the Marxian prediction of increasing with industrialization, but appears to be sharpest in the agricultural countries.

QUESTIONS

1. Distinguish between caste and class.
2. In the *damay* type of society would you expect to find rapid change in class status? Why or why not?
3. Explain the relationship between the class system and agrarian uprisings.
4. Why has a strong middle class failed to develop in the Philippines?
5. What factors in the present scene work for and against basic change in Philippine class structure?
6. What features of the class system do you feel have contributed to the rise of Communism in Asia?
7. Is awareness of class status a good thing? Should people refrain from mentioning class interests in the hope that they will hereby become less important?
8. Do you feel that restricting the business activities of foreign investors will increase Filipino prosperity? Why?
9. Primitive tribes seldom show signs of class conflicts; why?

PROJECTS

1. Make a report on the attitudes and beliefs of different classes in your home communiy. Show those attitudes which influence school attendance, health, mode of dress and use of leisure time.

2. Analyze the class structure of a community with which you are familiar. In doing this, see if you can discover any groups of people who have either risen or fallen in class status in recent years.

3. Members of differnt social classes are sometimes able to unite in common activities. Make a report showing the activities in which one can find approximately equal participation by different social classes.

SUGGESTED READINGS

Alip, Eufronio M.: *Philippine History: Political, Social, Economic*, Alip & Brion Publication, Inc., Manila, pp. 61, 62.
Brief description of social class in Pre-Spanish Period.

Davis, Allison: *Social Factors in Learning*, Harvard University Press. Cambridge, Mass., 1949.
A brief treatment of the effect of social class upon student attiiudes.

Davis, Allison; Garner, Burleigh; Garner, Mary R.: *Deep South*, University of Chicago Press, Chicago, 1941.
Study of class status in the southern part of the United States in which white and Negros authors collaborated.

Du Bois, Cora: *Social Forces in South East Asia*, University of Minneota Press, 1949.
A small, highly readable book which contains an excellent discussion of the role of social class in this area.

Macaraig, Serafin E.: *Sociology*, University of the Philippines, Manila, 1948.
Pages 274 to 286 are devoted to a discussion of social class in the Philippines.

Pelzer, Karl: *Pioneer Settlement in the Asiatic Tropics*, American Geographical Society, New York, 1945.
This book gives a deailed treatment of the relation between class alignments and various types of land tenure, pp. 81-159.

Warner, Loyd, Marchia Meeker, and Kenneth Eells: *The Measurement of Social Status*, Chicago, Science Research Associates, 1951.
A discussion for the research scientist, but of little interest to the general reader.

———————— and ohers: *Yankee City Series*, Vols. I-IV New Haven, Conn., Yale University Press, 1941-1947.
An analysis of class status in various American cities by the foremost American authority on social class.

Zaide, Gregorio F.: *Philippine Political and Cultural History*, Volume 2, Philippine Education Company, Manila, 1949, pp. 81-82.
Brief description of social class in Spanish Period.

CHAPTER EIGHT

RELATIONSHIP OF ETHNIC GROUPS

"I have seen, at the same table, Spaniards, mestizos and Indios, priests and soldiers. To the eyes of one who has observed the repugnance and misunderstandings caused by race in the various parts of the Orient and who knows that race is the great divider of society, the contrast and exception presented by so mixed a population as that of the Philippines is admirable."

— Statement of Sir John Bowring on a visit to Manila in 1859. Cited in "The Other Manila," *Philippine Free Press*, December 13, 1952, p. 59.

Ethnic Factors in Intergroup Behaviour

The role of racial consciousness.

The last two hundred years have seen the rise of a consciousness of race to an extent never before known in the world's history. This rise in racial consciousness accompanied the increase in travel and the consequent growth in contacts between peoples of different physical appearance. Since the difference in physical appearance was accompanied by a difference in culture, it seemed a logical step to assume that the two were related. As all men have a tendency to assume that their own culture represents the highest possible values, the conclusion usually followed that other cultures were inferior, and this inferiority was explained on the basis of hereditary traits associated with specific races. Thus one of the first results of large scale contacts between different groups was a natural assumption of the inferiority of the other party.

This initial reaction of in-group egotism was modified by the undeniable fact that the white peoples had developed a type of technology which gave them unquestioned superiority in commerce and warfare. This fact supported the assumption of superiority on the part of the whites and drove other peoples to desperate rationalizations of their own cultural systems in an effort to escape an admission of their alleged inferiority. In colored peoples, this effort was expressed either by extreme claims of their assimilation of western culture or in a frantic "nativism" which sought to glorify their historic past and to minimize the importance of the white man's technology. Among whites, it resulted in an attitude of condescension epitomized in the phrase "white man's burden."

In recent years, the idea that cultural development is an index of racial superiority has been challenged on many grounds. Perhaps most powerful in this respect is the realization of the influence of environment on cultural characteristics. As the environment of individuals changed, we found that Orientals or Africans were perfectly capable of acquiring either the mechanical or the intellectual traits of western culture.[1]

Another influence which weakened the idea of a casual link between race and culture was the realization of historical variation in the culture of different groups. A review of history brought to light the fact that the position of various peoples has fluctuated widely over a period of time. Four thousand years ago when Europe was sunk in barbarism, the Chinese had an advanced civilization. At the time of the birth of Christ, the countries of Western Europe were still backward, but civilization had reached an advanced stage in Southern Europe, Northern Africa and parts of Central and South America. If race explains Caucasian dominance today, then the question arises—how could one explain the historic superiority of other races?

We still do not understand all the causes which lead to the rise and fall of civilization, but since this seems to happen to peoples of all physical types, we have no reason for believing that it is related to alleged racial char-

---
[1] See discussion of Negro-White differences in Chapter three, p. 50.

acteristics. The present tendency is to regard the association between culture and race as being the result of social environment rather than inborn, hereditary traits.

Comparison of terms "race" and "ethnic".

Racial categories are usually the result of an attempt to classify groups of people on the basis of distinctive physical characteristics which are passed on by biological inheritance and not subject to social influences. Since the number of physical traits is great, the combinations which can be drawn up are practically without limit. Because of this, there is no possibility of agreement on the exact number of races to be found on the earth. One scientist may find three races, another thirty and yet both scientists may be equally competent and conscientious. Their classifications are different because they have chosen to regard different groups of traits as important for racial classifications, and no one can say that one is right and the other wrong.

The popular emphasis on color has been considered inadequate by biologists because of its lack of precision. It is easy to distinguish the extreme shades of black, brown, yellow and white, but large numbers of men fall in between the extremes. For example, Filipinos and American Whites are usually regarded as belonging to different racial groups, yet no one can say how white a man must be to qualify as a Caucasian or how brown to be considered a Malay. If one adds such traits as shape of nose, size of lips, texture of hair, shape of skull, and stature, the situation does not become any less confused. None of these characteristics necessarily go together and one may have a white skin color and also the short stature associated with the Malay or *vice versa*.

In practice, people are usually classified on a basis of extremes of physical traits with those in intermediate categories identified by the group with which they associate. In the Philippines, there is a tendency for those of light color and mestizo ancestry to identify themselves with the

Spanish. In Brazil, a man of brown skin who is socially successful is considered Caucasian, otherwise, he will be considered Indian or Negro. In the United States, light-skinned people of Negro ancestry may choose to associate only with Caucasians and thus "pass" as white. Jews may change their group affiliation by changing their friends and taking a non-Jewish name. Thus Isidore Cohen who lives in a Jewish district is considered Jewish, but if the same man moves to another neighborhood and becomes Joseph Cook, he will usually be accepted as a member of the local group.

For purpose of popular classification, without attempting to make exact biological distinctions, it is now common to divide the world into three main racial classifications with various subtypes. These classifications are Caucasoid (white), Mongoloid (yellow or brown) and Negroid (black). These categories still lead to some uncertainty as: the Hindu, who is brown in color but whose facial characteristics resemble the Caucasoid; the white-skinned Japanese Ainu who fits neither Caucasoid nor Mongoloid categories and the straight haired blackman of Australia whose skin color is Negroid, but who has other features which defy classification. The major defect of this threefold division, however, is not the presence of many obvious exceptions, but the failure to include all that is popularly meant by race. The biologist may content himself with three major classifications, but the man in the street has a much more elaborate system which he uses in his thinking. He is quite sure of the difference between Jew and non-Jew, Chinese and Filipino, American and Spaniard, Bohemian and German, Moro and Tagalog, French and Italian. Nor is it enough to say that these differences simply represent nationality, for most Jews live outside the state of Israel, most Bohemians live outside of Czeco-Slovakia and Tagalogs and Moros are both Filipino.

These distinctions are a vital part of our social life and there must be some way to describe them. Nationality does not serve our purpose, since groups may still be regarded as distinct, even though not a part of separate countries or may be considered the same when they live in different territorial units. Race is rejected because it implies physical distinctions which may not exist. Religion enters the picture, but many of these groups are still considered distinct even though they follow the same religious practices and a change in religion does not change group status. A Hindu does not become a European merely by conversion to Christianity, nor does a Moro become an Ilocano by ceasing to be a Moslem. The term "ethnic" is used to indicate a distinction which may be a compound of religious affiliation, social habits, language, physical features and national background, even though it does not depend upon any one of these factors. It represents a "consciousness of kind" which is recognized both by those inside the group and those outside of its confines. The term defies logical definition, but it indicates a type of distinction which is a social reality. Since "ethnic" does not carry the false claims to precise biological differences which are imputed to "race," it seems a more useful concept in this discussions of social differences.

Patterns of Ethnic Behavior

Patterns of conflict.

The long list of massacres, race riots, lynchings and wars based on ethnic differences give ample testimony to the tendency of people to feel that difference implies hostility. No country can boast of its freedom from this type of conflict and no group is guiltless. At times, the hostilities have flared immediately upon initial contact, as in the first encounters of Spaniards and Filipinos; and at other times, conflict has come up after long years of comparative tranquility, as in the case of Jews and non-Jews in Germany.

Ethnic conflict may be designed to eliminate the opposing group from the geographical area. This may be accomplished by violence which kills off the weaker groups or by an agreed separation and division of territory. Examples of elimination through violence would include Hitler's extermination of the Jews, the Turkish attacks on the Armenians and the treatment of American Indians by the early settlers. Instances of separation and division of territory can be seen in the peaceful separation of Norway from Sweden in 1905 and in the more recent partitions which separated Jews from Arabs in Palestine and Moslems from Hindus in India. The methods may differ, but the basic motive is simply the belief that the attitudes of the two groups are so divergent that it is undesirable for them to live together in a common territory.

Immigration policies also reflect this attitude. In the Orient, this can be seen in the "white Australia policy" which bars all non-Caucasians from coming to that continent and in the Filipino immigration laws which seek to reduce Chinese immigration to an insignificant amount. In the west, the most dramatic example is the United States, which for a long time welcomed all who wished to come from any part of the world, but which later adopted a strict control of immigration. This control reduced Oriental and African migration to a nominal token figure of 100 or less per country per year and sharply restricted the number coming from Europe. Immigration controls were relaxed after World War II to allow the entry of 400,000 European refugees, but this was a temporary move which did not change the basic policy. Prior to 1924, there were occasions when more than a million migrants entered the United States in a year's time.

Segregation and discrimination.

More frequent than the attempt to eliminate other ethnic groups from the area, is the attempt to confine them to specific areas of the national life through discriminatory measures. In this case, the minority group is welcome as long as it occupies the status which the majority feel is proper. Negroes in the United States were welcomed as unskilled workers in the cotton fields, but encountered opposition when they wished to compete in more desirable occupation. Chinese and Indian merchants were at first welcomed in most Asiatic countries, but became an object of hostility when the native population developed a desire to engage in trade.

Attempts to keep the minority in their status take many forms. Residential and occupational segregation will automatically eliminate them from some types of competition. Stratification, which implies that different ethnic groups follow different class levels with appropriate occupational patterns, will tend to freeze an economic pattern. Legislation such as imposing special taxes and making the buying of property difficult, is often introduced as in the case of measures to "Filipinize" the economy. None of these measures attempts to oust the minority from the country, but they all imply that the minority ethnic group is welcome only as long as it refrains from economic or social competition with the dominant group.

Extreme examples of this attitude are the segregation laws of South Africa which deprive the non-Caucasians of education, political voice and economic opportunity and Negro-White relations in the southern part of the United States. There is also a growing tendency for Oriental nations to place restrictions both on westerners and on other Asiatics.

Friendship and equality.

In most instances, different peoples have learned to live together in a peaceful relationship. Frequently, their differences are reduced to the vanishing point through the process of assimilation by which they combine their previous cultures to produce a new culture which is then common to both groups. A similar process is that of amalgamation through intermarriage which reduces physical differences and makes the two peoples biologically one. These processes usually operate even in periods of conflict and constantly tend to bring different groups together. The United States is known as a "melting pot" because of the extent to which it has united many ethnic groups.

An entirely different technique of peaceful relationship is involved in cultural pluralism. In this situation, the two groups maintain their own identity with a minimum of assimilation and amalgamation. They may occupy the same general geographical area and yet follow different customs and religions, speak different languages and maintain some difference in physical appearance. The essential element here is a desire of each group to maintain its own culture without destroying the culture of other groups.

Examples of cultural pluralism would include Canada, Belgium, Switzerland and Russia. In Canada, Quebec, a French Catholic section, has preserved its unique character in the midst of a country which is predominantly English and Protestant. In Russia, the Communist party allowed different groups to follow their own peculiar customs, speak their own languages and have local self rule. Current reports indicate that this policy is being disregarded and that the Communists are returning to the Czarist policy of attempting to "Russify" the entire country.[2]

Switzerland is outstanding in the length of time which the pattern has endured and in the friendly feeling between its different groups. The Swiss have no common language and are divided into French, German, and Italian sections. They are also religiously divided between Catholics and Protestants. In spite of these divisions, the Swiss people have an intense loyalty to their country and have had relatively few instances of severe ethnic conflict.

Is there a group relations cycle?

Several sociologists[3] have maintained that there is an inherent cycle of inter-group relationships which passes through several stages of friendship and conflict. The suggested cycles vary in form, but the following pattern is fairly representative:

---

[2] See discussion in Berry, Brewton: *Race Relations*, Houghton Mifflin Company, Boston, Mass., 1950, pp. 327-351.
[3] *Ibid.*, pp. 132-154.

Chapter VIII. Relationship of Ethnic Groups

(1) Curiosity and friendliness in first contacts.
(2) Suspicion and limited conflict as numbers of new groups increase.
(3) Growing awareness of different interests and preparation for conflict.
(4) Serious conflict on a large scale.
(5) Efforts to mediate conflict and develop common bonds between groups—to some extent, this develops at the same time as No. 3.
(6) Some type of peaceful settlement or *modus vivendi* which enables the groups to live on a cooperative basis.

In the modern world, the best examples of a race relations cycle can be seen in the adjustment of European immigrants to the United States. In this situation, there is little chance for a distinction between immigrant and native on the basis of physical differences and as the immigrant acquires the American culture, it becomes difficult to distinguish him from the majority group. In cases where groups are distinguished by color as well as culture, it is much less certain that such a cycle will operate and the chances are greater that a peaceful solution may collapse and give rise to new conflicts.

Ethnic composition of the Philippines.

From a standpoint of distinctive physical appearance, four groups have influenced the local scene in a fairly substantial manner. These include the Negritos, usually considered the group which has resided in the Islands for the longest period; the Malayan-Indonesian strain which predominates in the majority of Filipinos; the Chinese, who comprise the largest group of foreign nationals and who, Beyer[4] estimates, share in the ancestry of about ten per cent of the total population; and the Caucasians, mostly Spanish and American.

---

[4] H. Otley Beyer: Table of Philippine Racial Ancestry, cited in Tangco, Marcelo: "The Christian Peoples of the Philippines," *Natural and Applied Science Bulletin*. University of the Philippines, Vol. XI, No. 1, January-March, 1951, p. 110.

Culturally, one will also find sharp differences between the majority group, the mountain tribes and the Moros. These last two groups combined include about six per cent of the population.

Less sharply defined than these, are a variety of regional groups which developed before the Philippines were considered a united country. The various regional groups have developed different customs, attitudes and languages. The 1939 census lists some 70 tongues, while Professor Tangco lists 55 language-dialects and 137 sub-dialects, exclusive of English, Spanish and Chinese.[5] Some of the dialects are spoken only by a few hundred, others by several million. Even discounting the minor groups, the variety of major dialects is impressive; however, the different languages have much in common and some degree of bilingualism is present in at least half of the population. Many who speak one of the major languages also utilize one of the minor dialects as a basic language.

Major Filipino Languages	No. of Speakers in 1939	Percentage of Population
1. Tagalog	4,068,565	25.43%
2. Cebuano	3,854,299	24.09%
3. Ilocano	2,353,318	14.71%
4. Hiligaynon	2,063,744	12.89%
5. Bicol	1,289,424	8.06%
6. Samar-Leyte Bisayan	1,051,438	6.57%
7. Pampango	621,455	3.88%
8. Pangasinan	573,752	3.59%
[6] Total	15,875,995	99.22%

Ethnic lines in the Philippines separate the various regional groups as well as Oriental-Caucasian, Filipino-Chinese, American-Spanish, Christian-Moslem, Negrito-Malayan and Mountain-Lowland. Upon first glance, this bewildering variety of peoples would seem to present a fertile ground for the development of ethnic conflict. On the

---

[5] Tangco, Marcelo: *Op. Cit.*, pp. 105-109.
[6] Clifford H. Prator, Jr.: *Language Teaching in the Philippines*, United States Educational Foundation in the Philippines, 1950, p. 1.

CHAPTER VIII. RELATIONSHIP OF ETHNIC GROUPS 173

other hand, there are elements of uniformity which unite many of these different sectors. These bonds would include some degree of intermarriage between most groups, the predominance of the Christian religion, the heavy numerical preponderance of the Indonesian-Malay Stock and the prevalence of a roughly similar agricultural economy in most areas. The language disparity is also mitigated somewhat by a widespread use of English and the gradual growth of the National Language.

The Philippines present the unusual picture of a country with a large number of ethnic divisions which are united by common interests that cut across ethnic lines.

Social distance as a measure of ethnic relationships.

Social distance is a concept coined to express a situation in which a feeling of social difference is more important than geographical proximity in determining relationships. If there is a feeling of essential similarity between groups, then there is a tendency for them to intermarry, join the same clubs, live in the same neighborhood and share the same leisure time activities. A sense of strangeness, however, will tend to limit this type of interaction even though they may live quite close to each other. In the United States, Bogardus attempted to measure this tendency by means of a social distance scale designed to measure the mutual acceptance of various groups. In general, he found that acceptance by the majority depended largely upon similarity in culture, religion, language and physical type. Thus he found that in the United States the preferred group were English speaking, Protestant Caucasians.[7]

The author gave a somewhat similar questionnaire to students at the University of the Philippines in an attempt to discover the pattern of social attitudes which prevailed in this group of Filipino students. The questionnaire was given to 200 students in seven different classes and showed a high degree of agreement between the different classes. A summary of the results is shown in tabular form:

---

[7] Emory S. Bogardus: *Immigration and Race Attitudes*, Boston, D.C. Health & Co., 1928.

NATIONALITY GROUPS	Husband or Wife	Roommate in Dormitory	Business Partner	Important Gov't Official	Citizen of Philippines	Average In All Categories
American White	1.72	1.40	1.42	1.92	1.41	1.52
Spanish	2.28	2.16	2.42	2.69	2.14	2.24
Dutch, English	2.42	1.90	2.23	2.79	2.00	2.16
Chinese	3.04	2.90	2.05	3.32	2.95	2.84
Japanese, Indonesian, Korean, Bombay	3.18	2.77	2.73	3.34	2.85	2.83
American Negro	3.53	2.87	2.96	3.41	2.89	2.94
REGIONAL GROUPS						
Tagalog	1.47	1.31	1.58	1.50	—	1.54
Ilocano, Samareño, Ilongo, Cebuano, Pampangueño	2.24	2.05	2.14	2.19	—	2.22
Moro, Igorot, Negrito, Ibanag	3.40	3.07	3.24	3.00	—	3.40
RELIGIOUS GROUPS						
Catholic	1.08	1.11	1.17	1.08	—	1.19
Protestant	2.63	2.35	2.24	2.05	—	2.23
Aglipayan	3.11	2.37	2.32	2.37	—	2.51
Iglesia Ni Kristo, 7th Day Adventist	3.39	2.85	2.87	2.96	—	2.92
Jewish, Moslem, Buddhist	3.52	2.49	3.23	3.08	—	3.08

Marking: (1) Desirable in this relationship (2) Indifferent (3) Mild hostility (4) Extreme resistance to this relationship

Average in all categories includes three items not listed here for reasons of space.

Like all groups, the U.P. students show a high degree of ethnocentric feeling and since the majority are Tagalogs and Catholics, it is natural that these categories had a highly favored rating. Other ratings require a more detailed explanation. In the case of nationalities, Americans ranked highest with European groups next in line. It is interesting to note that ethnocentric prejudices did not extend to racial lines. All colored groups, including the American Negro, received a low rating. In some instances, this antipathy to colored groups may be caused by unpleasant experiences, but the overall tendency can only be

Chapter VIII. RELATIONSHIP OF ETHNIC GROUPS

explained on the basis of a generalized identification with Caucasians. The Chinese rating reflects tensions between them and Filipinos and the higher rating they received for association in commercial activities indicates a Filipino recognition of Chinese abilities in these lines.

Regional ratings indicate a degree of rivalry between Tagalogs and the other major groups which is significant, but probably no greater than the usual sectional differences likely to be found in any country. The difference between these major groups and the smaller units; however, is great and is comparable to the feeling of distance in respect to the least favored nationalities. When students were asked for an explanation, they usually based their attitude on the opinion that these groups were less advanced in cultural development and hence, less desirable as close associates.

Religious attitudes give a heavy preference to Catholics with Protestants second, Aglipayans (Philippine Independent Church) third; and all others receiving unfavorable ratings. Among the Christian churches, students reported having had the most contact with Protestants and Aglipayans and felt that these were more similar to Catholics than were Seventh Day Adventists or the *Iglesia Ni Kristo*. Some students indicated that the American associations of Protestants added to their prestige. All of the non-Christians ranked low, presumably because of the preference for those who shared a religious viewpoint at least to the extent of following the same basic tradition. Jews did not rank differently in business relations than in other areas and were apparently regarded simply as non-Christian rather than as commercial competitors.

To summarize these results, one would conclude that these students showed a preference for those who were assimilated to western culture, followers of the Christian religion and leaning toward the Caucasoid in physical appearance. This tendency is in harmony with the history of the Philippines, but in direct contrast to its geographical environment. The preference for western culture conflicts with the oriental culture of surrounding countries and the Christian bias is in sharp contrast to the fact that nearby areas are predominantly Moslem, Buddhist or Hindu. The preference for persons of the Caucasoid type is not only in contrast to the Mongoloid character of surrounding peoples, but with the Indo-Malayan origin of the majority of Filipinos.

Prejudice and Ethnic Relations

The cultural setting of prejudice.

Prejudice is derived from a combination of *pre*, meaning *before*, and *judge*, meaning *to render a decision*. The word carries the idea that one has made a decision about an individual or group before knowing all the facts. On this basis, a great deal of effort has been spent in attempting to show people that their prejudices were ill founded and should be altered in the light of more complete information. At best, any prejudice is an attempt to apply a group description to individuals, many of whom are exceptions to the general rule and at worst, prejudice may unjustly attack the reputation of an entire group. The most common way of expressing prejudice is by means of stereotypes.

We need to analyze our cherished beliefs about other peoples and find the extent to which we have been victims of misinformation. American whites need to learn that many Negroes have been distinguished scientists, diplomats, and businessmen, and that the general backwardness of the group is explainable by the lack of opportunity. Jews and Christians should learn about the common elements of both religions which caused Pope Pius XI to say, "Spiritually, we are all Semites." Lowland Filipinos should discover that the mountain peoples are no longer headhunters and possess one of the oldest and best integrated cultures of any Filipino group.

This type of enlightment is desirable and should be encouraged by all educated people, but it is futile to hope that, by itself, it will eliminate prejudiced feeling about ethnic groups. The difficulty is that no individuals possess the complete information needed for an impartial appraisal of other ethnic groups and hence, they necessarily accept the notions which are handed to them as part of their culture. These notions can be improved by better education, but the element of prejudice can probably never be entirely removed.

Another difficulty is that we tend to accept the notions about other peoples which suit our own purposes. Western beliefs about the inferiority of Oriental and African peoples cannot be explained without realizing the need of western nations to justify an imperialistic rule over "backward" peoples. The ideas of whites about Negro inferiority are related to a desire to confine Negroes to the status of unskilled labor doing work which other people find distasteful. Charges of the "unscrupulousness" and "sharp dealings" of the Chinese are related to a desire of other Orientals to eliminate them as business competitors. The tendency of Filipinos to minimize the importance of the mountain tribes is inexplicable unless one understands the fear that foreigners will underestimate Filipino acquisition of western culture.

Factual analysis of specific prejudices is likely to be futile when these prejudices are linked to group attitudes or individual emotional difficulties. Such prejudices form an inherent part of the psycho-social structure and cannot be fundamentally changed without attacking its roots. The phrase, "I am not prejudiced, but..." in which one then goes on to attack another group indicates that simply deploring prejudice does not eliminate it as a factor in society.

To reduce prejudice will require the joint efforts of the social reformer and the psychiatrist. The former will alter the social system which produces group rivalries; the latter will seek to bring health and insight to the sick mentality which rationalizes its inadequacy by blaming unpopular ethnic groups.

The technique of greatest help in this area is the association of members of different groups on an equal basis. In this fashion, they gradually learn to judge each other as individuals, rather than as members of a group. In this process the stereotypes are eventually recognized as false by the different individuals. The greatest obstacle to changing prejudice is a system which either limits contacts or confines all relationships to a stereotyped master-servant; storekeeper-customer; ruler-subject basis.[8]

Economic Basis of Ethnic Patterns

Throughout this chapter, frequent reference has been made to conflicting economic interests of various ethnic groups. This economic struggle is only one of the factors involved in group relationships, but it is a basic cause of difficulty and economic competition usually enters into ethnic conflict. In this discussion, we shall deal first with some of the general aspects of economic struggle along ethnic lines and then attempt to analyze the specific form which this factor assumes in the area of Southeast Asia.

Social mobility and ethnic competition.

When immigrants move to a new locality, they often bring with them economic contributions which are welcomed by the natives. These contributions vary in nature and would include both skilled and unskilled labor and the capital and expert advice essential for hitherto neglected industries. These contributions may be of great aid to the native economy, but they invariably involve some degree of competition with local workers and businessmen. Also the immigrants are seldom content to confine themselves to specific fields and feel they should be able to enter any activity which appeals to them. Likewise, the native will not long be content to leave the newly developed enterprises in the hands of other nationals. The result is a

---

[8] One of the best discussions along these lines is to be found in an inexpensive little pamphlet by Arnold Rose entitled, *Race and Prejudice*, 1951, issued by UNESCO, 19 Avenue Kleber, Paris.

Chapter VIII. Relationship of Ethnic Groups

struggle between individuals for profits in which they will appeal to their ethnic groups for aid in their efforts to rise in the social scale. In this fashion, what might be a healthy competition between individuals is changed into bitter rivalry between large groups.

If the immigrant group and the local inhabitants are similar in physical appearance and not too divergent in culture, assimilation takes place and conflict ultimately disappears. Examples of this kind would include the Irish immigrants to the United States, who, for a period of time, were in sharp conflict with native Americans, but, with the loss of their distinctive cultural characteristics, became accepted as part of the general population. Similar experiences have often occurred to Tagalogs and Ilocanos as they moved into areas of the Philippines inhabited by other regional groups. When the immigrant group has distinct physical traits or clings tenaciously to sharply different cultural patterns, then the course of affairs is less favorable. In his case, the immigrant group remains identifiable and is under constant attacks from competitors in the native group. The Japanese in California probably absorbed American culture as rapidly as the Irish, but their physical appearance continued to set them apart. The result was that Caucasian groups kept up a steady pressure to reduce Japanese competition through hostile legislation. This eventually resulted in restrictions on landholding and in an exclusion act which completely ended the mass immigration of Japanese settlers to the United States.

Ethnic stratification in Southeast Asia.

The different position of various ethnic groups in this area can best be understood by analyzing their respective roles in the change from a subsistence to a monetary economy. In the older subsistence economy, agricultural crops were consumed in the immediate vicinity with very little use of money in the process. The peasant provided for his own needs and also raised the food supply for a small upper class and their servants. In the monetary economy, a large percentage of farm production went into the export market on a cash basis to provide money for luxury goods for the aristocracy, dividends for the foreign peasant.

This change in the economy brought a need for services which the local population could not easily furnish. These needs included better roads and public health facilities, which the native government was ill equipped to provide, and large scale capital investment which exceeded both the resources and the inclinations of the local aristocracy. The new capitalistic development also called for a host of small shopkeepers, processors and bankers—occupations for which the local population lacked special aptitude. These needs were supplied by westerners who took over the administration of government and provided capital and by Chinese or Indian migrants who established retail stores, processed farm products and supplied small scale credit.

The change in the economy not only brought new ethnic elements into the picture, but the pressure for money led to credit practices which imperiled the security of both peasant and aristocrat as they struggled for money to pay taxes and buy the factory-made goods which now seemed a part of their life. The resulting economic difficulties led to ethnic antagonisms which Jacoby describes in the following terms:

> For the majority of the farming population, the foreign middle man and the money lender is the representative of a hated economic system. His frequently doubtful activities and the high price of his services enrage the peasants and result in tension and riots. Consequently, the middle man may be the first object of agrarian unrest, and where he is the representative of a racial minority, as in Burma, racial riots occur frequently. He is the immediate enemy, easier and less risky to attack than the white man or the native landlord. Smart political propaganda may make use of him as a scapegoat for the misery of the peasants, thereby diverting them from a demand for efficient agricultural reorganization to a fight against the foreign money-

lender, though his existence is merely a function of the dependent system as such.

The class of foreign middle men, based economically on the absence of adequate credit and marketing institutions, has created a status of racial tension and conflict, previously unknown among the tolerant and hospitable Oriental peoples. Agrarian unrest in Southeast Asia thus gets a touch of racial warfare which endangers political understanding among the peoples of the Pacific area.[9]

Resentment against the dominant role of the white man gave rise to nationalistic movements which changed the political control to native hands, but which still required the services of the western investor and technical expert. The next object of nationalism was the Chinese or Indian middleman. As Jacoby points out, this group of people is closer to the populace and also less protected so that violence against them is usually more extreme than against the representatives of colonial powers. On the other hand, the local populations still lack the skills and attitudes required in these occupations, and the usual result of an attack on alien elements is simply to slow down economic activity and cause greater suffering to all concerned.

The solution of these difficulties is far from easy, since it involves the reorganization of the traditional agricultural system; a change which is opposed by the landlords and not fully understood by the peasants. If this could be accomplished, there would still be tension unless local peoples could acquire the attitudes and skills essential to business activity, thus enabling them to compete with migrants in the role of middlemen. The cautious, frugal handling of money, which is required in modern commerce, is entirely foreign to a way of life based on subsistence farming spiced by profligate expenditures on fiestas and weighed down by family obligations. Such a change requires a complete alteration

---

[9] Erich H. Jacoby: *Agrarian Unrest in Southeast Asia*, New York, Columbia University Press, 1949, p. 24.

in the basic values of the Oriental peasant and would require generations to accomplish.

Ethnic stratification in the Philippines.

In the Philippines, the first wave of western influence was brought in by the Spaniards, who controlled the government and stimulated the production of export crops. The Spaniards intermarried with the *Caciques*, who formed a mestizo group that became the dominant element in the landlord class. When the Spaniards lost political power, their place was taken by the Americans who greatly increased the production of export crops, but did not intermarry in great numbers.

The Chinese have conducted trading relations with the Philippines for centuries. Their numbers increased slightly under the Spaniards and they developed retail trade to a greater extent. With the greater economic activity under the American rule, the Chinese merchants found new opportunities and increased considerably in numbers, although their growth was limited by immigration restrictions.

One of the best descriptions of the role of the mestizo group is furnished by McHale in a discussion of Philippine economic development:

> The intermarriage of the *datu* class Filipino and the Spanish colonists was parallel by another important intermarriage pattern: that of the Chinese traders and skilled craftsmen with the native Filipinos...
> While little information is available on the subject, it seems reasonably safe to assume that the majority of Chinese who did marry Filipino women married into either the small Filipino trading class or into the class that had left the subsistence village because it was economically possible for them to do so. This suggests that the Chinese, like the Spanish, married into the higher levels of Filipino society rather than into the lower;
> The development of a Chinese-Filipino and Spanish-Filipino mestizo class in the Philippines

Chapter VIII. RELATIONSHIP OF ETHNIC GROUPS

brought forth a peculiar ethno-economic cleavage within the Philippine society in which the upper class, both socially and economically, is not only ethnically distinguishable from the rest of Philippine society but has solidified as a class apart without a true Filipino middle class to bridge the gap. By intermarriage within the existing mestizo group or with other Chinese or Spanish and by perpetuating a system wherein social mobility is all but impossible, the ethno-economic schism in the Philippines has increased over the years rather than decreased.[10]

The present situation may be seen in the following table:

Table I — Economic Role of Ethnic Groups

Group	Economic Role
European and American	Capitalists, Technical Experts, Export-Import traders.
Spanish and Chinese Mestizos	Landlords, Government Officials, Professionals, Export-Import traders.
Chinese	Laborers, Skilled Craftsmen, Sari-Sari Operators, Retail and Wholesale Businessmen, Export-Import traders, Agricultural Processors.
Filipinos of Native Ancestry	Mostly Taos or urban laborers; some have made gains in business, professional and governmental activities.

Relations between these groups have followed the usual pattern in Southeast Asia with the exception that the American withdrawal from governmental control was accomplished without bloodshed and has left a friendly feeling between them and the Filipinos. The gap between

---

[10] Thomas R. McHale: "Economic Development in the Philippines," *The University of Manila Journal of East Asiatic Studies.* Vol. 1, No. 3, April, 1952, pp. 7-8.

Tao and landlord causes constant strife, but does not seem to result in a conscious stressing of ethnic differences between the mestizo and those of indigenous stock.

Chinese business success has aroused resentment of all classes of Filipinos and tension is manifested by occasional riots and constant legislative discrimination which now prevents Chinese from buying land, eliminates them from city owned markets and hampers their import-export activity. Since the Filipino business class has only begun to develop, these restrictions have slowed down economic development, but have not diminished the economic importance of the Chinese. Their main effect has been to divert Filipino interest from more important economic problems and to make the Chinese business men resort to bribery in order to overcome unfavorable laws.

Filipino-American Relationships
In the Philippines.

When the end of the Spanish-American war found the Americans in the Philippines, they were faced with the problem of determining their role in a new situation. They had never seriously considered the addition of a colonial area of this size; they were not inclined to hand the Islands back to Spain and they felt that the Filipinos were not yet prepared to conduct the government of an independent nation. The ultimate decision which governed American policy was expressed in the words of President McKinley:

> There was nothing left to do but to take them all and to educate the Filipinos and uplift and civilize and Christianize them, and by God's grace, do the very best we could by them, as our fellowmen for whom Christ also died.[11]

Most of the world regarded this statement as merely the attempt to cloak imperialistic motives in pious terms.

---
[11] Frank Charles Laubach: *The People of the Philippines*, Duran and Company, New York, 1925, p. 123.

Chapter VIII. Relationship of Ethnic Groups

Filipinos regarded themselves as already civilized and Christian and only the force of arms persuaded them to accept American rule. Americans, for the most part, accepted the doctrine in good faith. They combined a dislike of colonial empire with a deepseated faith in the superiority of their own culture. To them, the obvious procedure was first to "Americanize" the Filipinos and then let them run their own affairs.

The result was that Americans did not regard their somewhat unwilling wards either as equals or inferiors, but as potential carriers of western culture to be made over in the American image. In this sense, all Americans had the "missionary" spirit. Some endeavoured to spread Protestant versions of the Christian faith; others were carrying the gospel of universal education, public health and sanitation, democratic government and modern business.

Filipinos responded rapidly to increased opportunities in government and education and, in some degree, the American pattern became accepted as a desirable goal. Friction did not center on ultimate objectives, but on the timing and procedure required in attaining political independence. In general, the Filipino politicians wanted to get independence at once and were willing to accept the risk of inefficient government. Americans felt that a long period of preparation was required and that early independence would lead to disaster. This point of friction was settled by the decision to grant independence in 1946.

In personal relationships, Americans manifested neither the tendency to intermarry and become a part of the country which characterized the Spanish, nor the complete aloofness which is typical of the British in colonial situations. The permanent residents usually brought their wives and children with them and settled down in self sufficient colonies in the larger cities. Their official and business contacts were conducted upon a friendly, informal basis, but social contacts were limited.

Intermarriage was not common between permanent residents and Filipinos and the intermixture which did occur was often the result of illicit unions between American soldiers and Filipino women. The American has never manifested much personal responsibility for illegitimate children, and the mixed offspring were frequently ignored by their fathers and thrown back upon the resources of their mother's families. As a result, the American mestizo has many social handicaps and has never gained the favored position of the Spanish mestizo.[12]

The traditional prejudice attitude toward colored peoples, which is especially strong in the southern parts of the United States, was less of a factor than might have been expected. Prejudice is usually related to the environment and, in the Philippines, Americans were dependent upon good will which could easily be lost by racial arrogance. A more potent cause of friction was misunderstanding based upon Filipino concern for "honor" and the American tendency for direct and blunt expression. These differences, however, became well known and both parties were able to adjust on a friendly basis.

American-Filipino relationships were seldom intimate and involved contrasting cultural patterns, but have been increasingly characterized by a respectful friendship. The only cloud on the horizon at present is the prospect that upper class Filipinos may become irritated at American advice and resentful at their continued dependence upon American financial and technical assistance. In this respect, the revival of interest in Spanish culture may be classified as a kind of upper class "nativism" which seeks a counterbalance to American influence. In summary, though, it is probably true that few peoples have come through a colonial experience with as great a measure of friendly feeling as have the Filipinos and the Americans.

[12] The American-Philippine Guardian Association was founded by Gov. General Leonard Wood to alleviate the plight of illegitimate American mestizos. Its 1951 report estimated that upwards of 5,000 World War II G.I. babies in the Philippines lived without paternal support.

CHAPTER VIII. RELATIONSHIP OF ETHNIC GROUPS   187

Filipinos in the United States.

Since the turn of the century, an increasing stream of Filipinos have come to the U.S. on a temporary basis. This group, composed of students, business men and government officials, did not come into competition with the local residents and were generally received on a friendly basis. Their numbers were not restricted by immigration quotas and much of this travel has been aided by American groups. In this fashion, many of the educational, political and business leaders received part of their training in the United States.

Those who came to the United States seeking employment had a somewhat different kind of experience. During the period of American rule, Filipinos were allowed to come to the United States without regard to immigration restrictions. At first, this movement was a mere trickle, but in the nineteen twenties, prospects of remunerative employment in Hawaii and the west coast of the U.S. attracted thousands. They found work in the plantations of Hawaii, the salmon fisheries of Alaska and the agricultural areas of California. Others were readily accepted in such personal service occupations as bellhops, stewards, waiters and cooks.[13]

This type of migrant was welcomed because he supplied labor of a kind which was needed in the American economy, but his experience was not altogether favorable. Some Filipinos adjust easily, made substantial amounts of money and became American citizens. Many others found they were unable to enter the most attractive occupations, and that the native population was far from friendly.

The Filipino migrant came to America on the bottom rung of the economic ladder, but his training made him reluctant to accept a position of inferiority. Americans in the United States were free from the pressures for good relations which forced them to equalitarian conduct

---

[13] Benicio T. Catapusan, "The Philippine Labor Cycle in the U.S.," *Sociology and Social Research,* September, 1934, pp. 61-63.

in the Philippines, and they sometimes regarded the Filipino migrant as being in the same subordinate category in which they placed all colored peoples.

Relationships with the opposite sex also brought about ill-feeling. The typical Filipino migrant was young, male and unmarried. At one time, the sex ratio was 143 to one and even in 1940 was estimated at seven to one.[14] If he was to have any contacts with women, he must turn to American women, and this aroused the animosity of American men, who deeply resented any crossing of the color line, even though the women might be receptive. The place of least resistance was the house of prostitution or the taxi dance hall and this, of course, classified the Filipino as immoral. Actually, he was about as conventional as other men of the same age and marital status, but social pressure placed him in an extremely difficult situation.

The consequence of these factors was the existence of considerable distrust between Filipinos and native Americans which resulted in riots, fights and hostile legislation. As a result of independence, immigration was restricted to one hundred a year and Filipinos desiring to return to the homeland were repatriated at the expense of the United States government. This ended the era of large scale immigration and it appears that the number of Filipinos in the U.S. will be stabilized at a figure of about forty thousand.

Although still not completely assimilated in American society, the migrants have found their lot easier in post war years. Increased prosperity diminished the resentment of local labor and gave Filipino-Americans a better chance to improve their fortunes. Legislation against landholding has been declared unconstitutional and the Filipino migrant has benefited from a general movement toward better treatment of minority groups.

American development of Pacific bases caused the employment of many Filipinos in Okinawa, Guam and else-

---

[14] John H. Burma: "The Background of the Current Situation of Filipino Americans," *Social Forces*, Vol. 30, number 1, October, 1951.

CHAPTER VIII. RELATIONSHIP OF ETHNIC GROUPS 189

where. This employment is of a temporary nature and the assumption is that workers will return to the Philippines when their work is finished. Both the American and Filipino governments seek to protect the worker from friction and exploitation. Migratory workers of this kind contribute their labor to this development and, in return, receive wages large enough to permit substantial savings.

Hawaiian development has also been advanced by Filipino workers, several thousand of whom were admitted as laborers in World War II. Immigration here is again restricted, but Hawaii has 61,040 Filipinos, comprising the eighth largest ethnic group. Hawaii, with one of the world's most mixed populations, has never had the racial frictions of the mainland. Intermarriage is common and open racial discrimination is absent.[15]

The condition of Filipinos in America ranged from homesickness and despair to adjustment and success. Today, large scale immigration is ended and the Filipino-American is becoming an integral part of American society. The bitterness of the earlier days is fading as both the migrant and the older residents of his adopted homeland learn to live together.

Trends in Intergroup Relations in the Philippines

Stratification: its strength and weakness.

Stratification, in the ethnic sense, may be regarded as existing when class divisions are based on ethnic groupings. This seems to be the situation to a large degree at the present time. In the upper class, one would find the European and American settlers, Spanish mestizos and some Chinese; in the middle class one would find the same groups with the exception of the Europeans and Americans; the upper-lower would find a high proportion of Tagalogs and Ilocanos with a minor representation of those from other regions and the

---

[15] Ch'eng-K'un Cheng: "Assimilation in Hawaii and the Bid for Statehood," *Fookien Times Yearbook*, 1952, pp. 91-94.

lower class would consist primarily of comparatively pure-blooded Filipinos from all regions. Tagalogs and Ilocanos would form a heavy proportion of this class even though also comprising most of the next higher category.

There are various considerations which make one hesitate in assuming that stratification will continue to be this pronounced. One of the major weaknesses of the system is that intermarriage is continually changing the ethnic lines. Another weakness is that ethnic stratification does not have a social sanction as strong as that of Negro-White relations in the U.S. and in South Africa, or in the caste system in India. Ethnic groups do overlap class lines and some members of each group are to be found in all classes, although not in the same proportions. The ethnic class structure is more the result of variations in cultural background and economic opportunity than of deliberate effort to impose a definite status.

Those of foreign origin are more likely to have inherited the capital and to have learned the economic know-how which made for financial success. Ilocanos, the most frequent migrants in the Philippines, found new opportunity in many areas. Tagalogs had similar advantages due to their predominance in the largest city with its greater cultural and economic advantages. These social advantages of the different ethnic groups are considerable, but their importance should lessen with the increase of education and the spread of commerce and industry throughout the islands. Further, when one from another group does achieve success, he finds that he is usually accepted in upper class society with only a minimum of regard to his ethnic origin.

Assimilation and amalgamation between regional groups.

Assimilation and amalgamation refer to the tendency for people to acquire a common culture and to marry across ethnic lines. We do not have exact indices of the extent to which all Filipinos have a common culture, but several

CHAPTER VIII. RELATIONSHIP OF ETHNIC GROUPS

factors are obvious. These would include the use of English and, to an almost equal extent, Tagalog, as a common language; the unifying factor of Filipino nationalism and the widespread loyalty to the Roman Catholic Church plus many common traits of material culture. On the other hand, the majority of the population does not share a common language after fifty years of attempting to absorb English, and it is doubtful that Tagalog can make much more rapid progress. Local loyalties are still preserved by the use of a distinctive dialect, modes of dress and particular customs. Pressures for assimilation exist, but counter forces are also at work to keep alive a variety of somewhat different cultures.

Amalgamation through intermarriage, tends of course, to break down concepts of the distinctiveness of various groups. The increase in internal migration tends to bring members of different regional groups into more frequent contact and thus increase the chances of marrying across traditional lines. Two studies which have been made on this subject indicate that while endogamy is the rule there is a considerable trend toward the crossing of regional lines.[16]

One of the best descriptions of the Filipino attitude toward intermarriage is given by Professor Tangco in his monograph, *The Christian Peoples of the Philippines.*

> In a sense, he is endogamic in his innate feelings, but without any characteristic spirit of racial prejudice against any nationality. For example, he would not approve heartily the marriage of a Tagalog to an Ilocano, or that of a Filipino to a Chinese, a Japanese, an American, a Spaniard or any other foreign nationality; but if these mixed marriages occur, he tolerates them and does not

---

[16] Severino F. Corpus, "Patterns of Regional Intermarriage and Language Usage in Middle Class families in Manila." *Manila Times Sunday Magazine,* February 28, 1954, pp. 20, 21.
Chester L. Hunt, "Cotabato: Melting Pot of the Philippines." *Philippine Social Science and Humanities Review,* March, 1954, pp. 39, 72. Both studies found that approximately thirty percent of the marriages studied involved spouses from different regions.

consider the participants and their children as social outcasts.[17]

Assimilation and amalgamation of the Chinese.

The Chinese in the Philippines are in the paradoxical position of a group which has little desire to be absorbed in the Filipino culture, but which has experienced an amazing degree of both assimilation and amalgamation. Both Chinese and Filipinos feel that their own language, religion, physical type and cultural traditions are superior; yet both people have become mingled in spite of their inclinations.

The most obvious reason for this situation is that the goal of the Chinese in the Philippines was to become a business man and to achieve this goal, he had to learn how to serve a predominantly Filipino clientele. To do this, he had to learn the language and understand the people. Thus, Chinese have learned the local languages and these, in turn, that have been infiltrated by words of Chinese origin to express concepts not adequately conveyed in the indigenous tongue. Manuel has made a study of Chinese influence on Tagalog in which he finds that three and one half per cent of the most commonly used Tagalog words are of Chinese origin.[18] Similarly, the association of the two peoples has caused Chinese methods of preparing food to be practically a part of Filipino culture. Such dishes as *pancit, siopao, lumpia* and *lechon* are known to most Filipinos.

Residents of the Philippines classified as Chinese Nationals in the 1948 census numbered only 150,000 or less than one per cent of the population.[19] On the other hand, Beyer estimates that at least ten per cent of the population has some degree of Chinese ancestry.[20] This points to the

---

[17] Tangco, *op. cit.*, pp. 36-37.
[18] Arsenio E. Manuel: *Chinese Words in the Tagalog Language*, Manila, Philippinians Publications, 1948, p. 117.
[19] This figure is frequently challenged as being too low because of the number of illegal immigrants who conceal their status. Purcell acknowledges this, but feels that an estimate of 200,000 is probably too high. Purcell, Victor: *Chinese in Southeast Asia*, London, Oxford Press, 1950, pp. 652-653.
[20] Beyer, *op. cit., p.* 110.

view that there has been a high degree of intermarriage and that evidently, the natural history of the Chinese is to intermarry and find that his descendants become more Filipino and less Chinese with each generation. The explanation of this situation lies in a disproportionate sex ratio which makes it impossible for most Chinese men to acquire wives of their own nationality. In 1918, the sex ratio was one to thirteen and by 1939, was still one to four.[21]

This change to a more nearly equal ratio may indicate the possibility of a slowing down of the rate of intermarriage, but it is still true that most Chinese men have little opportunity to marry Chinese women. Social prejudices discourage intermarriage, but have little effect against a situation of this type. In spite of animosity between the two groups, some of the most prominent Filipino leaders including Jose Rizal and Sergio Osmeña have some Chinese ancestry.

Pluralism: Is This the Filipino Pattern?

Pluralistic factors in the Philippines.

In our earlier discussion of pluralism in this chapter (see discussion on page 152) we cited the Swiss as an example of a pluralistic society which was united in national feeling, but divided in language and religion. This situation would seem to be even more true in the Philippines. The Swiss have three major regional languages and one minor dialect. The Philippines have eight major regional languages and at least seventy-two minor dialects in addition to English, Spanish and Chinese. The Swiss are divided between Protestant and Catholic and although Catholicism is predominant in the Philippines, there are large groups of other Christians in addition to a considerable non-Christian population. Swiss cultural patterns have only a limited degree of variation, while groups in the

---

[21] See discussion in Purcell, *op. cit.*, pp. 575-577. Taking the figures for the group 15-54, the 1939 census showed 67,815 **males** and 13,675 females or a ratio of 5 to 1.

Philippines run the gamut from primitive food gatherers to those who participate in advanced industrial enterprises.

These differences are preserved through education, the press, radio and specialized religious agencies. One finds in Manila an American school which exists for the main purpose of preparing American children for schools in the homeland; Chinese schools in which the language and history of this group form a major part of the curriculum and several institutions which pride themselves on preserving Spanish patterns of instruction. Cemeteries, churches, temples, magazines and radio programs in many languages: all these give testimony to the fact that group differences have a practical effect and are preserved by many agencies. In a cosmopolitan city such as Manila, these groups will be separated by their specialized agencies, but brought together by common interests in economic and social activities. Even in this type of area, distinction persist and there is a tendency for members of different groups to live in separate districts. The Chinese section of Manila is well known, and while there is some dispersion through the city, most Chinese tend to live in two or three compact areas.[22] The distribution of regional groups is less visible, but a recent study of squatters indicated that those from the same region were grouped together.[23]

Outside of the larger cities ethnic distinctions are more apparent, but are weakened by internal migration which produces a mixed population. Most of the major regional groups are united by a common orientation toward western culture, and consider their differences less significant than their role as "modern" members of the Philippine Republic.

Do minorities have rights?

One of the most difficult questions in a mixed society concerns policy toward the minority peoples who deviate

---
[22] George Weightman: *The Chinese Community in the Philippines*, Unpublished Master's Thesis, University of the Philippines, 1952.
[23] Fe Rodriguez: "Manila Squatters," unpublished paper written for Sociology Department, University of the Philippines.

CHAPTER VIII. RELATIONSHIP OF ETHNIC GROUPS 195

Photo shows one of the claimants to the title of Sultan of Sulu with members of his court. The position now carries no political power but is still important because of the social and religious prestige of the Sultanate. Variety of clothes in the picture indicates the type of cultural transition now taking place among the Moros. Photo by courtesy of the Manila Times.

drastically from the dominant culture. Are they to be allowed to follow patterns which differ sharply from the political, religious, moral and economic convictions of the majority or must they be brought into line? If they must be assimilated, will this be accomplished by force, economic pressure or educational activity? Does the majority have any obligations to preserve a culture which it regards as not only different, but definitely inferior?

Prominent in this category, are the so-called non-Christian tribes (some of which include many converts to Christianity) such as Negritos, Igorots, Bagobos, Tinguians and Moros. Must they be "Filipinized" in the sense that their culture resembles that of the dominant group or can they be allowed to follow their traditional patterns? Can we refrain from attacking their particular cultures and still bring them the benefits of better sanitation, peace and order and higher living standards?

In previous years, technologically advanced groups took it for granted that their only concern with minorities of this type was to persuade or force them to adopt "modern" practices. Recently, this belief has been brought into question as circumstances have made us less certain that "modern" culture was completely good or that "primitives" were altogether bad. Also, we find that people suffer from a drastic cultural change and that there is a tendency for them to acquire the vices of both cultures and the virtues of neither.

In the United States, there was a strenuous effort for many years to "Americanize" the Indians. In this attempt, efforts were made to break the power of the tribal chiefs, eliminate the native languags, destroy the Indian religions and force the Indians to work for wages or practice farming in the usual American manner. The result of this policy was that the Indian became an extreme example of the "marginal" man, unable to live in the older pattern and unwilling to adopt the new. Disease, vice and general demoralization were rampant. Through western influence, the ideals and practices which safeguarded Indian life were destroyed and Indian morale was destroyed along with them.

In 1933, John Collier, chief of the Indian bureau, broke with this policy and attempted to give the Indians some of the benefits of modern society *within the framework of Indian culture*. This policy is still not completely accepted, but it marks a basic turning point in cultural attitudes.[24]

In an article in the *Free Press*, Professor Tage Ellinger raises a similar question in regard to the Negritos in the Zambales area. Due to the Huk menace, these people had been ordered to leave their traditional mountain homes and attempt to adjust in an entirely different setting. Ellinger points out that the Negritos had worked out a good adjust-

---

[24] The reasoning in back of Collier's beliefs is eloquently expressed in a recent book. John Collier: *Indians of North America*, American Library of World Literature, New York, 1947.

CHAPTER VIII. RELATIONSHIP OF ETHNIC GROUPS 197

The mountain peoples of Central Luzon, often known as Igorots, are separated from the lowlanders by a distinctive type of culture. Top left panel shows Igorot man pounding rice and right panel shows women in native costume. At the bottom are the famed Banaue rice terraces which constitute one of the great engineering achievements of all time. These terraces are sometimes called the "Eighth wonder of the world" and it is estimated that stretched out lengthwise they would reach halfway around the world. These terraces were probably begun a thousand years before the birth of Christ and represent a high degree of utilization of natural resources. Photos by courtesy of the Manila Times.

ment to migratory mountain living but would become demoralized in another environment. Under these circumstances it seemed that the welfare of the group of Negritos was being ruthlessly sacrificed in favor of military considerations.[25]

Professor Fred Eggan, an anthropologist who has spent several years in the study of the Igorots, feels that progress has been made toward assimilation but that successful adjustment requires a changed attitude on the part of the majority group and a greater understanding of local culture on the part of government officials.

> Perhaps the most important single task in connection with the mountain peoples is to bring about a change in the attitudes of lowlanders toward them. Differences anywhere in the world are frequently expressed in terms of superiority by the dominant group and the attitudes of lowlanders have a long and complex history. But these differences are cultural for the most part—not biological—and are being reduced by greater communication and education. Unless there are corresponding changes in attitude, however, the policy of assimilation will fail: the mountaineer does not look forward to being a second class citizen in the Philippines... The Philippine government utilizes experts in other fields—now that it is responsible for the continual welfare and development of the mountain peoples it needs all the expert advice it can find. Filipino social scientists would be particularly helpful in evaluating changes involved in reorienting social institutions and basic cultural beliefs. They might also prevent the application of policies which may have disastrous or costly effects.[26]

At the present time, most minorities in the Philippines are given a considerable degree of freedom. The continuance of this policy in the future depends upon two factors.

---

[25] Tage U. H. Ellinger: "Negrito Tragedy," *Free Press*, January 31, 1953.
[26] Fred Eggan: "Comments on Assimilation in the Mountain Province," *Philippine Social Science and Humanities Review*, March, 1954.

First, we can recognize that nationalism does not demand absolute uniformity and that groups, as well as individuals, have the inherent right to exist? Second, can we bring schools, sanitation and economic development to these peoples without destroying their cultural base? An affirmative answer to these questions will require a maximum of broadminded tolerance of cultural differences and skillful social planning in the handling of schools, churches, government agencies, hospitals and commercial enterprises.

Unity in diversity.

Cultural pluralism implies not only that differences exist, but that they are to be tolerated. A growing nationalism which will inspire and fortify the populace is a prime concern in the Philippines and many people claim that such a nationalism demands a common culture. Others would say that the Swiss example indicates that patriotism does not depend upon uniformity, and that both groups and individuals should have freedom to develop as they see fit.

Democracy implies not only the rule of the majority but also respect for the rights of the individual. It is difficult to respect the individual personality unless society also respects the culture of which the individual is a part. In this sense, cultural pluralism seems to be a logical expression of a democratic philosophy.

Summary

The term, "race," is rejected in this discussion because it implies the existence of clear-cut biological groups. The less pretentious and more inclusive term, "ethnic group," has been substituted. Ethnic prejudice is related both to the general cultural trend and to individual neurotic difficulties. Causes of prejudice are found in socio-economic relationships and in individual frustration. Treatment of prejudice requires both a psychiatric and a sociological approach. Social distance tests indicate that Filipino students are inclined to identify themselves with Caucasian

Christians who have adopted western culture. This contrasts sharply with the racial composition of the Philippines and their location in an Oriental area dominated by Buddhist, Hindu and Moslem religions.

Relations with Americans in the Philippines have been friendly without being intimate. Filipino migrants to the United States who went as temporary visitors found a friendly reception, but permanent migrants were frequently involved in ethnic conflict. Large scale permanent migration has now ceased, and the position of Filipino-Americans is being stabilized on a more harmonious basis.

The association of ethnic groups with each other produces a number of rather clearly defined patterns: open conflict, segregation, assimilation, amalgamation, stratification and cultural pluralism. These patterns are closely linked with economic activities, and class lines are sometimes identical with ethnic lines. All of these processes operate in the Philippines, with open conflict most likely to occur between the Chinese and the native inhabitants. At the same time, the Chinese have intermarried to a great extent, due to a disproportionate sex ratio, and a high degree of assimilation has taken place. Stratification is apparent in Filipino society. Filipinos without noticeable foreign blood are heavily represented in the lowest economic group and the Spanish and Chinese mestizos are predominant in the upper class. Social change may lessen this stratification, and the prevailing trend is toward a pluralistic society which, however, may run counter to a nationalistic desire for uniformity.

Chapter VIII. RELATIONSHIP OF ETHNIC GROUPS

PROJECTS

1. Make a list of contributions and the problems brought to the Philippines by contact with Chinese, Spanish and Americans.
2. List the ethnic groups present in your hometown and describe their economic and social interaction. On the basis of this analysis, prepare a prediction of the future course of ethnic relationships in your town.
3. Report on one of the suggested readings.

QUESTIONS

1. What is the difference between racial and ethnic? Why does the author question the idea that large groups of people are separated by definite physical distinctions?
2. Distinguish between the following terms: segregation, stratification, assimilation, amalgamation, pluralism.
3. Do you feel that cultural pluralism applies as well to the Philippines as to Switzerland? Why?
4. Should the mountain peoples abandon the G-string and the *tapis* for the clothing of the majority group? What advantages and drawbacks can you see from such a change?
5. What factors do you think are important in explaining the difficulties of Filipino migrants to the United States?
6. What are the main trends of Filipino attitudes as shown in the social distance test? How would these trends affect Filipino relationships with Oriental countries?
7. Is there any similarity between the "White Australia" policy and Filipino restrictions of Chinese immigration?
8. Does national patriotism demand a common language, religion, code of morals, mode of dress and economic attitudes? What arguments do you see in favor of each view-point?
9. What are basic causes of friction between Chinese and Filipinos? How would you decrease such friction?
10. What is racial prejudice? What things have to be considered in attempting to reduce the extent of such prejudice?

SUGGESTED READINGS

Adams, Romanzo: *Interracial Marriage in Hawaii*, The Macmillan Company, New York, 1937.
   Analysis of adjustment patterns in a cosmopolitan society.
Berry, Brewton: *Race Relations*, Houghton Mifflin Company, Boston, Mass., 1950.
   An analysis of race relations on an international basis from a sociological point of view.

Burma, John H.: "The Background of the Current Situation of Filipino Americans," *Social Forces*, Vol. 30, No. 1, October, 1951.
   Best available summary of current situation of Filipinos in United States.

Collier, John: *Indians of North America*, American Library of World Literature, New York, 1947.
   Eloquent plea for preservation of minority culture by the former chief of the United States Indian Bureau.

Fookien Times Yearbook, 1952, Manila, Philippines.
   This yearbook has a number of interesting articles dealing with intergroup relations in the Philippines.

Jacoby, Erich H.: *Agrarian Unrest in Southeast Asia*, Columbia University Press, New York, 1949.
   Pages 20 to 40 give an analysis of interrelation of economic and ethnic factors.

Felix and Marie Keesing: *Taming Philippine Headhunters*, Stanford University Press, 1934.
   In spite of its lurid title this is a scholarly account of cultural change in the mountain province.

Lind, Andrew W.: *An Island Community: Ecological Succession in Hawaii*, University of Chicago Press, Chicago, 1938.
   A discriminating analysis of one of the world's most harmonious interracial areas.

Linton, Ralph, ed.: *The Science of Man in the World Crisis*, Columbia University Press, New York, 1945.

————: *Most of the World*, Columbia University Press, New York, 1936.
   Descriptions of intergroup adjustment in various parts of the world.

Locke, Alain and Stern B. J.: *When Peoples Meet*, Progressive Educational Association, New York, 1942.
   Case studies of various intergroup relationships.

MacIver, R. M., ed.: *Group Relations and Group Antagonisms*, Harper and Brothers, New York, 1949.
   Program for improving race relations. Geared to United States situation, but also relevant to other areas.

Manuel, Arsenio E.: *Chinese Words in the Tagalog Language*, Philipiniana Publications, Manila, 1948.

Montague, Kate Bigelow: *Send the Wise Wind*, John Day, New York, 1952.
   Novel about a Bontoc family.

Prator, Clifford H. Jr.: *Language Teaching in the Philippines*. United States Educational Foundation in the Philippines, 1950.
   Report of the investigation of social background and educational influence of language teaching. Good analysis of current research.

CHAPTER VIII. RELATIONSHIP OF ETHNIC GROUPS 203

Purcell, Victor: *Chinese in Southeast Asia,* Oxford Press, London, 1950.
Authoritative study of Chinese in Southeast Asia. Most complete work on this subject. Page 569 to 672 are concerned with the Philippines.

Social Science and Humanities Review, University of the Philippines, Manila, March, 1954.
This issue contains twelve articles on ethnic relations in the Philippines and was produced under the auspices of the Philippine Sociological Society. Subjects include, Social Distance, Language Usage, Interregional Marriages, Social Patterns of Mountain tribes, Moro-Christian Interaction and papers on the role of the Chinese, Indians and Jews in the Philippines.

Tangco, Marcelo: "The Christian Peoples of the Philippines," *Natural and Applied Science Bulletin,* University of the Philippines, Vol. XI, No. 11, January-March, 1951.
Summary of current impressions of the various Christian regional groups in the Philippines.

UNESCO SERIES:
   Dunn, L. C., *Race and Biology*
   Klineberg, Otto: *Race and Psychology*
   Rose, Arnold: *The Roots of Prejudice*
   Leiris, Michel: *Race and Culture*
   Comas, Juan: *Racial Myths*
      Published by United Nations, Educational, Scientific and Cultural Organization, 19 Avenue Kleber, Paris-16.
      UNESCO publications on racial issues; brief, scholarly, readable and inexpensive.

Warner, W. L. and Srole, Leo: *The Social Systems of American Ethnic Groups,* Yale University Press, New Haven, 1945.
Ethnic-Economic cleavages in the American scene.

Weightman, George: *The Chinese Community in the Philippines,* unpublished Master's Thesis, University of the Philippines, 1952.
A significant survey of the Chinese group as found in the Philippines, with particular emphasis on Manila.

CHAPTER NINE

RELIGION AND SOCIETY

...In the Philippines there are three branches of Christianity; Aglipayanism, Protestantism, and Catholicism. All are one in the recognition of the fatherhood of God, the neighborliness of nations, and the brotherhood of man. Aglipayanism tends to be more efficacious in nationalizing Filipino spiritual life; Protestantism, in democratizing it; and Catholicism, in internationalizing it. All are contributive to the people's striving for the highest and best in human life, for the divinely righteous, for godliness itself.

— Osias, Camilo: *The Filipino Way of Life*, Ginn and Company, New York, 1940, p. 272.

Social Influence of Religious Bodies

This brief description by Osias of the contributions of major Christian groups has been used as an introduction to this chapter because it stresses the social contributions which these groups have made to the Philippines. By itself, this statement does not constitute an exhaustive analysis of the contributions of the various churches, but it does direct our attention to the fact that religion and secular society (secular in this sense, refers to social life not directly controlled by the church) are simply different aspects of our common life. Religion cannot be understood apart from other aspects of man's life nor can society be analyzed without considering the religious element.

It is not within the field of the sociologist, as such, to judge the truth or falsity of the claims of various religions or to analyze the strengths and weaknesses of various doctrinal positions. In this chapter, we are not writing as theologians, but simply as observers of the

Chapter IX. RELIGION AND SOCIETY

social scene who must include the religious institutions along with the other institutions which have made man the kind of person he is. One could not begin to describe Filipino society without considering the important contributions of the Roman Catholic Church, the challenge of Protestantism, the Moslem culture of the Moros, and the influence of religious practices and concepts which antedate either Islam or Christianity.

Many factors bring the churches into a close relationship with secular activities. Religious institutions must have a building for holding services, support their clergy, instruct the young in the tenets of their faith and carry on the works of mercy enjoined by religious idealism. This means that religion is inevitably involved in the getting and spending of money, the holding of property, and the conduct of social welfare and educational institutions. These activities may be regarded as means to an end, but they are also important by themselves.

The participation of religious groups in social activities depends upon the level of cultural development in the society, the specific beliefs of the religious group and the historic pattern of development. Frequently, these categories overlap; thus, churchmen have supported schools partly on the basis of simply making educational opportunities available and partly because of a belief that churches should play an influential role in the teaching of the younger generation. In underdeveloped areas, the church may be the only agency capable of carrying on educational and welfare activities. As the culture develops, governmental or private non-religious groups enter the picture, but the early pattern of religious institutions also tends to persist. Thus, in most countries, one finds that some educational and welfare institutions are supported by churches and others by non-religious organizations. In this sense, the church is both a pioneer initiating activities which eventually are taken over by other agencies, and also a group carrying on enterprises which it feels should remain in the control of church authorities.

The most controversial issue has been the involvement of churches in commercial and agricultural activities. In the early days, churchmen were often the best informed in economic matters and the establishment of industries and farms was a part of their contribution to the general culture of the area. The economic assets of the church also grew as church members made gifts for the support of church activities. These gifts are made in whatever type of wealth is prevalent in the society; in an industrial society, churches may come to own stocks and bonds and in an agricultural society, they will naturally come into the ownership of farmland. The purpose of this economic participation is simply to provide funds for religious activities, but an indirect result is to involve church authorities in the actual management of a portion of the economy.

When a church operates haciendas or business enterprises, it inevitably becomes involved in all the problems of landlords and tenants, capital and labor, etc. This means that the church authorities are apt to be plagued by economic disputes and perhaps identified with one social class rather than with the entire population. Resentment against churches as holders of property has led to anti-clerical activity in many countries.

In the Middle Ages, practically all education was under religious auspices, the church courts were as important as those of civil government, the arts of drama, painting, sculpture and music were nearly monopolized by the church; social welfare and religious charity were practically synonymous and the church was an important landholder. Recent developments have placed a large share of these activities in secular hands, but the role of the church in these fields is still the greatest of any institution apart from government.

In Philippine society, the social influence of religious groups has an important place. In education, we would think of Santo Tomas and San Carlos, the oldest universities in the Philippines, and of the more recent Silliman

University, which is the most outstanding Protestant University in the country. Along with these, which are probably the most famous religious schools, are a host of others which play a major role in education.

Other types of institutions also indicate the importance of religious influence. Hospitals and orphanages have been established by all important religious groups. Credit unions sponsored by churches form a major non-governmental type of credit cooperatives while the agricultural and commercial holdings of religious groups are a noticeable factor in economic life. In the southern part of the Philippines, Moslem law still dominates many aspects of life which have been taken over by the government in other areas. Historically, the Spanish Friars settled the population in towns, developed haciendas, taught the art of large scale building and established numerous industries.[1] The activities of the Friars provoked resentment as well as appreciation, but whatever the reaction, there can be no doubt that Filipino culture owes much to their efforts.

Probably more important than the direct activities of religious bodies are the attitudes and practices they encourage in the general society. The severe and rather drab New England pattern of thrift and simplicity grew easily out of the Puritan religious emphasis, while the Philippine fiestas are intimately connected with Catholicism. In a broader sphere, such scholars as Weber, Troeltsch, and Tawney found that, on the European scene, capitalism made slow headway in Catholic countries and progressed most rapidly in areas where the Protestant Reformation had been most complete.[2]

The same type of influence is frequently found in non-Christian religions. In Burma, the Indian money lenders

---

[1] E. Bazaco: *The Church on the Philippines*, Sto. Tomas Press, Manila, 1938.

[2] R. H. Tawney: *Religion and the Rise of Capitalism*, Harcourt, Brace and Co., New York, 1926.

Max Weber: *The Protestant Ethic and the Spirit of Capitalism*, tr. by Talcott Parsons, George Allen and Unwin, London, 1930.

Ernest Troeltsch: *The Social Teachings of the Christian Churches*, Macmillan Co., New York, 1930.

have nearly a monopoly in the field of credit. There are many reasons for this development, but religious differences certainly affect the situation. The Burmese religion prohibits the taking of interest, while the Indians belong to the Chettyar caste which has religious beliefs that clearly support the role of the banker. Other socio-religious links would include the spur to military activity given by the promise of paradise to those who die in defense of Islam, and the Buddhist indifference to social reform which is linked to the emphasis on escape from the world that is found in this religion.

The Ecclesia and the Sect

Troeltsch has endeavoured to distinguish two types of religious influences in what he terms the "ecclesia" and the "sect." The ecclesia is a dominant religious body which comprises the greater part of society and which thereby has come to either dominate or accept most practices of the society. The sect is a small group which includes only a minority of the society and which may be sharply critical of the practices of most of the people. Examples of the ecclesia would include the Anglican church in England, the Lutheran Church in Sweden, the Catholic Church in Spain, and state Shinto in pre-World War II Japan. A prime example of the sect is the Quakers who feel that both religious ceremony and military activity are wrong and thus sharply challenge the beliefs of most of the people of any nation. The Jehovah's Witnesses are a locally conspicuous group which approximates the sect type.

In a changing society the ecclesia is usually tied up with the older social arrangements and thus may be regarded as a foe of change. Under these circumstances, those advocating change regard the church as an obstacle and endeavor to weaken the influence of the church in social life. This has led to the phenomenon known as anti-clericalism which may be defined as an attempt to restrict the authority of the church to purely "spiritual" matters and oppose efforts of the clergy to exert influence on governmental and econ-

Chapter IX. RELIGION AND SOCIETY

omic life. Some European countries have "Catholic" parties which seek to extend the power of the church in political life and also anti-clerical parties which seek to minimize religious influence in secular affairs. Similar controversies may be noted in the state of Israel concerning the role of the Jewish rabbis and in Moslem countries in regard to the role of the Islamic religious institutions. Local instances of anti-clericalism occurred during the time of the Philippine revolution when the Spanish Friars were driven from their lands and, in some cases, subjected to physical violence. Parenthetically, it may be observed that organized anti-clericalism seldom develops in countries which have accepted a separation of church and state.

In the Philippines, the ecclesia can best be seen in the Roman Catholic church in the days of the Spanish regime and in the Moslem area of the south. In both these areas, church and state had become inextricably mixed so that it was hard to tell where one ended and the other began. Under these circumstances, an attack on the state was automatically regarded as an attack on the church. Rizal, for instance, could hardly have criticized Spanish policies and practices in the Philippines without also criticizing the Friars.

Since the end of the Spanish regime, the situation has changed drastically. The Moros find their institutions challenged by the migration of Christian to Mindanao; while Catholics, who comprise a heavy majority of the population, have accepted the separation of church and state. The Protestant groups have some of the characteristics of sects, but, to a degree, have become an accepted part of the Philippine life. Yet another development of importance is the rise of sects with a purely local character such as the *Iglesia Ni Kristo, Moncadistas,* and others.

Religious survivals.

No discussion of the Philippine scene would be complete which limited itself to an analysis of the major religious groups of the present day. Behind these groups are a host of pagan deities whose worship dominated life for thousands of years and whose influence is still present today. This type of religion may be seen in its purest form in the groups outside of either Christian or Moslem influence who still cling to the formal observance of the ancient rites. For these people, the various tribal deities constitute the only religion. Features of these religions include a belief in *anitos*, a group of spirits who roamed about and directly caused pain or pleasure to man. Sacrifice and prayers accompanied by feasting, the *cañao*, were the most common type of worship. Magic was used to force the spirits to follow human requests, while omens and divination based on the entrails of pigs and chickens warned protected one against evil spirits. The baliti tree was given special reverence, while any tree might well be the home of an *anito* and must be treated with special care.[3]

The most important effect of pagan religion is not its influence upon the small minority who consider themselves believers in these deities, but the persistence of pagan practices and beliefs among those who consider themselves to be Christian or Moslem. Religious conversion seldom involves a complete discarding of the older religious forms, and so elements of these tend to persist along with the new faith. Sometimes the old forms are modified and incorporated in the newer religion as in the fiestas, which include many elements of the older type of religious celebration or the Christmas tree which was taken over by Christian peoples from the pagan religion of the ancient Germans. Other times, in spite of the opposition of the clergy of the new religion, they persist simply as cultural traits too deepseated to be easily removed. Fauconnier describes this process of religious overlap in one area as follows:

> The conversion of a people to a new religion does not modify the character of that people. It is

---

[3] Laubach, *op. cit.*, p. 49. A more detailed discussion is found in Blair, Emma H. and Robertson, James A. *The Philippine Islands 1493-1898*, Cleveland, Clark, 1903-1909, volumes V and XLVII.

Chapter IX. RELIGION AND SOCIETY

a process of painting wood to look like wood. Man is incapable of abjuration. Beliefs are superimposed within him like coats of paint; they do not mix, and they are not effaced. The original colour remains and shows through. Christians are pagans white-washed with Judaism and Christianity. Theirs is a triple faith and they explain this anomaly by a mystery. They have a predilection for Christ, but they fear Jehovah in God the Father, and they have baptised the Great Pan under the name of the Holy Spirit. The Malays, too, have their three soul-coatings: animism, Hinduism, and Islam. They are obstinate Mussulmans, but quite unorthodox. Their invocations, that start and finish with the name of Allah, are really addressed to countless demons discredited by the Prophet. Allah is very merciful, and they do not fail to remind him of the fact every day. But a subordinate spirit has a narrower intelligence. He is also more sensitive to compliments. He does not disdain a few little offerings, but he is prompt to take offence. The Malays life is passed in trying not to tread on the invisible toes of some irritable deity.[4]

LeRoy cites the observation of a traveler to the Philippines in 1841 on the persistence of earlier practices and beliefs.

> In disregard to the monks, the Indians circumcise their children, the Bayan tree is held sacred... "There is no driving out of them," says a padre, "the cursed belief that the spirits of their ancestors are in the woods and among the roots of the bamboos."[5]

That this is not an obsolete complaint may be seen from the statement of a modern teacher.

> I found a group of students in a college class in literature heavily believing in superstition... They could not understand how terribly inhibiting

---
[4] Henry Fauconnier: *The Soul of Malaya*, Penguin Books, Ltd., C. Nicholls and Company Ltd., London, England, 1948, pp. 62-63.
[5] LeRoy: *op. cit.*, p. 127.

of spiritual growth superstition can be... They could not understand the 'unbelievers' who must be either a snob or a charlatan... They must have felt I was betraying our old customs and traditions; or so their youthfully reproachful faces looked when I debunked their cherished beliefs in the old man of the mountains, the *asuangs*, (witches), the *mankukulams*, (wizards).[6]

In a somewhat similar vein, the late J. C. Laya commented on the persistence of these beliefs in his own mother.

One of those who mentioned Kal-la is my own mother. Now my mother is as Christian as any woman I know, but yet when she gave vent to the emotion of grief, she spoke the idiom of our father's father and turned for assuagement to pre-Spanish God. For Kal-la is the name of the old God of the underworld which our forefathers believed in. He and other gods, as well as fairies of our pagan past, still hover over our dark rural communities, occupying the dark trees, the rivers, the depth of the sea, the loneliness of the islands, the anthills and the subconscious of our people.[7]

Filipinos were somewhat offended when Katherine Mayo stressed the influence of these older religious elements in her book, "The Isles of Fear."[8] The picture in this book was overdrawn, but its major defect was that it stressed something that is world wide as though it were primarily a Philippine problem. In many countries, supernatural beliefs which antedate modern religious development may cause supposedly faithful Christians to speak of "casting a hex," as in some areas of the U.S.; to reject medical science for various types of "faith" healing; to use good luck charms and to patronize fortune tellers and spirit mediums.

---
[6] Pura Santillan Castrence, "Women Sense, The Viewpoint of a Filipina," *Manila Bulletin*, October 20, 1952.
[7] J. C. Laya, *Little Democracies*, Inang Wika, Manila, 1951, p. 4.
[8] Katherine Mayo: *The Isles of Fear*, Harcourt Brace, New York, 1924.

Modern skeptics emphasize the difficulty of having the faith required to accept a belief in God, but this is only part of the picture. In every country, people cling to religious survivals which the dominant religious groups reject and which have no basis in either Christianity or Islam. Hence, they continue to patronize fortune tellers and astrologers, to fear ghosts and spirits, to look for mediums who can contact the unseen world and to accept miracles which have been denounced as fraudulent by church authorities.

In their opposition to these religious survivals, the major religions and scientific thought are more nearly allied than they realize. Both movements seek to persuade people to more rational beliefs than many individuals are able to accept. The old Gods die hard.

Effect of Urbanization on Religious Institutions

To some extent, the persistence of pre-Christian religious forms is an evidence of the strength of what may be characterized as a religious point of view in the *damay* type of environment. In this setting, the power of religion is as dependent upon the strength of tradition as upon the specific activities of churches and clergy. Thus, the earlier religious elements have persisted even in areas where a pagan priesthood no longer exists.

Urbanization and the development of *gesellschaft* attitudes may be expected to weaken the hold of these pagan elements, but it also produces a society in which any type of religion has greater difficulty in holding its adherents. In the *gesellschaft*, traditions of all types lose their power and every type of belief has to establish its validity in constant competition with other points of view. The influence of urbanization extends beyond the city limits as modern communication permeates the countryside with urban attitudes.

The reaction of religious groups to this situation is characterized by less reliance upon customary procedures

Top panel shows Roman Catholic Cathedral in Baguio, middle panel is Central Methodist Church in Manila and at bottom is a typical Roman Catholic chapel in a rural barrio. Barrio chapels are used primarily for private devotions and may have a public service only at time of annual fiesta.

and a greater emphasis upon the "efficiency" of religious efforts. Thus, churches are located at strategic corners, and the clergy learn to utilize the radio, newspaper, magazines, drama, etc. in the effort to reach a mass of people who have no roots and are easily distracted. Religious organizations expand in numbers and offer a variety of activities. Clergy become experts on labor relations, courtship and marriage and any other theme current at the moment. All this represents the adjustment of religious institutions to an era in which traditions are no longer sacred, family control weakened and change the order of the day. In the *damay* situation, religion grows naturally with little conscious effort; in the *gessellschaft* grouping, a less sturdy variety requires an elaborate promotion geared to the shifting tastes of the metropolis.

Contemporary religious institutions in the Philippines.

Religious groups reflect the historical circumstances which led to the introduction of various faiths. The oldest groups are those which still follow the tribal faiths that prevailed before the coming of either Islam or Christianity. These people are usually found in mountainous areas which have resisted the impact of either Arabic or European influence. In the southern portions of the Philippines, the Arabic traders introduced the faith of Islam in the Fourteenth Century and it is still a major influence in this area at the present time. With the Spaniards, Christianity and conquest went hand in hand and, as a result of their influence, the majority of people are adherents of Roman Catholicism. Chinese migrants were usually Buddhists and their temples have been found in the Islands since an early date.

At the beginning of the Twentieth Century, the revolt against Spain included an attack on the alleged Spanish domination of the Catholic church which resulted in the formation of the Philippine Independent Church, commonly known as the Aglipayan movement. The entry of the

Americans produced conditions favorable to the spread of Protestantism. Through the work of American missionaries and of Filipino converts, numerous Protestant churches were established; the two largest groups are the Methodists and the United Church of Christ, which is a union movement including several denominations. The *Iglesia ni Kristo* is a strong church, similar, in some respects, to the Protestant churches; but is entirely Filipino and is not connected with any foreign group. From time to time, spectacular groups which seem to be somewhat outside of the Christian tradition, such as the *Moncadistas*, the followers of Moncado, have also appeared.

Table 1. Membership in Religious Organizations *

Roman Catholics	15,941,422
Philippine Independent Church	1,456,114
Protestants	444,491
Mohammedans	791,817
Iglesia ni Kristo	88,125
Pagans or No Religion	353,482
Buddhists	42,751

* Census of religious bodies in the Philippines as of October 1, 1948, Bureau of Census and Statistics, Manila.

Religion as a source of international contacts.

The Philippines are in the singular position of being the only predominantly Christian country in the Orient and also a country in which foreign influence is prominent in religious circles. In part, this is due to the international nature of most religious bodies which makes it entirely natural for their clergy to cross national lines; but to a greater extent, it is due to the specific nature of religious development in the area.

The involvement of the Roman Catholic Church and the Spanish colonial regime was so great that placing Filipinos in important ecclesiastical positions was nearly as difficult as giving the local population a role in political affairs. The shift at the time of American rule was partly in the direction of more Filipino priests and partly toward replacing Spanish clergy with those from other countries. Thus, an American prelate, Michael J. O'Doherty, became Archbishop of Manila and American, Australian, French and Belgian clergy entered the Islands in substantial numbers. At present, about half the Catholic clergy are Filipino and the remainder come from a variety of other nations. Filipinos have become Bishops and Archbishops, but foreign clergy are still represented both in the hierarchy and in the lower clergy, especially in certain clerical orders.

Organized Protestantism dates back to the American entry, and the initial impetus was dependent upon the efforts of American missionaries. The missionaries felt strongly the need to establish locally controlled, self-supporting churches. By 1941, this goal had been largely achieved so that Protestantism was able to survive the wartime period when it was cut off from American aid. With the end of the war, missionaries returned to the Islands but most of them operated under the control of the Filipino churchmen and served in advisory or educational functions. More than eighty per cent of local Protestant preachers are Filipino and most funds are raised locally, although these are supplemented by American contributions for special purposes; close ties are maintained with churches in the United States and American influence is still strong.

In terms of cultural background, one might speak of Catholicism as developing on the basis of interaction between Filipinos and Spaniards tempered in later years by the influence of clergy from other European nations and the United States. Protestantism owes its existence here to the joint efforts of Filipinos and Americans, with a rapid move toward complete Filipino control. The Aglipayan church is a group which has a completely Filipino clergy who have been influenced to some degree by American Unitarians and Episcopalians. This influence is along advisory lines and nationalism constitutes a major emphasis in the Aglipayan churches.

Islam was brought to the Philippines by wandering Arab traders and contacts with predominantly Moslem countries continue to this day. Arab merchants still come to Mindanao and Sulu and frequently function as teachers of the Koran. A few Egyptian and Indonesian missionaries also visit the area and teach in Mohammedan schools. The greatest source of contact is the yearly pilgrimage to Mecca when hundreds of Filipino Moslems journey to the holy city of Islam and meet other Moslems from all parts of the world.

From the standpoint of cultural diffusion, religious institutions are a major means of bringing Filipinos into contact with the culture of other nations and, together with education, diplomacy and commerce, serve as a mechanism of international collaboration.

Moslem worshippers in a rural mosque. While predominantly Christian, the Philippines has about three quarters of a million Moslems, mostly living in Mindanao and Sulu. They are intensely loyal to their faith.

Problems of religious pluralism.

The action of the Revolutionary Congress in decreeing the separation of church and state was followed by the American authorities and later incorporated in the Philippine constitution. It has become the basis for the legal position of religion since that time. This represents a shift from the position in which, as LeRoy says, "the Crown of Spain was the royal patron of religion," to one in which the government was officially neutral and church and state were separate.[9]

The constitutional provision for the separation of church and state has had the effect of causing government officials to make a sharp distinction between their personal beliefs and their role as government officials. One example of this distinction may be seen in the reaction of the late President Quezon when he was invited to participate in a Roman Catholic Eucharistic Congress held in Manila during his term of office. In a letter to the Archbishop of Manila, President Quezon requested that all references to himself and to the Philippine government be removed from the program of the Eucharistic Congress. He explained this request as follows:

> I hope that I am a good practical Catholic. As such, in my individual capacity, there is nothing that I shall not be glad to do to give added solemnity to the celebration of the Eucharistic Congress... but as President of the Philippines, I am not in a position to do what your program calls for.[10]

In theory, the separation of church and state means that all religious groups have the same legal status and that the government neither hinders nor promotes specific religious activity. The basic assumption of religious pluralism is similar to that of cultural pluralism in general. This is that national loyalty does not require a uniformity of religious belief or practice and hence, that the state should give equal treatment to all religious groups. In practice, such a belief marks a great advance from the days in which religious conflict produced both persecution and civil wars, but it also raises many specific issues which are difficult to decide. These issues appear to be most prominent in

---
[9] LeRoy, *op. cit.*, p. 127.
[10] Cited in Hayden, *op. cit.*, p. 569.

the fields of education, legislation and community cooperation.

Religion and education.

In education, the Philippines has a dual philosophy: the American emphasis on the responsibility of the state for training its citizens, and the Roman Catholic belief that only the church should be entrusted with the schooling of the younger generation. The effort to satisfy both viewpoints has resulted in both church and governmental schools with voluntary religious instruction in the latter institutions. This compromise has not been completely accepted and its operation continually raises points of conflict.

In many European countries, the government supports religious schools, while in the United States and the Philippines, the churches support their schools without government aid on the basis of keeping religious and political institutions separate, and of maintaining the freedom of church operated schools from direct government control.

Aside from financial support, there is the question of religious education as part of the school curriculum. In the Philippines, parents may arrange to have students receive voluntary religious instruction, but there has been a steady demand for the schools to make this instruction an integral part of the school system.

An even more difficult issue concerns the teaching of items which are not labeled as strictly religious, but on which the various religious groups tend to disagree. Here, the question is whether these items should be taught on the basis of sectarian viewpoint or on the teacher's appraisal of scholarly evidence. This question is not simply one of science versus religion, because on many issues, equally competent scholars may take opposite positions. The point at issue is whether churches should seek to force teachers to follow the scholars who take the position most harmonious with church doctrines, or whether they should simply

Chapter IX. RELIGION AND SOCIETY 221

permit the truth or falsity of these propositions to demonstrate themselves in free inquiry and debate.

The difficulty of determining the proper role of religious and secular institutions may be appreciated when we mention a few of the areas in which no clear line of responsibility has been established between educational and religious authorities. The following types of issues are often a point of controversy in the Philippines. What may the schools teach about the authority of the retraction of Rizal, the virtues and vices of the Spanish Friars, the causes and effects of the Protestant Reformation? May economists candidly examine the operation of church controlled haciendas or sociologists make an impartial inquiry into the effect of divorce legislation or population increase? Must biologists follow an approved line in teaching the origin of human life? These and many other issues bring educational questions into the field of religious controversy; and frequently, churchmen are unwilling to leave them to the judgment of the educators.

Legislation and Religious Viewpoints.

Since religion is the source of most social idealism, it is natural that much legislation should owe its inspiration to religious ideals of moral living and brotherly obligation. Difficulty arises when churches fail to agree on what constitutes moral principle and then attempt to persuade the state to make the moral principles of one group of citizens mandatory on the entire nation.

In the United States, most Protestants were strongly convinced of the complete evil of alcoholic beverages and used their numerical superiority to force through a prohibition law which adherents of other churches did not consider a matter of religious idealism. In predominantly Catholic countries, Catholics frequently try to use legal means to outlaw divorce and birth control. In both cases, the result is to use legal power to force the moral concepts of one church on an entire population. The question is complicated both by deep feeling on these and kindred matters, and the fact that conflicting views on the desirability of such legislation may also arise from non-religious sources.

Community cooperation.

The same religious idealism which affects legislation is both an aid and a barrier to effective cooperation in the effort to improve community conditions. It is an aid through the religious impulse to unselfish service, but becomes a problem when a community is divided by sectarian strife.

Some difficulties in this area come from a tendency of members of their own groups to support their co-religionists in any organizational activity. An example of this is shown in a student's description of cleavages between Catholics and Aglipayans in her hometown.

> Even in civic organizations like the "Carpa Club" (an all-male society of prominent professional and businessmen in town), the Senior Women's Club, (an association of some middle-aged women who work for the support of the local puericulture center) the Rural Improvement Club, (a branch project of the Bureau of Plant Industry to encourage home industries), and the Junior Women's Club (an association of young ladies which performs a function corollary to that of the Senior Women's Club), the religious question becomes an issue every now and then. In the election of their officers and taking in of new members, very often they vote along religious lines—Catholics for Catholics, and Aglipayans for Aglipayans.[11]

A situation of even greater intensity is shown by an article in the *Philippines Free Press* in which a member of the *Iglesia ni Kristo* refers to the disagreeable experiences which have come his way as a result of religious intolerance.

---

[11] Student's paper in Sociology class, University of the Philippines.

Chapter IX. RELIGION AND SOCIETY

Since I embraced the Iglesia ni Cristo (after separating myself from the Catholic faith), I have become virtually a social martyr. I have suffered undue humiliation, lost a number of friends and, on a not a few occasions, received physical harm.

Yes, I have been literally regarded as social surplus by the people around me — because I am an Iglesia.

In school I am almost friendless. I find myself the subject of malicious anecdotes. Students and former friends delight in calling me unprintable names; insults are frequently hurled at me and my church. 'Iglesia ni Kulafu!' they jeer.[12]

Community factionalism of the type described in these articles is contrary to the Christian teachings of brotherhood and charity and is condemned by the leaders of all churches. It is not a feeling unique to religious groups, but occurs whenever a feeling of strong loyalty to one's own groups is diverted into a feeling of hostility toward those who are identified with other groups. While many such cases of intolerance and bitterness could be cited, it would be unfair to ignore the fact that, in many areas, members of different groups are able to work together in a spirit of tolerance and good will.

Problems which are more persistent and more difficult to solve occur when religious leaders feel that civic groups may compete with church loyalties or tend to minimize the claim of a particular church to be the only valid representative of the true faith. Or, to put it differently, can members of different religious groups work together in the same civic organizations, especially when such organizations attempt to capitalize on a generalized religious feeling? Situations of this type are likely to occur whenever there is a move to organize people for character building or re-

---

[12] "Because I am an Iglesia," *Philippines Free Press*, Manila, as told to Nicholas Prieto, July 29, 1950.

creational activities. Such activities may be carried out either by churches or by non-sectarian groups and there is no universally accepted criterion as to the proper sphere for each type of sponsorship.

Specific examples of such controversy would include disputes over the role of service clubs such as Rotary International, fraternal orders like the Masonic lodges and idealistic youth organizations such as the YMCA and YWCA. Catholic priests who had been officers or members of Rotary were informed recently that a papal edict discouraged such participation for members of the clergy. In the Philippines, the Masons had an important role in the movement for freedom from Spain and have always included members of all churches although condemned by Catholic authorities. The role of the YMCA and the YWCA has aroused discussion over a period of years. At the time of this writing, the archbishop of Cebu and the Apostolic Vicar of the Mountain Province had threatened to excommunicate members of the Catholic church participating in these organizations. On the other hand, many persons feel that such enterprises are simple types of community cooperation for civic betterment in which members of all religious groups can properly participate. Usually, this viewpoint is expressed in practice, rather than rhetoric, but recently, Dean Conrado Benitez expressed vigorous dissent from the position of the hierarchy on these matters.[13]

Social basis of religious pluralism.

During the Spanish regime, church and state were closely linked together and the Roman Catholic Church was the only recognized form of the Christian faith. Separation of church and state, which is closely associated with the growth of religious pluralism, was decreed by the revolutionary legislature and accepted subsequently by both the American authorities and the governments of the Common-

---

[13] Incidents cited in *Manila Bulletin*, December 1, 20, and 31, 1952.

Chapter IX. RELIGION AND SOCIETY

wealth and the Republic. It is accepted, in principle, by most Filipinos, but confusion arises over the role of church and state in various specific fields.

The question is complicated in the Philippines by the fact that, although other churches have won a considerable number of members, the Roman Catholic Church commands the allegiance of an overwhelming percentage of the population. In the United States, religious pluralism became inevitable because no one church commanded a majority of the population and, hence, all churches were forced to accept each other on the basis of necessity. A continuance of a pattern of religious pluralism in the Philippines will call for an unusual degree of understanding and tolerance from the members of the dominant religious group. In other countries, religious divisions have made tolerance a necessity, but here it can only be based on a type of brotherhood which combines loyalty to one's own church with a tolerance of those who are outside the fold of the major religious organization. It depends, not upon the force of circumstances, but upon an ingrained respect for those whose faith may differ from our own.

Since the relation of church and state is a perennial question one may well ask about the relation of this concept to that of religious pluralism. There are, of course, different degrees of separation between church and state and it may be possible for the state to aid one church and still tolerate the existence of other churches or it is possible for all religious groups to receive state support. Such a situation, however, is apt to lead to constant conflict since it is difficult for the state to give equal support to all religious groups, especially when they are unequal in numbers. A separation of church and state avoids the question of how many favors the states should extend to any particular church and forces all religious groups to rely on the voluntary support of their members. The separation of church and state minimizes the possibility of minorities being exploited and frees all churches from political control. It is the situation in which religious pluralism most easily flourishes.

Like cultural pluralism in general, religious pluralism is related to the concept of democracy. If one feels that democracy simply means majority rule, then there is no reason for the dominant group to give consideration to minority churches. On the other hand, if democracy implies a respect for individual freedom then the tolerance of religious diversity logically follows.

Religion and Social Policies

Impact of religious teachings.

While the activities of religious institutions are manifold, their greatest influence lies in their ability to mold the deals of their adherents. If faith in God, human brotherhood, righteous living and unselfish concern for others are effectively taught by the churches, these qualities may form the basis for a healthy national life. If the churches are ineffective in this major task, then moral cynicism and civic indifference are likely to make their appearance.

In many respects, the Christian outlook on life has become an accepted part of the folkways of the country, but in other areas, such as the persistence of pagan superstition among adherents of Christian churches, religious indoctrination is less than complete. In this respect, it is worthy of note that one may be nominally a member of a religious group and even hold an intense emotional loyalty to the group without governing his life by religious teachings. Religious teachings compete with other philosophies and require steady promotion to maintain or win a hold on the people.

In recent years, there has been a good deal of discussion and some research on the effect of religious education on the formation of character.[14] The usual assumption has been that, since religious teaching emphasizes virtuous living, this teaching would tend to produce virtue in those educated

---

[14] See Hugh Hartshore: *Character in Human Relations*, Scribners, New York, 1939.

Chapter IX. Religion and Society

under religious auspices. Critics of this viewpoint say that many persons trained under religious auspices fail to measure up to the highest ideals, while frequently, those outside of immediate church influence lead exemplary lives. On a broader scale, they can point to countries like Germany or Italy, where religious instruction in the schools did not produce a population which could resist the appeal of dictators who frankly opposed many Christian teachings.

Other questions raised about religious instruction in the public schools include concern about the adding of additional courses to a curriculum which is already overburdened and a fear that religious antagonisms will be increased if school children are separated into different groups on the basis of religious affiliation. There is also a feeling that the power of religion is based on the voluntary emotional loyalty of its adherents and that this power is lost when religion becomes a routine school subject like history or mathematics.

Actually, there is no simple answer to this question and only carefully conducted research can give us reliable information. The effect of religious education and, for that matter of church activities of all kinds, depends on many factors. These factors would include the impact of the total culture, the specific emphasis of the religious teaching which is offered and the resources and wisdom which the churches devote to the task of training the youth of the land. At one time, churchmen tended to regard inquiry into the functioning of religious institutions as an attack on the church, but they now recognize that intelligent research may increase the effectiveness of church activities.

In a preface to a book entitled *The Sociology of the Parish*, Cardinal Stritch makes the following comments:

> ...we recommend it to all who are really interested in the right sort of social progress in our times... it will stimulate thought and it will promote other studies in this same field, and if

the purpose of the contributors is accomplished, it will help greatly to promote the betterment of society in our times.[15]

Intensive social investigation of the operation of religious groups in the Philippines would doubtless produce an increased awareness of the social factors which influence their effectiveness. On an admittedly superficial analysis, the two most obvious factors are, on the one hand, the extent to which religion has permeated the total culture, and on the other hand, the relative scarcity of clergymen. Filipinos who never venture inside a church can still not escape the religious influences which have affected all phases of the nation's development. The ratio of clergy to members, however, is only one to 8,259 for Catholics and one to 3,265 for Aglipayans.[16] The proportion of clergy is lower than that found in most other countries and means that many members have little chance for personal contact with a parish priest.

In summary, we may say that the churches play a major role in the effort to influence the character of youth and help to shape the nation's ideals. There is much agitation for making religious education an integral part of the school system on the assumption that this step will strengthen the character of the students. Such a step may or may not be desirable, but we lack sufficient data on the actual effect of religious efforts in this direction. Because of this lack, it is impossible, at this time, to give a scientific answer as to the consequences of a great emphasis on religious instruction in the school setting.

Religious teaching on social issues.

All major religious bodies have indicated a concern for the carrying into practice of religious ideals in social re-

---

[15] Nuesse & Harte: *The Sociology of the Parish*, Bruce, Milwaukee, 1950, p. x.

[16] Figures obtained by computing ratio between membership of religious groups and priests registered with the Bureau of Public Libraries as of July 11, 1950.

Chapter IX. RELIGION AND SOCIETY

lationships. On the international scene, these ideals have been spelled out in Papal Encyclicals and in the statements of the World Council of Churches. Briefly summarized, these statements reject communism, but urge that society must give greater opportunity to the lower classes and make Christian ideals a reality in social life.

Such statements plunge religious bodies into the controversial field of questions concerning labor and capital, landlord and tenant, and sometimes cause distress to those who have been inclined to accept uncritically the prevailing social arrangements. A reaction to this criticism is seen in the newspaper story of a speech by Father Hogan, a prominent Jesuit priest.

> Speaking as a guest before the Manila Lion's Club at the Riviera, the Ateneo father pointed out that since the church must teach the moral law 'all the way' it was thus its duty 'to explain what is morally right and wrong in the relation between capital and labor as well as in the matter of family life.' [17]

Protestant groups have been equally interested in such questions as indicated in the statement of the Methodist Social Creed.

> The Methodist Church aims to view the perplexing times and problems which we face today in the light of the teachings of Jesus. Jesus taught us to love our neighbors; and because we love them, we seek justice for them. We believe that to be silent in the face of need, injustice, and exploitation would be to deny Him... We believe that it is our Christian duty to do our utmost to provide for all men opportunity to earn an adequate livelihood.[18]

While the churches can claim historical precedent for this interest in social issues, they find it difficult to make the "social gospel" a vital matter to their adherents. Many church members regard religion as primarily concerned with

---
[17] *Manila Bulletin*, April 27, 1952, p. 16.
[18] Methodist Church Publication, *Methodist Discipline*, Detroit, 1949, Paragraph 202, p. 583.

ceremonial observances, theological beliefs, a concern for future life, and a strictly personal morality. In spite of sermons, conferences, official statements and occasional books and articles, the religious concern for social righteousness has not yet permeated the great body of Christian believers. It is, however, increasingly becoming important to the clergy and to the better educated group of laymen. Usually, there is a considerable time lag between a shift in emphasis by the clergy and a response by the lay members, and it is at least conceivable that, eventually, the average Christian will be convinced of the need to guide his political and economic behavior by Christian principles.

This religious concern for social problems may be regarded as one aspect of adjustment to an urbanized *gesellschaft* type of society. If it arouses controversy, this reflects the fact that the *gesellschaft* gives rise to different and conflicting values.

Summary

Religion and social life exercise a reciprocal influence with each affecting the other. Filipino culture has been formed, in large part, by religious influence and the churches still play a major role in education and social service. In recent years, churchmen have made direct pronouncements on social issues, but these statements are not always accepted by laymen.

Religious pluralism is the pattern in the Philippines, although a majority of the populace is Roman Catholic. Separation of church and state is recognized in the constitution, but many difficult questions arise in carrying this policy into practice. On the community level, there is both a general spirit of tolerance and also many specific incidents of friction between members of different religious groups.

The leadership of the Filipino churches has been drawn in large part, from foreign nationals and the various churches are agencies of international contact. The majority of the people are either Christian or Moslem, although many prac-

CHAPTER IX. RELIGION AND SOCIETY 231

tices and beliefs persist which are foreign to either belief. The entire culture is permeated by religious patterns which appear in both sacred and secular situations, while the immediate influence of the churches is limited by the relative scarcity of clergymen. Religious institutions operate in a social setting and, in recent years, have welcomed sociological analysis of the cultural context in which they function.

QUESTIONS

1. Distinguish between the sect and the ecclesia.
2. What is meant by religious pluralism? What problem arises in carrying out this policy?
3. Contrast religion in the *damay* and the *gesellschaft* type of society.
4. How do pre-Christian survivals influence social thought?
5. Is religion related to labor unions, land tenure and social legislation?
6. Are religious principles best carried out by means of specific legislation? Why or why not?

PROJECTS

1. Write a paper describing the pre-Christian religious ideas and practices which survive in your locality. Explain their effect on the lives of the people and the type of people most affected.
2. Write a paper describing the economic, benevolent and educational institutions conducted by religious authorities in a given locality.
3. Write a paper describing the different religious groups in your hometown. Analyze the type of people who belong to the different groups and the similarities or differences in their social ideals. Describe patterns of cooperation and of conflict.

SUGGESTED READINGS

Bazaco, E., O.P.: *The Church in the Philippines*, Sto. Tomas Press, Manila, 1938.
  Description of Roman Catholic contribution to Philippine culture.
Grunder, Garel A. and Livezey, William E.: *The Philippines and the United States*, University of Oklahoma, Norman, 1953.
  Contains a chapter entitled "Friars and Friar Lands," pp. 122-130, which has interesting material on church-state relationships at the end of the Spanish regime.

Hartshorne, Hugh: *Character in Human Relations*, Scribners, New York, 1939.
An analysis of the effect of religious teaching on the development of character.

Hunt, Chester L.: "Religion and the Business Man," *Diliman Review*, Vol. I, No. 3, July, 1953.
A consideration of the relationship between religious institutions and business development in the Philippines.

Laubach, Frank C.: *People of the Philippines*, Doran, New York, 1925, History of religious developments in the Philippines from a Protestant point of view.

Nuesse-Hart: *Sociology of the Parish*, Bruce Company, Milwaukee, 1950.
One of several books seeking to make a sociological analysis of religious institutions.

Rivera, Juan A.: "The Aglipayan Movement," *Social Science Humanities Review*, Vol. IV, No. 4, Dec. 1937.
Historical Background of Aglipayan Movement.

Tawney, R. H.: *Religion and the Rise of Capitalism*, Mentor Books, Harcourt, Brace and Company, New York, 1950.
Relation between religious culture and the development of capitalism and democracy. Available in 35c paper bound edition. A classic in this field.

THE COMMUNITY

AN INTRODUCTION

In the next two chapters we shall examine the human groups which are related to a given territory. That is, we shall study communities. In sociology a community is usually regarded as a population in a given territory which is linked together by certain bonds. These bonds may come from a common government, language, or general culture. Following this general definition one could then say that a barrio, municipality, city, province, or nation would be a community since all of these groupings possess the described characteristics. However, in actual practice, the sociologist usually focuses his attention on communities which are of city size or less.

The community is generally regarded as the second most important human group. It is found that the community really represents an extension of the family, which is viewed as the group of first importance. Therefore, we say that the community completes our social training which begins in the family.

When one turns to the historical side of human community life, a sequence of development is found. After the human species had passed many centuries in a wandering stage, villages were founded. These villages came with the development of farming and fishing. Thus the village is mankind's oldest type of settled community. It is estimated that villages have been present on the earth for at least 10,000 years. At later stages, came the growth of towns and then cities. In the following chapters we will first examine the rural community as the oldest type of human community and then turn to the urban community which is a relatively recent development in the growth of civilization.

CHAPTER TEN

RURAL COMMUNITIES

We keep on telling the villager to take pride in his home, farm and village, to abandon his besetting sins of apathy, faction and extravagance, to sacrifice his case and leisure and to join with his fellows and work hard and eagerly to raise his standard of living. Our appeals leave him cold, and without strong persuasion he often will not even pick up money lying at his feet or stop wasting what he already has. He seems quite indifferent either to his happiness, his health, or his property. Laws are made to help him to ease his load of debt. Does he use them? No, he colludes with what we call his natural enemy the creditor to evade the law, and borrows still more money at even worse rates. At certain seasons and for certain purposes his ancient customs demand that he should spend money freely, and spend it he will, cost what it may to get. He does not even want to get out of debt, he knows that any improvement in his farm will mean more money, not for him but for his creditor, and so he is indifferent to the improvement of his farm, and he even seems indifferent to the welfare of his family. The only real, true incentive is an inborn desire for something better for its own sake and not to please some outside authority. No village can be permanently improved from outside and no home can be permanently improved until its inmates themselves want to improve it. For permanence we must have spontaneity, and spontaneity means a burning desire for better things in the hearts of villager themselves.

— F. L. Brayne, *Better Villages*, Oxford University Press, London, 1938, pp. 3-7.

CHAPTER X. RURAL COMMUNITIES 235

Culture of the Rural Communities

The Philippines is divided into provinces, municipalities and barrios. Usually, barrio residents are classified as rural, although frequently the municipality or *poblacion* also has a rural character. While the barrio is the smallest unit which has legal recognition, there are smaller neighborhood units known as *sitio* or *purok* which represent cohesive units within the barrio. The principal characteristic which distinguishes rural from urban communities is the extent to which the former have developed patterns of intimacy and mutual helpfulness. The rural barrio is a prime example of the *damay* type of interaction.

Neighborliness is a distinctive feature which continues to be an important part of social behavior. It is manifested in various situations. In farm communities the exchange of work and mutual helpfulness is a permanent pattern of social life. Economic cooperation on the barrio level is seen in mutual helpfulness at the time of harvesting and planting and on such special occasions as the building of houses. Every individual is closely bound to his neighbors; his contacts are intimate, personal and full of meaning. The sharing of joys as well as sorrows is the bond that links neighbors together. The neighborhood has had an uncontested function was emphasized during the Japanese occupation when neighborhood associations were organized for defense purposes.

In the municipality, in which a larger group occupies a bigger community area, the basic economy is still drawn from the soil but interests are more varied and numerous and social interactions play a greater role in the life of the group. Even in the *poblacion* though, the pattern is primarily one of the primary group relationship governed by traditional mores.

The following excerpt from the 1950 Yearbook of the Philippine Association of School Superintendents presents a picture of the rural community.

"The first thing that strikes even a casual observer in the average town is its somnolence. The streets are empty the greater part of the day. The houses which are of nipa, or cogon and bamboo squat unsteadily on bamboo poles and seem untenanted. The surroundings are overgrown with weeds, and mounds of carabao manure and wallows are everywhere around. It is not uncommon to see loose animals plastered with mud and malodorous matter roaming the plaza that is equally unsightly in spite of the imposing monument of a national hero overlooking the scene.

"In the evening life manifests itself in the town with the coming home of the farmers and the fishermen. Young people walk the streets. The tiendas become alive with customers who come to buy petroleum for the lamp, vinegar or *bagoong* and some fruits like limes, guavas, or tamarind for seasoning the stew, and bananas or *panutsa* for desert. Soon lights begin to flicker in the homes; some faint strains of a guitar or a song float in the evening air, and before long the town goes to sleep. In the morning the people repeat the same daily routine.

"Socially and economically the Philippine town is homogeneous. Except for a Chinaman or two, the inhabitants are Filipino nationals. The average family has its own house or lot, work animals and rice paddies. The people know one another and are friends. They eat the same kind of food, wear the same kind of clothes, and earn their livelihood in the same vicinity. More than 80% of the 3,143,886 families use petroleum and native oil for light, and only 1% own radio sets according to the 1939 census. The household furniture and equipment are few and simple, and there is hardly any item that may be classified as a luxury except perhaps a tin of face powder and a mirror for the young women, and a wooden chest or two that contain the family's belongings. Of the means of comfort, there are none to speak of, unless the hammock or the bamboo bench may be considered as such. Of decorations on the wall, there are colored lithographed prints of rural scenes and Catholic saints, besides rotogravure pictures from local and foreign magazines.

The average adult is believed to possess an education equivalent to grade one. He does not read any newspaper or magazine. He has no vision of the future although he has a secret thought of making his sons live a much better life than his, for which purpose he has no plan, much less means." [1]

Rural culture is partial to the practical and necessary and is often prejudiced against the things which are artistic and comfortable. It is sometimes thought that because the farmer is in constant contact with nature his aesthetic sense must be well developed. The contrary is true. The farm family is willing to forego comforts in the home in favor of buying an additional carabao to increase their supply of working animals.

Despite this age of extensive change our rural communities are characterized by the presence of persisting traditional culture patterns. Farming is premised on the idea that much of it is learned only through experience and example. Customary ways of seed selection, planting, storage of crop, and treatment of animal diseases are some of the processes which tradition passes on generation after generation. The practices that have withstood the ages are followed, while new theories are steadfastly refused.

In this picture the stark poverty, cultural backwardness and fatalism of the rural community are major obstacles to progress. On the other hand, the intense intimacy of neighborhood life and the habits of group cooperation might well be utilized in organized effort for community improvement. Such items as the interest in education, the frequent migrations to urban centers and occasional incidents of armed outbreaks indicate that the *tao* has aspirations for a different life and is not altogether contented with the traditional pattern.

---

[1] "Education in Rural Areas for Better Living"—1956 *Yearbook*, Philippine Association of School Superintendents, Bookman Inc., Manila, pp. 7-9.

Structure and Organization of Rural Communities

The structural pattern of rural life in this country may best be described by two general types—the municipal or *poblacion* and the barrio. The municipality, a political unit into which a province is divided, is a public corporation governed by the Municipal Law which defines its powers and duties. It has a government of its own with principal officials elected by the qualified voters among its population. There are five types of municipalities based on the amount of taxes raised.[2]

According to the census of 1939, there are 1,187 municipalities with an average of 3,170 population and there are 19,000 barrios with an average population of 724.

As far as political structure is concerned the barrio is a part of the municipality and is governed by municipal officials. Each municipal councilor is in charge of one or more barrios and he in turn appoints a barrio lieutenant, an unpaid official who acts as deputy of the councilor. In some barrios the barrio lieutenant is assisted by a council which represents different areas of the barrio. The barrio councilors are also unpaid and do not have any direct governmental power. Barrio residents do not have a direct voice in the selection of their officials and can only exercise their influence as voters within the municipality.

Most of the barrios are located five to fifteen miles from the *poblacion*. Many of them are not connected by good roads, and in any event automobiles are rare. During the rainy season the rivers may cut off the trails and the barrio will be completely isolated for long periods of time. The officials in the *poblacion* are isolated from the barrio both in communication and in basic concern.

All taxes are paid into the municipal treasury and the barrio itself cannot levy taxes for any purpose whatsoever. Their roads, schools, fire protection and other facilities are

---
[2] Arturo M. Tolentino: *The Government of the Philippines*, Manila. R. P. Garcia Publishing Company, 1950.

CHAPTER X. RURAL COMMUNITIES 239

dependent upon the action of municipal officials. These officials are usually under the influence of the large landowners whose concern with government facilities is limited to the *poblacion* and whose principal interest is to maintain order and keep down taxes.

This structure makes it difficult, if not impossible, for barrio residents to utilize local governmental action in solving their problems. Policies sponsored by the national government frequently stop at the *poblacion* level where the officials reside. The MSA-PHILCUSA survey of rural communities found that only two out of ten government programs seemed to be effective at the barrio level.[3]

This highly centralized structure of rural government is a factor which must be considered in any plans calling for governmental action. Programs which appear to be ideal in Manila are apt to be rendered impractical by difficulties of physical communications or sabotaged by the indifference or antagonism of municipal officials. This is especially true of programs such as the Rice-Share Tenancy Act which runs counter to traditional mores governing landlord-tenant relationships.

The trend away from centralization is represented by the effects of the community school movement to reach groups of less than barrio size. To do this, much of their work is centered in the *purok*, a voluntary neighborhood group which takes over civic functions on its own initiative. The *purok* is not a governmental unit but simply represents a small area in which neighborhood ties are especially close.

---

[3] Generoso F. Rivera and Robert T. McMillan, *The Rural Philippines*, Philippine Council for United States Aid and The United States Mutual Security Agency, Manila, 1952.

SOCIAL INSTITUTIONS IN RURAL COMMUNITIES

The Rural Family

The cultural contacts of the Filipinos with the other Oriental countries and the Western nations have influenced family life tremendously. Today, traces of Oriental influences are more apparent in the rural areas than in the urban communities.

In the rural family, the father is usually the recognized head of the household and principal breadwinner, a practice attesting to the general assumption that the farm family is patriarchal. Rural life demands physical strength and endurance. The wife readily accepts her role as second in authority as a matter of course. There is, however, a just compensation for the wife's subordinate role in that she is the uncontested treasurer of the family finances. Generally, there is mutual respect and confidence between the spouses. The traditional pattern of parental authority and parental control over the children are outstanding aspects of rural family life.

The extended family is more prominent in the rural setting than anywhere else. Besides the parents and the children, relatives such as grandparents, aunts and uncles live together as members of one big family, each one contributing what he can for the common welfare. The numerical factor in rural life is important in view of the fact that the nature of farm work is largely manual. Although the father does the major job of farming, other members of the family ordinarily perform such tasks as babysitting for the couple or feeding the chickens and the pigs. The wife and the daughters, besides keeping house, help in the planting and harvesting of the crops. The sons learn farming by working with their fathers in preparation for taking over the job later. This spirit of mutual aid and interdependence is carried far into the years so that parents expect their children to support them in their old age.

A rural family in transmitting the biological heritage through the natural processes of birth and child-bearing

CHAPTER X. RURAL COMMUNITIES

not only replenishes its own numbers but provides a surplus. Early marriage and the nonpractice of birth control are probably the main reasons for the big families in the rural areas.

The rural family is noted for its stability. The presence of many children, as well as the fact that the rural environment fosters fewer of those family crises, partially accounts for this stability. The presence of the grandparents, taken for granted in the rural household, also may prevent the dissolution of family ties.

The problem of projection often occurs in a rural family. Parents have a strong tendency to impose their own ambitions on their children. They may dictate the vocational choices of the latter without considering individual capacities.

Family influence is strong in economic life. On the farm the entire household pools their labor in the common task of working the fields and caring for animals. Many tenants rent from relatives and most farms are acquired through inheritance or marriage. The inheritance system is a definite factor in the decreasing size of the acreage farm unit as custom decrees that land should be distributed equally among children.

In the relation between the sexes, the rural family is less subject to western influence than the city family. Strict chaperonage of the unmarried girls is practically unchallenged and marriages tend to be arranged through intermediaries and dependent upon parental approval. In the rural community, economic life is close to the subsistence level and education, organized religion and government exercise only a limited influence while the family is the major institutional influence in all areas of life.

The Rural School

The progress and enlightenment of a country is largely dependent upon the educational opportunities offered to its people. The school is the principal agency in this process.

Four-fifths of the barrios have elementary schools. The school is the center of most community activities. Attendance is obligatory but not compulsory through the fourth grade. Most schools have a Parent-Teacher's Association which helps to provide buildings and equipment.
Photo and caption from *The Rural Philippines*.

The Filipinos as a people have a deep and pervading passion for education, a trait which the Bell Mission acknowledged in its Report in 1950. The rural family often goes into debt in order to send its children to school.

The typical rural school is a four-grade school housed in a four-room temporary building situated in the center of a barrio. This school is taught by two or three teachers who are graduates of a normal school, and it is populated by about a hundred pupils. The aim of the primary level is to equip the pupils with the fundamentals of reading, language, writing, and arithmetic. Although the primary level of education is supported by the government, facilities are far from satisfactory.

In the municipalities, the six-grade elementary school level is offered by the government-supported school which is usually housed in a concrete Gabaldon structure and supplementary wooden annexes. Courses offered in addition to the four fundamentals are the social studies, health, and music.

Over and above the elementary school level, the secondary schools offer opportunities for educational advance-

CHAPTER X. RURAL COMMUNITIES

ment. The secondary schools, both public and private, are established in large centers of population. The types of curriculum offered in such schools are the academic type intended for those who expect to go to college, for others the trade and technical training type, and the agricultural curriculum. The Filipino is partial to college attainment; hence the agricultural and technical schools have not been overly popular. In a few rural communities private normal schools and preparatory schools have been established in an effort to reach the rural population.[4]

A recent innovation in the field of education is the current trend towards the establishment of the community school. A community school is one which, in addition to performing the basic academic tasks, is directly concerned with the improvement of living in the community. To attain this objective, the curriculum of such a school consists of subjects that meet the demands and needs of that particular community.

Community schools have sponsored reforestation, community libraries, adult dressmaking classes, home beautification and sanitation, improved agricultural practices and better methods of preserving food. In general, the school tries to help the community apply the knowledge which would be of only academic value if confined to the school room.

The community school is part of a general effort to make education more effective in the rural community. The expansion of schools has been rapid in comparison with Oriental countries, but many barrios still lack elementary schools and nearly all barrio children have to travel a considerable distance to high school. After fifty years of educational development, illiteracy is still widespread and even those with some education have a cultural outlook which is extremely limited.

The typical rural student does not progress beyond the fourth grade and here his efforts are mainly devoted

---

[4] See Coller, Richard W. "Role of the Philippine Rural High School," *Philippine Sociological Review*, Vol. II, No. 2, July, 1954, p. 42.

to an unsuccessful effect to master English. In this setting many students never gain the ability to read or write effectively in any language and do not have enough training in arithmetic to handle simple farm bookkeeping. School efforts to encourage sanitation and understanding of political processes are even less successful. Rural schools have made a considerable advance but are handicapped both by insufficient financial support and by a curriculum remote from the life of their students.

The Rural Church

The quality of rural religion.

Sociologists agree that religion is related to the economic and social code of a people. It is also generally accepted that one who has been reared in a rural environment views life differently from one reared in a big city. The rural man is more intensely aware of the natural powers which control his life such as the weather, the seasons, growth and life. The urban man attributes his troubles to his fellowmen rather than to nature.

Conclusions reached concerning rural religion reveal that the religion of the rural man is more personal and less social than that of the urbanite, more conservative, more local in its applications, less missionary in spirit, more stable, clinging to traditional emotional values, less intellectual, more supernatural and less humanistic, looking toward the ultimate outcome of life, more contemplative and less dynamic in social action.[5]

The rural areas also keep the firmest hold on traditional pre-Christian folk beliefs. Lowie, speaking of the Polish peasants says:

> In true animistic fashion they assign spirits to the house and the water, believe that the soul leaves a dreamer's body and may find it difficult

[5] Compare J. R. Williams, *Our Social Heritage*, A. Knopf, Inc., N. Y., 1925, pp. 151-152.

CHAPTER X. RURAL COMMUNITIES 245

to reenter it. Such a mentality is apt to give a quaint twist to Christianity.[6]

Speaking of magic and witchcraft survivals he cites cases in the United States:

> There is the case of the white parents in Louisiana whose child suffered from shingles (a skin disease). For a remedy they cut a cat's tail and with the blood made the sign of a cross over the patient's chest. In recent years the people of a village of Illinois of predominantly British descent —were found carrying potatoes in their pockets as an antidote for rheumatism... Not even in rural America, then, has the modern spirit gained complete sway.[7]

The churches scattered over the rural communities in the Philippines are predominantly Roman Catholic. Many of them are elaborate affairs of Spanish architecture which were built over two hundred years ago and are still used as places of worship. They give testimony to the devotion and skill of the religious orders responsible for their building. The larger communities on the major islands generally have Catholic churches adequate to meet the needs of the group but some of the more distant and isolated barrios are still without churches. The people may have to travel great distances to reach the Church in the *poblacion*, and during the rainy season their regular attendance is not expected. Many rural communities have a parish priest in charge of the local church; others must rely on visits from the clergyman in the *poblacion*. The priest is a community leader whose main work is to take care of the spiritual needs of his group. The church still retains some of the age old functions such as welfare work and educational work.

The most popular occasions for social contact within the church group consists of the Sunday masses, the church feast days and other occasions celebrated by the church. The two church organizations, which are most effective in

---

[6] Robert H. Lowie, *Cultural Anthropology*, Rinehart & Co., New York, 1940, pp. 530-531.
[7] *Ibid.*, p. 53.

helping the church fulfill its mission are the Legion of Mary and the Knights of Columbus.

Many Philippine Independent Churches (Aglipayan) are also found in rural communities. The Aglipayan church is usually a building made of wood and galvanized iron big enough to accommodate the congregation in a particular area. Except in the Ilocos regions, it seldom attracts a majority of the community but it usually has an intensely loyal congregation. The ritual in these churches is similar to that in Roman Catholic parishes although there are many differences in theology and in emphasis. In spite of their similarity it is not uncommon for Aglipayans and Catholics to form distinct groups which are separate in most community relationships.

Protestant churches show a spotty distribution. In a few barrios they may be the dominant religious groups; in others a small minority, and in many districts they are totally absent. *Iglesia ni Kristo*, Jehovah's Witnesses and Seventh Day Adventists likewise have a strong following in some districts but in most others they are either numerically weak or non-existent.

The minority religious groups are regarded by their adherents as the churches embodying the true faith, and by others as disturbers of religious harmony. From a more objective standpoint they offer a strong sense of community to their adherents, and bring not only controversy but also a religious awareness to the total community. The majority group is impelled by their competition to further its own evangelistic efforts and to increase its social services. In this fashion the traditional piety of the rural community is sometimes changed into a more active and intellectual religious activity such as is prevalent in urban centers.

Rural Health

One of the outstanding advantages of rural life is the superior healthfulness of the open country. But this is not the only factor which affects the health of the population. The traditional attitudes of the people towards health and

CHAPTER X. RURAL COMMUNITIES 247

sickness, the availability of health facilities and the distribution of physicians in the rural areas are other factors upon which rural health depends.

A survey of health conditions in the country reveals that 4,000 physicians are distributed throughout the rural areas.[8] In the provinces of Bohol, Camarines Sur, Capiz, Catanduanes, Iloilo, Lanao, Leyte, Misamis Oriental, Romblon, Samar, Sorsogon and Surigao, there is only one physician for every ten thousand inhabitants.

The country has some 3,000 dentists who follow the pattern of distribution of the physicians. The rural people in general are not much concerned about their teeth and mouth hygiene; so the rural dentists, though scarce, may still lack patients.

This obvious maldistribution of physicians can be attributed to the following reasons: first of all, young doctors would rather not practice in rural communities where the "horse and calesa facilities are not in consonance with their training." They prefer to concentrate in Manila where laboratory conveniences are handy. Second, doctors are aware of the attitude held by the majority of rural people which places faith in the healing powers of the "herbolario" and supernatural elements, thus making medical practise inadequate to maintain a decent livelihood. Although the country is divided into sanitary divisions under the charge of a charity physicians, such health centers have not received complete public acceptance.

In many rural areas the barrio dweller is still superstitious. Some of the common beliefs which conflict with medical practices are the following: a mother who has just given birth is required to use a high pillow to prevent the flow of blood to her head; nails, no matter how long, are not supposed to be cut on Tuesdays and Fridays, chicken and squash should not be eaten in a meal together as this may develop disease; windows should be closed at night to keep out evil spirits.

---

[8] Salvador C. Meñez: "Medical Manpower in the Philippines," *Sunday Times Magazine*, May 4, 1952, pp. 8-9.

Some municipalities have puericulture centers established by civic spirited citizens. A center nurse with limited equipment is the usual condition. Puericulture centers have done a commendable job in caring for maternity cases and reducing infant mortality. The small town *hilot* is still the greatest obstacle to widespread use of the puericulture center.

The MSA-PHILCUSA Community Survey found that only one of the 13 barrios visited had a medical doctor but that every village had its *herbolario* and *hilot*.[9] Ninety-six percent of the births in the barrios were attended by someone other than a trained physican. Less than half of the barrio population had received the supposedly compulsory vaccination even though this is given free of charge by the municipal sanitary inspector. Only one-fifth of these barrio residents received their water from artesian wells; the majority were dependent upon surface wells with several households often using the same well.[10]

Recreational and Cultural Activities

A recent innovation in the way of enriching rural culture in the Philippines is the establishment of reading centers in the municipalities and barrios. The reading materials are daily newspapers and vernacular magazines donated by the leading citizens. This is a means of spreading general information that is especially intended for the adult group.

Occasional literary and musical programs offered by the schools form the core of activities for artistic development.

Radios and movie houses are not found in all rural communities because electric power is installed only in big population centers. A small handful of the inhabitants are subscribers to the dailies, and a less significant portion are interested in reading standard magazines.

---
[9] The *herbolario* is an untrained man who applies native remedies. The *hilot* is a midwife, usually untrained, although some have attended classes arranged by the government.
[10] *The Rural Philippines. Op. Cit.,* p. 141.

Chapter X. RURAL COMMUNITIES

Metropolitan
1-20

Provincial
1-90

Each figure represents ten people

Daily newspaper circulation in metropolitan Manila is about one copy per twenty people. In the provinces it is about one to ninety people and if the *poblaciones* were excluded the figure would be still greater. Daily contact with the news is still mainly an urban characteristic.

Some data on communication facilities in rural communities is furnished by the MSA-PHILCUSA community survey.[11] The *damay* characteristic of the communities is indicated by the fact that neighbors were the most important source of news, and that forty-one percent of the households reported that they read no newspaper or magazine regularly. In the majority of the households which did utilize printed matter was restricted to popular fiction in the vernacular press. Approximately half of the informants reported having seen a movie during 1951, and the average frequency was ten times during the year. Only three percent of the households had radios, but one-fourth reported that they had listened to one sometime in the week preceding the interview. This survey would seem to indicate that most barrio residents are still not reached by the type of communication facilities which are taken for granted in city life.

One of the big problems of rural living is the lack of wholesome recreational centers. The sari-sari store, the market place and the barber-shop provide a meeting place

---

[11] *Ibid.*, pp. 156, 157.

for rural people who are not actually working. Gossip is a favorite pastime among the women, and for the men drinking or cock fighting is popular. Most time is spent in casual talk and informal activity within the family or neighborhood.

Occasions that call for big celebrations are weddings, baptisms and death anniversaries. It is not surprising to find farmers spending their produce ahead of time to celebrate with an ostentatious party. The town fiestas are occasions which give the farm people a good excuse to spend freely.

The "fiesta complex" has often been criticized by social reformers because of the strain it places on family finances. From another point of view it may be regarded as the major organized effort to relieve the drabness and monotony of rural life. This stand is concisely expressed in a statement by J. O. Masa:[12]

> The fiesta spirit is the rural Filipino's answer to deep seated demand for relaxation and recreation... Thus, the Philippines today not only has patron saint's days but a series of celebrations that are related to the birth of a child, the death of a person, the marriage of a young couple, or similar events that may lend excuse for this desire to overcome the monotony and drabness of rural life. We often make a big mistake of casting aspersions on these fiesta celebrations,—leaders should realize that people do not operate in a vacuum and unless we have adequate substitutes there is no reason to disregard the folkways of a people without which they would cease to be themselves.

Rural culture is limited and recreation is expensive, sporadic and usually far from constructive. Improvement in social life may come with higher standards of education, greater community activity by schools and churches, improved roads making access to the *poblacion* easier, and

---

[12] J. O. Masa, "Components of Philippine Rural Culture," *Philippine Christian Rural Fellowship Bulletin*, No. 17, 1st quarter, 1953, p. 2.

better power distribution, facilitating the spread of the *cine* and the use of radios.

This type of "improvement" means that the country is being urbanized and that rural recreation patterns are shifting from the *damay* to the *gesellschaft* pattern. While this shift may produce a more varied pattern of recreation is traditional in nature, carried on in a pri nary group setting and subject to fairly rigid social controls. Urban recreation is more subject to innovation and is often carried on in an impersonal setting where the individual is not protected by his friends.

Many peasant societies, for example, have institutionalized occasions when heavy drinking is condoned by the group. In the Philippines this is often true of the drinking of *tuba* or *basi* at the time of weddings or other festive occasions. While the resulting intoxication may offend the sensibilities, it is not ordinarily a cause of social disorganization. The participants are protected by others in the community from accidents and the drinking is usually restricted to special occasions. Thomas and Znaniecki noted this practice among the Polish peasants and commented that when peasants moved to an urban setting drink became a major social disturbance.[13] Urban drinking represents a shift from rice wine to gin, from festival occasions to routine indulgence and from the care of intimate friends to the impersonal setting of the waterfront dive.

Rural recreation may be criticized because of its limited variety and its often destructive character. On the other hand it does operate within the supervision of the kinship group and maintains a degree of social unity. Reforms here should attempt to add the stimulus of new ideas while retaining the unity and social control of a family centered society.

---

[13] William J. Thomas and Florian Znaniecki, *The Polish Peasant in Europe and America*, Alfred A. Knopf, Inc., New York, 1927, Vol. II, pp. 1691-1692.

Rural Economic Activities

The basic economy of the country is agrarian. However, there are a few rural communities whose principal income is derived from small scale handicraft industries such as shoe-making, hat-weaving and the like.

The different rural regions raise products suited to their soil, climate, and topography. The following is a table showing the distribution of the principal products as of 1948.

Table 1 — Rural Economic Activities. *

Product	No. of people depending upon the product	Place where product is raised
Rice	5,000,000	C. Luzon, Iloilo, Occ. Negros, Cotabato, Lanao
Corn		C. Luzon, E. Visayas, C. Valley
Sugar	1,900,000	Negros, Cebu, Panay, Pampanga, Bulacan, Tarlac, Batangas, Laguna.
Coconut	4,000,000	Quezon, Laguna, Masbate, Oriental Misamis, Zamboanga.
Abaca	2,500,000	Bicol, Leyte, Samar, Davao, Masbate, Catanduanes
Tobacco	600,000	Cagayan Valley, Cebu, Negros, Pampanga.

* Based on Andres Castillo, *Philippine Economics*, Manila, 1949.

The farmer raises his own livestock to provide animals for farm work and to supply him with meat. The most common of such livestock are carabaos, cattle, horses, goats and sheep. Poultry raising is another activity which not only supplies food for the farm but also adds to the family income.

A considerable number of the rural population are engaged in the extractive industries such as mining, lumbering and fishing. The mining towns are located in the Bicol regions and the Mountain Province. The lumber

CHAPTER X. RURAL COMMUNITIES 253

towns are located in Mindanao. Fishing towns are along the coasts of the different islands.

The most striking characteristic of the rural economy is the utter poverty of most of the inhabitants. It is estimated that the owner of an average size farm cultivated area = 2.16 hectares) would produce about 27.4 cavans of rice per hectar with an estimated gross return of ₱590 per year.[14] The return of the share tenant is much less and in some cases outside income is negligible.

This means that many farmers operate on a subsistence economy and, in addition, have to borrow money at extremely high rates of interest in order to live between harvests. The MSA Community Study found that less than one tenth of the tenant farmers they interviewed sold any rice after creditors were paid.[15] Obviously this means that most farmers simply do not have the income to educate their children, pay for medical expenses or purchase any of the luxury items usually included in a modern standard of living.

Cottage Industries.

Although the Philippines remains predominantly an agricultural country, it is considered as having many potential cottage industries. The abundance of various raw materials and the substantial supply of labor, especially during the long interval between the planting and the harvesting season, make possible such industries as weaving, hat making, embroidery and the manufacture of slippers, shoes, and novelty articles.

Cottage industry is frequently regarded as a method of making use of the idle manpower caused by the seasonal nature of farm labor. This period of unemployment has been estimated to run as high as 200 days a year and offers an obvious opportunity for work which can be carried on in the home during the off season. At present about 300,000

---

[14] Philippine Land Tenure Reform Report of Mutual Security Agency, U.S.A., Manila, 1952, p. 4.
[15] *The Rural Philippines, Op. Cit.*, p. 121.

people are estimated to be employed in this type of work. Their net annual income is small, usually under a hundred pesos a year per family but many authorities are convinced this can be substantially increased. Various agencies are making efforts to find markets, improve techniques and designs and stimulate the growth of these industries.[16]

Personality Traits and Farm Experience

Personalities can be classified on the basis of those characteristics that develop in response to environmental circumstances. The individual raised on a farm therefore develops a personality which is influenced by farm life.

The experience of the farmer usually emphasizes direct contact with nature. His logic is sound in dealing with the phenomena of direct experience. Farm people have an almost unlimited patience and endurance which are developed by the requirements of hard farm work.

The "marginal" man is seldom found in rural communities and the farmer is usually well-integrated in his cultural setting. This gives him a stability often lacking in urban dwellers. Mental disease and personality disorders are uncommon in rural areas and stable, balanced personalities are the rule. The rural dweller has the calm confidence which comes from a traditional way of life and a unified set of folkways and mores.

When the rural dweller moves to the city, however, he may appear bashful, shy and reserved. His background has prepared him for a natural consistent type of life and he is not adept in the verbal skills which the urbanite uses in adjusting to a changing artificial type of world.

Conservatism is the mark of a farmer in the matter of adopting new methods of farming. This trait grows out of the fact that the farmer works for himself and therefore he can persist in following his old methods without pressure from an employer.

---

[16] Data based on report of MSA Handicraft Development Project. June 30, 1952.

Chapter X. RURAL COMMUNITIES

In the field of expenditures, the farmers belong to two types. One type would be slow in spending because his income is dependent upon the natural factors that affect production, and he does not want to take the risk of exhausting his finances before the next crop is due. To the other type belongs the farmer who is willing to splurge during a fiesta or one who seeks recreation and sudden wealth through gambling.

The farmer is habituated to resignation to circumstances instead of adopting the urbanite's philosophy of social manipulation. The farmer often develops submission to the forces of his environment and holds to the idea that no amount of manipulation will change things as nature meant them to be. In contrast to this view is the idea of the urbanite that one can fix things if he knows the right people and pulls the right strings. Therefore the city person frequently concentrates on cultivating the right connections to get what he wants, while the farmer often accepts what fate bestows upon him.

People whose major attitudes have been shaped by an urban background sometimes are discouraged by the personality traits of the farmer which make difficult the improvements in rural life that otherwise would be easy to accomplish. The fatalistic acceptance of the situation, the persistence of spending habits which render thrift impossible and the resistance to scientific planning are attitudes often associated with the rural personality pattern.

H. Welton Rotz makes the following analysis in an article entitled "The Rural Resistance":

> A worker with rural persons can speak for hours on end about cleanliness, pride in his barrio, to become diligent about health and sanitation, to give up his extravagance in gambling and cock-fighting, and get busy with his neighbors to raise the level of the living of his barrio. But the worker is dismayed that among all these presentations there is nothing that seems to have strong persuasion enough to change even one behavior pattern... Why does the rural person so often seem indifferent

to his own health, financial security and enjoyment of life? ...We find some part of the answer in the past of the farmer. For centuries he has been a victim of many adverse forces. Ignorance has caused the misuse of the land and a decreasing productivity. He gathered less and less from his fields and became more and more desperately at the mercy of the money lender. Bad weather, typhoon, swarms of insects, bands of rats have all continued to defeat his efforts. No matter how hard he tried, something would happen to reduce or destroy his crops. For generations he lost over one half of his children, his own health was poor... After hundreds of years of such experience he has developed a fatalistic outlook on life, and a tremendous characteristic of resistance to any change.[17]

Mr. Rotz goes on to point out that laws, agricultural demonstrations and even education do not seem to change the picture. His own proposals involve a change in community spirit through close association and patient work by those with a scientific viewpoint. This involves the transformation of the entire community mores—a task which, while not impossible, demands the personal attention of one willing to live in the barrio, motivated by love and guided by an understanding of social organization. He sees the smaller churches as important factors in this process, but the same analysis would apply to educators, businessmen, landlords and government officials.

Rural Improvement Programs

Numerous proposals have been made for rural improvement and even a summary of their effects would require a book by itself. They seem to be divided into two major types: those concerned with some specific type of economic improvement and those directed to securing a change in the basic attitudes of the rural community. The two approaches are not antagonistic and may both be regarded as essential elements in rural progress.

---

[17] Rotz, Welton H., "The Rural Resistance," *Philippine Christian Rural Fellowship Bulletin*, 5th year, No. 14, May, 1952, p. 2.

Under the first heading we have the effort to improve the *tao's* share of farm income through tenancy laws and land distribution. Other measures seek to increase the total income by expanding irrigation, providing proper fertilizer, using better seeds and similar technical improvements. Basic to this approach is the development of an extension service which will be able actually to reach the rural barrio and to keep the farmer aware of the latest technical knowledge. Further economic measures include power development, encouragement of cottage industries and development of rural credit facilities.

The other approach seeks to change the total tone of community life and to lessen "the rural resistance" to effective selp help. This type of movement is represented by a desire to improve the work of the rural health services and to make church and school more vital factors in social life. Newer agencies working for change in community life include the Philippine Rural Reconstruction Movement and the Philippine Rural Community Improvement Society which aim to analyze the problem of rural life and bring the entire community into a cooperative effort to better its condition. Another organization, the NAMFREL is seeking to make free elections to reality in the barrio and help rural people to participate in government.

In the past, rural apathy has been matched by urban cynicism based on the belief that nothing could change the outlook of the *tao*. These forces are still strong but a growing discontent in rural life is bringing a renewed effort to change the basic pattern of rural society. A study of social life makes one aware of its traditional character but should also make one realize that every social pattern is subject to change. The task today is to accelerate the rate of change and guide the change into constructive channels. The American and the Philippine government together are spending millions of pesos toward rural reconstuction but the success of these programs demands the cooperation of thousands of people who are not in government positions.

Summary

The rural community is the prime example of the *damay* society in which tradition is strong and change is relatively slow. Rural government is controlled by authorities stationed in urban centers and the local people have little voice in the governmental affairs. Farming methods and sanitary facilities reflect the hostility of the rural areas to change and keep close to ancient patterns. Health facilities are inadequate and their usage is impeded by superstition which relies on unscientific medical practices. The average income is low and poverty handicaps efforts to improve the tone of rural society. Many barrios lack adequate roads and this isolation is increased by a limited use of reading matter, widespread illiteracy, and the absence of electricity in a majority of barrios which makes the operation of radios difficult.

Efforts to improve rural communities are being made by both private and governmental organizations. These efforts are based on a desire to utilize the cooperative patterns of the barrio in the improvement of social and economic conditions.

QUESTIONS

1. Define a rural community.
2. Give the impressions that a casual observer gathers as he passes through a rural community.
3. What are the manifestations of neighborliness in a rural community?
4. Name some of the rural traditions that govern social life.
5. What personality traits result from a rural environment?
6. What are the distinguishing characteristics of the rural family?
7. Describe a typical community school. Evaluate the effect of education on the rural resident who spends only four years in school.
8. What suggestions would you make for improvement of barrio government?
9. How do you account for the popularity of the *herbolario* in the barrios?
10. What attitudes in conflict with science are possessed by barrio people?

Chapter X. RURAL COMMUNITIES

11. Evaluate the cultural and recreational facilities of our rural areas.
12. What are some of the most popular cottage industries in our country?
13. What are the fundamental problems of rural communities?
14. What are the suggested solutions to such problems?
15. What advantages do you see in rural living? What disadvantages?

PROJECTS

1. Analyze a rural barrio from one of the following standpoints: education, religion, agricultural practices, health, recreation, housing and family life, land ownership and tenancy patterns, credit facilities. First describe carefully the actual operation of a particular phase of barrio life and then indicate possible methods of improvement.

2. From your own knowledge and interviews with barrio residents list the major changes during the last twenty years in the items mentioned in question one. Indicate the factors which seem to have caused these changes and the differences which they made in community life. Designate any items in which you expect to see change in the near future and indicate the factors on which your prediction is based.

SUGGESTED READINGS

Agricultural and Industrial Life, P. O. Box 2062, Manila. Subscription — four pesos a year.
  A semi-popular type of farm magazine with interesting articles on a wide variety of topics.

Aguilar, José V.: *This is Our Community School*, Bookman, Inc., Manila, 1951.
  Exposition of the practices of various community schools.

Brayne, F. L.: *Better Villages*, Oxford University Press, London, 1937.
  A discussion of Indian village life which has many suggestions applicable to the Philippine scene.

Castillo, Andres V.: *Philippine Economics*, Manila, 1949.
  A general economics text with several chapters definitely relating to the Philippines. An especially good discussion of rural credit and landlord-tenant relationships.

Journal of the Philippine Soil Science Society. Soil Conservation Building, Florida Street, Manila. Subscription — three pesos. Usually devoted to articles on soil analysis and similar topics but includes a fair proportion of more general material.

Landis, Paul H.: *Rural Life in Process*, McGraw-Hill Publications, New York, 1949.
Good discussion of social patterns in rural communities.

Loomis, Charles and Beegle, J. Allen: *Rural Social Systems*, Prentice-Hall, New York, 1950.
Has a good discussion of primary and secondary group concepts as applied to rural communities.

Philippine Association of School Superintendents, 1950 *Yearbook*, Bookman Inc., Manila.
Contains several articles dealing with the relationship of the schools to the Community.

Philippine Christian Rural Fellowship Bulletin. 726 Taft Avenue, Manila. Published by the Philippine Federation of Christian Churches. Subscription — one peso a year.
Devoted to a consideration of the rural scene from the religious viewpoint.

Sanderson, Dwight: *Rural Sociology and Rural Social Organization*, Wiley & Sons, New York, 1949.
A general rural sociology which pays particular attention to social change in rural areas.

The Rural Philippines, Manila. Mutual Security Agency and Philippine for U.S. Aid, 1952.
The famous McMillan-Rivera Report which presents data from a survey study of thirteen rural communities selected to afford a cross section view of Philippine rural life.

Tolentino, Arturo M.: *The Government of the Philippines*, R. P. Garcia Publishing Company, Manila, 1950.
Has a good description of rural government.

CHAPTER ELEVEN

THE URBAN COMMUNITY

"For Manila is the city like all cities—changeless and changing. Giving and taking back. Harsh and yet tender as a child's caress. And unlike other cities, it is the east and the west meeting at last. It is the Malay and the Latin. The American and the Chinese. ...The city with the strident voice and the brick and cement jungles, and the city with the hidden lullabies and the warm hand. Cankered by ugliness and evil, spiked with violence and sudden death, it has its moments of breathless beauty and primal innocence. And if a man could see his way clear through to the very core of the city, he might yet apprehend the final meaning which could be the germ of his fulfillment."

— Vicente Rivera, Jr., "This is Manila," *Sunday Times Magazine*, November 20, 1953, pp. 9-10.

History and Growth of City Life.

The growth of great cities is often mentioned in accounts of world history. However, the fact is that city life is a relatively new experience in the history of the human species. It is estimated that the first appearance of people on the earth was about 500,000 B.C., or possibly even earlier, while the first settlement of city size is dated at 3,500 B.C. So human beings as a group have now experienced at least 496,500 years of life without cities, but only 5,500 years with cities. Because of this we say that the urban community is a relatively new environment for mankind.

The best known cities of ancient times are located in the Asia Minor and Mediterranean areas. Among them would be Ur in Summeria, Memphis in Egypt, Carthage in northern Africa, Babylon and Nineveh in Asia Minor,

Tyre and Sidon in Phoenecia, and Rome—the greatest of all. Greece also had the cities of Athens, Syracuse, Corinth, and Sparta. However, ancient urban centers were also found in other parts of the world. Thus in the 16th century B.C. China had the city Shang in the lower Huang Ho valley while Indian had such urban communities as Mohenjo Daro and Harappa in the Indus valley at about 3,000 B.C.

However, although there were these ancient cities, it still is a fact that the ancient urban communities were fewer and smaller than those of today. It is now generally agreed that no ancient city ever had a population of more than one million. This is because transportation facilities could not bring in the food and other necessities fast enough for a larger population. In those times animal caravans, carts, and boats were the only means of carrying goods to the cities and the methods of storing and preserving food were not highly developed. Today, on the other hand, Manila is already over one million population. There are now also at least 40 other cities in the world which have population of more than one million.

The great growth of cities has accompanied the development of modern technology since the Industrial Revolution. Although many towns and cities began to grow in the Medieval period (from the 11th to 15th centuries), the huge cities did not appear until the use of steam power for transportation and factories. As industrialization and world trade grew, so did the cities. However, this urban growth has not been evenly distributed around the world. Europe still has the greatest proportion of cities and city dwellers; while South America, Africa, and parts of Asia have more people on farms and in villages.

The percentages of people in the city have changed greatly in the industrialized nations. For example, in 1790 about one per cent of the population in the United States was classed as urban. Today about 60% of the United States population is defined as urban. In England about 80% of the population is now in the city. Germany comes second

Chapter XI. THE URBAN COMMUNITY

with an urban percentage of 70%. On the other hand, the Philippines is estimated to have between 15 and 20% of its population in the cities. Thus the Philippines and England are almost opposite in this respect.

As the effects of modern technology have increased in the Philippines, the greater growth of cities has also become evident. So we find that in 1903 there was actually only one city—Manila—and it had a population of 219,928. All of the other communities had less than 20,000 people and so were classified as "towns" by the census bureau. This means that in 1903 only 3% of the population in the Philippines could really be regarded as urban dwellers.

Table 1. City Growth in the Philippines *

CITY	1903	1918	1939	1948
Manila	219,928	285,306	623,492	983,906
Cebu	18,330	65,502	146,817	167,503
Davao	8,560	13,300	95,546	111,263
Iloilo	19,054	49,114	90,480	110,122
Zamboanga	3,281	30,798	131,455	103,317
Bacolod	5,678	19,360	57,474	101,432
Ormoc	5.419	38.174	77.349	72,773

* The selection of these particular cities was based primarily on the availability of recorded material.

The figures are taken from the following census materials:

1. *Census of the Philippine Islands*: 1903, Volume II, Second Edition, 1905, pp. 38, 123, 129, 154, and 209.
2. *Census of the Philippine Islands*: 1918, Volume II, 1921, pp. 99-110.
3. *Census of the Philippine Islands*: 1939, Volume II, Summary for the Philippines and General Report for the Censuses of Population and Agriculture, 1941, p. 59.
4. *Facts and Figures About the Economic and Social Conditions of the Philippines*, 1948-1949, Bureau of Census and Statistics, 1950.

In 1948, the year of the latest official census, there were 21 legally chartered cities in the nation with a total population of 2,445,651 people. Moreover, six of these twenty cities had a population of more than 100,000 people. Thus the

Philippines has changed a great deal in the last half century in regard to the presence of large cities. It is also of interest to note that Manila has more than tripled its population from 1918 to 1948, and that most of the other Philippine cities have at least doubled their population in the same period. The process of city growth in the Philippines has been definitely accelerating through the years.

Urban Social Relationships

As a particular type of human community, the urban centers have also developed a particular sort of culture. And, since there has been this great growth and spread of cities in modern times, the urban culture has likewise become of greater significance. As previously mentioned, the large city is considered to be the best example of a *gesellschaft* social setting. Thus most of the social contacts in the city are of the secondary type. This situation is a natural and logical result of the city's size. It would be impossible to form primary relationships with all of the one million people in Manila, for example. Hence because of the very nature of the city itself this condition exists.

Many people who leave a *damay* sort of community and come to the urban area often remark that the city is so cold and unfriendly. For them this difference is undoubtedly disappointing, but for the city-raised person it becomes accepted as an inevitable and unavoidable trait of urban life. Some writers even say that the city person has such limited primary contacts that his intimate relationships are confined to the family and a small group of friends.

This impersonal, secondary nature of most urban relationships is also fostered by the influence of commerce. Almost every large city is a center of trade as well as other functions. This trading relationship emphasizes a businesslike, somewhat cold-blooded way of dealing with people. Therefore, the urban dweller tends to think more of cash values rather than sentiments in his contacts with others.

CHAPTER XI. THE URBAN COMMUNITY

Damay and *Gesellschaft* social settings. At top, is the Escolta, prominent Manila business street, and at bottom is a scene from a rural barrio.

As a result, the impersonal *gesellschaft pattern* of city life is thereby re-enforced.

Another important factor in the social experience of the urban resident is the variety of peoples and cultures which are found in most large cities. Thus a city person sees many others who are following folkways and mores different from his own. This existence of varied cultures in the same community means that there is often no definite set of folkways and mores which prevails in a city. As a result, the relationships between people in the city tend to be controlled more by formal laws than by the mores. So we find that laws, courts, police, and other such agencies of control receive more emphasis in city life.

An additional effect which comes from the secondary, impersonal nature of urban life is the formation and maintenance of stereotypes. In the section on stereotypes it was noted that in a *gesellschaft* situation stereotypes are a natural product. People, especially in a large city, try to simplify their social relationships. Therefore, in the complex urban setting people have a tendency to develop stereotypes and react to each other on that basis more than rural residents would. It is both an effect of the impersonal character of urban life, and also a partial cause of impersonal attitudes.

Some sociologists have observed that the urban culture also often leads to the development of certain special attitudes. Thus city dwellers are frequently described as being more "broad-minded" or sophisticated. This is linked to the experience of living in a "melting-pot" of many different peoples and cultures. In fact one might say that in the city unusual things become commonplace. The city person accordingly learns to tolerate and deal with person of very different backgrounds from his own as a matter of practical necessity. This makes the city a place of refuge for non-conformists and others who are not accepted elsewhere.

Also, since the urban dweller is living in a largely man-made environment, some say he is more inclined to be cynical about the supernatural. It has been pointed out that "humanistic" or "mechanistic" philosophies are more frequently found in urban areas. Thus the city culture has been described as "secular" while the rural culture is characterized as "sacred."

In addition to developing distinctive attitudes, the urban resident is often said to experience certain special influences on his personality. Most of this idea rests upon the fundamental concept that "culture conflict often brings personality conflict." This is to say that a person who is living with such a variety of cultural patterns as we see in the large modern city is likely to feel uncertain and become confused. Since there is so much variation in folkways and mores between the different groups it may lead to individual problems. This could particularly happen in a seaport city such as Manila where peoples from all lands are found.

There is still another influence on the individual's personality development in the urban area which comes from the great numbers of people and groups. Since the person has more secondary contacts with many different groups, his social experience is more divided. His home life is perhaps not related to work or school, and his religious life may be very distinct from his recreational experiences. His life frequently becomes "compartmentalized," or to say it differently, his social experience becomes "fractional." As a result the individual may have a difficult time in unifying his various experiences and developing an integrated personality.

Two other outstanding characteristics of the urban community are specialization and interdependence. We find that in the modern city, functions of individuals and groups may be very specialized. This is again related to the great numbers and varieties of peoples in urban communities. It is usually only in a big city that operas, art galleries, brain surgeons, and stadiums are found. This is because such specialized persons and facilities require a large population to support them.

Individual specialization shows up most in the occupations of city residents. The employed urban person usually works at only one specialized task or set of tasks. The result of this individual and group specialization is interdependence. The city dweller depends on other specialized persons or groups to serve his needs, just as he serves them. This can be easily seen in urban building construction where there are many specialized workers, unlike rural construction where one man often builds an entire structure alone.

Family Life and Marriage

Urban marriage and family patterns also usually differ greatly from those in the rural areas. In regard to marriage, the general difference is that city people, as a whole, marry less and later than rural residents. Moreover, even if city people do eventually marry, they are less likely to remain married. For example, in the U.S. census of 1940 the data for married women shows this trend. Between the ages of 15 to 19 years, 8.9% of urban women were married, while 14.6% of the farm women were married. For the ages of 20 to 24 years the figures were 45.6% and 59.2% respectively.[1] This then shows that urban women married later than rural women and were more apt to remain single. For men the differences are not so distinct or consistent.

This variation in women's marriage rates is commonly explained in terms of the urban culture. One influence is the commercial emphasis in most cities which opens more jobs to women outside of the home. Another factor is that in the city one can live alone and enjoy it. This is often regarded as part of the urban tendency toward a so-called "individualism". There are so many facilities such as hotels, boarding houses, restaurants, and theaters that some feel no particular need to marry and establish a family. Hence career opportunities for women and the special facilities of

---

[1] Noel P. Gist and L. A. Halbert. *Urban Society*, Third Edition, 1948, p. 402.

Chapter XI. THE RURAL COMMUNITY

the city for single individuals are usually given as the two most important factors in this situation.

The U.S. census also gives us some enlightening figures on the urban divorce situation.[2] As mentioned previously, 60% of the U.S. population is urban, yet out of all the divorces in the nation, 72% were granted to urban persons. Moreover, in 1940 for the U.S. 1.4% of the urban population over 15 years old and 0.8% of the similar rural group were divorced. This is almost a ratio of 2 to 1. This difference in marriage breakup is probably true for other countries as well, although we have no ready data on this point.

The city usually has a great variety of family patterns. However, in general, the small, "simple-independent" type of family receives more emphasis in the city than do the other kinds. This means that the *gesellschaft* type of city culture has been able to influence even the family relationships. In many cities the feelings of kinship between cousins and other such relatives often become very weak, so that the interaction is more impersonal. Another factor which sometimes reduces the size of the urban family is the birth of fewer children. It is now well-known that the urban populations do not produce enough children to maintain themselves. Therefore, a city family often has fewer children and fewer relatives in the home, and so is smaller than the rural family.

The family functions all show a strong tendency to decline in the urban setting. This is to say, the family functions are often greatly modified or abbreviated although they still exist. As one goes down the usual list of the traditional family functions a change can be seen in every one for the urban family. As noted above, even the reproductive function shows a change.

In such things as protection, education, and economic activities we find that outside agencies and institutions

---

[2] From Gist and Halbert, *Urban Society*, Third Edition, p. 340.

are now serving some of the urban family's needs. This means that the city family does less in these fields and the outside groups do more. The most concrete examples are found in the economic field.

City families in the Philippines now rarely pound their own rice to husk it. The usual urban practice is to buy rice which is already cleaned and hulled. Thus the rice mill is doing a task which rural families often do even today. The chief effect of this partial transfer and abbreviation of functions is that the urban family now has less interdependence between the family members. Since the family functions are reduced there is less reason for keeping the family together. This situation can accordingly contribute to a family break-up.

Other factors which foster the small family type in the urban community are the higher standard of living and greater cost of living. Except for certain specialized and imported products, the absolute cost of living is higher in the city than in the rural areas. This is natural since the city does not grow such items as its own food, but must have them brought in. As a result the city resident pays for the transportation and handling through higher prices.

However, in addition, the city dweller also tends to seek a higher standard of living. For example, he may want to have a better house, suit for clothes, and set of furniture than his rural compatriots do. As a result the city family is spending more for its needs both because of the cost of living and the higher standards which it desires. This all means that urban dwellers are less willing to assume the responsibilities of a large family and the expenses which it entails.

Urban social structure.

The other urban institutions outside of the family also show certain common characteristics. The first thing is that they are more distinct than their rural counterparts.

In a rural area the amount of overlapping between such institutions as government and economic organization is often greater. For example, the same persons may hold key positions in both groups. However, in the urban community there is much less of such overlapping, or there may be none at all.

Specialization is another general trait of urban institutions. It is in the city where such specialized types of institutions as the international bank, graduate school of social welfare, trade school, and publishing company are ordinarily located. This specialization is linked to the greater number and variety of urban institutions. As mentioned previously, specialization and interdependence characterize urban life, thus we find that the institutions merely follow the general trend. Probably the most striking illustration of this point is the comparison between the number and variety of schools in Manila and the schools in a smaller town of the Philippines.

The urban community has also been known for a greater degree of social mobility. A general definition of social mobility is given as a movement from one social position to another. In this discussion the focus will be on changes of status. This greater social mobility in the urban area stems from several factors. The first one is that in the city there are more channels for movement. That is, there are many such opportunities as schools, government jobs, and commercial careers which may aid one to raise in the social scale.

Another factor is the more rapid degree of social change in the city. Since there is always a great deal of shifting and movement within the urban social structure, many change places. Then those who are fortunate are able to rise as the change occurs.

Then lastly, but perhaps the most important of all, is the greater emphasis on individual traits in the city. In the anonymous and impersonal *gesellschaft* city, one's family and social background often mean much less than in a rural *damay* area. The individual is frequently judged more on personal characteristics. This is, of course, linked to the previously mentioned changes in family functions and the trend towards individualism.

The effects of this greater social mobility are of some interest. One result is a greater "striving and straining" for social positions. Thus the social competition may be stronger in the city. Since there is less security of position, those on the lower levels are often hoping and struggling to rise on the social ladder. It must be remembered that the mobility can be either up or down, and therefore, one may go either way.

In addition, since the individual is judged more on personal traits, there is a special interest in this matter of social mobility. In the city there seems to be more attention given to such personal symbols of status as fashions. This is because in the city it is more possible to influence people by displaying certain symbols of prestige, ("putting up a front"), than in the rural *damay* community. One may deceive others in the city about one's background, whereas in the small town or village the truth is known. This use of certain prestige giving materials and symbols to influence others was called "conspicuous consumption" by Thorstein Veblen.

Some mention should be made about the special population features of the urban community. The two so-called "vital processes" of birth and death show some distinct trends in urban areas. It was previously noted that city people as a whole do not reproduce their group. The crude birth rates, (births per 1,000 population for a given time period), for some cities illustrate this tendency quite dramatically. For example, the crude birth rate of Vienna in 1937 was 5.4, that of Paris (1934) 12.3, London (1934) 13.4, New York (1938-40) 13.6, and San Francisco (1938-40) 12.2.[3] These rates contrast with a crude birth rate of 51.2 which apparently existed in the Philippines in 1886 and

---

[3] Warren S. Thompson: *Plenty of People*, Ronald Press, New York, 1948, p. 32.

which was more than nine times that of Vienna in 1937. The current (1951) Philippine birth rate of over 30 is also more than five times the 1937 Vienna rate. Cities therefore grow by the inward migration from outside areas. For example, it has been calculated that any large American city would probably have 27% decrease in population in 28 years if no inward migration were permitted.[4] There is probably also a similar situation in the other urban communities of the world, since city life everywhere has many common traits.

It may seem extremely strange, but the cities generally also have a lower "life expectancy" rate. The average urban dweller dies at a younger age than the average rural resident. This is apparently caused by the greater possibilities of contracting diseases in the city crowds, certain hazzards of urban industrial work, and the greater opportunities to wear oneself out in the hurry and over-stimulation of the urban community. In the U.S., for example, the average life expectancy of rural residents in 1930 was at least four years greater than for urban dwellers.[5]

Since the city depends on migration for much of its growth, the kind of people who move to the city is noteworthy. The only detailed information on this subject is furnished by the U.S. Census Bureau.[6] It was found that 68% of those who went to a city had come from small towns and villages. Therefore it is the rural town or municipal people who go to the city most in the United States, not the farmers.

Another finding is that it is the young adults who go most to the U.S. cities. This means that many of the small-town high school graduates go to the big urban centers. Since they are young, most of them are still unmarried. Then the last point is that there are more women than men who are migrating to the U.S. cities. It is perhaps in this

---
[4] Ogburn and Nimkoff: *Sociology*, Second Edition, pp. 347-348.
[5] Gist and Halbert, *Urban Society, op. cit.* p. 223.
[6] *Ibid.*, pp. 225, 232 to 240.

respect that the migration to Philippine cities would differ the most. A casual observation, plus some preliminary surveys, seems to show that there are more males than females migrating to the cities in the Philippines. Such a trend, if it exists, would be more in harmony with the traditional family attitudes in the Philippines towards young people who wish to leave home. Therefore, the average migrant to the city in the Philippines could probably be described as a young unmarried man about the age of 20 who has come from a provincial town or municipality.

Urban Disorganization and Reorganization

It has been said that the very conditions of urban life itself lead to the growth of social disorganization. For one thing, we find that the urban area is traditionally a center of social change. This means that the constant and rapid change can bring a lack of consistency in the folkways and mores. As a result some parts of the social "rules" may be in conflict or even contradict each other. So the mores may thus lose their power and meaning for the individual.

Then, in addition, because of the multitude of groups and culture patterns in the city the individual finds less of a solid "anchor" in the mores. Therefore the individual is often uncertain as to what is the best line of action. This process occurs in the *gesellschaft* atmosphere of the modern metropolis, so that the individual often feels alone and adrift. This again illustrates the saying that "culture conflict often leads to personality conflict."

This individualization in the folkways and mores then brings a problem of what has been termed social control. In the *damay* life of a small settlement the folkways and mores are usually enough to provide for the regulation of the community life. However, since the folkways and mores are neither consistent nor universally accepted in the large urban centers, they can not be relied upon alone to regulate the community life. We thus find a greater

Chapter XI. THE URBAN COMMUNITY

emphasis in the city upon *formal* agencies of control such as police and law courts.

However, the formal agencies of control can never fully cope with the situation. As a result, the urban centers have generally shown higher rates in all those factors which are supposed to indicate some maladjustment in a community. We find that the urban areas have more divorce, desertion, crime, suicide, and insanity than do the rural settlements. The detailed statistics vary of course, but that is the general trend in all cases.

The basic factor which is related to all of these indices of disorganization is naturally the great crowding of people into the urban areas. The large numbers of people produce anonymity which is often a strong influence in crime, suicide, and insanity. It is also possible that the large variety of people in the city may be a factor leading to some of the tensions and distractions which foster divorce and desertion. This is, of course, what is meant by the earlier statement that city life itself by its very nature tends toward disorganization.

On the other hand, it should also be recognized that the city may play a leading role in social reorganization. For one thing, the city is often the home of new organizations. Many of our most useful associations and institutions had their beginnings in urban centers. Another urban contribution to reorganization may come from the development of new folkways and mores, better known as "technic ways." For example, the modern probation system which is generally a part of the folkways in westernized areas was an urban development. It is also in the city that individuals who have had some unfortunate experiences may be able to seek a refuge and rebuild their lives. Thus someone who is disgraced elsewhere may flee to the city where he can shed his shame and gain a position of respect. Therefor, although the urban community may have a greater degree of disorganization, we must also realize that the city can be a powerful force in social reorganization wherein new values and new patterns of behavior are created.

The Urban Ecological Structure

Although the urban community is a population grouping and a cultural unit, it also has a territorial location. Thus the location and growth of a city in its geographic setting is another way of analyzing the urban community. This view of the city is called "urban ecology" and is a part of the field of human ecology. Human ecology is defined as the study of the relationships between human groups and their natural or geographic environment.

Most of the studies in urban ecology have been made in the United States. Because of certain historical rea-

DIAGRAM I.
THE AREAS OF A CITY

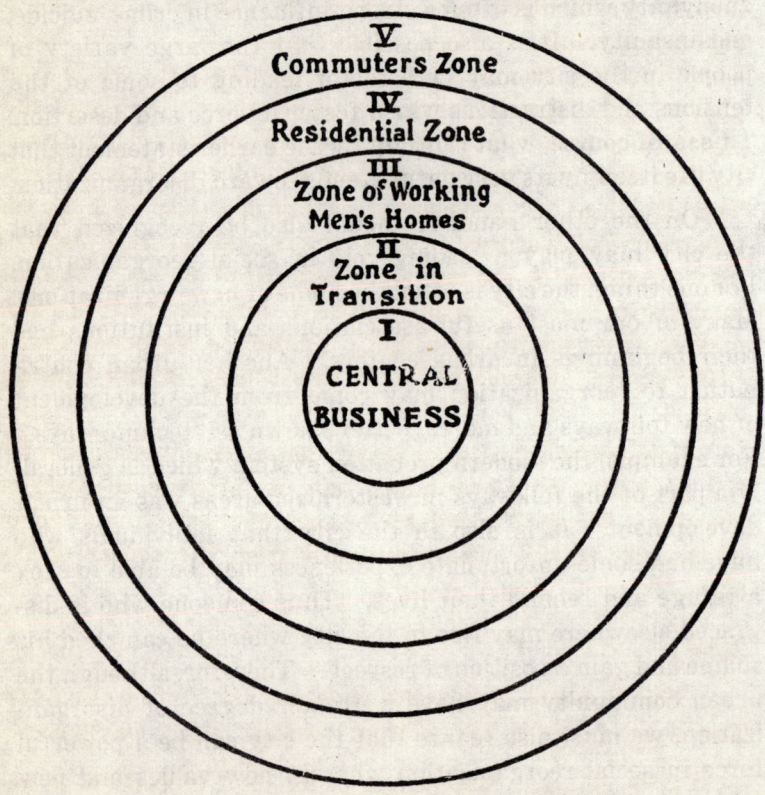

V Commuters Zone
IV Residential Zone
III Zone of Working Men's Homes
II Zone in Transition
I CENTRAL BUSINESS

Chapter XI. THE URBAN COMMUNITY

sons almost no research in urban ecology or human ecology in general has been done elsewhere. One of the first discoveries made in urban ecology was that cities show certain patterns in their growth and the distribution of their populations and facilities.

Ernest W. Burgess, a well-known sociologist in the United States, made a pioneering contribution to urban ecology in 1925. In that year, Burgess set forth the "Concentric Circle Theory of City Zones" in an effort to describe the formation of a city.[7] This theory, which was based on observations of Chicago, has now become a classic part of urban sociology and so will be examined in detail.

According to the "Concentric Circle Theory of City Zones," westernized cities tend to develop in a pattern of concentric, circular zones. This means that a city has a sort of pattern like an archery or rifle target if viewed from above. The diagram found in this chapter is the usual way of depicting this theoretical pattern. However, Burgess also realized that no city is a perfect example of this pattern. The effects of the geographic setting of a city such as the topographical features of hills, rivers, valleys and plateaus may greatly alter the ecological pattern of a city. The human works such as canals, highways, bridges, and railroads may have an additional effect. Therefore we never find a "100% pure" demonstration of this theory in any existing city.

Remember that this theory is *not* a recommendation for the formation of a city but is only an attempt to describe the city. We shall now describe each of these circular zones of the city in turn, going outward from the center of the city.

Zone I:

This is called the *Central Business District* or the *Loop*. The word Loop is taken from certain cities, particularly

---

[7] E. W. Burgess: "The Growth of the City" in Park, R. E. and Burgess, E. W., *The City*. 1925.

Chicago, where the buses and streetcars make a circle or loop in the downtown area. This zone usually has certain distinct characteristics. It ordinarily has the highest land values and the highest rents of the whole city. One also finds large office buildings and some hotels in this area. Specialized stores such as those selling jewelry and luggage ordinarily cluster there as well.

The large department stores are traditionally located in this zone along with these other facilities. In and around this area are also found banks, exclusive restaurants, the higher priced theaters, and some government offices. This central business district has the greatest daily movement of people in the city. Everyday hundreds of workers and shoppers come and go in the area. In Manila the central business district would center on the Escolta, but also include the areas around Plaza Goiti and Plaza Moraga.

Zone II:

This is titled the *Zone in Transition*. This name is applied because it is typically an older residential area which is now "in transition," or on the way to becoming a business district. This zone is characterized by the second highest land values in the city, but some of the lowest rents. One usually finds that this zone has manufacturing establishments which are mixed in with old, dilapidated dwellings. Boarding houses are often found on the outer edges of this zone where it meets Zone III.

The population of the Zone in Transition also usually has some distinctive traits. Newcomers to the city and single persons who are away from home often reside there. Thus Zone II often has wanderers, homeless old people, and non-comformists of all sorts. This area is also usually the home of immigrant groups who desire a low rent area where they can follow their homeland customs without interference. Because of the changing character of the area and the resulting lack of a unified social atmosphere the Zone in Transition is traditionally the center of disorganization. Thus we find that the highest rates of crime, disease, and

Chapter XI. THE URBAN COMMUNITY

social breakdown are in this area. The districts in Manila which are closest to this pattern are Binondo and San Nicolas.

Zone III:

For want of a better name this area is called the *Zone of Workingmen's Homes*. The land values and rents in this area are fairly moderate. There is often found a patterns of multiple-family dwellings such as duplexes and apartments. Many times these dwellings have been remodelled from older structures which were former single-family homes. Most of the residents of this area are renters rather than owners of property.

In this zone are usually local markets and business centers which have such establishments as bakeries, pharmacies, cafes, hardware stores, and special grocery stores. The residents of this area are generally low-salaried workers who want to live near to their place of employment in a low rent area but one which is better than Zone II. In contrast to Zone II, we find that Zone III has more stability and emphasis on family life. In Manila the districts of Sampaloc, Paco, Pandacan, and Sta. Cruz are fairly close to this pattern.

Zone IV:

This area is designated as the *Residential Zone*. Here are found rent and land values which are fairly high. The dwellings of this zone are frequently either the more elaborate sort of apartments or else large single-family homes. In this Residential Zone there is generally a high proportion of home ownership. The residents of this area are usually persons of considerable means who are willing and able to pay the higher rates of rent and land purchase. This area offers the advantages of having newer and better facilities, less crowding, and yet being still quite close to the central facilities of the city. The rates of crime, disease, and social disorganization are generally low. The districts of Malate, Ermita, and Santa Ana plus other neighborhood areas near the Manila city boundaries would be included in such a category as Zone IV.

Zone V:

This area is entitled the *Commuter's Zone*. It stretches outward from the city boundaries. The outer limit of this zone is usually calculated as being the distance covered in one hour's ride from the center of the city. This naturally means that, if the transportation system is well-developed, this Zone V will be very large. On the other hand, if the transportation system is not well developed, the zone will be small.

In Zone V we find small cities, towns, and villages which are linked to the central city in a social-economic relationship. The land and rent values are usually lower than those of Zone IV. The residents of this area are usually office workers, businessmen, and professionals who travel to the central city for work every morning and return every evening. These people obtain the advantages of being in a newer, less crowded and less expensive area; but they also face the difficulties of being far away from many conveniences and facilities. The growth of the Zone V area has been a striking aspect of the Manila region since World War II. We now find such enters as Cavite, Grace Park, Quezon City, Pasig, Marikina, and San Juan del Monte appearing as important suburban centers of this type.

This completes the description of the urban ecological structure as set forth by Burgess. However it must be remembered that this theory of city zones was developed for westernized cities. Therefore it seems to apply best to the modern industrial type of city. In cities such as Manila there are many districts where this scheme does not apply. For example, we often see in Manila a different type of residential pattern. In some of the districts there occurs a mixture of large elaborate homes together with small humble dwellings of nipa, sawali, or thin lumber. In fact, these very different structures might be located beside each other. Mexico City is also said to have this pattern of residence.[8] This pattern is a great contrast to the theory of

---

[8] Norman S. Hayner: Mexico City: "Its Growth and Configuration," *American Journal of Sociology*, Vol. 50, Jan. 1943, pp. 295-304.

CHAPTER XI. THE URBAN COMMUNITY 281

Burgess which is based on the idea of similar structures and peoples grouped together. So we find that there are definite limitations on the application of this theory. As a result, other sociologists have proposed certain additions and corrections for this theory. However, it must be recognized that this theory still is useful as general, fundamental view of the urban ecological structure.

The Urban Ecological Processes

Sociologists have noticed that certain general processes could be observed in human ecology and so they applied them to the study of the urban community. Although these processes have been named and described, it should be realized that they are also generalized descriptions. Therefore, just as in the case of the concentric city zones, it is difficult to cite any specific examples which are a perfect illustration of these processes. The processes and their description follow below.[9]

1. Concentration

This refers to the increase of a *population* at certain geographic centers. This is the basic process found in the growth of towns and cities.

2. Centralization

This is defined as the clustering of certain specialized *institutions* and *facilities* at centers of transportation and communication. In every large city this process is very evident. For example, in Manila we have a centralization of banks around Plaza Moraga and a clustering of theaters along Rizal Avenue near Plaza Goiti and along Quezon Boulevard in the Quiapo area.

3. Decentralization

This refers to the opposite tendency for some institutions and facilities to follow the outward growth of a city. Good

---

[9] These processes were first fully described by McKenzie, R. D. in "The Scope of Human Ecology" in *The Urban Community* by Ernest W. Burgess, 1926.

examples of his process are found in the way that certain service establishments such as barbershops, gasoline stations, and cafes follow the spread of the city population. Residential districts also tend to move away from the center of the city.

4. Invasion

This is defined as the entrance of a new population and/or facilities into an occupied area. This is a very common feature in the growth of any modern city. In fact, it seems very likely that invasion is a universal process in the growth and development of all urban communities. Manila offers many classic illustrations of invasion. The central post-office, for instance, is located approximately on the site of a former school. Also as the city of Manila was founded and grew it gradually displaced some fishing settlements along the Pasig River and the coastline of Manila Bay.

5. Succession

This is described as the result of a complete invasion. Succession is generally said to have occured when the *majority* of the population and/or facilities of an area are replaced by the new type. Therefore it is not necessarily a matter of a total change. It should also be added that not all invasions lead to succession. Some invasions die out before they can run their course and become a succession. The examples given for invasion above are also cases of succession since in both instances the change has definitely been accomplished.

These are given as the major ecological processes which influence the growth and development of urban communities. There are others, but these processes are regarded as the chief factors. It is by the operation of these processes and the general influence of the tendency toward the concentric circle pattern of city zones that the modern city develops its specialized sub-areas. Thus these factors in urban ecology are frequently used to explain the rise of the distinctive sections of the city and the changes that they undergo.

CHAPTER XI. THE URBAN COMMUNITY

The Metropolitan Area

In recent years there has been a change in Zone V which has come from two developments, namely: the widespread use of the automobile and the truck, and secondly, the increased use of electric power. This situation encourages the movement of more families and light factories into the commuter's zone. This shift to the suburban areas means that the social-economic ties between the Zone V settlements and the central city are becoming much stronger. Therefore the central city plus the commuter's zone is now viewed as a whole community unit by itself. Thus the terms "Metropolitan Community" or "Metropolitan Area" are often used to describe this new settlement pattern.

This growth of the metropolitan area brings some significant changes to the general urban community. One effect is that the greater spread of the city brings added difficulties in administration. The problems of supplying such services as adequate water, electricity, and police and fire protection are greatly increased. This is particularly true because these suburban settlements are often independent political units and so the central city has no official jurisdiction over them.

The other general effects are an intensification of most of the general traits of urban life. Such a widespread distribution of people and facilities will increase the *gesellschaft* nature of the community life. This will in turn, of course, bring all of the related social features with it. Thus one could hardly expect that the development of the metropolitan area would bring any significant decrease in the disadvantages of urban life.

City planning.

Actually, city planning is nothing new. Many ancient and medieval cities are known to have been planned before their construction. In the more recent periods there have been some famous examples. The first is the remodeling of Paris which was done in the 1860's under Napoleon III by Baron Haussmann. This project centered on that age-old concern of city life—the traffic problem. Some of the great boulevards of Paris were built at that time. Other cities in the European area which had some planning were Edinburgh in Scotland and Mannheim and Karlsruhe in Germany. In the United States two well-known examples of city planning are Philadelphia and Washington, D.C. William Penn laid out Philadelphia in 1682 while L'Enfant came over from France to design Washington in 1791.

However, the basic theory of city planning has shifted a great deal in the more recent times. The planners now emphasize a long-range planning which tries to anticipate future changes. Thus the plans must now be both well-designed and flexible. This relatively recent trend is generally dated from the Chicago World's Fair of 1893. At that time Daniel H. Burnham presented the now famous *Chicago Plan*. This effort of Burnham and his associates caused a great surge of interest in city planning which then spread to the Philippines. This brings us to a consideration of how city planning has operated in the Philippine setting.

City planning in the Philippines.

In 1903 Daniel H. Burnham and his assistant Pierce Anderson came to Manila on request. After one year had passed a plan was proposed for the remodeling of Manila. The main features of this plan included the following:

1. Development of waterfront parks and parkways. Dewey Boulevard is the outgrowth of this idea.
2. Construction of certain main thoroughfares through the city to speed communication.
3. Construction of a given area for public buildings.
4. Improvement of harbor, river and shore areas.
5. Development of resort areas in areas near Manila such as Tagaytay.

These recommendations of Burnham have so far been partially carried out in Manila, so that the plan did have

CHAPTER XI. THE URBAN COMMUNITY 285

some effect. Another planning effort of Burnham in the Philippines concerned the basic planning for Baguio City. Burnham Park in Baguio stands as a tribute to this pioneer in modern city planning.

In the succeeding years the Philippines has generally maintained its interest in city planning. The Bureau of Public Works was responsible for town and city planning for sometime. In the post-World War II period the National Urban Planning Commission was formed to continue the effort. Thus there has been a fairly continuous development of city planning in the Philippines.

Recent trends in city planning.

One of the most noticeable traits of modern city planning is the wide range which it attempts to cover. Thus an ordinary plan for an urban community today is expected to include plans for:

1. The regulation of traffic and transportation means such as railway tracks, stations, and routes; streetcar and bus lines; airlines, highways; waterways.

2. Regulating the types, patterns, and uses of streets.

3. Designating and restricting land and building use.

4. The design and construction of private and public buildings.

5. Recreational facilities such as parks and playgrounds.

6. Financial arrangements such as bonds and assessments.

7. Public services such as water, waste disposal, and utilities.

Such a detailed regulation of the urban community has now become essential if cities are to be both healthful and efficient with the effects of rapid growth and modern technology. Actually, most of the difficulties of urban life stem from the basic factor of the over-concentration of large numbers of people. Thus the city planner's problems and the general urban problems are all related to such questions as health, housing, and traffic which must always be faced in any large, growing urban center.

The growth of the metropolitan area has now also multiplied and complicated the problems of city planning. The recent trend is now to plan for a metropolitan region rather than just for an isolated city. Thus not only the functions but the actual geographic area of city planning has been increased.

In conclusion it should be noted that effective city planning rests upon certain absolute essentials. These are that the planning must be continuous, based on adequate research, and cover an area which is significant and inclusive and yet still small enough to be workable. Then the last but perhaps most important essential is that the plan must be implemented or applied. It is unfortunate but true that there are many splendid city plans which are never used or followed but are only set aside to gather dust.

Summary

The rise of great cities is a relatively recent occurrence. The Industrial Revolution which brought changes in technology is generally regarded as the turning point in urban history. Thus today the improvements in such fields as transportation and food storage have fostered the growth of cities which have populations exceeding one million.

This growth of urban communities has also brought the development of certain special patterns of life in the cities. So we find that the urban centers possess distinctive characteristics in regard to their populations, institutions, social organization, and culture. Most of the prominent urban traits are summarized in the descriptive term *gesellschaft*, which refers to an impersonal, complex type of community life.

Since the city has always been a center of social change and variety, we find that cultural inconsistencies and conflicts are common there. This great urban diversity of peoples and culture patterns often leads to problems of individual and group adjustment. Some of these difficulties

Chapter XI. THE URBAN COMMUNITY

are probably preventable, but others stem from the very nature of urban life itself and so are unavoidable.

The great increase of cities means also that the urban way of life will have a greater influence on the life of nations. Thus the urban attitudes and values may come to predominate in most countries of the world. Viewing this trend objectively, one may see two different roles of the urban centers. On one hand, the cities may act as disrupting or disturbing elements in the social heritage of a nation because of their function as centers of change. On the other hand, however, the cities also may act as the innovators of newer culture patterns which improve the social organization.

In addition to the social traits of the urban community there is also the ecological aspect. Cities are said to develop in certain characteristic spatial patterns. Thus human ecologists have set forth certain theories about the urban ecological structure and processes. These theories are additional aids in understanding and interpreting the nature of the urban community.

Recent trends in urban life show some distinct patterns. The most significant development of recent times is the rise of the metropolitan area. This outward expansion of the city has brought new patterns of living and the necessity of making new adjustments. One of the chief techniques of readjustment in urban life today is the use of city planning. By means of city planning cities hope to reshape the urban area to provide for better living. The chief handicap in this effort at city planning is the difficulty in getting the plans actually implemented. Thus the technical problems of planning are also linked to problems of statemanship. ship.

Some writers even mention the possibility that cities as we now know them may eventually disappear. This idea rests upon the assumption that we are still experimenting with city life. Therefore, our final results as the experimenting and planning advance, may be greatly different. In any case, it is certain that the increased complexity of modern urban life does require some fresh thinking and planning, otherwise the future city may become an expensive and inefficient bedlam of social and technical development which is not in harmony with human needs.

QUESTIONS

1. Why were cities before the Industrial Revolution generally under one million population?
2. Why are cities regarded as so important in the present social system?
3. What is the significance of urbanization in the modern world?
4. What are the causes of the impersonal relationships which prevail in urban life?
5. What are the typical characteristics of the average urban family?
6. Is urban life better or worse than rural life? How much does ethnocentrism influence your answer?
7. What are the special features of the urban population in such traits as age, sex, and marital status?
8. What is the difference between invasion and succession: between centralization and concentration?
9. What are the names and characteristics of the five zones which Burgess described?
10. Why does it seem easier to observe the ecological processes at work in the urban community than in the rural community?
11. Are slums an inevitable accompaniment of urban growth?
12. How may decentralization affect the problems of urban adjustment in the future?
13. Is there any evidence that the area in which you live is becoming part of a metropolitan area?
14. What problems of urban life are unavoidable? What urban problems can be remedied?
15. What is meant by saying that the urban dwellers' life is often "compartmentalized" or "fractional"?

CHAPTER XI. THE URBAN COMMUNITY 289

PROJECTS

1. Describe an example of one of the ecological processes such as an invasion which you have either observed or read about.

2. Write a comparison of a rural family to the life pattern of an urban family. Use examples and illustrations from your own experiences.

3. If you know of some persons who migrated to the urban centers, try to discover their reasons for doing so. What are their reactions to the urban environment? Do they want to remain in the city? Why?

4. Make two comparison lists showing the disadvantages and advantages of urban life.

SUGGESTED READINGS

Burgess, Ernest W. Editor: *The Urban Community*, University of Chicago Press, Chicago, 1926.
This is composed of a series of short articles on special aspects of the city. It furnishes both a fresh perspective on city life and theoretical possibilities for research.

Gist, Noel P. and L. A. Halbert: *Urban Society*, Third Edition, Thomas Y. Crowell Company, New York, 1948.
One of the standard texts on the subject which contains some of the most careful documentation of the various facts of urban life.

McKenzie, R. D.: *The Metropolitan Community*, McGraw-Hill Company, New York, 1933.
The most comprehensive and systematic study available of the rise, structure, and problems of the total functional area dominated by the large city.

Mumford, Lewis: *The Culture of Cities*, Harcourt, Brace, New York, 1938.
An original and stimulating book on the modern city and human living. It is written from a general rather than strictly sociological point of view and endeavors to show the unfavorable aspects of modern metropolitan living.

Park, Robert E., Ernest W. Burgess, and R. D. McKenzie: *The City*, University of Chicago Press, Chicago, 1925.
A series of essays on the possibilities of ecological studies, with special reference to the city of Chicago. This early classic in urban ecology has stimulated a whole series of concrete research projects in this field, and is still valuable for anyone having a special interest in the subject.

CHAPTER TWELVE

POPULATION GROWTH AND DISTRIBUTION

"A given population phenomenon may or may not be considered a problem... A large family under one condition of living may be viewed as an undesirable thing; in another culture, it may be looked upon as highly desirable, involving no problem whatever. 'Multiply and replenish the earth' is the motto of one age; 'check increase or live in misery,' the stark alternative set forth in another. Among one people abortion may be practiced without any sense of moral guilt; among others it is considered a social evil and/or a crime. Rapid growth in a population may be looked upon with optimism or, on the contrary, it may be viewed with foreboding. Immigration was encouraged for many years in the United States; it became a problem when the public began to consider it a threat to general welfare."

— Paul H. Landis, *Population Problems*, New York; American Book Company, 1943, pp. 6-7.

Population has long been a topic of interest in human society, but it has only been possible to analyze populations with any exactness with the widespread adoption of the general population census. At the present time, with a general amount of available data, the analysis of population has become a special field of study. However, even today there are many areas of the world where a complete population census is not taken. Thus the analysis of population at present is limited to those nations where records of population data are maintained. Usually it is the industrial-commercial nations with a *gesellschaft* type of culture which place the most emphasis on careful census-taking and the accurate recording of such data as births, deaths, and marriages. In the rural *damay* type of societies,

CHAPTER XII. POPULATION

the people in general seem to have less appreciation of and need for such records.[1] Now since any analysis is only as good as its basic data, the student of population is also often handicapped by certain errors and omissions which frequently occur in the collection of population data.[2] This means that although much has already been done in this field, there is still much more which remains to be accomplished. In sociology an attempt is made to analyze the biological facts of population and to view them in regard to their social meaning. Thus population is considered as both an influence on society and also as a phenomena which is subject to social influence. The following pages will endeavor to present population data within this frame of reference.

Population growth.

The population of the world has been growing at a gradually increasing rate. During the last three centuries the world population has increased four-fold (400%), while in the last century the world population has doubled. These rates are based on the estimates of world population as being one-half billion in 1650 and almost two and one-half billion in 1950. This sort of rapid increase seems to be unusual in the history of human civilization, however. All available estimates indicate that prior to about 1650 the world population fluctuated a great deal and so showed a slow, irregular rate of growth.[3] This suggests that perhaps this present rapid rate of increase is only a temporary spurt

---

[1] Amos H. Hawley: *Human Ecology*, Ronald Press, New York, 1950, p. 92.

[2] This is especially true for the population data concerning isolated rural regions. In the United States, for example, certain discrepancies have been noted in the age records for the rural states of the south. (See Paul H. Landis, *Population Problems*, New York, 1943, p. 286). Several investigators have remarked that the same difficulties appear to operate in similar portions of the census of the Philippines. See Amos H. Hawley, "The Philippine Census of 1948" in *Papers in Demography and Public Administration*, Institute of Public Administration, University of the Philippines, January 1954 for a penetrating analysis of the difficulties prevailing in the 1948 Census.

[3] Warren Thompson: *Plenty of People*, Ronald Press, New York, 1948, p. 23.

which will subside in later centuries. However, although this increase has a certain theoretical interest, the growth of population in specific areas of the world is of more practical concern.

In any given part of the world there are two general ways in which population can grow. The first way is by migration, which would refer to the entrance of new-comers in an area. The effect of migration can often be of great importance. For instance, in the chapter on the urban community it was noted that most cities grow more by migration than by other means.

The other way for population to grow is by natural increase, which is defined as the excess of births over deaths. For example, if a barrio had 100 births and 75 deaths in a year then the natural increase for that period would be 25. This means that a large number of births would not always bring population growth, for the deaths may equal or exceed the births. The only way that the world population is growing is by natural increase of course, since there are not as yet any interplanetary migrations to the earth from such places as Mars.

Some writers have further classified the various factors which restrict the natural increase. The following categories are often used.

1. Limiting Factors in the Natural Environment
    A. Sickness
    B. Disasters (flood, fires, earthquakes, etc.)
2. Socially Related Factors
    A. Restrictions on Reproduction
        a. Sex Taboos
        b. Contraception (Birth Control)
        c. Celibacy
        d. Legal Restrictions on marriage
    B. Reduction of the Living
        a. Wars
        b. Infanticide
        c. Abortion
        d. Executions

CHAPTER XII. POPULATION

The various socially related factors have operated with different degrees of influence according to the time, place, and culture. Thus wars have greatly reduced some primitive peoples whereas celibacy had a great effect in Ireland and contraception has had a noticeable effect in certain cities of Europe and North America.

For these reasons population almost never grows at its maximum rate. If the world population all other forms of life and occupy every available piece of land. As it is, we find that in many areas of the world there have been groups which apparently had little, if any, natural increase until modern times. In fact there are some dramatic cases where a tremendous natural *decrease* was experienced, as in Europe during the great plagues for example.[4]

Population growth and culture.

As the reader will notice, the greater part of the factors which limit population increase are the *socially* related influences. This point is given particular emphasis by the sociologist. This point is given particular emphasis by the sociologist. Thus we see that for one thing, the physical equipment of the human species has changed little since the appearance of *homo sapiens*. Also the geographic environment has not undergone any tremendous alteration in a way which would affect the growth of population. This means that culture more than anything else influences the growth or decline of a population. It is true that population growth is a biological fact, but it is a process which is *culturally controlled* and which in turn can have profound effects on a culture. This has led population analysts to regard population changes as one of the most useful indicators of social change.[5]

Perhaps the most obvious relationship between population and culture is found in the economy of a society. It is commonly observed that a growing population brings

---

[4] Warren Thompson: *Plenty of People*, Ronald Press, New York, 1948, pp. 63-66.

[5] Amos H. Hawley: *Human Ecology*, Ronald Press, New York, 1950, pp. 78 and 104.

a demand for an expansion in the economy of that area. Now if the economy is capable of expansion and the people possess the knowledge necessary for such development, the society may experience a period of great prosperity. However, on the other hand, if the population grows and the resources are not capable of expansion and/or the people do not know how to develop the economy, this increase of population may only lead to the development of serious problems.[6]

The question of what cultural factors have caused the rapid growth of world population since 1650 naturally follows from the preceding discussion. Warren Thompson presents an answer which is perhaps the most concise and adequate given anywhere.

> In the writer's opinion the fundamental factors in bringing about the unprecedented growth of population in the last two and a half centuries have been the development of science, i.e., knowledge, and the application of this knowledge to the practical problems of production and health.[7]

This, of course, again points out the fact that cultural factors, more than anything else, account for changes in populations. The development of science is a part of human culture, and the application of it is a matter of change in the folkways and mores.

Now let us examine the population growth of the Philippines and the cultural factors which have influenced it.

Philippine population growth.

Population growth in the Philippines shows an intimate relationship to the general patterns of population increase in all of South East Asia. This general pattern is related to the particular direction and order of culture change in

---

[6] The above discussion is largely drawn from Thompson, *op. cit.*, Chapter 10 and 11 *passim*.

[7] Warren S. Thompson, "The Growth of Population" in O'Brien, Shrag, and Martin, *Readings in Feneral Sociology*, Houghton Mifflin Company, New York, 1951, p. 201.

Chapter XII. POPULATION

that area.[8] In Europe and in other Western nations, the invention and application of better food-producing devices entered the culture at the same time that more lives were being saved by modern health measures. Thus the greater number of people were readily cared for by increased food production. However, in South East Asia, this parallel advance of food production and measures for extending and preserving life did not occur. Instead, South East Asia still retains an economy which has a non-industrial, peasant type of agriculture with a typical low food production. Hence, the economy of South East Asia has thus far not been expanded to meet the needs of its rapidly growing population.

Thus modern medicine and health measures came in but the rest of the culture remained unchanged. This was possible because as Hawley remarks:

> It is a peculiarity of mortality that sharp reductions can be achieved by relatively simple, externally applied, and non-controversial methods withuot immediately disturbing the *status quo* in other sectors of society. And while the death rate is systematically lowered, the birth rate continues at its characteristically high level for a generation or more after mortality decline begins.[9]

This means that the rapid introduction of medicine could and did reduce death rates in South East Asia dramatically. However, at the same time, the pre-modern *damay* culture with its emphasis on familism and an accompanying large number of children remained undisturbed. As a result the population of South East Asia grew at a rapid rate. This, of course, is a *cultural* condition, hence the rapid

---

[8] The writer is greatly indebted to Dr. Irene Taeuber for the ideas used in the following analysis. Dr. Taeuber presented this material in the Eighth Pacific Science Congress, Manila, November, 1953 in a paper titled "Population Growth in the Western Pacific: The New Demographic Revolution."

[9] Amos H. Hawley, "Demographic Factors in Public Administration" in *Papers in Demography and Public Administration*, Institute of Public Administration, University of the Philippines, Manila, January, 1954, page 8.

population growth of South East Asia can not be properly understood unless one takes the social setting into account.

The Philippines has shared in this general experience of South East Asia. The Spanish introduced smallpox vaccination to the Philippines and so began to halt the ancient plague which formerly had devasted the islands so often. This was followed by the American efforts to install modern sanitation equipment and pure drinking water systems. Modern medicine was brought in along with the construction of hospitals and clinics. This work has been continued by various private and government agencies up to the present. The results of such efforts have been of the same general pattern that occurred in all of South East Asia. The Philippine death rate dropped abruptly while the birth rate remained relatively high. This means, therefore, that the Philippines now has in common with most of the rest of South East Asia a "Western death rate and an Eastern birth rate," to use the expression of Dr. Taeuber. Now let us turn to the specific data on these developments in the Philippines.

The Philippine Birth Rate

The usual manner of analyzing births is to view them in terms of the crude birth rate. The crude birth rate is defined as the number of births per 1,000 population during a given time period. Hence a barrio with a population of 2,000 which has 20 births in a year would have a crude birth rate will merely be referred to as the "birth rate."

A general survey of the population data in the Philippines shows that there has been a gradual decline in the birth rate. The highest general period occurred between 1876-1898 when the average rate was 47.9. The peak was reached in 1885-1887 when the birth rate rose to 51.2.[10]

---

[10] Serafin E. Macaraig: *Introduction to Sociology*, Revised Edition, 1948, pp. 177-178.

Chapter XII. POPULATION

Since that time the birth rate has been considerably lower. This can be seen from the following selected years.

Table 1. Philippine Birth Rate in Certain Selected Years.*

Year	Rate
1920	34.50
1925	33.99
1930	32.78
1935	31.32
1940	32.28
1946	28.50
1951	30.85

Yearbook of Philippine Statistics, 1940 and Bureau of Census and Statistics files.

However, although the Philippine birth rate shows a gradual drop, it is still a great deal higher than that of many European or North American countries.

In fact, it is possible that the Philippine birth rate may be even higher than the table indicates. It has been pointed out that in a rural nation such as the Philippines there is frequently an under-registration of births. Even in the industrial countries this is a problem and Thompson points out that population analysts discovered certain discrepancies in the birth registration in the United States.[11] The Philippine birth rate may be actually be closer to 35 than 30.[12] In the following table, the Philippine is exceeded only by Chile, Ceylon, Puerto Rico, and Mexico in birth rate.

---

[11] Warren Thompson, *Plenty of People*, op. cit.
[12] Amos H. Hawley, *Papers in Demography and Public Administration*, op. cit., 8.

Table 2. The Birth Rate in Certain Selected Populations for the Period 1938-1947 *

Country	Rate
Belgium	15.3
France	16.0
United Kingdom	16.7
Sweden	17.8
Switzerland	17.9
Austria	18.0
United States	20.3
Ireland	21.1
Spain	21.2
Italy	21.5
New Zealand	21.8
Bulgaria	22.8
Japan	28.4
India	29.5
Philippines	30.8
Chile	33.0
Ceylon	37.3
Puerto Rico	40.2
Mexico	44.5

* Ogburn and Nimkoff, *op. cit.*, Table 17, p. 335. Philippine birth rate for that period is calculated from the *Yearbook of Philippine Statistics* 1940 and data in the files of the Bureau of Census and Statistics.

Culture and the Birth Rate

In this case the sociologists again emphasize the social aspects of population. The three cultural factors of most importance which seem to affect the birth rate of any given group are:

1. Attitudes which come as a reaction to a particular economic situation.

2. Attitudes which come from individual whims and psychological makeup.

3. Attitudes which are related to the "climate of opinion" which in turn is shaped by tradition and fashion.

Chapter XII. POPULATION

In general, it has been observed that the attitudes and resulting behaviour which favor a high birth rate are ordinarily found in a *damay* type of culture. On the other hand, the attitudes and resulting behaviour which favor a low birth rate are usually present in a *gesellschaft* sort of society.

Thus a *damay* group with a rural economy, little emphasis on formal education, and a general acceptance of what fate has in store accordingly favors a large family size. The urbanized *gesellschaft* type of society favors the effort to control every aspect of the environment including the size of the family. It seems to be equally difficult to introduce contraception in the *damay* setting or to oppose contraception in the *gesellschaft*. We have already noted that the culture of the Philippines is primarily of the *damay* type. Thus in the Philippines we find an emphasis on familism and hence a relatively higher birth rate. Two specific types of behavior observable in most *damay* cultures and also in the Philippines are early marriage and little use of contraception, (birth control).

According to a very limited sample study, the median age of marriage in the Philippines is approximately 20 for women and 23 for men.[13] For most of the industrialized nations of Europe and North America the median age of marriage is somewhat higher. For example, the median age of marriage in the United States during 1940 was 21.6 for women and 24.3 for men.[14] The chances of having more children are, of course, increased with an early age of marriage. The English scientist Galton estimated that a woman who marries at the age of 18 is likely to have twice as many children as one who marries at the age of 28.[15]

---

[13] Calculated from the *Journal of Philippine Statistics*, Vol. V, No. 9, pp. 2-5.
[14] Meyer F. Nimkoff: *Marriage and the Family*, New York, 1947, p. 460.
[15] Quote in Landis, *op. cit.*, pp. 64-65 from Davis, Barnes, and others, *An Introduction to Sociolog*, p. 351

The limited use of contraception in the Philippines may be partially due to ignorance of it, but probably is mostly due to a genuine desire for large families. Although there is much argument about the reduction of family size on political or religious grounds, the evidence indicates that neither governments nor churches have as much influence as does culture on this phenomenon. For instance in Table Two, you will note that Catholic Belgium has a lower birth rate than Protestant New Zealand. In Japan, a government campaign in favor of "birth control" has made little progress although there is no organized opposition of any consequence. In the United States, on the other hand, Catholic clergy have not been able to keep their flocks from the general urban trend toward smaller families. However, as noted, a small family size may be obtained by several means, and contraception is only one of them.

The Philippine Death Rate

Although the Philippines has had a generally high birth rate the amount of natural increase has been fairly low until more recent times. This is explained by the fact that formerly the Philippines also had an extremely high death rate. In this discussion we shall also use the crude rate for deaths, that is, the number of deaths per 1,000 population for a given time period. Between the years of 1876 to 1898 the average death rate was 39.7. The highest level was reached in 1879 when the death rate rose to 106.3 because of a cholera epidemic. It is estimated that 400,000 people died in that period.. The highest point reached in this century came in 1903 when the death rate was about 50.[16] Thus the Philippine birth rate was nearly equalled by the death rate in the atter part of the 19th century. This condition is usually the case in a country which is relatively untouched by modern influences. There is apparently established a sort of natural balance in such a situation. The technical term for this type of balance is "equilibrium."

---

[16] Macaraig, op. cit., pp. 181-182.

As following figures indicate, the Philippine death rate has shown quite a steady decline since the World War 1 era.

Table 3. Philippine Death Rate in Certain Selected Years. *

Year	Death Rate
1918	36.63
1920	19.68
1925	18.11
1930	19.32
1935	17.46
1940	16.50
1946	16.27
1951	11.56

* *Yearbook of Philippine Statistics*, 1940 and Bureau of Census and Statistics files.

Since 1924 the death rate has been below 20, and since 1946 the rate has been below 15. However, again the under-registration of deaths in a rural society such as the Philippines may influence the above data. Hence it is estimated that there was a 14.4% under registration of deaths for the years 1918 to 1939 in the Philippines. This would mean that the Philippine death rate may actually be closer to 17 than the lower figure.[17] Even so, the decline in the death rate has altered the position of the Philippines in comparison with the rates of other nations. As Macaraig so aptly described it, in the 1930's the Philippines had a semi-Occidental death rate.[18] However, today the death rate of the Philippines is apparently approaching that of the United States. Since 1921 the death rate of the United States has fluctuated between 10 and 12.[19] This of course emphasizes the fact that when a certain level is attained, it becomes extremely hard to decrease the death rate any further. This is because

---
[17] Amos H. Hawley, *Papers in Demography and Public Administration*, op. cit., pp. 20-23.
[18] Macaraig, *op. cit.*, p. 182.
[19] Landis, *op. cit.*, p. 185.

the first gains are made by reducing infant mortality, but further gains can only be obtained by decreasing the adult death rate, which is a more difficult task.

This striking drop in the death rate of the Philippines has been largely accomplished through the use of modern medical and sanitation measures. This means that the increase of population in the Philippines has been due to a lowering of the death rate rather than an increase of the birth rate. This also explains why it is that some countries can still show a great natural increase although their birth rates have shown a sharp decline. The following table and chart shows the population growth of the Philippines. As one may note, the results of the lowered death rate in recent times are quite evident.

Table 4. Population Growth in the Philippines

Year	Number
1800	1,561,251
1845	3,488,258
1903	7,635,426
1918	10,314,310
1939	16,000,303
1948	19,234,182*

* Hawley estimates that the actual population in 1948 was probably closer to 18 million. See *Papers in Demography*, pp. 25-26.

Philippine life expectancy

The reduction of the death rate through the use of modern medical and sanitation methods has also brought an increase in the length of life. The usual way of expressing the length of life is in terms of the "complete life expectancy," or it is often called simply the life expectancy. Th meaning of life expectancy is the number of years which the average person at birth can expect to live.

Research on the expectation of life in different times and places shows a considerable variation. Although the data are frequently not accurate, the approximate figures are nevertheless enlightening. For example, an ancient

CHAPTER XII. POPULATION 303

Rome the estimated life expectancy was 22 years. Thus the old adage of "a short life and a merry one" surely would apply to those times! During the Middle Ages the life expectancy rose to a point somewhere between 30 and 35 depending on the particular area.

As one may note in the accompanying tables, life expectancy has shown a striking rise since the turn of the century. Yet, despite the great strides that have been taken, the life expectancy of the average Filipino today is still considerably less than for the inhabitants of European and North American nations.

Table 5. Rise of Life Expectancy in the Philippines and the United States.*

Year	Philippines	United States
1900-1902	17.91	49.2
1918-1920	26.59	55
1938-1940	46.19	63.8
1948-1950	50 + (approximate)	67

* Sources: For the Philippines by years; 1902 and 1918, "Life Expectancy in the Philippines in 1902 and 1918" by A. G. Sison, H. Lara, M. M. Herbosa and A. A. Lozano, Institute of Hygiene, University of the Philippines. This manuscript is in the files of the demography division of the Bureau of Census.

1938, "Statistical Application of the 1938 Philippine Life Table" by Dr. T. J. Jaramillo. This manuscript is also filed by the demography division of the Bureau of Census.

1948, An estimate made from some preliminary calculations of Dr. Eliseo Perez, Jr., the chief of the Demography Division, Bureau of Census and Statistics.

Landis, op. cit., pp. 314-319.

Ogburn and Nimkoff, op. cit., pp. 340-341.

Statistical Bulletin of the Metropolitan Life Insurance Company, Volume 31, No. 10, October, 1950, pp. 2-3.

Table 6. World Life Expectancy *

Country	Period	Expectancy of life at birth
New Zealand	1931	65.4
Netherlands	1931—1935	65.1
United States (white)	1940	63.8
Norway	1921—1930	61.0
Germany	1932—1934	60.0
Austria	1930—1933	54.5
Philippines	1938	46.2
Bulgaria	1925—1928	46.0
Japan	1926—1930	49.0
U.S.S.R. (Europe)	1926—1927	42.0
U.S.S.R. (Siberia)	1926—1927	39.2
British India	1921—1930	27.0

* All figures except that of the Philippines, taken from Landis, op. cit., p. 218.

For Philippines: "Statistical Application of the 1938 Philippine Life Table" by Dr. T. J. Jaramillo. This manuscript is filed by the Demography Division of the Bureau of Census and Statistics.

Since the Philippines has shown such a rapid extension of the life expectancy in the last half-century, and the medical facilities are constantly improving, it is reasonable to assume that the Philippine life expectancy will continue to rise until it is similar to that of the technologically advanced nations. However, we could not expect an indefinite continuation in the length of life. Although it may be theoretically possible to elevate the life expectancy to 100 years, some believe that an increase of much over 75 is doubtful.[20]

The Distribution of Population

In the world as a whole, it is found that population is distributed unevenly. The most densely settled parts of the world are in Southern Asia, Europe, and the eastern United States. Those world areas which have a low density

---
[20] Amos H. Hawley: *Human Ecology*, op. cit., pp. 113-114.
Warren Thompson: *Plenty of People*, op. cit., pp. 76-77.

CHAPTER XII. POPULATION 305

of population are northern Asia, Canada, Africa, South America, Australia, and the western United States. The following table compares the distribution of the world's population for two different periods. It will be observed that some continents have shifted noticeably in relative position.

Table 7. World's Population by Continents,
1650 and 1947, by Percentage
Distributions.*

Continent	1650	1947
Europe	18.3	23.2
North America	1.2	8.9
South America	1.2	4.5
Oceania	.4	.5
Africa	18.3	8.1
Asia	60.6	54.8

* Taken from Ogburn and Nimkoff, *op. cit.*, p. 306.

It is generally held that the two particular elements which lead to any given pattern of population distribution are the natural environment and human culture. Writers accordingly have observed that the areas where the world population has concentrated are ordinarily also places where transportation, technology and resources have permitted a better living for more people than would be possible elsewhere. Now let us turn to the various aspects of population distribution as they are seen in the Philippines and elsewhere.

Distribution of Population in the Philippines

A rapid survey of the distribution of population in the Philippines reveals two general areas of concentration, namely, the lowlands of Luzon especially in the vicinity of Manila, and the Central Visayas. The areas of least population density are generally the provinces of Mindanao, the more inaccessible sections of Luzon, and two undeveloped islands (Palawan and Mindoro). The specific areas of greatest and least population density are indicated by province in the following chart:

Taking the three general divisions of the Philippines, the estimates for 1948 show the greatest density in the Visayas. "...in the Luzon division, there are 81 persons per square kilometer; in the Visayas, 85 persons; and in Mindanao and Sulu (with Palawan), 30."[21] Perhaps a

---

[21] The President's Action Committee on Social Amelioration Assisted by United Nations Consultants, *Philippine Social Trends*, Manila, 1950, p. 17.

comparison of two areas would be a better illustration of this pattern of population distribution. In 1948 the five provinces of Cavite, Laguna, Batangas, Rizal, and Quezon contained more than 11% of the Philippine population, and yet these provinces comprised only 6.1% of the national land area. On the other hand, Mindanao has almost 1/3 (32%) of the national land area but in 1948 contained only 14.6% of the Philippine population. These figures indicate the variation in the distribution of the Philippine population. Now let us turn to the population movements which influence this pattern of population distribution.

Population Movement

The movement or migration of people is just as important as their increase or decrease in number. As mentioned previously, a particular area in the world may grow in population by either natural increase or migration. However, there is much more significance to population movement than the mere shift of population size. Migration also is frequently accompanied by changes in the physical and cultural character of the population and shifts in the age and sex distribution. These basic alterations can then, of course, bring a whole host of other changes in turn, so that a migration may set off a "chain reaction" as it were. However, although migration may be viewed as a force which brings social change, it is also true that migration itself is a symptom of social change. For example, the groups of people who fled from Europe during periods of political and religious persecution were a clear indication that their homelands were in a social turmoil.

In general there are three basic factors which operate in every migration. These factors have been termed as "push, pull, and transportation." Push refers to whatever conditions exist that make a place unattractive to a group. For instance, a group may leave a place because of adverse geographic conditions such as drought or because of an unfavorable social situation such as war. Pull designates the attractions which draw people to one particular place instead of another. Again, the attractions may be of different sorts such as free land, good climate, or a peaceful and tolerant society. Now let us examine the Philippines in regard to the two general types of population movement, international migration and internal migration.

The sort of international migration which has the most interest for people in the Philippines is immigration. Immigration is defined as the peaceful entry of citizens of foreign countries into a nation for purposes of permanent residence there.[22] The movement of people *out* of a nation is emigration. Both of these movements are included in the general term of migration. In general one may say that large scale immigration to the Philippines is a relatively modern development. Following the lead of Dr. Macaraig, we shall discuss this topic by historical periods.[23]

The Pre-Spanish Era. In the days before the Spanish came to the Philippines, there was apparently very little immigration. (However, one must not forget that the Philippines did have several distinct waves of peoples who came to the Islands from the neighboring regions in ancient times and formed the basis for the present population). Most contacts between the neighboring nations and the Philippines were evidently only those of a loose sort of trading arrangement.

Spanish Era. During this period the only group which came in to the Philippines in significant numbers were the Chinese. In fact, from the Spanish era onward, any discussion of immigration would of necessity focus on the Chinese since they were and are still the most prominent immigrant group to the Philippines.[24] The Spanish had a vacillating policy towards the Chinese. At one period, they admitted them freely on the grounds that they were needed

---

[22] Landis, *op. cit.*, p. 390.
[23] This account is largely based on pp. 190-197 of his text, (1949 edition).
[24] See Victor Purcell: *Chinese in Southeast Asia*, Oxford Press, London, 1950, pp. 569-672, for a detailed account of the Chinese in the Philippines.

Chapter XII. POPULATION

in agriculture. This, of course, was a natural step since Spain was trying to promote the growth of certain crops such as tobacco for export.

However, in 1789 and 1804 most of the Chinese were expelled from the Philippines. The reasons were that the Spaniards did not want any political or commercial rivals in the Islands and began to see the Chinese as entering that position. But, after a while, the former interest of promoting certain crops and international trade became again dominant and so in 1850 the Chinese were again admitted. This then remained the policy of Spain until the American government entered the Philippines.

The American Era. During this era the so-called "Exclusion Act" was applied to the Philippines. This act greatly reduced the numbers of people from Asia (principally Chinese, of course) who could be admitted to the United States or the Philippines. However, the Act did permit the entry of students, teachers, clergymen, traders, and dependents of resident Chinese. So the only ones who were really excluded were unskilled laborers. The number of Chinese in the Philippines in 1940 was estimated at 117,000.

During the American era the immigration of groups other than Chinese was small. The Japanese who came to the Philippines totalled only 20,000 at that time. The primary reasons for this small number of Japanese immigrants seem to be the cultural differences between Japan and the Philippines and the strong attachment which the Japanese are reputed to have for their homeland. The peoples of India and Indonesia were then under Great Britain and the Netherlands, respectively. They were at that time restricted in their entry to the Philippines by both their governing powers and the United States.

The Present Era. Since the Republic of the Philippines was established in 1946, small scale Chinese immigration has continued. There is also now a small influx of peoples from other nations such as India. In 1950 the estimates of the numbers of Chinese in the Philippines ranged from 150,000 to 300,000.[25] However, even if we take the maximum estimate, the proportion of Chinese is still under 2% of the national population. Therefore in numbers the Chinese still constitute a small minority in the population. However, they are the largest foreign population in the Philippines and so are considered as posing certain social problems. Table 9 shows the relative proportions of the alien groups in the Philippines as of 1952.

Table 8. Number of Registered Aliens in The Philippines By Nationality: As of December 31, 1952.*

Nationality	Number
Chinese	150,670
American	13,101
Spanish	2,566
Indian	1,619
British	1,143
German	531
Belgian	298
All Other	2,940
TOTAL	172,868

* Bureau of Immigration, printed in the *Journal of Philippine Statistics*, Volume VI, January-March, 1953. Nos. 1-3, p. 83, Table 66.

In the retail trade of the Philippines the Chinese have had an extremely influential role. The estimates of Chinese participation in the retail trade vary from 40 to 85 per cent.[26] If one takes the median figure of about 65%, it is still a considerable proportion. This predominance of an immigrant group in the retail trade seems to be explained by three factors:

1. Historical events. The Chinese were apparently the first small retail traders here and so have an early start.

---

[25] George H. Weightman: *The Chinese Community in the Philippines*, Unpublished M. A. Thesis, University of the Philippines, 1952, pp. 22-24.
[26] Weightman, *op. cit.*, pp. 73-75.

2. Legal Restrictions. According to Philippine law, Chinese are excluded from the exploitation of natural resources and the owning of such lands as haciendas. Trade then remains the only possible outlet, since the professions and the ranks of unskilled labor are already overcrowded.

3. Selection of Migrants. Traders are one of the most frequently migrating groups. In the Philippines the natural tendency of Chinese businessmen to seek entry was strengthened by the Exclusion Act during the American Era which shut out the unskilled laborers.

Today, with the rising Filipino middle class coming into direct competition with the Chinese retailers, there are many evidences of a greater feeling against the immigrant traders. Judging from experience elsewhere, the conflict could be eased gradually if other occupations were opened for the Chinese group. However, if there is haste on the part of those who would alter the situation, the usual processes of assimilation will probably be disrupted and a more bitter and severe feeling will arise. It seems reasonable to expect that Chinese immigration will be restricted to a small figure. The present legal quota of permanent immigrants is 500 a year, which is swelled by an uncertain amount of illegal entry.

External Migration (Emigration)

Between 1920 and 1930 a fairly large movement took place between the Philippines and the United States with about 50,000 Filipinos going to the mainland of the United States and a somewhat greater number going to Hawaii. This movement was checked by the granting of Independence to the Philippines which reduced the number of quota migrants to 100 per year. Immigration was, however, permitted to Hawaii immediately after World War II, although restrictions were restored shortly afterward.

This migration increased Filipino ties with the U.S. and resulted in a steady flow of dollars coming back to the Philippines. Present American immigration laws have halted this movement, and today there is no pattern of large scale movement out of the Philippines.

Internal Migration

The movement of population from one part of a country to another is called internal migration. The amount and direction of internal migration will naturally have a great effect on the distribution of population within the nation.

In general the two directions of internal migration in the Philippines are toward the cities and toward the South. There is a considerable amount of material which provides some measure of these migration trends. For the movement to the cities we have first of all the figures which show the rapid increase in the size of certain Philippine cities. Thus, as noted in the chapter on urban communities, the rapid growth of such centers as Manila, Cebu, Iloilo, and Bacolod during recent years could hardly be attributed to natural increase alone. Manila, for example, showed an increase of over 60% between 1939 and 1948.

A different approach is that of estimating the movement to a city itself. Manila is the only Philippine city at present for which an analysis is possible. The data for other cities are not yet available. Now if there were no unusual events or migration occuring, one would expect that a city would be composed of nearly equal numbers of males and females in every age groups. However, in 1948 for the age group of 25 to 34 there are 88,622 males and 83,746 females in Manila, a difference of 4,876.[27] This suggests that the migrants to Manila are usually young men. It seems likely that the same pattern would also be true for other Philippine cities, although there is no data available at present.

In connection with this movement of males to the city it is of interest to note the proportions of the two sexes

---

[27] *Journal of Philippine Statistics*, Vol. V, No. 8, Tables 6 and 7, pp. 13-16.

CHAPTER XII. POPULATION

in the provinces which are near Manila. By calculating the "Sex Ratio" for the various provinces we obtain a standard measure for comparison. In this case, we calculated the sex ratio on the basis of those over 10 years of age. This was to eliminate the presence of babies and small children from the sample, since they seldom migrate. The following table shows the results in terms of males per 100 females.

Table 9. Sex Ratio for Persons 10 Years Old and Over in Selected Provinces: 1948.*

Province	Ratio
Batangas	94.8
Bulacan	94.4
Cavite	93.9
Laguna	96.5
Pampanga	96.7
Pangasinan	92.9

* Calculated from the *Journal of Philippine Statistics*, Volume V, No. 9, Table 9, p. 16.

The province which immediately adjoins Manila, Rizal, is omitted because its population is actually in the metropolitan area of Manila. These figures show that the provinces adjoining Manila have a lack of males. It seems most probable that this condition is caused by the movement of young men from the towns and cities of these areas to Manila.

Moreover, for *married* people it was found that in 1948 Manila had 39,633 men who did not have their wives with them in the city. This means that approximately one-fourth (25%) of the married men in Manila had apparently come in from outside areas and had left their wives behind them.[28] However, it must be remembered that a certain proportion of these married men would be foreigners who have come to Manila on a temporary basis.

Another way of noting the migration of peoples toward the cities and to Manila in particular is by the reports on

---

[28] *Journal of Philippine Statistics*, Volume V, No. 9, Table 7, p. 17.

the "mother tongue," or most used language that was learned in early life, of the population. It is revealing to note that although 576,000 people in Manila listed Tagalog as their mother tongue, there were 407,221 additional people or over 40% who listed other languages.[29]

There are several important implications which stem from this trend in migration. One is that this movement means a transfer of people from the *damay* community life of the rural areas to that of the *gesellschaft* culture of the city. This, of course, entails a complete reorganization of life in many respects. The adjustment of rural migrants in the urban setting is a complex and often neglected study.

Related to the above point is the task of learning which this movement poses. Many who come to the city are ill-prepared vocationally as well as socially for urban life. The question is then often raised concerning what can be done to prepare young men, for they are apparently the ones who migrate most, before they leave the rural areas.

The migration southward is also demonstrated by the different sets of data. For one thing, there is the matter of population gain and loss between the various census periods. The accompanying table lists certain selected provinces which show clearly the effects of migration.

---

[29] *Journal of Philippine Statistics*, Volume V, No. 10, Table 5, p. 9.

CHAPTER XII. POPULATION

Table 10. Gain and Loss of Population in Selected Provinces: 1948 *

Provinces	Year 1939	Year 1948
Decreasing:		
Abra	87,780	86,000
Albay	432,470	394,690
Mt. Province	296,870	278,120
Increasing:		
Agusan	99,020	126,450
Cotabato	298,940	439,670
Davao	292,600	364,850
Zamboanga	355,980	521,940

* Source: Frederico B. Moreno, "Population" in *Manila Times Mid-Week Review*, January 26, 1949, pp. 8-9.

It was previously noted that Mindanao was one area in the Philippines which had an extremely low population density. From the above table one can observe that it is precisely these low-density areas which are showing a considerable growth. Therefore one part of the "pull" in the migration to the South is evidently composed of the opportunities which such a lightly populated but fertile area can offer.

When one examines the age and marital distributions of certain provinces there also seems to be evidence of the workings of migration. To be specific, for single persons only in each of the provinces of Cotabato, Davao, Lanao, Negros Occidental, and Zamboanga males over 9 years of age exceed the females over 9 years of age by more than 17,000. On the other hand, in Cebu and the Ilocos provinces there are several thousands more of females.[30] Since these differences appear in provinces which are evidently strongly affected by migration according to other measures, they are also probably due to the effects of population movement.

[30] *Journal of Philippine Statistics*, Volume V. No. 9, Table 7, p. 11.

Referring to the sex ratio index again, the provinces show some significant variations. In the accompanying table, the fifteen provinces at each end of the distribution are listed with their sex ratios. Remember that the ratios are expressed in terms of the number of males per 100 females, and in this instance, it is only for those over 9 years of age.

Table 11. Sex Ratio for Persons 10 Years Old and Over for Selected Provinces: 1948.*

Province	Ratio	Province	Ratio
Ilocos Sur	82.3	Samar	102.6
Ilocos Norte	84.4	Sorsogon	102.6
La Union	88.6	Masbate	102.7
Batanes	91.0	Misamis Oriental	102.9
Romblon	91.3	Isabela	102.9
Capiz	91.4	Quezon	105.0
Bohol	91.6	Mindoro	105.2
Abra	92.3	Palawan	105.9
Cebu	92.4	Cotabato	106.1
Iloilo	92.8	Negros Occidental	106.8
Pangasinan	92.9	Zamboanga	106.8
Cavite	93.9	Agusan	109.0
Bulacan	94.4	Lanao	113.3
Batangas	94.8	Bukidnon	113.5
Nueva Ecija	95.2	Davao	118.7

* Source: Calculated from *Journal of Philippine Statistics*, Volume V, No. 9, Table 9, p. 16.

The impressions gained from the figures for single persons over 10 years of age and their distribution in the various provinces are strengthened by these sex ratios. From the table one can readily see that the provinces in northern Luzon tend to have a larger proportion of females of 10 years or older. This is in accord with the impressions which others have gained, namely, that the Ilocos provinces especially have been a traditional area of out-migration.[31]

---

[31] For a historical description of this movement see Tomás S. Fonacier. "The Ilokano Movement: A New Frontier in Philippine History." *Diliman Review*, University of the Philippines, Quezon City, Vol. 1, No. 1, pp. 89-94.

The low sex ratio in the western Visayas is apparently due to out-migration also. In the succeeding passages some further evidence to support this conclusion will be cited. Mindanao and the Visayan provinces near it which have a high sex ratio are most probably affected by a heavy in-migration of males into these frontier areas. These patterns would again be consistent with the theory that the internal migration of the Philippines largely consists of young males.

Using the data for "mother tongue" there are at least two significant patterns which are discernible.[32] The first of these pertains to the Iloko speaking people. Outside of the provinces of Ilocos Sur and Norte, the Iloko speaking group has become primarily distributed in the provinces of Central Luzon and in Manila. In fact, the number of Iloko speaking people in Manila is equal to almost 1/6 of the combined populations of two Ilocos provinces.

The other outstanding pattern is in regard to those speaking Bisaya-Cebuano as a "mother tongue." It will be recalled that the western Visayan areas generally had a low sex ratio. This fact is now clarified when the distribution of this language group is analyzed. It is found that there are more people who speak Bisaya-Cebuano in all of Mindanao than there are in Cebu province itself! By totalling the figures for the 9 provinces of Mindanao proper the number of residents for that island who speak Bisaya-Cebuano was found to be 1,483,721. However, in Cebu province there are only 1,095,121 people whose "mother tongue" is Bisaya-Cebuano.

Two generalizations follow from this finding. The first is that the Visayans who are in Mindanao are probably predominantly male judging from the ratios of Cebu and the provinces of Mindanao. The second is that Mindanao seems to be drawing its new settlers from the adjacent or nearly adjacent islands rather than the more distant areas. This is a rather obvious and natural development, but it is apparently often forgotten if one may judge from the

---

[32] This is calculated from *Journal of Philippine Statistics*, Vol. V, No. 10, Table V, pp. 9-10.

frequent discussions of Mindanao as an outlet for the peoples of densely settled portions of Luzon.

The question is often raised as to why these internal migrations are taking place in the Philippines. The following reasons seem to account for most of it.

1. Changes in the Economy. This would include the decline in certain rural and urban industries and the rise of others.

2. Social Disruption. This would refer to the effects of World War II and the struggles against the dissident groups in the immediate post-war period.

3. Natural Disasters. Here are meant such crises as floods, typhoons, and volcanic eruptions which have devastated certain areas in the nation at times. One could also put the locust plagues and plant diseases in this category.

4. Weakening of old cultural ties to home areas. This includes the change from *Damay* to *Gesellschaft* attitudes.

Age Composition

One topic of particular interest in any country is the age composition of the population. Age composition merely refers to the relative proportions of people at the various age levels. A table comparing the percentage distribution of ages in the Philippines and the United States is given below.

Table 12. Age Distribution of the Philippines
and the United States
Selected Years. *

Age Groups	Philippines: 1948	U.S. 1940
0 — 4	16%	8.0%
5 — 19	38.3%	26.4%
20 — 44	32.5%	38.2%
45 — 64	9.3%	10.5%
65 over	3.1%	7.0%

* Calculated from *Journal of Philippine Statistics*, Volume V, No. 8, pp. 9-11 and from Landis, *op. cit.*, p. 281.

CHAPTER XII. POPULATION

From these figures one can see that in some respects the Philippines and the United States populations were almost opposite. Thus in the ages 0 to 4 the Philippine percentage was double that of the United States. However, on the other hand, for the ages over 65 the Philippine percentage was less than half of the United States. Let us consider the significance of these differences.

If one reads the current population literature dealing with the United States it will be noticed that there are frequent references to the effects of an aging population. However, in the Philippines one could certainly say that by comparison the Philippine population is definitely young. Even putting comparisons aside one could still say that any population which has more than half of its people below age 20, and over 85% below the age of 45 is young. It is interesting to note that the age composition of the Philippines in 1948 is very similar to that of United States in 1850.[33]

Although the Philippines has a youthful population and is not burdened by the care of a large number of aged, it also has more dependent children and a smaller percentage in the active working years. Fifty seven per cent of the U.S. is between 19 and 64 compared to forty-one percent for the same age group in the Philippines. This means that the Philippines has a smaller proportion of "producers" than the United States. Better health conditions would both "age" the population and increase its productivity.

Many writers point out that the age composition of a population can have profound social effects.[34] For example, a nation which has a large proportion of small children would probably spend more for toys, while a nation which has many old people would spend more for wheel chairs or false teeth. This difference in age composition can therefore have a great effect on business. An example would be that of a manufacturer of baby cribs who may lose business

---

[33] Landis, *op. cit.*, pp. 278-279.
[34] See Amos H. Hawley: *Human Ecology*, op. cit., pp. 143-148 for an excellent analysis of this topic.

and become poor if the birth rate drops and the population accordingly has a smaller percentage of infants.

Therefore, in a modern population which has many young people and children there would be a demand for many elementary schools, canned milk, playgrounds, toys and doctors specializing in children's diseases. On the other hand, in a modern population which has many old people there would be a demand for old age pensions, reading material, tobacco, eye-glasses, adult education, and doctors specializing in the diseases of old people. Furthermore, these variations in age composition and their effects can also exert a great influence on the total culture of a society. They can affect the ways of life and the attitudes of the members of the society. Now interestingly enough these differences in age composition are, of course, due to changes in the culture such as the use of modern medicine and contraception. So here again we see an illustration of the principle that population both influences society and is also subject to social influence. Thus some of the differences between nations may be due in no small part to their varying types of age structure.

Population and Level of Living

Some people believe that a large population which causes a high density of human settlement will automatically result in a lowered level of living. Now it is true that the size of a population can have a great effect on the level of living of a given country. For example, in Japan, China, and India the population appears to be too large for the land area to support at a high plane of living. In the Philippines such areas as Cebu and central Luzon appear to have a population pressure, whereas in Mindanao, Palawan, and Mindoro an increased population might well bring an improved level of living.

However, population analysts now recognize that population is only one factor among four which bring about a given level of living. The four factors are:

CHAPTER XII. POPULATION

1. Natural Resources
2. Invention
3. Social Organization
4. Population

This explains why it is that, although the American Indians were a small population and were living on a continent which we now know has excellent natural resources, they had a low level of living. An opposite case would be that of Belgium which has an extremely high density of population but maintains it at a distinctly high plane. The operation of the four factors also accounts for the fact that some *conservative* writers have estimated that the Philippines could support 50 million people on a higher level of living than exists today. Italy is an instructive comparison in this respect.

The land areas of the Philippines and Italy are almost the same. The natural resources of Italy, however, are generally regarded as being less than those of the Philippines. Yet, Italy is able to maintain a population which is more than double that of the Philippines on a noticeably higher level of living. (Although one should also add that Italy does have difficulty in coping with its growing population.) Nevertheless, the comparison still demonstrates the lack of any absolute relationship between a high density of population and a low plane of living. Therefore, one should always realize that population and natural resources cannot be considered alone as leading to a given living condition. Rather, it is the complex inter-relationship and interaction of all the four factors which operate to produce a particular level of living.

Summary

As a special subject of sociological study, population is viewed as a biological phenomena which is interrelated with human culture. This viewpoint is especially brought forth in the discussion of population growth. It is now generally recognized that such culturally-based factors as medical developments, contraception, and celibacy overshadow the biological factors in the increase of population.

The Philippines, as does the world as a whole, shows an increasing rate of population growth in recent years. However, this growth has come from the saving of life rather than increased birth rate. Although the birth rate of the Philippines has shown a gradual decline since the turn of the century, the rate is still one of the highest in the world. Today the increased use of modern medicine has prolonged the life expectancy of the average Filipino, but the present level of approximately 50 is still below that of many other lands.

Migration is viewed as the other great aspect of population. The movement of peoples can bring great changes to an area. Some specific effects of migration would be changes in language, customs, and physical type of the population. The movement of peoples is seen as both a cause of social change and as a result of social change. For example, migration may bring changes in a culture. But, on the other hand, migration may be a response to such a change as war. The two most outstanding types of population movement in the Philippines are immigration and internal migration.

Immigration to the Philippines has consisted predominantly of Chinese. From the Spanish times onward, the Chinese immigrants have been prominent in the retail trade of the Philippines although they are only a small fraction of the population. This predominance of a foreign group in one part of the economy has led to certain tensions and conflicts. This then poses a problem of adjustment in the future.

Internal migration in the Philippines shows two trends; going toward the cities and toward the South. This has resulted in a distinct pattern as far as sex ratio and language distribution is concerned; the areas of in-migration showing

Chapter XII. POPULATION

a preponderance of males, especially Mindanao, and the areas of out-migration showing a higher proportion of females. The two most densely settled areas are the lowlands of Luzon and the Central Visayas. The most lightly settled regions on the other hand, are the outlying areas of Luzon and the islands of Mindanao, Palawan, and Mindoro. The two language groups which show the most evidence of movement are the Bisaya-Cebuano and the Iloko-speaking peoples.

This movement of peoples can bring great changes in the lives of individuals and groups. The most significant of these shifts is the movement from the *damay* rural communities to the *gesellschaft* atmosphere of the urban centers. This particularly poses the problems of readjustment to a greatly different social and physical environment.

In regard to age composition, this has a definite influence on the social life of the nation. Such things as the general outlook on life, the organization of the economy, and the provision of social welfare services are all affected.

QUESTIONS

1. Which is more important in accounting for the numbers of human beings on the earth at the present time, the biological or cultural factors? Why?

2. What were the ages at which your married relatives were wedded? What percentage were married below the age of 20?

3. If you know of any very large family try to learn at what age they were married. Was it below or above 20 for the wife?

4. How has your home neighborhood grown, by natural increase or migration?

5. What factors lead people to migrate? Which is the most important factor of all?

6. What factors account for the movement from rural to urban areas? Will this trend continue?

7. What proportion of the people in your home neighborhood are from other provinces? from other nations?

8. What sort of adjustments would a person have to make who migrates from a rural *damay* community to the urban *gesellschaft* setting?

9. Describe the probable nature of a community where there is an excess of males. Compare it to the opposite situation where there is an excess of females.

10. In comparison to the United States the Philippines has a "young" population. How would this influence the social and economic life of the nation?

PROJECTS

1. A case history of a migration, either of a family or an individual.

2. The present age composition of your home community and its social significance.

3. Analyze the problems which both an individual immigrant and an immigrant family would face in the Philippines today.

4. Make a list of the various resettlement programs which the government has promoted as a means of redistributing the population.

SUGGESTED READINGS

Bureau of Census and Statistics, *Journal of Philippine Statistics*. This publication appears monthly or quarterly and provides current data about population and commercial activities. Material from the most recent census is also included from time to time.

——————————, *Yearbook of Philippine Statistics*: 1946. This work contains a summary of pre-World War II data in addition to the first collected data for the immediate post-war era.

Hawley, Amos H.: *Papers in Demography and Public Administration*, Institute of Public Administration, University of the Philippines, Manila, 1954. (Pamphlet form).
This contains three papers dealing with various aspects of population and public administration. However, they are also of great value for anyone interested in the study of the Philippine population, since they cover a wide range of material.

Landis, Paul H.: *Population Problems; A Cultural Interpretation*, American Book Company, New York, 1943.
This represents one of the more consistently sociological works on human population. The discussion is technical but rewarding for the serious students of population.

Ogburn, William F. and Meyer F. Nimkoff: *Sociology*, Second Edition, Houghton-Mifflin Company, New York, 1950. Chapters 17 and 18. In this standard work on general sociology the reader will find a comprehensive but simple explanation of the basic principles in the sociological study of population.

Chapter XII. POPULATION

Thompson, Warren S.: *Plenty of People*, Revised Edition, The Ronald Press, New York, 1948.
Supplies a thorough yet non-technical discussion of the various aspects of population by one of the well-known authorities on the subject.

CHAPTER THIRTEEN

SOCIAL ASPECTS OF INDUSTRIALIZATION

In economic development we may distinguish between the *seeds* of development, such as the accumulation of industrial capital, the spread of modern technological methods, and the rise in standards of education, and the *fruits* of economic development, such as better nutrition, lower death rates, luxury consumption, progress in social security, the development of highly complex administration and multiple state intervention. The awkward fact is that it is very much easier to transplant the fruits of economic development, or at least to go through the motions of doing so, than to transplant the seeds... It is fatally easy to transplant them not as end products but in isolation, divorced from the process which has created them in the industrialized countries. Treated in such fashion, these fruits of economic development have a way of putrefying and even checking development itself. Transplant medical improvements in isolation, and you increase the population which is being maintained at stationary standards rather than raise *per capita* standards; transplant advanced social legislation and it either remains a dead letter or proves positively detrimental to economic development; create a desire for luxury consumption, and the foreign exchange resources available for the import of capital goods are reduced; set up an elaborate machinery of state planning, and under the conditions obtaining in many underdeveloped countries such machinery often becomes absurdly irrelevant to real needs and possibilities.

— H. W. Singer, "Economic Progress in Underdeveloped Countries," SOCIAL RESEARCH, March 1949, pp. 4-5.

Chapter XIII. Aspects of Industrialization

The historical background.

In every society, the activities connected with the provision of material needs are a basic part of man's social life. There is no such being as an "economic man" concerned only with financial profit. Whenever man works for a livelihood, he also strives to gain status with his fellows by working in ways they approve and in a fashion which promotes human companionship. In seeking group approval, the Hindu refrains from using the cow as meat; the capitalist may employ close relatives rather than more competent outsiders, and the factory worker governs his output by what his fellow laborers think is a "fair amount of work," rather than the amount of work which would bring him the greatest financial return. The non-economic factors which influence industrial activity are a part of the total culture and can only be interpreted in terms of the total setting.

In primitive societies, there is usually no separate work group and one labors either as part of a family or with the total community. Husband, wife, children and more distant relatives carry family patterns into the gathering of food and its distribution to individuals. In larger enterprises, such as big scale animal hunts, the whole community shares the work and divides the product. Religious officials spend much of their time asking the blessing of the heavenly powers on the hunt or the fertility of the fields. Family, community, church and economic enterprise are blended together in a fashion in which it is impossible to separate the one from the other.

In the handicraft societies, typical of medieval Europe and still prevalent in some parts of Asia today, more specialized economic activities began to appear. Accordingly, we find craftsmen and workshops, storekeepers and peddlers, markets and money lenders. Usually, the number of individuals engage in any unit of activity is so small their geographical range is limited and the responsibility to the community clearly defined. Relationships are highly personal and family influence strong. Some extra-family influence in the form of guilds and municipal laws begin to develop. The unity of all social institutions is still strong, but is somewhat less apparent than in primitive societies.

The industrial society brings in highly specialized economic activity in which large groups of men work together in one unit of production. The relationships seem to be less personal and there is sharper division between economic activity, family influence, religious rites and community control. Primary groupings appear to be of lesser importance and work relationships are organized on the basis of secondary relationships.

The following table illustrates the changes involved in the transition from a handicraft to an industrial society.

guild	union
workshop	factory
handcraftsman	machine operator
sari-sari store	cold store and super market
peddler	salesman
owner proprietor	stockholders and manager
family enterprises	corporations with thousands of stockholders

Large numbers of people are involved in these operations which reach beyond the control of a single family, international labor unions, world-wide business corporations and international governmental agreements. The worker may be better paid, but feels the lack of the security of the companionship of a close knit social group; rather than economic activity pulling the family together, it tends to place them in numerous specialized types of work which separate family members during the working day. A large factory may be forced to employ workers from different family backgrounds, different religious affiliations and different ethnic loyalties. These workers may have nothing in common except their labor in the same place.

Another effect of industrialization is to provide opportunities for the growth of a large middle class, demands

CHAPTER XIII. ASPECTS OF INDUSTRIALIZATION 329

for skilled workers, factory managers, engineers, accountants, clerical employees and other specialized workers and the big capitalist. Other men find a place as independent merchants in the collection of raw materials and the sale of finished products.

Industrial development in the Philippines.

At the present time, the Philippines is still largely in an agricultural-handicraft stage of development with seventy percent of the population directly dependent upon agriculture; according to the 1939 census, only 104,000 persons were employed in manufacturing concerns which had an output of over 5,000 pesos.[1] The basic aspect of the economy is a situation in which the Philippines produces farm crops for home consumption with a surplus for export and imports manufactured goods.

The effect of import control has been to increase, to a small extent, the number of processing industries, and there seems little doubt that the future trend will be toward an emphasis on increased industrial production. The major reason for this is simply the fact that greater industrialization is one way in which a growing population may find employment for its labor. McHale estimates that if the total amount of potential agricultural land was utilized, this would still only amount to about one and a half hectares per laborer, and this estimate makes no allowance for the growth in population or the increased used of labor-saving machinery on the farm.[2] Thus, one may say that, while at present, the Philippines has only the beginning of industrial development, the prospects are that the future will see an effort to stimulate growth in this field. Hence, this area may soon be faced with the same types of problems which have been encountered by other industrial societies.

---

[1] *Philippine Census*, 1939, Vol. II, p. 989.
[2] Thomas R. McHale: "Economic Development in the Philippines," *The University of Manila Journal of East Asiatic Studies*, Vol. I, No. 3, April, 1952, p. 8.

Folkways of the industrial society.

In general, the social attitudes related to an industrial society are those suited to a *gesellschaft* type of environment. These would include the shift from small scale, family controlled subsistence type of enterprises to widespread, corporate organizations in which people are dependent upon wages or monetary profits and find their economic welfare tied up with that of total strangers. The folkways of the industrial society are usually best developed in a commercial, middle class group and the lag in the development of these folkways locally is related to the factors that have slowed down the development of such a group on Philippine society. At this point, Lasker's comparative analysis of the development of European and Filipino society is of interest:

> In Europe,... the small shop which became the factory was a place where master and journeymen and apprentices labored together at common tasks. The idea that it was unbecoming for the master or members of his family to dirty their hands would have been inconceivable to a class whose dignity and independence even the lords and princes had respected for centuries. But in the Philippines, anyone whose industry, thrift, or luck had placed in possession of money almost invariably invested it in land and thus changed his social status. To engage in any kind of physical labor would have held down his social position. The process of industrialization thus was greatly handicapped not only by the export of potential capital, but also by the absence of a class of manual workers who, when successful, would invest their savings in technical training for themselves or their children and thus build from the ground up enterprises of growing complexity. Instead, the successful man became an *illustrado* whose son, if of a progressive frame of mind, might prepare himself for a career of industrial management or teaching, but always with a view to functioning in the office or the classroom, never in the shop. Those who blame the Filipinos for this propensity do not understand the historical

Chapter XIII. Aspects of Industrialization

background. The idea that a manual worker may be a free man is spreading slowly. The "social justice" movement, ... connected the ideas of political and economic freedom and thus tended to dignify the position of the wage-earner. But all economic and social, as well as political, progress in the Philippines still is held back by a psychological heritage which continues to divide society. This, to some extent, is true of all societies that have but lately come within the orbit of modern economic life.[3]

In all fairness, one should also point out that the development of attitudes consistent with industrialism took place in Europe and the United States over a period of centuries and that, even in these areas, many unsolved problems still remain. The Philippines, thus faces the problem of accomplishing major changes within a short period of time, changes which are opposed by basic elements in the culture. This area is building up a supply of capital, labor and industrial knowledge, but these will only be profitable if the basic folkways are congenial to their use.

Money for capital investment, for instance, depends not only upon the accumulation of surplus wealth, but on the manner in which this wealth is invested. In the past, money has been invested mainly in farm land and, to a lesser extent, in retail facilities, urban real estate, amusement centers and private educational enterprises. Attitudes inimical to business enterprise include a distrust of the stock exchange which confines business there largely to foreigners, and a distrust of banks which leads to savings being hoarded rather than deposited in banks where they become the basis for credit. It is estimated that a half billion pesos have been withdrawn from circulation by hoarders.[4] Money invested in stocks or bank accounts is used to finance business.

---

[3] Bruno Lasker: *Human Bondage in Southeast Asia*, University of North Carolina Press, Chapel Hill, under the auspices of Institute of Pacific Relations, p. 235.

[4] *Manila Daily Bulletin*, March 3, 1953.

Savings hoarded in the house may give security to the individual but do not finance commercial expansion.

Industrialism requires a group of investors who will take the risk of loss in the hope of large profits from long-term manufacturing projects where management is outside of any one family group. Filipinos have not been altogether lacking in business enterprise as shown by the growth of small *sari-sari* stores and similar retail establishments. The problem in economic development is how such profit-making activity can be channeled into *manufacturing* enterprises of a size commensurate with the possibilities of modern machinery.

The promotion of business enterprise requires an ambitious group of young people who will look to industry rather than to professions, government service or agriculture. This means that ambitious young people will strive to become aggressive salesmen, engineers, office workers and business organizers who have the initiative to venture into the new fields and the courage to take the risk of failure.

For the labor, it means the recruitment of a group whose work meet the pace of the machine and who are willing to work at a rapid rate in return for more adequate wages. It also means that the distinction is blurred between managerial, white collar and manual work and that the business executive is one who knows from his own experience, the requirements and problems of the worker in the shop. There will be less of a tendency to operate from the top down and more of an inclination to work from the bottom up with business managers being men whose hands actually carry the callouses of manual labor.

In the past, most men with this type of attitude have come from an American, Chinese or European background, but there is some evidence of the development of Filipino businessmen of this caliber. By way of specific examples, we might refer to Toribio Teodoro of the Ang Tibay shoe company who developed a large corporation from a cobbler's shop; Max Jimenez, whose entry into the restaurant business was based on skills developed while working his way through college; L. R. Aguinaldo, who built up a large mercantile establishment; Fortunato Halili, whose career is based on the transition from peddler to large scale business operator; and Gonzalo Puyat, at one time a laborer, who established an important furniture factory. The list is not exhaustive, but is cited to give some idea of the occupational procedures which must become more common if industrialization is to succeed.

What makes workers work?

Maximum production depends on a combination of machinery, management and labor. The most elaborate machines and the most highly trained production engineers will be helpless unless they have the cooperation of a labor force willing to work diligently and carefully. Much thought has been spent on the question of how such a labor force could be obtained.

At first, it was thought that economic motives were the only ones which were effective and attempts were made to increase production by material rewards such as better wages, profit sharing or paying extra money for a faster rate of work. Such methods were only partially successful and then attention was given to the physical aspects of work —the spacing of machinery, the lighting and ventilation of the factory. These measures helped, but they too, seemed to be only a partial answer.

On a more sophisticated level, factory managers began to realize that workers brought their total personality to the factory and that psychological problems affected the rate of work. It was thought that the worker who was depressed, unhappy, and insecure would lower his output and that the man who was well adjusted, contented and emotionally balanced would be an efficient worker. This theory led to the introduction of industrial counseling, psychological testing and similar efforts to match the job to the worker's personality type and to improve his emotional state. Like the other approaches, attempts of this type seemed worthwhile, but also left many questions unanswered.

The sociology of the factory.

Much of the pioneer work in this type of research has been done by Elton Mayo of the Harvard Business School. Mayo began his work at the Harvard Business School. Mayo began his work with a distinct leaning toward the psychological explanation and in 1925, he wrote: "When we talk of social problems, we are apt to forget that every social problem is ultimately individual." [5] By 1945, his thinking had shifted to a sociological basis as shown by the statement, "Economics, psychology, physiology, all... ignore the fact that complex group association is the distinguishing character of human beings." [6]

The change in Mayo's thinking seems to be related to a rather striking experiment conducted in the Hawthorne plant of the Western Electric Company where an effort had been made to measure the effect of changes in light on worker's output. The interesting thing about this experiment was that, within wide limits, output seemed to increase whether the amount of light was increased or decreased!

Mayo and his associates then proceeded to make an extremely thorough study of the effect of the changing of a wide type of working conditions in the same plant. Like the preceding experiment, they found that, no matter what changes were introduced, output seemed to increase— even when the changes were of a type though to be unpopular or to handicap the worker's performance.

What was the explanation of this perplexing result?

Evidently, the experiment had changed the very nature of the work group. Before the experiment, they had been merely an anonymous group of employees doing a routine task according to directions dictated by superior authority. After the experiment had begun, they had become a group

---
[5] "The Fruitful Errors of Elton Mayo," *Fortune*, November, 1946, p. 241.
[6] *Ibid.*, p. 242.

Chapter XIII. ASPECTS OF INDUSTRIALIZATION

with a unique importance: their wishes and opinions were consulted by distinguished scientists. They were the object of special scrutiny and were no longer anonymous, unimportant individuals, but members of a highly integrated group whose importance had been recognized by respected authorities.

The factory had been thought of as a secondary type of association in which workers were united by impersonal considerations of factory routine and achieved their desire for the security of intimate primary associations in the family or other groups in which they participated outside their working hours. It was found instead, that each unit of the factory formed a primary group type of contact with its own pattern of folkways and mores, its leaders and subordinates, its frustrations and rewards. Output was not determined either by the authority of the foreman or by the individual desire for gain, but by what the group folkways considered a "fair day's work." Worker satisfaction was related to psychological adjustment, but was primarily affected by the manner in which he was either accepted or rejected by the group of fellow employes.

Viewed in this light, employee relationships were not just the specific problems of unrelated individuals, but the relation of a particular group of workers to the total manner in which one studies functioning of other group relationships. In this function, sociology moved into the factory and gave rise to the discipline now known as industrial sociology.[7]

---

[7] Excellent brief descriptions of the Hawthorne experiments may be found in Miller & Form: *Industrial Sociology*, Harpers, New York, 1951 and in Chase, Stuart: *Men At Work*, Harcourt, Brace, New York, 1045, pp. 9-27. A complete report is found in Roethlisberger & Dickinson: *Management and the Worker*, Harvard University Press, 1939.

Industrialization and Social Problems

Types of problems.

An agricultural society may suffer from many ills including extreme poverty and a large amount of idle time. Complete unemployment, however, is rare and usually the family will assume responsibility for the aged and infirm. In an industrial society, changes in business are likely to produce frequent unemployment, while those unable to work because of age or illness may find that the family group is unable to care for them. The laborer has little control over conditions of his work and may find himself working long hours in unsanitary surroundings for meager pay.

To meet these problems, four types of approach have been developed: employer paternalism, private charitable organizations, collective bargaining and social legislation. While, in a sense, these approaches are competitive, they exist along side each and also supplement the traditional system of family responsibility for welfare needs.

Employer paternalism.

Even as the more benevolent landlords assume responsibility for the special needs of the tenants, so do many industrial corporations attempt to alleviate the lot of their employees. Provisions of this type include the furnishing of recreation facilities, low cost insurance, special grants to help in illness; loan funds available at low interest rates and occasionally, special help in building houses or educating children.

In a sense, this means that the corporation executive becomes a type of "benevolent father" to his employees to whom they can turn and has the advantage that, in a wisely administered system, the employer may know the special needs of his workers better than any outside agency. The successful operation of such a system will boost employees' loyalty to the company and produce better feeling between the boss and the workers. While such a system seems especially adaptable to a situation in which class divisions are sharp, it is worthy to note that it has also persisted, to some extent, in heavily industrialized societies such as the United States and Western Europe.

In saying that this system is compatible with Filipino tradition we might point to the provisions of the civil code which give legal recognition to the subparental type of authority exercised over apprentices by the directors of trade establishments (Chapter 6, Article 349, Sec. 4, Civil Code of the Philippines, Republic Act No. 386). This article is in line with the pattern in which the authority of the father is transferred to the employer and workers are regarded somewhat in the category of dependent children. In this pattern the worker places himself under the guidance of the employer who, in turn, has an obligation to care for the more pressing needs of his workers. Just as the authoritarian father may be either harsh and demanding or kind and indulgent so the paternalistic employer may be either a severe tyrant or a kindly overseer who is a "soft touch" for improvident employees.

The contrast between the paternalistic pattern and the development of democratic attitudes is obvious. A system which looks to the generosity of the "boss" as a way of meeting emergency needs does not develop either self-reliance or group participation. Self-reliance would mean that the worker received an adequate wage and in turn developed habits of thrift which helped him to cope with his economic problems. Group participation implies that, through co-operative planning with his fellow employees, he works out group arrangements for protection against the hazards of life. Either of these techniques requires the individual to take an active responsibility in determining his own destiny. On the other hand, even the best employer paternalism carries some resemblance to the subservience which characterizes the relationship of *cacique* and *tao*. This pattern may be inevitable in a transition period but it is of doubtful value as a permanent feature of economic life.

Another weakness of such a system is that it varies from company to company and not all employers have either the financial resources or the social concern to make such paternalism an effective way of meeting welfare needs. In fact, such a paternalistic welfare program is likely to best be developed in plants paying high wages and assuring fairly stable employment. Companies subject to intense competition, whose employees may see frequent unemployment, are often the least able to carry this type of program.

Private charity has some similarity to all the other methods, but this will be discussed at length in the chapter on social work.

Social legislation.

Every industrial society has seen an attempt to meet the ills of industrialization by legal measures. Laws of this type in the Philippines, include minimum wage legislation, rules for working conditions of children and women, requirements that employers give maternity leaves, and special provision for the compensation of workmen injured in industrial accidents. The major difference between the Philippines and more industrialized countries is that Philippine laws are not as comprehensive nor as liberal financially speaking.

The advantages of such social legislation are that they cover entire categories of workers without imposing heavy burdens on the finances of any one company. They are regarded as more democratic, since they are passed by the national legislature which presumably represents both workers and employers. They represent an attempt to protect employees who may suffer because of the indifference or the financial troubles of a particular employer.

The drawbacks of this type of legislation lie in the realm of costs, administration and enforcement. If the effect of social legislation is to impose a heavy burden on all Filipino industry, then this industry faces difficulty in foreign competition and the end result may be bankrupt employers and to throw laborers out of work. In this connection, it is fair to note that such legislation did not appear in other countries until they had reached a stage of industrialization far in advance of the present developments in the Philippines.

Speaking of the type of labor laws passed recently in underdeveloped countries, Wilbert E. Moore makes the following comment:

> Often they appear to be those standards that have been gradually worked out in the most industrially advanced countries, which have levels of production and productivity per worker that allow the enforcement of minimum material and social standards. It is doubtful if all existing legislative standards in China, India and Latin America could be immediately enforced without a greater economic disruption than the good accomplished for the workers. The first effect would almost certainly be widespread loss of employment.[8]

In the matter of administration, a major shortcoming of this approach is the difficulty of taking into consideration local and regional differences. It is also true that, unless given strong support by the public, such laws may become only "paper legislation" without real effect. Reformers in this field tend to exaggerate the extent to which law may change social habits and forget that arbitrary legislation may simply lead to wholesale violation of the law and consequent corruption of government agencies. Eventually, social security legislation seems certain to be extended in the Philippines, but a premature introduction of such measures may cause injuries greater than the benefits they confer.

Collective bargaining.

The basis for collective bargaining is the weakness of the individual employee compared to the power of the large

---

[8] Wilbert E. Moore: *Industrialization and Labor*, Cornell University Press, Ithaca, N. Y., 1951, p. 144.

corporation. The individual has few alternate chances for work and may be confronted with the alternative of accepting what his employer offers or facing unemployment. The corporation, however, may be able to recruit labor from distant area, can readily replace any single employee and thus, be able to hire labor on its own terms. One remedy for this situation is for laborers to combine into unions which represent a large number of workers and have the power to completely withhold a labor supply from a company or even from an entire industry. This is accomplished by means of the strike—a technique by which a group of laborers refrain from work until their demands are met or a compromise agreement is reached. As compared to individual bargaining, the labor union controls a large part of the labor force and thus, forces the employer to share with the union the determination of wage rates and conditions of work. As contrasted to social legislation, collective bargaining means that wage rates and extra benefits and conditions of work will be determined for a specific concern or industry by those close to the scene; that is, by the employer and his workers. Like social legislation, collective bargaining is present in most industrialized countries and a high percentage of laborers in such countries work under agreements, usually called contracts, reached between the union and the employer.

While labor unionism and collective bargaining has advantages, it also has some drawbacks. Perhaps the most serious drawback is that a dispute which results in a strike may cause a work stoppage for a long period of time. Such a work stoppage may bankrupt employers, reduce laborers to destitution and seriously inconvenience the general public. The destructiveness of a long strike means that effective collective bargaining requires a great deal of wisdom and a readiness to make concessions on the part of employers, workers and union leaders. Employers who insist on complete domination, workers who demand benefits the industry is unable to pay or labor leaders who use strikes to enhance their own power may bankrupt an entire industry.

Chapter XIII. ASPECTS OF INDUSTRIALIZATION

Just as businessmen have been inclined to over emphasize the purely economic role of business enterprise, so there has been a tendency to view the labor unions as purely economic agencies. Actually, the union is more than a bargaining mechanism to settle wage rates. It represents the struggle of workers to gain status and have their voice heard in places where frequently, their wishes have been disregarded and they have been viewed as impersonal parts of the productive enterprise. Through the union, the worker meets and associates with his fellows and participates in a democratic process which proves that he is an important member of society. In a fully developed union, he finds social activities and recognition from his fellows which gives him a place in society and offers him both a sense of social solidarity and of individual importance. Viewed in this fashion, the union is another example of the worker to regain the group affiliation he lost when the workshop changed from an intimate family enterprise to a large scale industrial corporation.

The matter of leadership is a delicate point. It is supposedly democratic, but workers may be indifferent to union affairs or may be threatened by gangsters in the pay of union leaders. Since the average worker does not have much knowledge of complicated economic questions, he must place a large share of discretion in the hands of his leaders and these leaders may either ask for impossible demands or, on occasion, may "sell out" to the employer. In other countries, labor leaders imbued with the communist ideology have attempted to use the union to promote the ends of the communist party. On the other hand, progressive labor leaders are often smeared unjustly on charges of being communist. In the Philippines, communist leaders have never attained sufficient power to enable them to use industrial labor unions for subversive purposes, but a considerable number of alleged labor leaders have frankly exploited unions for their own financial gain. The causes of this situation are rooted in the social background of Philippine industry.

Philippine labor unionism developed in a land which had long been used to extreme variations in the wealth and power of different social classes with the power and authority of the upper class taken for granted. Labor unions under the leadership of the early social reformers began as a protest against this situation, but at the same time, other unions arose which simply sought to take advantage of the existing mores. These latter unions were of two types, the company union and unions operated by the *Capataz* or labor contractor.[9]

The company union is an organization which is run either by the employer himself or a close relative. It may promote recreational or welfare activities and even bring to light minor grievances but it can hardly function as an independent bargaining agency in situations in which there is a major disagreement between employer and workers.

The *Capataz* is simply a labor contractor who agrees to provide a certain amount of labor for an employer. He is paid a flat sum by the real employer and then reimburses the workers. He may claim to be a union leader but his real function is to corner the supply of available labor in such a fashion that he can gain large profits for himself. It is to the interest of the *Capataz* to discourage the participation of workers in the control of union policies and he may terrorize both workers and employers by the use of gangsters. The *Capataz* has long been prominent in waterfront unions, and it is interesting to note in this connection that the U.S. Army cut its Manila stevedoring cost in half by requiring stevedoring companies to pay wages direct to the workers.[10] The legitimate union is one which has no connection with the employer and whose membership determines policies and elects the union officers. The officers work for a

---

[9] *Capataz* in some areas of the Philippines simply indicates a foreman. Here it designates one who is a labor agent or supplier of labor.

[10] *U. S. Economic Survey Mission's Report*, distributed by Philippine Book Co., Manila, 1951, p. 109.

Chapter XIII. ASPECTS OF INDUSTRIALIZATION

stipulated salary and their major function is to gain benefits for the workers through negotiation with the management of the companies concerned.

Labor unions which functions as bargaining agencies did not develop until the period of American rule. Mutual aid religious guilds did appear in the early parts of the 19th century but these seem to have been confined to fraternal, religious, and welfare activities. Serquiña traces the rise of an important labor union movement to the formation, by De Los Reyes in 1902, of the Union Obrera Democratica Filipina.[11] Growth through the years has been far from steady and has fluctuated with changing government policies and economic conditions. Statistics in 1948 showed 622 registered unions with 131,144 members.[12]

These figures give some idea of union strength but are far from reliable. They include a large number of "paper unions" which have no membership and represent only an attempt on the part of some ambitious men to claim a political influence over a fictitious group of workers. On the other hand, they omit some unions which conduct business without having registered with the secretary of labor. It is, however, true, that the total membership of labor unions includes only a small number of workers and that no one union is a major economic force. Even this picture must be further qualified by the fact that some of the alleged labor organizations are really either company unions in which the employer negotiates with himself or fronts for a *Capataz*.

Most of the unions are small and, while they have played an important role in specific industries, there are few seasoned leaders and the majority of workers have had little experience in the responsibilities and privileges of union membership. The existence of a large pool of underemployed and poorly paid workers outside of the unions has weak-

---

[11] Conrado A. Serquiña: *A Sociological Analysis of Labor Unionism in the Philippines*. Unpublished Master's Thesis, University of the Philippines, 1952, p. 62.
[12] *Ibid.*, p. 144.

ened their position, facilitated strikebreaking by employers and encouraged by desperate union members.

The Philippine government has legalized the position of labor unions and their right to existence and has enacted numerous laws to facilitate the settlement of labor disputes. At the present time, employers are compelled to bargain with the union of their employee's choice and prohibited from any kind of action against employees which might discourage union activity. Unions also have to bargain with the employer and must give thirty days notice before going on strike. If the President of the Philippines considers that the strike has created a "national emergency" he may certify the dispute to the Court of Industrial Relations for decision. Such a decision is binding on both parties and is an example of compulsory arbitration. Except in cases certified by the President to be of this nature, the government has no power to end a strike and management and labor are expected to work out their own solution.

The present law is a change from the older provisions which gave much greater power to the Court of Industrial Relations. It assumes that industry has matured to the point where Capital and Labor can settle their disputes without government dictation. Some labor attorneys question the timeliness of this act pointing out that Filipino folkways make it difficult to retreat from a bargaining position without "losing face." Thus a union or an employer may yield to a judge's decision when they would never consent to back down on their own volition.

Admittedly, some unions are weak and many employers have been accustomed to run their employee relations in an autocratic manner. Present labor legislation assumes that growth will only come with responsibility and that, in most instances, the heavy hand of the government is no longer required. Labor unions came to the other countries when industrialism had reached a fairly advanced development. In the Philippines, a nascent industrialism has been forced to accommodate itself to labor unionism at an early stage.

Whether or not this development is desirable is a debatable question but, for better or worse, it is the situation which prevails.

The future of labor unionism will be less influenced by governmental policies than by the growth of industry. When industry grows to the point where workers lose intimate contact with the employer, the development of labor unions provides them with a sense of security and an opportunity for group action. In an industrialized Philippines, one may expect a strong labor movement to develop in the normal process of social change. Labor unions are a normal part of a modern economic society and a realization of their importance should help to promote wise governmental policies.

Production and Social Problems

In the emphasis on labor unions, social legislation, charity and government intervention, we are apt to forget that it is the businessmen who do the most to eliminate poverty. This is true because it is the businessmen who set in motion the forces that increase production and give employment, while other elements can do little more than distribute what the businessmen have produced. The Philippines is a poor country, not because a few rich people keep all the money, but because business activity is limited and total production is low. In 1953, the Central Bank estimated the per capita income at ₱342 a year as compared to an American income of about seven times as much. With such a low per capita income, dire poverty is bound to be the lot of the majority of the inhabitants, regardless of how the money is distributed. To increase the national income we must build factories, develop plantations, increase agricultural production and improve transportation.

Some people raise the question, Why can't the government do all this? The answer is that this has been tried both in the Philippines and elsewhere and the result is often a type of graft, corruption and inefficiency which costs the taxpayers money, lowers the standard of living and prevents government projects from succeeding. A private businessman has to make money or go out of business while a government bureaucrat finds that he can lose money and still keep going by tapping the national treasury. Even the best government official is apt to find that many employees are apathetic and that civil service regulations and government red tape keep him from running an efficient organization. It is probably because of these considerations that President Magsaysay, shortly after assuming office, directed that his administration should consider selling government corporations to private business.

If we realize the importance of private enterprise, the question then arises, how can we encourage private business to increase the country's income?

The answer to this question is simply to do everything possible to assure businessmen that they have a chance to make a profit. When businessmen see an opportunity to make money they invest their funds, employ large numbers of people and the national income rises. When businessmen are afraid of the future they stop making investments, employment diminishes and the national prosperity declines. Factors which help businessmen to feel that investment is safe include the maintenance of peace and order, industrious and peaceful labor, low taxes, the freedom to use money and labor in any way the businessmen see fit and a feeling that the government is friendly to business enterprise.

The profits of business do not represent money taken from the workers, but are the source of capital which will employ more workers and increase production still more. It is the businessman, drawn by the lure of profits, who serves his fellow man by using his savings in business enterprise which make it possible for all of us to lead a better life. In this fashion, the businessman who invests in a new factory or develops a new mine may actually do more for his country than the individual who gives a fortune to

CHAPTER XIII. ASPECTS OF INDUSTRIALIZATION   347

charity, for the businessman's investment makes it possible for others to earn a better living.

The reason that the Philippines is often called an underdeveloped country is that the natural resources of the country have not been utilized to the greatest possible extent. Hence, many people live in poverty in a land which is potentially wealthy. One reason for this slow pace of development is that Filipinos as a group do not have enough savings to provide investment funds for the rapid increase in the country's wealth. Another reason is that relatively few Filipinos have the training or experience as businessmen which would enable them to take advantage of the opportunities around them.

Many people in the Philippines are friendly to business development as long as it is in the Philippine hands but are afraid that development by Americans, Spanish or Chinese capitalists will mean the loss of the country's heritage. Here we should bear in mind that the main point is not that a particular businessman makes a profit but, that in the making of that profit, he develops the country's resources. Baguio, for instance, is immensely richer because Judge Hauserman made large profits in the development of the gold mines, and another American venture, the Caltex refinery, will mean not only profits for a foreign company but jobs for Filipino workers and lower priced petroleum for Filipino consumers. Similarly, when the Sycip brothers made profits in banking they helped hundreds of Filipino businessmen to establish profitable businesses and gave employment to thousands of people. Business development makes everyone richer and no one poorer whether the businessmen are natives or aliens.

Perhaps the United States may be a case in point since it too was once an underdeveloped country, and the early Americans were short of capital and limited in business experience. The United States developed rapidly because capitalists from England, Germany and France invested large funds and because clever businessmen from all parts of the world swarmed into the country. These businessmen often competed with local merchants but the net result of their activities was to bring every possibility of profit to a maximum development so that the United States became a prosperous country able to send out capital and skill to the rest of the world. The United States did not develop by shutting herself off from the world but by inviting capital and business skill from all the rest of the world to come into the country and go to work. Today Americans feel less need of outside help but the amount of immigration permitted is still many times that allowed in the Philippines and foreigners are entirely free to enter most American business activities.

A case closer in time and space concerns the situation in Hongkong after the communists had gained power in the Chinese mainland. Fear of the communists caused thousands of Chinese merchants to flee to Hongkong at a time when the trade of the country with China was greatly reduced. This might be thought to cause more competition and hence bring difficulty to the people of Hongkong. Actually, the increased number of businessmen invested their money in trade and manufacture so that Hongkong was more prosperous than before they entered the country. When the Chinese merchants made money the English merchants also profited and the whole country experienced a time of prosperity. The moral to the illustration is simply that it is the businessmen who keep the economy going and the more businessmen in a country the more prosperous the country will be. The Philippines needs, and is gaining, a larger number of local businessmen but its development will also profit greatly by help from alien businessmen utilizing foreign sources of capital. The phrase "social justice" is a mockery unless the activity of the businessmen have brought production to the point where it can support a decent livelihood. The encouragement of business will bring prosperity to all parts of the population but the effort to saddle it with high wages, big taxes and cumbersome rules leads to unemployment, suffering and a further lag in the develop-

BUSINESS LEADERS IN THE PHILIPPINES

John W. Haussermann
Benguet Consolidated Mining Company and Balatoc Consolidated Mining Company

Andres Soriano
San Miguel Brewery and allied enterprises

Albino Sycip
China Banking Corporation

Gonzalo Puyat
Puyat & Sons Furniture

Don Toribio Teodoro
Ang Tibay Shoe Company

L. R. Aguinaldo
Aguinaldo's Merchandise

Picture includes a few of the men who are helping to build a modern Philippines. Three of these men are of Filipino origin, the rest are of Chinese, Spanish and American ancestry. All are working to establish more prosperous country through business enterprises and civic service.

ment of the country's resources. A free business is the best foundation for a Philippines which is free in every sense of the word.

Summary

The industrial process is one phase of social life. In an earlier stage of development, industry was identical with family and community, but in modern society it operates outside of these groups. Under these circumstances, laborers look to their work unit for intimate primary group associations which bind men together. Thus, the informal work group becomes a control mechanism setting rates of output and determining employee's satisfaction on the job. Industrialism has been delayed in the Philippines, but efforts are now being made to expand manufacturing. This expansion of industry requires a shift in traditional folkways to favor capital investment in long range manufacturing enterprises, the development of local businessmen and a changed attitude toward manual labor. Industrialism produses social problems which may be alleviated by private charity, business paternalism, social legislation and collective bargaining. Collective bargaining represents an attempt to integrate more fully the social life of the workers, but has only rudimentary beginnings in this area. Opinion, at this time, is divided on the need for compulsory arbitration and close union supervision. Social legislation in the Philippines has not included much provision for social security, and it is questionable whether or not this step is desirable at the present stage of industrial development.

CHAPTER XIII. ASPECTS OF INDUSTRIALIZATION

QUESTIONS

1. How did the transition from primitive to industrial society affect man's life?
2. What are the chief methods of coping with social problems of industrial society? Give the merits and drawbacks of the three methods discussed in this chapter.
3. Is compulsory arbitration of industrial disputes desirable? Why?
4. What was the significance of the Haythorne experiment? How would you distinguish between the psychological and the sociological approaches to factory life?
5. What changes in Filipino folkways might facilitate industrialization?
6. How did the class structure of European life promote a more favorable attitude toward manual labor?
7. News stories frequently carry reports of individual Filipinos being robbed of large sums of money. What does this indicate about the folkways concerning business practices and methods of saving money?
8. Do high profits hurt the laborers? Justify your answer.

PROJECTS

1. If you have worked in a factory give a description of the informal social groups which developed. What was their attitude toward the foreman, the management, the rapid worker and the slower than average worker? If there was a union, describe its functions.
2. Follow through newspaper reports the history of a specific labor dispute. Write up the story in outline form.
3. Report on one of the references in the bibliography.

SUGGESTED READINGS

Chase, Stuart: *Men at Work*, Harcourt Brace, New York, 1945.
A good popular discussion of industrial Sociology.

Chiong, Ernesto E.: *A Critical Study of Philippine Labor Laws*. Unpublished Master's Thesis, Far Eastern University, 1952.

Kurihara, Kenneth: *Labor in the Philippine Economy*, Stanford University Press, 1945.
Discussion of Organized Labor in the Philippines.

Miller William H. & Delbert C. Form: *Industrial Sociology*, Harpers, New York, 1951.
A very comprehensive textbook type of treatment.

Moore, Wilbert E.: *Industrialization and Labor*, Cornell University Press, Ithaca, N. Y., 1951.
Written by a member of the Princeton University Office of Population Research. An exhaustive analysis of the social attitudes affecting labor in underdeveloped counries.

Serquiña, Conrado A.: *A Sociological Analysis of Labor Unionism in the Philippines*. Unpublished Master's Thesis, University of the Philippines, 1952.

Thompson, Virginia: *Labor Problems in Southeast Asia*, Yale University Press, New Haven, 1947.
A comprehensive study of labor problems in the area which brings out the relationship of the Philippines to other countries in Southeast Asia.

Tupas, Rodolfo: "The Case of Free Labor," *Sunday Times Magazine*, March 1, 1953 and Lanting, Juan L. "The Court and the Workers," *Sunday Times Magazine*, February 15, 1953.
These two articles give divergent viewpoints on the merits of present day Philippine labor legislation.

U. S. *Economic Survey Mission's Report*, distributed by Philippine Book Co., Manila.
This is the famous Bell Report. Pages 69 to 82 and 105 to 113 deal with some of the problems raised in this chapter.

Whyte, William F.: *Industry and Society*, McGraw Hill, New York, 1946.
A brief and quite readable book which contains essays on a number of aspects of industrial sociology.

CHAPTER FOURTEEN

AGRARIAN CONFLICT

...land reform is important not only because of its potential effect on incentives to production. It has a far larger significance. It can mean the difference between explosive tensions and stability, between apathy and hope, between serfdom and citizenship. A nation of farm owners and of tenants who have the opportunity to become farm-owners has the basic elements of a stable society. The farmer who owns his land, who retains an equitable share of his production, who is able to combine in voluntary associations with his neighbors to improve their common lot, knows the meaning of human dignity. He has a stake in his community. A nation of insecure tenants and rootless laborers, who see little hope to better their lot, is an unstable society, subject to sporadic violence and easily persuaded to follow false leaders.

— Extract from *Land Reform Challenges The Free World* by Isador Lubin, U.S. Representative, Economic and Social Council of the United Nations.

Rural Unrest

Frequently, observers of rural life describe the ordinary *tao* as one completely bound by tradition who has no longing for a better life and is perfectly content to live in a very humble manner. It is true that the *tao* does not always have the same ideas about his welfare as the city reformer, but to describe him as perfectly contented is evidence either of wishful thinking or of gross misunderstanding. Indications of rural discontent are to be found in the demonstrations, strikes and armed revolts which have erupted periodically for many years.

In the last forty years, much of the world's surface has been plunged into conflict between landless peasants who wished to become farm owners and the landlords who held title to considerable areas of property. The Communist Revolution in Russia in 1917 was successful, in part, because its leaders promised land to the peasants, and similar promises were influential in unseating the Nationalist government in China. In Mexico and Spain, land distribution has agitated politics for years. In Italy, government and opposition parties compete with each other in promises to end landlordism and give the peasant a plot to call his own. In Japan, the American occupation authorities sponsored a drastic program of land distribution. Korea had a land distribution program in progress at the outbreak of the conflict which began in 1950 and similar programs are currently under way in Formosa and parts of India. Throughout the rest of the Far East, the demand of the ordinary farmer for land ownership underlies all present conflicts.

Since the peasant is a many sided human being, his revolts may be concerned with several issues, but always the claim to land of his own will be a prime concern. Thus some uprisings are linked to religious fanaticism, others feature a demand for national independence and still others may be influenced by communist agitators. Undue attention to the variation in the form or the leadership of peasant uprisings brings more confusion than understanding, especially if this conceals the basic point that a landless peasant is always a threat to the stability of any society.

Peasant revolts have been known for centuries, but they seem to be increasing in frequency and intensity at the present time. One explanation of this development is the manner in which the entry of the modern *gesellschaft* type of society in rural areas has shattered the security of older institutions while simultaneously stimulating new demands and ambitions in the landless peasant. In Southeast Asia, this tendency is most apparent in the shift from a subsistence to an export type of economy. This means that, whereas

Chapter XIV. AGRARIAN CONFLICT

at one time, the farmer's efforts were devoted to raising food for himself and a small group of landlords, traders and government officials; he may now be producing cash crops for a foreign market and, in turn, be forced to buy his own food on the open market. This means that a humble but secure type of livelihood has been exchanged for one equally humble, but now subject to all the insecurity of fluctuating markets and uncertain prices.

The landlord has also been influenced by new developments and, he too, is caught in the grip of a cash economy which demands money for taxes and for the maintenance of an urban style of living. Frequently, the landlord responds to this situation by turning over the management of the farm to a hired agent and moving to the city where he and his family can enjoy a more luxurious type of living. The possibilities of conflicts are always present in the landlord-tenant relationship and these are accentuated when the landlord changes from a benevolent patriarch with a personal concern for his tenants to an absentee owner interested in ready cash. In this event, the personal ties between owner and tenant are weakened at the very time when the chances for friction are increased.

The same forces which rob the peasant of his security also cause him to be discontented with the life he formerly led. Even if the shift to an export cash crop economy causes no actual hardship or perhaps increases slightly the income of the peasant, this still does not eliminate unrest. The type of culture which makes possible world markets also brings increased communication which enables the present to learn the utility of factory made clothes, commercial amusements, and household conveniences. Furthermore, he learns that these luxuries are not simply for a privileged few, but the proper expectation of all men. Thus he fights not only for his vanished security, but also for the perennial dream of owning his own land and for the modern hope of a comfortable livelihood.

Conflict in the Philippines.

The close of World War II found landlord-tenant relationships disrupted in many areas of the Philippines. The Japanese had effectively occupied the cities, but never had sufficient troops to garrison the entire country and suppress guerrilla opposition. Under these circumstances, a major technique of guerrillas was the effort to prevent the Japanese troops from securing a normal share of the harvest. Since the landlord was well known and could not openly defy the Japanese, the guerrillas encouraged the *taos* to seize the crops themselves rather than follow the usual procedures of marketing. This meant that the landlord was almost inevitably placed in the position of either collaborating with the Japanese or of giving up his usual source of income. On the other hand, the guerrilla's motivation combined the element of patriotic opposition to an occupying power with a long standing resentment of tenants against farm owners.

One of the most effective guerrilla movements was the *Hukbo ng Bayan Laban sa Hapon* or *Hukbalahap*, a Tagalog abbreviation for People's Army Against the Japanese. After World War II this organization became known as the *Hukbong Magpapalaya sa Bayan*, meaning The Army to Free the Nation. Led by Luis Taruc, the Huks became a militant peasant's organization and some of the leaders appear to have definite ties with communist movements. Possibly because of the Communist link, no definite agreement was reached with the American forces and the Huks (except for a few units) were not given the monetary benefits afforded the "recognized" guerrillas. At the close of the war, the Huks comprised an armed group of considerable strength whose relations with the liberating Americans and the reconstituted Filipino armed forces were far from satisfactory. The Huks were in no mood to welcome back the landlords, many of whom they considered to be collaborators, and, in any event, they were as much interested in changing the land system as in eliminating the Japanese. Following a

CHAPTER XIV. AGRARIAN CONFLICT

period of uncertainty and attempts to reach a compromise, the *Hukbalahap* were officially outlawed on March 6, 1948 under a proclamation by President Roxas. After the death of Roxas, his successor, President Quirino, offered an amnesty which was first accepted by Taruc and then broken in a few months with mutual charges of bad faith.

Since that time, the Huks have been engaged in an intermittent guerrilla type warfare with the armed forces of the Republic. The Huk activities include a systematic campaign of terror which has forced farmers to flee from many sections of the country and caused thousands of hectares of land to be left unused. They have systematically taxed the residents of barrios, raided towns, engaged in major robbery and occasionally, even attacked army posts. The most sensational activity was an attack on a convoy enroute to Baler which resulted in the death of the widow of the late President Quezon.

At this writing, February, 1954, official reports indicate that the Huk movement is losing strength and is confined to scattered bands in the more inaccessible areas. Several of the Huk leaders have been arrested and a considerable number of followers have surrendered. In spite of these reverses, the Huks can still muster enough force for occasional raids and are a constant menace in many areas of Central Luzon. Personnel of the *Hukbalahap* is drawn from a variety of sources and, in the early days, included many who had joined it simply as a means of opposing the Japanese. The postwar group includes a sprinkling of professional communists together with discontented *taos*, adventurous youth, ordinary bandits, confused idealists and a number of wartime guerrillas who find the ways of peace dull and boring; in other words, the type of motley group of mixed motives who are attracted to any extremist movement. The motives of the individual Huks are undoubtedly too mixed to be described by a simple formula, but the social situation which made their existence possible was the combination of wartime confusion with tenant unrest. The unrest has been in existence for years. The war broke down the previous social controls and the Huk leaders gave direction to a discontented group.

Military operations may result in the elimination of the Huks, but a final solution to the problem of agrarian revolts will require major changes in the whole system of landlord-tenant relationships.

Historical Background of Filipino Agrarian Troubles

While the wartime conditions allowed the formation of a particular type of agrarian revolt, it would be a grave error to assume that tenant unrest is of recent origin. The Spanish period saw literally hundreds of uprisings in which agrarian unrest was coupled with religious controversy and patriotic grievances. Incidents of this type include agrarian revolts in 1743 and 1745 in the provinces of Cavite and Tayabas.[1] This type of unrest was manifested in the revolution of 1896 in which the lands of the Friars were seized by the tenants and many of the Friars killed or driven away. Nor did the purchase and resale of the Friar lands end such difficulties. During the American regime, we find a large number of petty controversies and such incidents as the *Tayug* incident and the *Sakdal* uprisings in 1931 and 1935 respectively. In the *Tayug* incident, armed peasants looted the city hall and destroyed land records. The Sakdal uprising involved 5,000 to 7,000 people and was only put down after bloody fighting. The *Sakdalistas* advocated immediate independence rather than a commonwealth government and independence was linked in their minds with the ability to eliminate the landlords. Hayden quotes from a report made by American members of the Malacañan advisory staff as follows:

> The rank and file of the radical wing of the Sakdalistas now believe that the establishment of the Commonwealth Government is a move to es-

---

[1] Macaraig, *op. cit.*, p. 262.

tablish and maintain in power a group of Filipino leaders who represent the upper classes and who will oppress the lower classes. They believe that immediate independence will enable the economically depressed classes to eliminate these leaders from politics.[2]

In addition to the violent and relatively large scale incidents of agrarian conflict, there have been a constant number of disputes which have resulted in riots, discontent and court action. These disputes are based on arguments over landownership, allegedly excessive interest payments, requirements of extra work by landlords and disagreement over proper division of the harvest. By itself, no one dispute is particularly serious, but the cumulative total, 4,194 cases between 1937 and 1941, indicates a serious undercurrent of unrest.[3] In considering these figures, one should bear in mind that in only a minority of cases would the tenants have the courage to make an open complaint about allegedly unjust practices.

Pattern of landlord-tenant relationships.

The prevailing pattern of land distribution may be traced back to pre-Spanish days in what is very nearly an unbroken pattern. Before the coming of the Spaniards, the population was divided into *datus*, free men, serfs and slaves. Pelzer describes the pattern as follows:

> Each village, or *barangay*, as the Tagalog called it, had its own chief, or *datu*. Under the aristocracy, which was represented by the *datu* and his family, there were three classes of people: free men, serfs, and slaves. The free-born members of a barangay usually paid no taxes or tribute to the *datu* were obliged to follow him in war and to help with the cultivation of his land, the harvesting of his rice and the construction of his house. In a tropical climate this last task is repeated every few years. The serfs were obviously what today we

---
[2] Hayden, *op. cit.*, p. 393.
[3] Based on Table 128 *Yearbook of Philippine Statistics*, 1946.

should call tenants or *aparceros*. They had their own houses and turned over to their masters the yield of half the land that they cultivated. The slaves lived in quarters provided by the master, could not marry without his permission, and could be sold at any time.

The cleared land of a barangay was divided among the free-born, each one recognizing the rights of the others. There were no titles. The forested land was not divided but was held by the barangay other than his own unless he had purchased or inherited the right to do so. The position of *datu* was usually held by one family through hereditary right. This gave the family definite economic and social advantages over the other families of the barangay.[4]

The Spaniards professed to recognize the rights of the peasants to the lands they were actually working, but divided the most desirable land into grants or *encomiendas* in which the native population were forced to pay tribute to Spanish settlers who were known *encomenderos*. Eventually, conflict between the *encomenderos* and religious authorities and complaints of native exploitation led the Spanish government to replace the *encomenderos* with political appointees and to favor the development of large estates belonging to the church.

In all these changes, the Spaniards attempted to leave the social structure of the village in its original form and to use the *datus* as intermediaries between the ruling power and the native population. In the process, the power of the *datus* was enlarged by their role as tax collectors and further strengthened by intermarriage with the Spanish. Freeholders, on the other hand, were reduced to the status of tenants. The American authorities attempted to alleviate conflict between the Roman Catholic Church and the tenants by purchasing the Friar lands, but this did not eliminate all church owned lands and church estates were

---

[4] Karl J. Pelzer: *Pioneer Settlement in the Asiatic Tropics*, American Geographical Society, New York, 1945, p. 88. Used by permission of the publishers.

Chapter XIV. AGRACIAN CONFLICT

increased by later acquisitions. The descendants of the *datus*, who had now become known as *caciques* or sometimes as *hacenderos*, were left undisturbed in their claims to land ownership. Not only was the landowning class left undisturbed in their possessions, but as the most intelligent and best educated class in the country, they were able to obtain national as well as local political power, a position strengthened by intermarriage with the Spaniards.

As the Spanish, American, and later, the Philippine governmental regimes proceeded to impose a more westernized type of control on the country, they aggravated the problem through their policy on land titles. To quote Pelzer:

> To the great majority of peasants, accustomed to unwritten rules of land tenure, the land law was too involved, the idea of a land title too strange. In the opinion of the Spaniard and the American, most Filipinos were without individual legal rights to the land, but in their own opinion they were the actual owners of this land that their forefathers had cleared and that had been in constant use by their families. The comparatively few people who acquired legal titles were mostly persons belonging to the *cacique* group, and these often laid claim to more land than actually they had a right to. Thus in many cases peasants who had felt secure in the possession of their land and had not known or cared about titles were suddenly confronted with the fact that a wealthy person, with the law behind him, was claiming their land. These peasants were then driven from it or forced to become tenants.[6]

Thus the pattern of land holding dominated by a comparatively small group of landowners with tenants in an inferior social and economic position was present in the Islands at the time of the arrival of the Spanish, and has remained dominant during subsequent changes in government. The

---
[5] *Ibid.*, pp. 89-91.
[6] *Ibid.*, p. 90. Reproduced by permission of the publishers.

officials in Malacañan might change from Spanish to American and then to Filipino, but to the man who tilled the soil these shifts in governmental power made very little difference in his social and economic position. Before the Spanish period, one spoke of *datus* and serfs; in the Spanish regime, the terminology was likely to be *cacique* and *tao*; while from the latter period of Spanish rule to the present, one was more likely to think of *hacenderos* and tenants. Whatever the nomenclature, the power, wealth and prestige belong to the land owner, while the peasant was characterized by servility and poverty.

Current landlord-tenant relationships.

At the present time, three major groups are found in the land tenure system: individual landlords, whose holdings vary from a few hectares to several thousand; farm owners, who till their own land, many of whom own an amount of land insufficient for a livelihood; and finally, a large group of landless tenants. In addition to these main groups, some land is still held by church estates and a considerable area is occupied by business corporations. On the basis of the 1939 census, the M.S.A. report on land tenure reform found that, considering cultivated land, farms operated by owners accounted for about 49%; by part owners, 15%; by tenants, 32% and by farm managers, 4%. This is an overall rate and in several provinces the proportion of tenancy is even higher. Thus in Pampanga, often a scene of disturbance, 70.4% of farms were cultivated by tenants.[7]

To gain an understanding of the relationship of agrarian conflict to land tenure, we shall now describe briefly the salient aspects of the tenancy system.[8] The landowner divides his estate into small units and has them tilled either by an *inquilino* or cash tenants or by a *kasama* or

---

[7] *Philippine Land Tenure Reform, op. cit.,* p. 2, A-5.
[8] This description is based on the discussion of Agrarian problems in *Report and Recommendations of the Advisory Committee on Large Estates Problems,* Republic of the Philippines, Office of Economic Coordination, Manila, April 1951.

Chapter XIV. AGRARIAN CONFLICT

share tenant. Under the *inquilino* system, a tenant agrees to work on a suit of land for a specific amount in cash or in kind called *canon* and agreed upon by both parties. The *inquilino* provides his own work animals, seeds and all other expenses for his agricultural operations. The amount of *canon* depends upon any or all of the following factors; namely, local conditions, population pressure, quality of land, and the crop raised on that particular farm.

In many cases, an absentee landlord enters into an agreement with an *inquilino* who, in turn, leases the land to share tenants who actually work the farm. In this system, the landlord does not need to supervise the work since a fixed *canon* is to be paid at the expiration of the contract.

The prevailing form of tenancy in the rice region where discontent is rampant is the *kasama* system. The most common form of this system is that one wherein the landowner provides the land, seed and cash for the agricultural operations, while the *kasama* provides the labor nad the work animals. The crop is equally divided after deducting in kind the expenses incurred during the transplanting and harvesting. In another form, the *kasama* receives two thirds of the crop and the landlord one third if the farmer bears the expenses for the seed, planting and harvesting as well as the labor and work animals. In the third arrangement, the landlord furnishes the tenant with land, work animals and seed. The harvest is equally divided after deducting the cost of operations.

This type of tenancy system encourages a number of practices which give rise to disputes between landlord and tenant. Such practices do not exist in all cases, and in some instances, the landlord may scrupulously avoid any kind of unfair dealing. The numbers of unscrupulous landlords, however, is large enough to give rise to many genuine grievances and, even more important, to create an attitude of distrust in the minds of many tenants.

Tenancy practices that produce friction.

The tenant is usually unable to take care of his needs between the time when the seeds are planted and the crop matures and is dependent upon loans received either from a landlord or from a merchant. The tenant is a man of limited income and has to pay an interest rate far above that which the urban business man pays for the financing of his business needs. A brief description of some types of loans will indicate the extent of the interest burden.

The *takipan* is a form of loan whereby the landlord lends the *kasama* two cavanes of palay to be paid in four cavanes. In this particular case, the rate of interest is 100%.

The *talindua* form of credit demands payment of three cavanes of palay for two cavanes borrowed. The interests is 50%.

The *terciahan* is a loan in which the interest demanded is 33-1/3%. This involves the loan of three cavanes of palay which is repaid by four.

These loan practices are aggravated by the fact that many tenants are illiterate and either have no written contract or must rely on the landlord for the interpretation of any contract which may be in force. Under these circumstances, the tenant can hardly question the landlord's account of crops produced or expenses incurred.

The tenant may be required to buy his supplies from a *cantina* (store) operated by the landlord which may charge exhorbitant prices. He is also apt to be in a position in which the landlord measures the amount of his harvest, charges him for storage and forces him to use transportation facilities owned by the landlord in moving the crops. In practically every aspect of his economic life, the tenant is dominated by the landlord in a fashion that leads to exploitation in some cases and misunderstanding in many others.

The above practices contribute to the impoverished condition of the tenant. Moreover, the system itself per-

CHAPTER XIV. AGRARIAN CONFLICT

petuates such a condition. The average holding of a tenant is two hectares, a number insufficient to yield a crop large enough to support decent living. The average annual income of such tenant farmers, assuming a crop of 27.4 cavanes per hectare and a rental basis of 30%, is only ₱365.70 a year with no allowance for pay of the laborer or his family.[9] It should be borne in mind that in many cases the yield is less, the farm smaller than two hectares and the tenant pays more than 30% of the crop in rent.

Proposals for Reform

Dating back to the abolition of the *encomienda* system, there have been numerous efforts to effect agrarian reform. These may be summarized under the heading of tenancy regulation, general rural improvement, mechanization of agriculture, development of new lands, purchase and and resale of large estates and the so-called Hardie recommendations to effect a major reduction in the scope of tenancy.

Tenancy Regulation.

An obvious method of dealing with the types of abuses which may arise in the tenancy system is to pass regulatory legislation designed to minimize or eliminate undesirable practices. Much legislation of this type has been passed; the most famous of which is the Rice Share Tenancy Act providing a set formula for sharing the crop between landlord and tenant. The difficulty of such an approach lies in the enforcement of regulatory legislation. If tenants were free to exercise their political and civic rights and were supported by an effective public opinion, such laws might be of real value; but the present social milieu is of an entirely different nature. Tenants compete with each other for land and willingly forego legal rights in a desperate effort to obtain a place to farm. Even aside from this economic pressure, tenants have long been the subordinate class in the community while the landlords usually

---
[9] Philippine Land Tenure Reform, *op. cit.*, p. 41.

have taken control of society for granted. Such a system is hardly congenial to the enforcement of laws which diminish the privileges of the landlord.

Large estate purchase.

This program can be said to have begun with the purchase by the American authorities of the Friar estates in the early days of the American occupation. The program implies that the government will purchase large estates and, in turn, resell them to small farmers. It is a plan which has received support from both the Philippine and American governments, but which has run into many difficulties. These difficulties include the enormous sums of money involved, which exceed the current governmental revenues available and which also frequently exceed the capacity of purchasers to repay. In addition, tenants may think that the original titles were fraudulent and feel that the demand of the government for repayment is unjust. Since other aspects of the farm system are left unchanged, the new owners are often unable to keep title to the property and it may again revert to landlord control. There is also the danger that prosperous landlords may demand exhorbitant prices while the owners of impoverished estates may actually seek government purchase as a means of easing their financial difficulties.

Development of new lands.

Since millions of hectares of undeveloped land are available for agricultural use, their development would seem to provide a possible answer to agrarian problems. Under the leadership of the then Secretary Magsaysay, military action against the Huks was combined with an offer of a chance to obtain land in the EDCOR project. Huks who would agree to surrender their arms and return to a peaceful life could thus start on the road to farm ownership. This type of approach would seem to offer tenants the chance for land ownership without disturbing existing relations in the settled areas of the Philippines.

CHAPTER XIV. AGRARIAN CONFLICT

The settlement of these lands does indeed afford a real opportunity to increase the production of the country and the prosperity of its people, but it, by no means, follows that migration to Mindanao and similar areas is a panacea for all rural ills. One obstacle is the fact that many tenants are closely attached to particular localities and reluctant to move to new areas. Aside from this reluctance to leave a district which has been their home for many years, there are numerous objective difficulties to be overcome. Large scale land resettlement requires the provision of credit, the construction of roads, the elimination of malaria, maintenance of peace and order and finally the efficient, just and speedy handling of applications for land titles. All of these problems are being attacked, but there is no speedy solution and years will be required before settlers in all areas can be assured of favorable conditions. The immediate prospect is for gradual improvement which will promote development of unsettled areas over a period of many years. Taking the most optimistic view of the possibilities of bringing new land under cultivation, this course seems better adapted to the alleviation of problems connected with population growth than to the adjustment of agrarian problems in areas which are already heavily settled. The population of the Philippines has nearly tripled since the end of Spanish rule and, at present, is growing at the rate of about two percent a year. It would seem that the most rapid possible rate of settlement could do little more than provide opportunities for the increment (annual increase) of population.

Mechanization of agriculture.

Since many Philippine farms are operated on the basis of carabao, wooden plow and unskilled labor, the possibilities of mechanization are obviously attractive. The widespread adoption of modern farming techniques might be expected to decrease labor costs, increase production and afford farm operators a larger return for their labor. Typical of this type of thinking is the proposal of the "Jungle Philosopher" who suggests that with ₱5,000 capital, one family could secure enough equipment to handle twenty-four hectares of land and easily make enough money to repay the capital cost.[10]

Mechanization is a method of changing the countryside in the direction of an urban *gesellschaft* type of culture. In this culture, the unskilled *tao* would be replaced by the number of laborers might be greatly increased. With a larger net return, rural life could be lifted above the poverty level and farm families could approximate an urban standard of living.

Pressure for rapid mechanization, however, ignores the adverse effects of such a change. At the present time, half of the farms are two hectares or less, approximately a million individuals are unemployed and an even larger number are under-employed. Under these circumstances, a sudden increase in the size of the average farm would spell unemployment and destitution for a large number of farm tenants and laborers. Mechanization would also have the effect of decreasing the number of independent small farmers, since the effective use of most types of mechanized farm equipment demands an area considerably greater than the farms of one to five hectares which are now an important part of the Philippine economy. The desirability of such a change depends not only on the possibility of such displaced farmers finding work in the cities but also on whether or not this shift from the status of small farmer to that of urban wage earner actually represents social improvement. Admitting the increase in productivity which may come from mechanization on the farm and industrialization in the city, many people would still maintain that a nation of small farmers has a type of stability and contentment which can not be attained in an urban society.

---

[10] *Philippine Free Press*, Manila, January 3, 1953.

CHAPTER XIV. AGRARIAN CONFLICT 369

Mechanization is often urged as a solution to rural poverty. These pictures contrast the use of tractors and carabaos on Philippine farms.

Eventually, a high degree of mechanization may be inevitable, but this would mean great economic suffering unless, at the same time, industrialization develops to the point where a large number of laborers can move to cities and find employment in industrial enterprises. Over a long period of time, mechanization may completely change the character of Philippine agriculture with benefit to all concerned, but its sudden development would give rise to social problems even more difficult than those with which we are now faced.

General rural improvement.

In speaking of the difficulty of solving tenancy problems by the division of large estates, we mentioned that the new owners might have difficulty in maintaining their position and be forced to sell out to landlords. This obviously points to the need of a broad scale attack on all the ills of rural society which hamper the development of independent responsible, moderately prosperous farmers.

Such a program would include greater civic awareness, better agricultural education to enable the *tao* to take advantage of modern methods, the provision of low cost credit facilities, better marketing agencies, improved sanitation and health services and a host of other changes. Changes of this type are essential regardless of the type of land tenure, but, by themselves, they are not a sufficient answer to rural discontent.

In the first place, these changes do not meet the "felt needs" of the common *tao*. They presuppose attitudes and concepts which as yet are developed. Furthermore, they ignore a need which is uppermost in his mind; the desire for land of his own. If society satisfies the land hunger of the *tao*, it may, by skillful planning, hold him to take advantage desire for a farm of his own is ignored, then the *tao* is likely to feel that alleged improvements are merely window dressing which force him to a painful change of life-long habits and, if valuable at all, would only serve to increase the income of the landlord.

General rural improvement is an indispensable ally of any program for change in the pattern of land ownership, but it is not a substitute for land redistribution.

The Hardie recommendations.

Although proposals for rural change have been common for many years, none of them produced a reaction as intense as that which greeted the publication of the so-called Hardie report. This was a report made by the U.S. Mutual Security Agency in the course of its investigation of rural problems in the Philippines. The report was largely based on previous investigations, and its analysis of current land practices contained little that was not already familiar to students of the problem. Its recommendations, however, were far more drastic than previous proposals which have emanated from high governmental circles.

The major differences between these proposals and previous ones lie in the scope of reform and in the time element. Previously, it has been fashionable to speak of tenancy problems as requiring generations for substantial change, while the Hardie report suggests that the entire situation could be allowed in two year's time. Similarly, the report departs from the usual concentration on the very large *haciendas* and calls for the redistribution of virtually all land which is not cultivated by the labor of the owner and his family. The report proposes that all farm land not actually cultivated by the labor of the owner and his family be purchased by the government and resold to tenants. A summary of the Hardie report may be found in the appendix.

Value of Hardie Report.

Although a similar project appears to have been highly successful in Japan, many questions have been raised about its prospects in the Philippines. One objection stems from a belief that tenancy itself is not really bad and that, with ameliorative legislation and general rural improvement, a tenancy system may actually be the type of agriculture best adapted to the Philippine scene. Even granting the undesirability of tenancy some may feel that so drastic and sudden a step may injure agricultural production.

Opposition also come from quarters who believe that the basic need of the Philippines is not a large number of small landowners but a shift to mechanized large scale farming. Perhaps the major objection to the recommendations of the Hardie report is that it is a direct challenge to local mores and vested interests. Land owners whose property would be placed on sale may number as many as 80,000 and they comprise the most powerful group in Philippine society. Land as an investment has long been considered the most desirable use of funds and large numbers of men prominent in business, government and the professions are also petty landlords. It is certainly an open question whether or not sufficient social pressure can be applied to force a change in this type of pattern.

Outcome of agrarian revolt.

In the chapter dealing with social class we mentioned that Communism seemed to make its greatest advances in rural areas plagued by conflict between landlord and tenant. This would certainly seem to be true of the Philippines where radicalism as an effective force has mainly been associated with tenant movements. In China communists appear to have won considerable peasant support and such an outcome in this area is at least conceivable.

From one point of view, it would seem paradoxical that tenants who desperately desire to own land should turn to a system which proclaims its opposition to all productive forms of private property. The answer to this paradox is that Communist leaders are not inflexibly bound by the writings of Karl Marx and that peasants are not political theoreticians but desperate men looking for help. The peasant desires a chance to own land which he calls his own and the Communist desires rural support; what could be simpler than for the Communist to promise the abolition of landlordism and the extension of private ownership to tenants in exchange for their support of the Communist movement?

The peasant hears varying comments on the ideological features of Communism, but he hears the Communist leaders say that they will give him land while leaders of other groups tend to evade the issue and talk in terms of long term amelioration. Further, the evidence is clear that in many areas of the world, Communists have launched energetic programs of land distribution under which onetime tenants have actually become owners of the land they till. The history of the Communist revolution in Russia illustrates how the Communist can harmonize immediate needs with the long term Communist policy.

At the time of the revolution in 1917, they seized the estates of the nobility and gave the peasants individual tracts of land, thus securing rural support while apparently abandoning their own principles of opposition to any kind of private ownership. By 1930, when the Communists had secured a firm grip on the country they reversed their policy. At this time, private ownership of land was practically outlawed and individual farmers were forced to join "collective farms" where they had no individual title to the land and the state became the new landlord.

This sequence of events should prove that Communist leaders are false saviors and that their promise of widespread farm ownership is a mirage which will disappear as soon as their political and economic control is established. Actually, however, the deceptions of Communism are known only to the relatively sophisticated. The ordinary peasant has little training in history and he may distrust those who attempt to teach him the historical proof of Communist treachery. He is inclined to judge on the basis of what he sees going on about him. If he sees Communists apparently talking and fighting for land reform while other groups are indifferent, he may be inclined to view the Communist as at least the lesser of two evils.

If this is the situation, how can non-Communists in predominantly agricultural areas stop the spread of the Communist party?

Three alternatives appear to be open in the fight against the Communist effort to utilize agrarian discontent as a means of coming to power; mild reform and moderate repression of dissidents, major reforms with military suppression of diehard elements and finally, a complete reliance on naked force.

Probably the first alternative is the easiest to follow. This appears to be the course pursued by the Nationalist government in China; namely, to make verbal offers of reform which have little real effect and to hope that remaining discontent can be put down by moderate use of military power. This method requires little adjustment of existing folkways and does not demand unusual imagination and creativity from government officials. Unfortunately, the effectiveness of this approach decreases rapidly with the passage of time.

The second alternative means that, at the same time it attempts to maintain peace and order, the government will convince the peasants that their demands for land ownership can be satisfied under the existing system. This cannot be accomplished by propaganda alone, but only by a program which can actually decrease landlordism and establishes small farmers on their own land. Such a program is directly opposed to the cherished beliefs of the most powerful members of the existing society. In addition, technical problems of administration are complex and require an unusual degree of integrity and wisdom on the part of government officials. It is an effort to beat the Communists at their own game by showing that a capitalist society is interested in exending the ownership of private property to the majority of its citizens. It means that the most powerful elements of society must be persuaded or coerced into giving up privilege for the sake of preserving the ideals of a free society.

The third alternative, reliance on naked force, is difficult for a democracy to follow. A dictator who makes no pretense of serving individual liberty may be able to intimidate his enemies for an indefinite period, but democratic governments seem to be handicapped by a concern for human dignity which is hardly compatible with long term military repression. Eventually, either the government loses its democratic character completely or the military effort is weakened by consideration for human rights. The choice of alternatives in any one country depends upon the political maturity of its inhabitants, the insight of its leaders and the ability of discontented groups to express themselves through legitimate channels. As to the type of action which is most effective, there seems to be little doubt. A social system may meet emerging needs within its own framework, but the effort to deny the deepest aspirations of large groups of people can only result in disaster.

In a stimulating article entitled "Riding the Whirlwind," Father de la Costa points out that the true genius of Catholicism requires it to work with the forces of history rather than trying to block them. This means that it must assist the changes required to meet the aspirations of the people instead of simply condemning Communists.

> "You cannot stop a social revolution. You may as well try to block a whirlwind.
>
> Yet that is precisely what certain conservative governments in Asia are trying to do today. They are opposing measures of social reform, relying on brute force to preserve existing arrangements, on the grounds that all such measures of reform are Communist-inspired and any concession made to the masses is a step nearer to Communist domination. They fail to see that by acting thus they are playing right into Communist hands. They are proving the Communist thesis that all non-Communist governments are by that very fact governments against the people. They are convincing the masses, as not even the Communists can convince

them; that the only hope for social justice lies in class warfare under Communist leadership.

We must go to the masses, as the Communists have gone to the masses and show them, by works and not by words alone, that their hope does not lie with Russia but with us. It is useless, besides being unjust, to try to stop social change in Asia. That is not the issue. The issue is, who is to control that changeé Who is to direct it? Who is to ride the whirlwind? The Communists or the men who are for freedom?" [12]

What de la Costa says about Catholicism is equally true of other religious groups and of democracy itself. The title of his article might well be paraphrased to read: They who ignore the wind of agrarian injustice will reap the whirlwind of revolution. The problem is not primarily how we can stop Communism, but rather how we can deal constructively with the demands of the rural populace. These demands led to armed revolt long before Karl Marx and the Communist Party appeared on the scene of history and they will continue to disturb the social order until the landless peasant becomes a full participant in the benefits of modern society. Peasant revolts may today be led by Communists, but their origin is less in the intrigues of the Kremlin than in the deep-rooted inequalities and lack of real opportunity which are found in many rural areas.

Summary

Revolutionary movements expressing the dissatisfaction of the rural populace have occurred periodically throughout recorded history. In Oriental countries, agrarian discontent has been aggravated by a trend toward an export cash crop type of economy which has diminished the security of the peasant, decreased the paternalistic role of the landlord and stimulated demands for a higher standard of living in all of the rural population. This agrarian discontent

---

[12] Horacio de la Cruz: "Riding the Whirlwind," *Social Order*, June, 1952, p. 246.

Chapter XIV. Agrarian Conflict

has been utilized by Communists in their drive for power even though the Communist program of collectivized farming is hostile to the demands of the peasant for individual farm ownership.

Programs to meet rural dissatisfaction have been developing over a period of years. These programs include; regulation of landlord-tenant relationships, breakup of large estates, development of new lands, general rural improvement, mechanization of farm work and, most drastic of all, proposals for a widespread shift from tenancy to owner operated farms. None of these programs stand alone and all are mutually dependent. Land redistribution is designed to meet the demands most keenly expressed by peasants and to effect a major change in the power relationships of rural society. Without effective action to give him a chance for farm ownership, the *tao* is apt to be indifferent to other types of reform and remain a threat to social stability. On the other hand, a new group of farm owners is apt to sink into tenancy unless far reaching changes can be undertaken in related aspects of rural society.

Effective programs to meet the discontent which stimulates agrarian revolt are difficult to operate and require a complex synthesis of knowledge based on the understanding of both rural culture and agricultural technology. Any effective program of this type seems destined to clash with traditional mores and vested interests and hence meets stubborn resistance. The urgency and difficulty of the problem makes the solution of rural ills a major test of free society.

SUGGESTED READINGS

De la Costa, Horacio: "Riding The Whirlwind," *Social Order*, June, 1952.
    Analysis of social basis of agrarian unrest by a Jesuit priest.

Jacoby, Erich H.: *Agrarian Unrest in Southeast Asia*, Columbia University Press, New York, 1949.
    Probably the most complete treatment of agrarian problems in this region.

Office of the Economic Coordination: *Report and Recommendations of the Advisory Committee on Large Estates*, Manila, April, 1951.
    A brief but interesting report drawn up by a group of Manila realtors.

Ortigas, Francisco, Jr.: *Planting Rice is Never Fun*, Alemars, Manila, 1953.
    Analysis of rice farming and marketing with proposals for changes. One chapter on tenancy system.

Pelzer, Karl J.: *Pioneer Settlement in the Asiatic Tropics*, American Geographical Society, New York, 1945.
    Contains discussion of agrarian attitudes in southeast Asia.

Philippine Land Tenure Reform: Analysis and Recommendations, Special Technical and Economic Missions, Manila. U S. Mutual Security Agency, 1952.
    The famous Hardie report and recommendations for land redistribution.

CHAPTER FIFTEEN

EDUCATION IN ITS SOCIAL SETTING

Our present educational system tends, in the main, to hold students to the customary, the existent, and the commonplace. It makes them merely participants with the present generation. In fact, it is often so full of dogmas, precedent, authority, and a thousand lesser cramping influences which retard progress, that it actually encourages reactionism. Instead it should, if it is really to "lead out," launch them from the shoulders of the present generation, passing on to them that which society has inherited, or wrought, or considers most contributory to its loftiest ideals, not as an end in itself or as a highest good, but a point of departure in a new process of discovery and invention.

— Joyce O. Hertzler, *Social Progress*

Education as the sociologist sees it.

In order to understand Philippine education today and its future, we have to view it from its social setting. This chapter, therefore, centers its study largely on the discussion of the social milieu as a strong background factor in conditioning the nature and role of education.

From the sociologist's viewpoint, education is a social process whereby the individual is prepared for successful participation in social relations. The phrase "successful participation in social relations" deserves more attention here because it conveys a different meaning to different people and no absolute standard of definition can be established. The variation of culture in different areas makes it impossible to develop a common yardstick which may be applied equally to schools in Ethiopia, Brazil, the Philippines, England, and the United States.

This cultural variation means that the pattern of "social relations" is not uniform and hence, the skills and attitudes required for "successful participation" will vary from country to country. Education which would be ideally suited to adjustment in England might be entirely irrelevant or even hostile to the social patterns of the Eskimo in the far north. Similarly, a type of school system which functions fairly well in relation to social life in New York City may be of doubtful value in the Philippines.

Some illustrations may help to clarify this viewpoint. In the matter of vocational skills, there will be an obvious difference between the educational needs of an area which is primarily agricultural and one in which urban occupations are predominant. The one area will have great need of men skilled on farming and in the processing of agricultural products, while the urban area will seek to develop large numbers of clerks, lawyers, accountants, factory workers, stenographers and other commercial, industrial and professional occupations. Some types of skills are equally helpful in either environment, but not all, and the general emphasis will be different. In the rural culture, the schools should seek to develop skills and attitudes which will enable their students to be happy and successful in the farm environment. The urban schools should also instill an appreciation of rural life, but their major task is to prepare students to cope with the impersonal, industrialized life of the city.

The same principle will apply in other areas. Education well suited to an area in which women are confined strictly to domestic tasks would be utterly inadequate in a region where women take an active part in the general social and industrial activities. Likewise, education which stresses conformity, memorization, obedience and submissiveness is well adapted to an authoritarian culture in which the people do not rule but simply obey. It is obviously less well suited to a democratic society which stresses initiative, freedom and social equality.

This somewhat overly neat classification of educational objectives in relationship to the culture in which they function is confused by the tendency of culture to change. An area which today is agricultural may be urban twenty years hence; women whose mothers seldom set foot outside of the home may be active in business and politics, and countries which have long been under authoritarian governments may seek to introduce a more democratic regime. Thus, education is not only related to the existing culture, but also to the direction of cultural change. It must prepare students for things to come as well as for the culture of the present.

Cultural change is never completely understood in all its implications, hence, the schools in a dynamic society can never do a completely satisfactory job. They are preparing students to find their place in a society which the educators themselves only partially understand. For this reason, schools in modern society always appear inadequate and are themselves subject to frequent change.

The task of the schools is also complicated by disagreement over the desirability of social change. Since some people welcome changes and others oppose them, they will differ accordingly in their attitude toward the schools. Some will wish the schools to accelerate the rate of change by abandoning older values and preparing students for a society different from that of their fathers. Others are suspicious of change and wish the schools to conduct a kind of rearguard battle in behalf of the older folkways. This type of clash brings the schools into the center of social conflict and means that, regardless of his specific approach, the educator can not feel that he is accepted by the total society.

From the foregoing, it becomes clear that the sociologist interprets education chiefly in its relation to culture. Applying this approach to Filipino education, we shall first seek to analyze the various cultural patterns which have influenced the schools of the Philippines; next, we shall seek to describe the type of synthesis (combination of different viewpoints) which has resulted from the interaction of various cultural influences; and finally, we shall point out the areas in which the inability to solve cultural conflicts causes confusion in educational procedures.

Education in Different Cultures

Education in primitive society.

Most primitive groups do not have institutions exactly comparable to the schools of modern society, but the education of the young is still an important part of primitive life.[1] This education is carried on by both formal and informal techniques with the family playing a dominant role. Since primitive society usually has a relatively slow rate of change, the goals of society are well defined, education has a distinctly conservative character and there is little conflict over either the objectives or the methodology of educational procedure. The subject matter of primitive education includs methods of hunting, fishing, agriculture, housekeeping and craftsmanship, along with a complicated pattern of folklore and religious practices.

While most of the learning in primitive groups is carried on by the process of interaction with members of the family, there are some groups who set aside a period of months or even years for formal instruction. Usually, this comes about the time of puberty and is the preliminary step to formal recognition of the individual as one of adult status. During this period, the youth live in a separate dwelling where older members of the tribe preside over their instruction emphasizes skills in craftsmanship or hunting and a mastery of religious and magical practices; girls are taught the role and duties of the wife and mother, in one African tribe, this is also a "fattening period" when girls refrain from exercise and eat rich food so that they will be pleasingly plump at the time of marriage. For both sexes, the instruction is climaxed with a final initiation which is one of the "rites of

---

[1] A good presentation of material on this topic is found in Woody, Thomas, *Life and Education in Early Societies*. Chapter I, "Primitive Life and Education," McMillan Co., N.Y., 1949.

passage" celebrating the transition from childhood to maturity.

An atmosphere is created of continuous excitement and novelty that catches the unabated and fervid attention of all the youth's senses. He is aroused and put on edge so as to furnish a helpless receptivity to the precepts, admonitions and didactic pageantry there set forth. It is all arranged to capture his attention and become engraved with a severe, unmitigated decisiveness that time will never erase nor circumstance expunge. This is effected by an accumulated discipline of sleeplessness, ingenious torments and trials, nerve-wracking frights and vigils of amazing variety... The whippings and torments are sometimes of incredible severity. They also attest to the crude "impressionistic" manner in which the culture is brought to bear upon the young. The Bechuana boys are arrayed in a state of nudity each morning. "The men of the town, all armed with long thin wands of a strong supple brush... are engaged in a dance named *Khoa*, in which questions are put to the boys, as, "Will you guard the chief well?" "Will you herd the cattle well?" and while the latter give an affirmative answer, the men rush forward to them, and each aims a full-length blow at the back of one of the boys—causes the supple wand to descend and bend into his back and every stroke inflicted thus makes the blood squirt out. At the end of the dance, the boys' backs are seamed with wounds and weals, the scars of which remain through life..." Thus arises the common saying that the neophyte learns the law while he is thrashed.

The immense accumulative force of these ordeals, privations, admonitions and instructions which in some instances are protracted for months, if not years at a time, is astounding in its effect upon the character of the youth. He emerges truly recast into a new mould, that of the mores of his folk. No longer indifferently interested in the life about, but keenly alive to the seriousness of his duties and the solemnity of his responsibilities, he emerges inwardly transformed.[2]

---

[2] Nathan, Miller: *The Child in Primitive Society*, Coward-McCann, Inc., New York, 1928, p. 189.

Many primitive tribes do not have such a period of formal instruction and initiation, but rely on the cumulative effect of normal contacts with the rest of the community. Most of the mountain groups of the Philippines separate boys and girls from their homes before adolescence and send them to sleep in a separate dormitory, but do not have either formal instruction or a special initiation ceremony. Even in groups of this type, it is often customary to utilize special signs of adult status such as tattooing, teeth-filing or the wearing of special types of jewelry.

Although there are few classrooms and no trained teachers, the primitive method of training the young seems quite effective in terms of passing on to succeeding generations the behavior patterns considered important for survival. Similarly, although there is little direct emphasis on what we call "discipline," the young usually accept the guidance of their elders and appear to fit easily into the prevailing social patterns. It is usually assumed that the success of primitive education is due to the direct relationship between the content of education and the demands of primitive life.

> Where one of our boys cannot understand why he should study grammar, for example, the savage child knows by personal, immediate, and hard experience that disobedience to the suggestions of an older hunter results in loss of life or injury, or, at any rate, the escape of the game upon which he has hoped to feed. This explains the apparent paradox presented by ethnographers: that the primitive child are not disciplined much or at all by their elders and yet are generally obedient and unspoiled. It is the protection from the consequences of inexpedient conduct that ruins a child's behavior; and in primitive life such protection cannot be extended very far.[3]

This somewhat idyllic picture of the relationships of the young and the old can only prevail in a stable unified

---

[3] William G. Sumner and Albert G. Keller: *The Science of Society*, Vol. 3, Yale University Press, New Haven, Conn., 1928, p. 929.

type of culture. Where primitives are in the process of rapid cultural change, they experience some of the educational problems of other groups. Thus, we find the Bontocs in Northern Luzon divided in attitude since their contact with another culture—some welcoming schoolroom education as the agency of desirable social change and others opposing it as destructive of their own culture. Also, there is complaint that the young no longer are always easy to train; they now doubt the expediency of older methods of getting a livelihood and the validity of older religious rites. Under these circumstances, they learn resentfully and under compulsion much as the western child who fails to see the utility of studying grammar.

The analytical observer will see in the educational practices of the primitives many elements present in modern society; in fact, modern progressive education is, in a large part, an emphasis on learning through experience and keeping the school close to actual social life. The family is the major of primitive education and is the place in which, even today, children learn most of their basic skills and acquire life attitudes. The concept of education as the indoctrination of the youth in the practices of the past, so prevalent among primitives, still receives support in many quarters today. Finally, the emphasis given initiation ceremonies at the time of puberty has some similarity to the debut of the society girl, the graduation ceremony at school and the religious observance of first communion, confirmation or baptism.

Educational Policies of Colonial Powers

The educational policies of colonial powers represent the influence of two conflicting sets of values: the desire to make money and retain power and the desire to spread western culture. Usually, the first desire is the one playing the major role in educational policy. Kennedy gives us a good picture of the results of this policy.

> The colonial governments until recently were either indifferent or opposed to native educational

improvement. The Europeans were in the area to make profits and to control the local populations for this purpose; and they were unwillingly to spend money for native schooling and to run the risk of sowing seeds of revolt by educating potential leaders in the knowledge, skills and human ideals of the Western world. The monopoly on economy and government, to be preserved, had to be accompanied by a monopoly on education, for ideas are the stuff of revolution. Although progress has been made in all of the countries, the figures on literacy show slow it has been. After three centuries of Dutch rule, the Indonesians were still 93 percent illiterate in 1930, and it is very unlikely that this proportion had dropped below 90 percent by 1941. Precise statistics for Indo-China are not available, but the rate of literacy there was probably not over 15 percent. In Malaya, literacy was more widespread, with 24 percent of the total population able to read and write in 1931.[4]

The general policy described by Kennedy was modified by the influence of Christian missions, the desire to train native officials for minor ranks in the government service and a need for a literate group of workmen. These factors promoted the rise of a small educated group, but, in general, the fear of education as a disturber of native contentment plus an unwillingness to bear the costs of widespread schooling sufficed to confine formal education to a small minority.

When education was provided, the policy was to confine higher education to an extremely small group suitable to the scarcity of professional opportunities open to the native population. Usually, available higher education was steeped in the language and culture of the occupying power. This was partly the natural result of European dominance and partly an effort to create an upper class native group which would identify itself with the colonial power. Primary

---

[4] Raymond Kennedy, *Southeast Asia and Indonesia* in Ralph Linton (editor): *Most of the World—The Peoples of Africa, Latin America, and the East Today.* Columbia University Press, New York, 1950, p. 673.

education had a heavy vocational emphasis and was frequently confined to the native vernacular with the objective of leaving the native social structure undisturbed and avoiding the creation of dissatisfaction which might have revolutionary consequences.

The Spanish government in the Philippines followed the general pattern of colonial educational policy which, in this case, was strengthened by the fact that education was not widespread in Spain itself. A few institutions of higher learning were established and scattered primary and elementary schools were founded. In actual practice, this meant that education along Spanish lines was available for the Spanish residents and the more prosperous Filipinos, but that the masses had little chance for schooling. The priests established some schools, but were divided in their attitude toward education of the *Indios* which many of them viewed viewed as likely to disturb religious faith and civil peace. In fact, opposition from the priests was often one of the problems of the early American school teachers.[5]

American Educational Policies

The educational policies of the United States were influenced by the major role of education in that country and the fact that it considered itself a trustee during an interim period of preparation for self-government rather than an imperialist power holding permanent possession. Unlike other western governments, it viewed the education of the Filipinos as a major responsibility which it proceeded to carry out in vigorous fashion.

The American version of public education in the Philippines had its historical beginning with the opening of the first public school by the American authorities on the island of Corregidor, at the mouth of Manila Bay, within less than a month after the destruction of the Spanish fleet by Admiral Dewey.[6]

---

[5] Antonio Isidro: *The Philippine Educational System*, Bookman, Inc., Manila, 1949, p. 16.

[6] *Report of the Director of Education* (Manila: Bureau of Printing, 1914), p. 9.

A few weeks after the occupation of the city of Manila, August 13, 1898, seven schools were reopened and a teacher of English was assigned to each under the supervision of the Reverend William McKinnon, Chaplain, First California Volunteer Infantry. At this initial stage of public education, the importance of education is clearly revealed, as pointed out in a report by General Smith as Secretary of Public Instruction:

> This work was in thorough accord with the policy of attraction marked out by President McKinley, and was offered to the Filipino people as the first earnest (demonstration) of the good intentions of the United States and of the serious purpose of the administration to benefit and advance the inhabitants of the possessions acquired as the result of the conflict with their former sovereign. Even after the insurrection broke out... free public instruction was never abandoned, but was adhered to wherever circumstances permitted and conditions were at all favorable to the building up of a school.[7]

The Schurman Commission stated in its four-volume report that "the priests who are in charge of the education of the people are interested in keeping the people in the dark as much as possible."[8] This educational policy was contrary to the purpose of the American government. In view of this situation, the Second Philippine Commission, appointed by President McKinley, April 7, 1900, gave serious consideration to the improvement of the system of education already inaugurated by the military authorities. "In doing this," it was pointed out, "they should regard as of first importance the extension of a system of primary education which shall be free to all, and which shall tend to fit the people for the duties of citizenship and for the ordinary avocations of a civilized community."[9]

---

[7] *Report of the Philippine Commission*, part 3 (Washington: Government Printing Office, 1903), pp. 673-74.
[8] *Report of the Philippine Commission*, Vol. II (Washington: Government Printing Office, 1900), p. 46.
[9] *Hearings before the Committee on the Philippines of the United States Senate*, 57th Congress, 1st session, part I (Washington: Government Printing Office, 1902), p. 108.

The rest of the story is well known. American teachers entered remote barrios. English became the language of instruction and a school system was established which was patterned, to some extent, on American lines. Gradually, the American teachers decreased in number to be replaced by Filipinos trained under their supervision or educated in the United States as *pensionados*. Seven thousand miles from the United States, a country steeped in a combination of Spanish and Oriental culture stepped into the twentieth century under the tutelage of American teachers. It was an epic experiment whose ultimate outcome is still to be decided.

Interaction of American and Filipino Culture

Nature of the interaction.

The American educational system did not completely transform the Philippine scene and the present educational system is the result of conflict and accommodation between the American educational emphasis and the dominant trends in Filipino culture. In one case, the outcome might be the complete acceptance of the American standard, in another, the prevalent Filipino practice might be preserved with little change, in still other instances, new methods might arise wihch had not been anticipated by either American or Filipino in 1900. Finally, some problems remain in which the clash of cultural values has not yet been resolved.

Cultural background of American education.

Although formal education is generally considered desirable in the United States, yet it is hard to say whether or not education is really held in respect. Education on the elementary basis is universal and it is widespread even at the graduate level of the university. On the other hand, many prominent business men and politicians boast of their lack of schooling and there is a widespread suspicion of the intellectual or "highbrow" attitude. Teachers feel that their status is inferior to others in the community and "Professor" is often a term of derision rather than respect. Perhaps Americans are so familiar with education that they feel they can afford to be a little irreverent towards it.

In the schools, the traditional classical type of learning has little support and the emphasis is on "practical" pursuits and a scientific emphasis. Here again though, the picture is mixed and one finds American engineers, physicians, lawyers and businessmen spending many years of college work in pre-professional training, studying general subjects with no direct utility in their vocational career. In fact, American professional men have more general cultural training than similar groups in many other countries.

American students take coeducation for granted as a normal part of a society which allows a considerable degree of unchaperoned association between the sexes. Athletics is a major school activity with much participation and an almost universal interest. Many students work their way through school and even boast of their experience as dishwashers, truck drivers, harvest hands, waiters, clerks, janitors, etc. Social distinctions, however, are preserved by a strong fraternity system which usually operates to strengthen a sense of class and ethnic differences.

The great majority of the people now live in cities with a tendency for the rural population to conform increasingly to urban standards. Many peoples have entered the culture, but the dominance of the English speaking, Anglo-Saxon, protestant group has still not been seriously threatened. Public support for all forms of education is generally accepted with the exception of parochial (religious schools) maintained by Catholics and one or two minor protestant groups. Practically all schools are subsidized either by public funds or private contributions, and it is taken for granted that schools cannot operate without some income in addition to that received from student's tuition.

Cultural background of Philippine education.

At the end of the Spanish era, education, although greatly revered, was restricted to a small group, with the bulk of the population illiterate. The American style of "self-made" man was unknown and leaders of all types liked to refer to either inherited prestige or educational achievement—preferably both. Manual labor was generally looked down on and working students were rare. Landholding was a mark of prestige, but actual farming carried little distinction. Business enterprise was dubiously regarded and professional, academic or governmental careers represented more attractive goals. Catholicism was the dominant religion and the area lacked a tradition of either public support or private charity as the basis of education.

The changes produced in the subsequent period of American control and later of independence modified these traits but did not completely alter the cultural pattern. Private education is now considered a big business and it is expected that a school is a commercial enterprise which will make profits for its investors. The schools have a tradition of emphasis on a memorization type of verbal learning with no scientific tradition and little development of either libraries or laboratories. Although the Malayan ethnic strain predominates, no one language is spoken by a majority of inhabitants and linguistic variation is a major problem of the schools. Compared to Western countries, the country is still largely rural and the per capita income is low.

Athletics is a recent development, somewhat inhibited by traditional sensitivity and face saving. Boys and girls have only limited chances for unchaperoned association and coeducation is still viewed with some suspicion.

Synthesis of Phil-American patterns.

As can be seen from the foregoing, some aspects of American culture would be eagerly welcome by Filipinos and others subjected to resistance. The general American enthusiasm for education found a ready response in the Philippines especially in regard to education as a preparation for professional, academic or government positions. Education has continued to be largely of a lecture-memorization type and the general educational enthusiasm did not extend to vocational or agricultural training. Public support for education was accepted wholeheartedly only at the primary level, with the secondary level relying largely on tuition fees, and the collegiate level being turned over, for the most part, to the private universities and colleges. Among the private schools, religious schools (many of which are also profit making) are outstripped by non-sectarian, money-making institutions. Athletics became popular and are thought to produce traits of good sportsmanship. Co-education is a fairly general pattern, although sometimes accompanied by such devices as separate stairs and entrances for the male and female. The government has found difficulty in finding money to match the nation's growing educational enthusiasm, and schools are not yet available for all the nation's youth. Language communication presents an unsolved problem with the schools now teaching Tagalog, English and Spanish; all of which are strange tongues to the majority of the people.

This presents a bird's eye view of cultural interaction in the educational field; now let us look at some problem areas in greater detail.

Culture Conflict and Educational Problems

How effective is Philippine education?

The Filipino educational system provokes both extravagant praise and vigorous criticism. One of the friendliest views is given by an American writer, Erich H. Jacoby:

> For the spiritual development of the Filipinos, however, American influence and education be-

came of decisive importance. The American creed of equality and liberty, and the confidence in progress and in a high standard of living for everybody, have changed the Filipino. He feels different from his ancestors and has accepted Western ideology and ways of thinking, not as an additional attribute, but almost as an inherited right. This process of mental assimilation cannot be emphasized too strongly. It explains the vigorous resistance of the Filipino peasants against the Japanese invaders and their "Asia for the Asiatics" propaganda... It was Abraham Lincoln—not Lenin—who became the prophet and hero for the oppressed and impoverished Filipino peasants, although some might say that it was a simplified Abraham Lincoln. It was the untiring American teacher who formed the psychology of the Filipino peasant at the same time when American economic policy stabilized the existing social order for another generation or two.[10]

A less enthusiastic view was given by the late J. C. Laya, a former superintendent of Bataan and one of the most candid Filipino educators. Laya implied that the schools serve only the select few who go on to high school, that most of the pupils get nothing from their attendance and that most of the money spent for school purposes goes for naught. He said:

> Is it true, I asked the teachers, that even after your pupils have finished the sixth grade they can not use English with any degree of effectiveness? (Answer: True). Do they forget the little English they learn soon after leaving school if they do not go to high school? (Answer: Yes.) Are sixth grade graduates capable of reading newspapers in English? (Answer: No.) Even the daily papers like the *Times* and the *Chronicle*? (Answer: We don't think so.) . . . Then I told them that the Joint Congressional Committee on

---

[10] Erich H. Jacoby: *Agrarian Unrest in Southeast Asia*, 1949, Columbia University Press, New York, pp. 221-222.

Education established the fact that graduation from the elementary grades is necessary in order to attain functional literacy. I told them further that only 6.23 out of the 100 first grade pupils who start in the first grade ever enter the first year high school. In other words, less than one fifteenth of all pupils that the elementary schools teach make use of most of what they learn in the elementary grades. The teachers also had to admit by inference that about nine-tenths of all they ever teach is wasted, that about nine-tenths of the ₱120,-000,000 spent annually for education, which is mostly elementary education, is also largely wasted.[11]

One could go on for an indefinite period of time citing such statements of criticism and defense, but for our purpose, it is enough to point out that, in spite of real accomplishments, the Philippine school system faces grave problems which seriously threaten its service to the nation. These problems are not due simply to technical or financial difficulties, but represent serious differences of viewpoint produced by clashes within Philippine culture. Problem areas will be treated under four headings, namely, language, diploma mills, distorted educational emphasis, and community relationships.

Distorted educational emphasis.

The tradition inherited from the Spanish regime left a preference for white-collar jobs and distate for productive manual labor. As a result, Isidro concludes that an academic type of curriculum had an overwhelming attraction, thus:

> To our people, no matter how poor and humble, the desire for a profession—to be a doctor, a lawyer, or an engineer—was irresistible... The sons of the poor and middle classes would rather be clerks and employees in the government or

---

[11] J. C. Laya: *Little Democracies (of Bataan)*, Inang Wika Publishing Co., Manila. 1951, p. 131.

CHAPTER XV. EDUCATION IN ITS SOCIAL SETTING   395

commercial firms than be farmers, blacksmiths, carpenters, or plumbers.[12]

This overvaluation of white-collar jobs has led thousands of young people to make heavy sacrifices in securing an education, which, for many of them, can only lead to unemployment and frustration. At the same time, the country's real manpower needs are being neglected. Unfortunately, the occupations which held the greatest prestige during the Spanish period are apparently not the ones most vital in a newly developing country. Intelligent farmers, well trained artisans, engineers and business enterprisers are in short supply; while doctors, lawyers, accountants and teachers are being turned out by the thousands only to accept positions with low income or face unemployment. The Bell Report summarizes the situation as follows:

> Only five per cent of all secondary school students are taking agricultural courses and an additional five per cent trade or vocational courses. The number preparing for a professional career is out of all proportion to the needs of the country. Instead of being well-provided with trained workers and managers for agriculture and industry, where they can be employed, the country will soon be faced with the problem of white collar unemployment. This is a misdirection of education that must prove costly to the Philippine economy and painful to the unfortunate victims.[13]

The demand for teachers can be estimated fairly accurately, we therefore, are able to gauge the extent to which this is an overemphasized profession. In 1952, some 33,500 teacher graduates were looking for about 8,500 jobs. If this rate continues into 1960, we would then have three times as many unemployed teacher graduates as we have teachers in

---

[12] Antonio Isidro: *op. cit.*, p. 142.
[13] U.S. Economic Survey Mission's Report, *The Bell Report*, Philippine Book Company, Distributor, Manila, 1950.

the schools. No other country has so great an excess of teaching graduates in proportion to its population.[14]

The neglect of agriculture is perhaps even more tragic than the overemphasis of the professions. It may be explained by the fact that a father does not send his son to school to become a better farmer, but to escape from farming. If the boy is capable and ambitious, he heads for a professional career, if he is satisfied with farming, then he sees no reason for going to school at all. In the schools, this has meant that little money is devoted to agricultural training, that few students are interested, the training offered is often considered "book learning" and that even the few agricultural graduates seldom make use of their training in the operation of farms. Orata feels that agricultural education has concentrated on setting up centers adopted to American practices which are of questionable relevance to Philippine conditions. This situation suggests that agricultural education has failed to interest the majority of students and also failed to develop an extension program to carry agricultural information to the farm. Even the few agricultural graduates give little evidence of applying their training to actual farm work.

> Our agricultural graduates, for the most part, who were doing any farming did not see fit to apply their scientific training to the cultivation of their little farms... they were waiting until they could have a hacienda and buy a tractor.[15]

In discussing the need for improved agricultural education, President Matela of Central Luzon Agricultural College gives some statistical data which indicates the extent the Philippines are handicapped by the failure of agricultural education.

---

[14] Pedro Orata: "Educational Trends," *Manila Daily Bulletin*, March 15, 1952.
[15] *Ibid.*, December 15, 1952.

CHAPTER XV. EDUCATION IN ITS SOCIAL SETTING 397

Table 1. Comparative Yields *

Average Rice Yield

Philippines	26.6	cavans	per	ha.
Philippine Ag. College Land	67.5	"	"	"
China	60.	"	"	"
Formosa	66.1	"	"	"
Japan	87.1	"	"	"

Average Corn Yield

Philippines	10.46	cavans	per	ha.
United States	41.46	"	"	"

* Arcadio G. Matela: "Agricultural Education," *Philippines Herald*, August 8, 1952.

It is, of course, true that ignorance of the best agricultural practice is not the only difficulty of Filipino agriculture, but it seems reasonable to assume that careless-

Law Students in the P. I.	Law Students in the U. S.	Agriculture Students in the U. S.	Agriculture Students in the P. I.

Proportion of Law and Agricultural Students in the United States and the Philippines.

The ratio of law students in the Philippines to the general population is 1 to 1818 while the United States has a proportion of only 1 to 2807. For Agricultural students the Filipino ratio is 1 to 6,666 of the general populace while the American ratio is 1 to 2701. The overemphasis on legal training and neglect of agriculture in the Philippines is accentuated by the fact that it is primarily an agricultural country which requires only a small number of lawyers but has a tremendous need for skilled farmers. The United States, on the other hand, is primarily urban and has far greater opportunities for lawyers than the Philippines, yet the ratio of law students is smaller than that of the Philippines and the proportion of agricultural students is much greater. These figures assume a population of 20,000,000 in the Philippines and 160,000,000 in the United States. The gross totals are estimated as follows: Philippines 11,367 law students, 3,000 college agricultural students; United States, 56,385 law students, 59,000 college agricultural students.

ness in seed selection, indifference to fertilization techniques and other evidences of backwardness hold down production in the country to an appreciable extent. Judged on the basis of its efficiency in disseminating knowledge essential to the nation's most important activity, Philippine education can hardly be considered a success. Considering the essentially urban focus of education, much justification can be seen in Dean Panlasigui's criticism that "the educational system is against the rural areas and in favor of urban communities." [16]

This problem of overemphasis on the professions and white-collar jobs and the neglect of trade and agricultural training cannot be cured by curriculum revision or increased appropriations. The situation represents a culture conflict in which the life attitudes of the most ambitious element of the populace are directly opposed to the life attitudes compatible with successful agriculture. This results in a "cutflower" type of civilization in which the brilliant life of the cities is cut off from nourishment in the soil. In other words, the culture is apparently friendly to an education which leads youth away from productive activity and hostile to education which would aid in the development of the country's greatest resources.

Diploma mills and educational standards.

Probably nothing on the Philippine educational scene shocks a foreign observer more than the major role played by profit making private institutions. In other countries, education tends to be the creature of either private charity or government subsidy. In certain private schools in the Philippines, the school is often a joint stock corporation paying fat dividends by offering an inferior brand of education. Such schools may go through the motions of schooling, but actually, they are merely a cheap imitation of the real thing. The apostolic nuncio to the Philippines summarized the situation thus:

[16] Isidoro Panlasigui: "Education for the Barrios," *The Sunday Times Magazine*, Vol. VIII, Number 196, March 1, 1953.

CHAPTER XV. EDUCATION IN ITS SOCIAL SETTING

Greed for money has in fact made many Filipino schools profit-making concerns for whom education is not a mission, but an invested stock. Consequently, their scholastic standards are below the level of decency and honesty, their students often have little time, energy, ability or motivation for higher learning.[17]

In a more detailed accounting, the UNESCO educational mission of 1949 noted:

>...the indiscriminate admission of unqualified students, inferior curricula of little value, passing of inferior students in order to continue fees, use of low-paid, part-time instructors, overloading of courses to put students through quickly, and unethical rivalry among schools for student business. The offering of so-called higher education on this low-grade basis is an imposition on an education hungry people.[18]

The existence of fraudulent educational institutions which purport to offer impressive degrees without actual work by the student is a problem in every country. Weird incidents occur in all nations of mail order institutions which will grant any kind of degree in return for a sufficient fee. The peculiar aspect of the Philippine situation is that here, the *diploma mills* are legal institutions, with imposing buildings and grounds and the sponsorship of leading citizens. Their existence is not due to clandestine evasion of legal requirements, but to the difficulty caused by a widespread desire for schooling in a country of limited income coupled with a general indifference to the importance of high educational standards.

Nor can one be completely sure that this trend is confined to profit-making institutions. Teodoro Locsin looks at the lowered standard of public education and says, "The government has become the biggest diploma mill in the country.[19] His point is that the elimination of the

---
[17] *Manila Daily Bulletin*, February 7, 1952, p. 5.
[18] U.S. Economic Survey, *op. cit.*, p. 107.
[19] Teodoro Locsin: "The Biggest Diploma Mill," *The Philippines Free Press*, September 15, 1951, p. 2.

seventh grade and the halftime basis of lower grades, together with the crowding of the curriculum by the addition of the national language, means that public school pupils are simply going through the motions without receiving a real chance for an education.

A summary of these critiques of both public and private education would be that the Philippines is spending enormous sums of money to produce graduates who have only a pseudo-education which fails to equip with the skills and knowledge usually acquired in the educational process.

The root cause of this situation is not the venality of private school owners or the corruption of government officials (although these play a part), but the dilemma faced by a country of limited income in which formal education is enormously popular. Let us look first at higher education. From the following table will be seen a comparison of per capita income with the percentage of the total population in colleges or universities. Here it will be seen that, while the Philippines rank close to the bottom in per capita income, they are next to the United States in the proportion enrolled in higher education.

Table 2. College Students and Per Capita Income

Ratio of College Students to the Population *		Per Capita Income in Pesos	
United States	1 to 88	United States	1,025
Philippines	1 " 88	England	917
Denmark	1 " 412	Chile	836
Switzerland	1 " 437	Denmark	821
Chile	1 " 758	Switzerland	753
Netherlands	1 " 784	Netherlands	469
England	1 " 841	Japan	310
Japan	1 " 972	Philippines	61

* Figures for Philippines computed on basis of 1948 census reports. Figures for other countries are for 1938 to 1940 computed from data in the Encyclopedia of Modern Education. Post war figures would give a larger proportion to the United States.

"Computed from "National Income Statistics 1938-1947" Statistical Office of the United Nations. 1938 figures used except for Chile which is for 1940. Population figures taken from "Statistical Yearbook of the League of Nations 1942-44." Geneva, 1945, Table 2 "Area and Population."

CHAPTER XV.   EDUCATION IN ITS SOCIAL SETTING   401

P. I.   U. S.   Denmark

Man = Proportion of college students to general population.
Bag = Per capita income.

The support of college education represents a heavy investment by the community. The Philippines and the United States have about the same proportion of college students to the general population but the relative' burden of support is easier in the United States because of a higher per capita income. Denmark has a per capita income midway between the Philippines and the United States but the proportion of college students is much lower; hence the Danes find it relatively easy to maintain their colleges and universities. Many educational problems in the Philippines stem from the combination of a big demand for education and limited funds to meet the expense.

The choice of an under-developed country interested in higher education would seem to lie between either restricting such education to a small minority of the population or devoting a major share of the country's income to this purpose. Neither alternative is pleasant and the Philippines seems to have discovered a third method. Under this procedure, the public colleges and universities and the non-profit private colleges are few in number and restricted in enrollment. The mass provision for higher education is made by profit-making institutions which do not ask for either charity or government subsidy.

High quality education cannot be supported on this basis, but it is possible to hold classes and give degrees which would satisfy the public demand. Unfortunately, this system not only produces thousands of half educated college graduates, but also exerts a downward pressure on legitimate institutions. If students in one school can graduate without work, then why should other students burn the midnight oil for a degree which seems to carry little more prestige? If some colleges operating on tuition fees alone, can offer instruction and still pay dividends, then why should philanthropists gave money to colleges or why should the legislature spend millions of pesos of tax money? Superficial education in one area tends to produce a trend toward mediocrity and superficiality in all areas.

Another result of this watering down of education is to give the country half-educated professionals whose potential ability is never reached because of inadequate training. The following statement of a Filipina doctor gives some idea of the inadequacies of one of the private medical schools:

> I finally finished my medical training. When I did, the only thing I was sure of was the fact that after graduation there were added to the incompetent medicos fresh from the factory... On graduation, few of us had seen a forceps delivery, much less had performed one. I doubt if half of the class knew how to tie a surgical knot or knew the difference between a Kelly and an artery clamp. The proper technique of doing an infusion was never explained to us, and maybe two or three knew the proper way to make an intravenous or intramuscular injection. It would be interesting to learn how many of the current internees can tell how much soap goes into an S.S. enema. These are some of the fundamental things I had to learn after I got through medical school. I learned them by bitter experience in private practice.[20]

While this ineffective training is especially shocking in medicine, the same principle applies to all other fields. Half-trained lawyers, accountants, engineers and teachers hold back the nation's progress by the dead weight of their own mediocrity.

---
[20] M. G. Mendoza: "What of the Medical Profession in the Philippines?", *Philippines Free Press*, Manila. May 7, 1949, p. 3.

CHAPTER XV. EDUCATION IN ITS SOCIAL SETTING 403

The problems which plague secondary and higher education also arise in primary and intermediate education, an area in which the public schools predominate. Here too, available funds are not equal to the public demand for educational facilities. This is true in spite of the fact that nearly twenty-five per cent of government revenues go for education, a proportion much higher than what is spent by other countries in the area. A glance at the statistics on illiteracy will illuminate this problem:

LITERACY LEVEL OF PERSONS TEN YEARS OLD AND OVER FOR THE YEARS 1903, 1918, 1939 and 1948 *

Literacy & Sex	1903 Number	Per Cent	1918 Number	Per Cent	1939 Number	Per Cent	1948 Number	Per Cent
Total, Philippines	4,973,526	100	6,381,261	100	10,903,879	100	13,300,961	100
Literate	1,002,588	20.2	3,138,634	49.2	5,316,146	48.8	7,960,050	59.8
Illiterate	3,970,938	79.8	3,242,627	50.8	5,574,254	51.8	5,024,482	41.2

* Bureau of Census Reports.

The 1948 census was taken at a time when the Huks had upset peace and order conditions and some observers feel its literacy data is questionable.

Here it will be seen that was very rapid advance in attacking illiteracy in the first twenty years of the American occupation, but very little progress after that time. About half of the population were literate in 1918 and the proportion seems to be about the same today. Since a school system reaching the bulk of the population should progressively reduce illiteracy, this would seem to be an anomalous situation. Apparently, the difficulty is twofold: in spite of a tremendous expansion, schools are still not readily available in all barrios and many students do not remain in school long enough to become literate.

As in higher education, the choice would seem to lie between allowing a portion of the population to remain outside the school system and keeping taxes low, or educating everyone and imposing heavy taxes on that country to bear the expense. In the education act of 1940, the government again looked for another way out and proposed changes whereby it was thought that the same amount of money could be spread so it would educate a larger number of children. These measures provided for the elimination of the seventh grade and the installation of the single double session in the schools, thus decreasing by more than fifty per cent the time spent in elementary education. This meant that the Filipino child would be expected to accomplish in six years of half time work what required the American child eight years of full time work. In deciding whether or not this change tended to turn the public schools into "diploma mills," it is interesting to note the appraisal of the Monroe commission in 1925 when the Filipino child had seven full years of elementary schooling. At this time, it was shown that fourth year high school students had a reading ability equal to American children in grade five and that in social studies, American children in grade four were better informed than Filipino children in the first year of high school. In arithmetic, there was less difference and Filipino and American children were about equal where no language usage was involved, with Filipinos lagging a half year behind when arithmetical problems involved the use of English.[21]

This lowering of educational standards was accompanied by a major post war increase in funds for primary schooling with the result that a much larger proportion of children is now in school. The question is whether they can achieve real literacy with the present limitations of the school curriculum.

Language problems.

In discussing the cultural backgrounds of Filipinos and Americans, we pointed out that, although Filipinos are predominantly of one racial stock, they speak many languages; whereas, Americans are of many ethnic backgrounds, but are predominantly English speaking. This confusion of tongues has been a major problem in Philip-

---

[21] Isidro, *op. cit.*, pp. 18-319.

pine education for many years, requiring the student to spend precious time in learning language before he can begin to tackle the content of basic subject matter. As Prator says:

> At present the Filipino child has the unenviable distinction of finding himself in a uniquely unfavorable situation with regard to his possibilities of obtaining a sound education. He carries a heavier linguistic burden than almost any other child in the world. He is now usually required to study three foreign languages, two of them throughout his entire school career. One of the three, English, is the medium through which he receives nearly all his formal instruction, so ideally he should master it to an extent that is unparalleled in the language classes of most other nations... On the other hand, his means of achieving what is asked of him are more limited than those of the great majority of other children. He goes to school for an unusually brief time each day and for an uncommonly short span of years.[22]

When the American authorities introduced a public school system, they chose English as the medium of instruction and sent over a thousand American teachers to begin the process of educational expansion and linguistic transformation. The result is that today, most of the serious literature of the country is in English. Its usage is universal among the better educated group and a larger percentage of the total population claim to speak English than any other language.[23]

Spanish still persists, and recent legislation makes it a required part of the secondary and college curriculum. Filipino nationalism has led to a demand for the development of an indigenous national language, and a revised Tagalog known officially as "Philippine Language" is

[22] Clifford H. Prator: *Language Teaching in the Philippines*, Report, U.S. Educational Foundation in the Philippines, Republic of the Philippines, June 28, 1950.

[23] English, 37.2%; Tagalog, 37.1%; Spanish, 1%; *Journal of Philippine Statistics*, Bureau of the Census, October, 1952, pp. 15-17.

now a part of the required course of study starting from first grade. Since the majority of Filipinos do not speak Tagalog, this too, can really be regarded as a foreign language. Thus one might say that the clash of cultures in Philippines has resulted in recognition for every major language with dominance for none, and with students forced to carry an impossible linguistic burden as a result of legislative attempts to conciliate various language pressure groups. During the Japanese occupation, Nippongo was added to the school curriculum, but the end of the war freed students from this particular requirement.

To appreciate fully the problem presented by the language pressures on the school, one must consider the amount of time which the average child spends in school. Education carried through college will probably enable the student to get a fair command of English and some understanding of Spanish and Tagalog, with no particular ill effects except a serious retardation in all his other courses because of the amount of time he is forced to spend in language study. For the majority of children, however, it is at least arguable that the language situation results not only in retardation, but also foreshadows a complete defeat of the educational process. About half of the school children do not go beyond the fourth grade and only one fourth finish the sixth grade as shown in the following table:

Table 3. Student's Academic Survival

	II	III	IV	V	VI
Per cent of survival of students entering grade I	79.92	65.32	51.15	34.22	22.69

Journal of Philippine Statistics, Sept., 1952, p. 31.

For three-fourths of the Filipino children, the language question must be viewed in the light of its effect on students whose school career is six years or less of half-time study. These children do not use English in the home or community, so the meager learning in school is quickly forgotten, while at the same time, a futile effort to master the medium of instruction makes it very difficult to give much attention to other subject matter.

This situation has led to a re-examination of the language question and given rise to some experimentation. In the Iloilo system, one school in which classes were conducted in the vernacular, Hiligaynon, was compared with another where the classes were conducted in English. The results of this experiment in vernacular education were a greater community satisfaction with the schools, work of about equal quality in arithmetic, and greatly superior work in reading and in social studies.[24] As Prator analyzed this experiment, the following pattern seemed to emerge as a tentative approach to languages in primary education.[25]

1. Postpone the study of national language by non-Tagalog pupils until intermediate grades.
2. Use the vernacular as medium of instruction in grades I and II.
3. Teach English as a separate subject in first two grades and shift to it as a medium of instruction in the third grade.

In the days of the early American teachers, the use of English was justified on the basis of the difficulty of making textbooks in all the various vernaculars and of securing trained teachers who could use the local dialect. Today, these difficulties are no longer insurmountable and it is possible to reconsider that decision. English seems to be secure as a medium of instruction in higher education, but its utility is doubtful in the lower grades. Scientific investigation seems to be establishing methods whereby the usage of the vernacular can enrich the early grades without working against the eventual acquisition of English.

While a reexamination of the language question requires scientific research, it is complicated by deepseated

---

[24] Prator, *op. cit.*, p. 27.
[25] *Ibid.*, p. 25.

value clashes between various groups. Some would subordinate everything else to a drive to make English a more popular form of expression, others would exploit the schools in behalf of Spanish culture by forcing students to spend years studying what is largely, in the Philippines, a forgotten tongue. Then, too, the advance guard of a rising nationalism feels that patriotism depends upon an indigenous language and demands that the schools attempt to produce graduates who speak a common language of Filipino origin. In the meantime, the basic vernacular of the people still keep their traditional dominance in home and community.

The way out of these difficulties is to concentrate on the needs of the student, rather than the abstract merits of different languages and cultures. Our educational experts can study the effect on student growth of various types of language instruction and devise programs which will better enable the student to cope with the type of world he finds on leaving school. To attain this goal, they must have the support of a public opinion which is aware of the blighting effect of using the schools as a field of combat in which the representatives of language groups wage war and make deals without worrying about what happens to education in the process.

School and Community.

The general reverence for education does not include the idea that what is learned in the school should affect the social life of the community. The usual attitude is that learning is a process of memorizing written material or lecture notes which must be disgorged on examination, but which are not assumed to have any particular importance for everyday life. Students may learn about tuberculosis, malaria, etc., but it is not assumed that such learning will change either dietary habits or community sanitation.

The "community school" attempts to involve the school directly in neighborhood affairs in such a way that the lessons of the schoolroom show results in better homes, more productive gardens, drainage ditches, clean-up campaigns, community meetings and many other types of civic activities.

The "little democracies" idea advanced by the late J. C. Laya, while Division Superintendent of Schools for Bataan, appears to have popular acceptance not only in educational circles, but also among members in the higher echelons of the government. The *purok* system of community organization, with the teacher in the background, is in itself a little democracy in action. It is a means whereby men, women, young boys and girls find satisfaction in working cooperatively to improve their own mode of living. Education for healthful living, a vital phase in social life, finds a prominent place in this *purok* organization. In this sense, the success of the school is demonstrated by changes in the community, and at the same time the improvement of attitudes and the building of character. All of these give assurance of an effective citizenry within the framework of a democracy.

Summary

Education is related to the prevailing culture and to the people's vision of possible change in the future. Filipino education reflects both the American pattern of widespread educational opportunity and an exaggerated concept of the value of white collar jobs. The schools have served to expand the general literacy of the population and to develop a sophisticated minority versed in the skills of democratic government. They have been less successful in producing the type of skills and attitudes required for the development of natural resources. Education as a means of general social improvement has been slow to appear but is now developing through the medium of the community school.

The existence of a variety of languages has led to conflict over school policy which seems to have been temporarily compromised on the basis of having students learn at least three languages. Difficulties caused by the disparity between the desire of the people for education and the limited wealth of the country have led to a dilution of the quality of education and the rise of alleged "diploma mills" under both private and public auspices.

Present trends point to a great increase in educational opportunity at the primary level with continued controversy about the role of various languages and continued uncertainty about the importance of high educational standards.

QUESTIONS

1. What are the main characteristics of education among primitive peoples? Are there any features of primitive education which might be applied in modern schools?

2. What are the distinguishing traits of educational policies followed by colonial powers? How would you appraise the values and shortcomings of this type of education?

3. What were the major differences between American and Spanish educational policies?

4. Discuss the extent to which the Philippines have followed American educational procedures? What features of American educational policy were difficult to apply in the Philippines?

5. Discuss the virtues and defects of the non-sectarian profit-making private schools? What do you think is the basic reason for the prominent place such schools hold in Philippine education?

6. Discuss the role of vocational and agricultural education. What measures would you suggest to increase the attention given to this type of education?

7. What is meant by the "Language Problem of the Schools"? What measures do you think the schools should adopt to improve this situation?

8. What is meant by the Community School? In what way does the Community School represent a shift in cultural values?

PROJECTS

1. Summarize and comment on one of the following: the UNESCO report on Philippine Education; Dr. Prator's Report on *Language Teaching in the Philippines;* J. C. Laya's *Little Democracies.*

2. Describe the work of a community school with which you are familiar.

3. Write an autobiographical report on your own adjustment to school. What factors either in the general Philippine culture or in

CHAPTER XV. EDUCATION IN ITS SOCIAL SETTING

your own family background do you think aided or hindered your school adjustment?

SUGGESTED READINGS

Bogardus, E. S., *Sociology*, Third Edition (New York: The Macmillan Company, 1949), pp. 255-284. Discusses the group function of education.

Corpus, S. F., "The Function of Education in Social Change," *Social Change in the Philippines During the Independence Movement*: 1898-1935 (Unpublished Doctoral Dissertation, University of Southern California, Los Angeles, 1951), pp. 188-306. Discusses the progress of education from 1898 up to 1948.

Hertzler, Joyce O., *Social Progress* (New York: The Century Co., 1928), pp. 269-291. Discusses education as the master agent of progress.

Laya, J. C., *Little Democracies*, Revised Edition (Manila: Inang Wika Publishing Co., 1951). The patterns of community school projects which are described in this little book are worthy of serious attention.

Lynd, Robert S., *Knowledge For What?* (Princeton University Press, 1948). This book is rather provocative and challenges both the educator and society.

Philippine Social Trends (Manila: Bureau of Printing, 1950). Basic documents pertinent to long-ranged social welfare planning in the Philippines.

The Community School (Series of lectures, mimeographed copy, under the auspices of the Institute on the Community School, University Extension Division, University of the Philippines, Manila, 1952).

Wahlquist, J. T., *The Philosophy of American Education* (New York: Ronald Press Company, 1942). This is a critical discussion of the different philosophies of education to the end that a democratic philosophy is structured and implemented to practical purposes.

Woody, Thomas, *Life and Education in Early Societies*, Macmillan Co., N.Y., 1949. Provides an analytic survey of educational systems in various cultures.

UNESCO Educational Mission, *Report of the Mission to the Philippines* (Paris, France: UNESCO, 1950). Gives a critical evaluation of Philippine education and points out the educational practices.

Prator, Clifford H., *Language Teaching in the Philippines* (Manila: U.S. Educational Foundation in the Philippines, June 28, 1950). A research study by a Fulbright scholar on the language problem in the schools.

CHAPTER SIXTEEN

SOCIAL WORK

I recognize that my greatest gift to another person may be an opportunity for him to develop and exercise his own capacities.

Linton B. Swift, A Social Worker's Creed

Social Amelioration

The consideration of social conditions naturally leads to a desire to take steps whereby our social life may be improved. Because of their knowledge about general social processes and specific social problems, sociologists have often been involved in projects designed to improve society. This is not necessarily a part of the sociologists job and one of the most famous of the early sociologists, William Graham Sumner, held to the position that any deliberate efforts at change were harmful. He believed that the mores and folkways could only change in response to a gradual social evolution and that deliberate attempts to alter society simply led to confusion and chaos:[1] a conclusion which is supported by the failure of the efforts of many well-meaning people and organizations. Nevertheless, most people are unwilling to accept such a view of human helplessness and feel that when anomalies are detected, men should make efforts to correct them. The sociologist may have reservations about the complete success of attempts at reform, but he is under obligation to present his analysis of the social situation so that reformers may be aware of the factors involved.

Efforts at social improvement take many forms and involve many agencies. The churches represent man's

---

[1] William Graham Sumner, "The Absurd Attempt to Make the World Over," *Collected Essays of William Graham Sumner*, edited by Keller, Albert Galloway and Davie, Maurice R. Yale University Press, New Haven, 1940, pp. 104-106.

CHAPTER XVI. SOCIAL WORK 413

highest ideals and play a continual role in the process of social improvement. The schools consider it their duty to work toward the development of a better society. Many private groups work toward special goals such as the improvement of rural communities or the prevention of juvenile delinquency. Business concerns change the nature of society by their operations as they develop new goods to satisfy human needs. Finally, most governments have accepted the idea that the state should work for the betterment of the total population.

As various people worked toward human betterment, they began to develop techniques which were helpful and a body of knowledge which came to be regarded as a necessary background. In the first days of the establishment of sociology as a separate science, sociologists were often directly involved in welfare activities. Later, a distinct group of people emerged who specialized in certain types of welfare activities and were known as *social workers*. The relationship of sociology and social work continues to be so close that we feel the subject is worthy of a special chapter in this text.

Purpose of social work.

Social work, known in the Philippines more often as social welfare, is the applied social science which deals with assisting individuals who have not been able to make satisfactory adjustments; who have been affected adversely by the impact of society, and who need help in satisfying their basic needs of food, clothing, shelter and emotional adjustment. Social work's primary objective is to assist persons, individually, in groups, and in the community, to attain satisfying relationships and standards of life in accordance with their particular needs and capacities. Social work has developed from charity and philanthropy and now seeks to offer services which aid people in reaching their goals.

When we speak of social work having developed from charity and philanthropy, we mean that it has advanced from the mere relief of distress to the attempt to help people cope with the causes of distress. The story of the good Samaritan as told in the Gospels (Luke 10:30-37) may be said to be an illustration of social work principles. The good Samaritan not only gave immediate attention to the man who had been wounded by robbers, he also made arrangements to have him restored to health so that he could again be an individual able to stand on his own feet and take care of his own needs.

Giving money to beggars, for instance, may be charity or philanthropy but it is not social work. The social worker seeks to find out why the individual is a beggar and what help he needs to be restored to independence. Perhaps the beggar is physically incapacitated and medical treatment will restore him to useful living, perhaps he has become so adjusted to panhandling that he needs a basic psychological change in his outlook so that he may learn to appreciate the values of self-respect, or possibly, the community attitudes make begging so profitable that men make more in this fashion than they could from honest work. On the other hand, it may be true that employment opportunities are so scarce that men are driven to mendicancy as the only way of staying alive. Finally, the individual beggar may be suffering from difficulties that, in our present stage of scientific knowledge, we are unable to cure; in this case, social work will seek to provide him with the essentials of life under conditions of decency and self-respect.

One of the frequent causes of distress is the break-up of families which robs the children of parental protection and destroys the family source of income. Obviously, mothers and children should be protected and society should arrange to meet their legitimate needs; the coming generation should not be demoralized because of the shortcomings of thir elders. Giving this help in such a way that it is adequate without being pauperizing (destroying self-respect) is no easy task and requires a high degree of professional skill and community organization. Such help

CHAPTER XVI. SOCIAL WORK 415

to broken families, however, is not the principal aim of family social work or child welfare agencies. These agencies seek to aid the family to be the type of social unit in which parents and children may find happiness and self-respect. Thus, social agencies not only deal with broken homes, but they provide counseling services designed to prevent the type of conflict which wrecks the family unit.

Illness is a basic cause of distress and, since early days, the provision of hospitals and medical treatment has been a major philanthropic activity. The difficulty here is that the treatment and prevention of disease requires more than mere access to hospitals and physicians. The sick persons may not recognize the benefits of medical care and he may be either unable or unwilling to follow the physician's advice. The physician, too, knows that it is not enough just to treat the physical symptoms of illness, for man's illness is a product of all the factors which go to make up his environment. Adequate diagnosis and treatment require a knowledge of the client's living conditions, his diet, his work, his home life, his state of mind and the emotional tensions which may aggravate physical causes of illness. Then too, illness may be a product of widespread social conditions related to hazards of work, inadequate diet, contaminated water supply and similar factors.

In this setting, the process has developed which is known as medical social work. The medical social worker is an auxiliary of the doctor and helps him in the task of dealing with the social and helps him in the task of dealing with the social aspects of illness. The medical social worker secures for the physician the social data which may affect his diagnosis and treatment. In turn, he interprets the plan of treatment to the patient and helps the patient to make the changes in his living conditions and attitudes which may be required. These changes are manifold and may involve a change in type of work, the following of different dietary habits, the solution of emotional conflicts the acceptance of changed method of living and securing the needed funds to pay for medical care and meet family expenses. In effect, medical treatment may require a complete change in the life of the patient which he is unable to make without guidance and assistance. Finally, the social worker helps the community to plan the type of medical institutions which are needed and to distinguish between those who are able to pay their way and the people who need financial assistance in meeting medical costs.

In our concern for dealing with basic causes of distress, we have to remember that it is impossible to construct a perfect society. What appears to be a happy and prosperous community may be ruined by natural disasters such as typhoons and earthquakes or devastated by social calamities such as war or large scale unemployment. In these cases, the provision of relief is needed so that people may be kept alive and have a chance to rebuild their society. For these emergencies, the social work profession offers a group of workers, aware of both the benefits and the hazards of charitable activity, who have some knowledge of techniques found useful in the alleviation of mass suffering. The social worker will see that relief is handled economically so that society is not bankrupt or the individual pauperized and yet is directed in such a way that people are not only kept from starvation but helped to reconstruct their lives and suport themselves. The Red Cross, for instance, has evolved plans for meeting disaster needs and has a corps of people especially trained in this type of work.

Basic techniques of social work.

Rehabilitation is inherent in the aims of social work. If real democracy is to succeed, social workers have to learn how to help meet social welfare needs, not by making decisions and doing things for others, but by helping others to come to their own decisions and to set upon them independently. For our purposes, a discussion of social work functions will be limited to a consideration of three basic methods: Case Work, Group Work and Community Organization.

Case work as a process of social work is characterized by the individualized, face to face, person to person relationship. The case worker, through a well-defined, but flexible set of principles, establishes a relationship with the individual client or recipient which is used as the basic tool of helping persons attain a definite goal. It is very different from the friendly, neighborly, or family relationship which is undisciplined and usually attempts to meet a need, or solve the immediate need, with little emphasis on the basic rehabilitation of the person.

Group work, like case work, is a basic method of social work; it is a way of helping individuals and groups in social, recreational and educational agency settings. Through groups, individuals are helped to relate to each other and experience opportunities from growth in accordance with their needs and capacities. This process produces personality development and change. Because of the identification process, the "we feeling" that a group engenders, the group is often able to fill needs that are more difficult to meet in an individual or case work relationship. Case work techniques are utilized by the social worker in group work to evaluate and understand the individual needs and capacities and the interests of the group with which he may be dealing.

Agencies making use of group work techniques include Boy and Girl Scouts, Y.M.C.A., Y.W.C.A., public playgrounds, 4-H clubs, religious youth clubs, etc. The principle of group work is that the agency does not exist merely to furnish recreation, or instruction but also to provide a social experience which will enrich the personalities of the participants.

In community organization, the social worker helps to stimulate and coordinate community services to meet local needs. Local communities have the resources to meet many of their problems but are frequently indifferent toward social needs or unaware of methods which have been helpful in other localities. The social worker has the difficult task of stimulating effective self help on the community level as well as with smaller groups. Community organization also exists outside of the formal shares of social work and one of the most effective examples of this type of approach is found in the community school movement.

Social work and related fields.

Although there is a close relationship between social work and other related social sciences, including sociology, social work has many distinguishing characteristics. A sociologist is not a social worker, although the social worker should have a broad and balanced background in the social sciences. Just as sociology furnishes much of the knowledge essential to social work, so religion stimulates the basic concern for the welfare of others. Yet, the religiously-minded person does not thereby become a social worker. Let us then consider the relation of social work to the rest of society.

Social work is concerned with social ills, it serves groups who need to be protected and at times defended, it serves society which also seeks protection through social work. The disadvantages in our society cause anxiety and discomfort to the more fortunate; thus arises the motivation to act on behalf of the deprived and oppressed. This concern for the less fortunate is known as social conscience. Historically, society has gradually developed this social conscience. The large number of handicapped individuals in society have always been a threat to the common good, causing feelings of guilt, helplessness, pity, hostility, superiority. These feelings have in turn motivated social action; efforts by the church, the state, individuals, and groups to help the less fortunate.

One of the distinguishing factors of social work is that it operates primarily through agencies and institutions which were traditionally established to educate, heal, and help people. More recently, it has begun to give counsel to the armed services and industry. Social work began with church philanthropies, and was concerned with the granting of individual or mass charity. Services and goods were generally administered in a condescending manner in which the more fortunate gave to the poor what they thought was good for them. In this sense, philanthropy carried a sense of superiority which assumed that, because of their need, the recipients had lost the right to direct their own lives. Charity thus gave the wealthy a sense of superior virtue while it robbed the recipients of their self-respect. Frequently, religious institutions stressed the emphasis on pity and the giving of alms but failed to develop a sense of stewardship and responsibility in the givers. This direction of social work activity from the top down also minimized the essential dignity of the individual even though his material needs might be recognized. Modern social work stresses the responsibility of all for a just social order and the duty of the social worker to assist the client in making his own decisions.

Motivations underlying the providing of social welfare services in most countries during the last 50 years have become less predominantly religious, charitable and philanthropic and more influenced by the belief that social welfare services are essential to the realization of a true democracy, and the fulfillment of basic human rights.

Religious welfare institutions are still important and have begun to make use of workers with specific social work training. While the current expansion of social service has been mostly under governmental or private non-sectarian auspices, this trend may be regarded as a general acceptance of one phase of religious idealism. In previous centuries, only those most active in religious institutions were concerned about social welfare; whereas today, there is general acceptance of the principle that man is his brother's keeper. The organization of a Catholic Charities Agency in Manila is an attempt to expand religious welfare service while using modern social work techniques.

Welfare Function of the Family

In every culture, and especially in the Philippines, the major task of relieving individual distress has been assumed by the family group. The widowed, the orphaned, the ill, the aged and the unemployed may all turn to their relatives with the assurance that they will freely be given whatever help the family can afford. The family group thus offers a haven of shelter in a stormy world.

In the Philippines, the emphasis on family responsibility has been so great that auxiliary welfare agencies have been slow to develop. Institutions for the aged, the orphans and the mentally ill house only a fraction of the number which are cared for in this fashion in other cultures. Likewise, private welfare agencies are almost unknown outside of Manila and all types of welfare agencies; religious, non-sectarian, and governmental, have been slow in their development. In view of the general acceptance of the family's welfare role, one may well ask whether, in this culture, there is need for the social work institutions which have developed in other countries.

It is not the purpose of social work to destroy the charitable activities of the family, but to strengthen these family functions and to extend them to areas which the family alone cannot cover. When we speak of strengthening the family in this respect, it is obvious that many families lack both the economic resources and the intellectual insight required for effective help. When this kind of family attempts to carry the welfare burden alone, the effect may be simply to spread poverty and prolong dependency by placing the support of the starving on those who are malnourished themselves.

Similarly, distress may root in social or natural disasters which impoverish not only occasional individuals but the total family group. Likewise, in the field of recreational services and community health facilities, there are needs which one family can meet only by cooperation with a large number of other families. In other instances, there are families which may be able to care for sporadic needs of their unfortunate members but which are unable to provide long-term expensive types of treatment. In all of these situations, the family group cannot stand alone but requires the assistance of the total community in meeting the needs of the family group.

To develop a wise social work program, we need a more accurate picture of the family's welfare role than is now available so that organized community efforts may cooperate with the traditional family pattern. We need this type of research to find out the results of family charity; does it produce rehabilitations or simply the continued dependency of the improvident? Also, we need more exact information on the types of social distress which the family can handle best by itself and the problems in which it requires help.[2]

Social work development in the Philippines.

Provision for the destitute and helpless in the Philippines has always been primarily a function of the family, but was supplemented to some extent by institutional care conducted by religious orders and its principal function was to aid beggars, orphans and the sick. Funds were secured from pious individuals who were encouraged to give to the unfortunate as a religious duty. The San Lazaro hospital, opened by the Franciscans in 1578, is usually regarded as the first example of organized charity. This hospital became the first treatment center for lepers and later was used for the treatment of other types of contagious disease. At the present time, it is operated by the government. Institutional care for the aged and orphaned began in 1810 with the establishment of the Hospicio de

---

[2] Some work of this kind has been done. *Philippine Social Trends,* previously cited, attempts an overall survey of the family's role. A more detailed study of this matter in one type of community has been made recently under the auspices of the University of the Philippines department of Sociology and Social Work — Cayetano Santiago, *Welfare of the Family in a Low Cost Housing Project in Quezon City,* unpublished Master's Thesis, 1953.

San Jose, founded by donations from private individuals and conducted by the Daughters of Charity.[3]

At the end of the Spanish regime, social work was confined to a small number of institutions operated by Catholic order. The emphasis was on relieving physical suffering and persuading people to fulfill their religious obligations; little attention was paid to the prevention of poverty or efforts to aid people to help themselves and rehabiliate their own lives. The total amount of social work activity was small and touched only a tiny fraction of the population.

When the American came to Manila, they brought with them a belief in organized methods of promoting human welfare which soon began to affect the Philippine scene. Medical social work, group work, private welfare work and government welfare all began to increase. Group work agencies were developed. Hospitals were built by government authorities. Protestant missions conducted free clinics and built hospitals which, in turn, stimulated further activity by Catholic agencies. Specific ailments attracted attention and the Tuberculosis Society, the Association for the Advancement of the Deaf and other medical care agencies appeared on the scene. The Red Cross became an important agency in many medical areas. The need for planning and organizing welfare activities brought about the creation of a Public Welfare Board to plan government activities throughout the Philippines and the Associated Charities to coordinate private and governmental charity in the city of Manila.

One of the most important of the new developments in this field was the creation of Welfareville in 1925. This was initiated by Governor General Leonard Wood who had a strong interest in social welfare and regarded the creation of the Welfareville as one of the great achieve-

---

[3] Virginia A. Paraiso: "Social Welfare in the Philippines," *The Survey*, April, 1952. Also see Maria Kalaw Katigbak, *A Survey of Four Major Catholic Social Welfare Agencies in Manila and Suburbs*, unpublished Master's thesis, University of the Philippines, 1953, pp. 88 to 123.

ments of his administration. It now offers a program aimed at preparing more than 1600 children under its supervision for useful, profitable and happier lives; in addition, it has under its charge some 117 aged and infirm. Welfareville is under the supervision and administration of the Social Welfare Administration. It consists of nine institutions: a home for orphaned and destitute children, a home for "negative" children of leprous parents, (for the care, training and education of children separated from their leprous parents) a home for mentally defective children, a nursery for "negative" infants of leprous parents, a Philippine Training School for Boys, (for the care, training, education, and rehabilitation of boys under 16 who committed offenses contrary to the law.) a Philippine Training School for Girls, (to care for the same group of girls), a Boys Home for the care, education and rehabilitation of homeless, displaced and neglected boys who are picked up by the police in Manila and its environs and those who are turned over by the armed forces, and a home for the aged and infirm.

In carrying out its program, Welfareville offer a variety of services. Academic and vocational training from kindergarten through high school is provided by 25 teachers from the Bureau of Public Schools. Catholic and Protestant clergy and lay workers are responsible for the spiritual instruction of the children. Medical service is provided through a hospital, dispensary and separate infirmary for the boys of the training school. A Child Guidance Clinic is operated by a part-time psychiatrist, a psychologist and two social workers.[4]

During the Commonwealth period, there was further progress is the organization of social work activities and the end of World War II brought a tremendous need for social welfare services of all kinds. Manila was the battleground of the war, and a great many lives were lost. Statistics indicate that with exception of Warsaw, Poland, Manila was the most devastated capital in the world. Homes,

---

[4] *Annual Report of Social Welfare Administrative,* 1951.

schools, industries, port facilities, roads, bridges and communications were wrecked. Many of the basic essentials of human existence were destroyed, leaving many people in need of help to carry on a bare existence. There were acute shortages of food, clothing, medicines and all types of consumer goods. The economy was completely disrupted. However, these material damages were not the most serious or the most lasting. The Japanese occupation did serious injury to the moral standards of the people; what was illegal in peacetime became acceptable and even admirable and heroic during the occupation.[5]

In the attempt to cope with these conditions, aid was given by the United States, the United Nations organizations and by various Philippine government agencies. Many of the activities of the Philippine government were eventually consolidated in the Social Welfare Administration, created by Executive Order Number 396 in January, 1951. The first head was Mrs. Asuncion Perez who had, at one time, been head of the pre-war Associated Charities. The Social Welfare Administration has a comparatively small appropriation which has to cover a wide variety of welfare services.[6]

In the field of private charitable activity, the outstanding event has been the postwar appearance of a Community Chest organization and Council of Social Agencies in greater Manila. The Community Chest is the fund raising unit for some twenty private social agencies while the Council of Social Agencies affords a means whereby those engaged in social work meet to plan their activities, avoid duplication of effort and devise ways to meet urgent needs in the community. Through the Community Chest, social agencies combine in one fund raising appeal and, in this manner, save time and expense in the soliciting of contributions. When the total amount has been raised the Chest board then apportions sums to different agencies in line with their needs.

---

[5] Paraiso, *op. cit.*, p. 17.
[6] See discussion by Golda Stander, "Social Work and Social Action in the Philippines," Vol. No. 3, *The Philippine Educational Forum*, 1952.

CHAPTER XVI. SOCIAL WORK 425

COMMUNITY CHEST

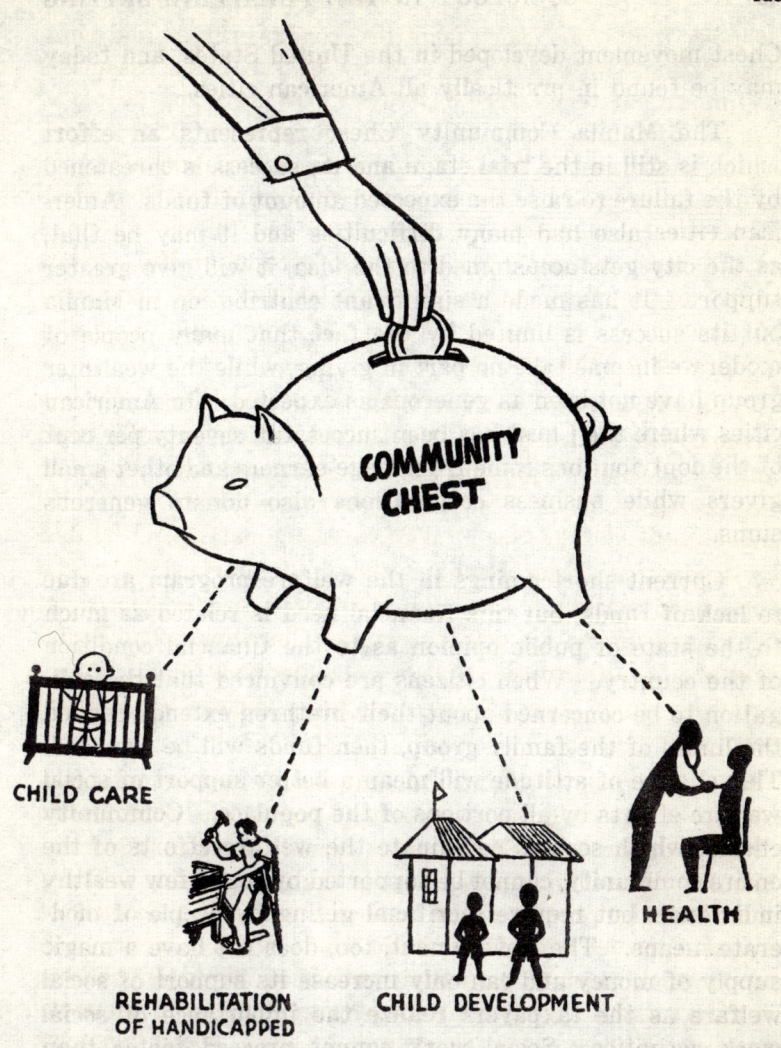

CHILD CARE

REHABILITATION OF HANDICAPPED

CHILD DEVELOPMENT

HEALTH

The Community Chest, along with the Council of Social Agencies, has been the best means of coordinating the efforts of private agencies yet discovered. It forces the different agencies to justify their programs before an impartial board and, at the same time, spares the community the commotion, expense and confusion attending a large number of charitable campaigns. The Community

Chest movement developed in the United States, and today may be found in practically all American cities.

The Manila Community Chest represents an effort which is still in the trial stage and its success is threatened by the failure to raise the expected amount of funds. American cities also had many difficulties and it may be that, as the city gets accustomed to the idea, it will give greater support. It has made a significant contribution in Manila but its success is limited by the fact that many people of moderate income take no part in giving, while the wealthier group have not been as generous as expected. In American cities where the Chest has been successful, seventy per cent of the contributions come from wage-earners and other small givers while business corporations also donate generous sums.

Current shortcomings in the welfare program are due to lack of funds, but this financial need is related as much to the state of public opinion as to the financial condition of the country. When citizens are convinced that the obligation to be concerned about their brethren extends beyond the limits of the family group, then funds will be provided. This change of attitude will mean a better support of social welfare efforts by all portions of the populace. Community chests, which seek to coordinate the welfare efforts of the entire community, cannot be supported by just a few wealthy individuals but require sacrificial giving by people of moderate means. The Government, too, does not have a magic supply of money and can only increase its support of social welfare as the taxpayers realize the importance of social work activities. Social work cannot proceed faster than the development of social conscience. Present social welfare efforts are largely the result of foreign influence. Their further development depends upon the acceptance of community responsibility in the mores of Philippine society.

Along with a more sensitive social conscience which will stimulate the financial support of social welfare, we need a larger number of people with technical training who are willing to devote their lives to social welfare work. Funds available for social welfare should be used in a way which gets the maximum results. A social welfare program without trained social workers is just as futile as a hospital without an adequate staff of physicians. The problems which lead to social welfare activities are complex enough to require the services of individuals with specialized preparation.

Social Work in the Treatment of Criminals

This field is treated separately because it is in this area that social work concepts have met the least acceptance. Indeed, if the approach to criminality is simply that of detention and punishment, then there is no need for people of social work training. Seen in this fashion, the criminal is one who wilfully violates the standards of society and the legal machinery functions only to terrorize potential criminals by the vengeance it deals out to those who are caught and convicted. In this philosophy, the police are human bloodhounds, the judge is one who looks up the rules of the law books and applies them according to the severity of the offense; while the function of the prison personnel is simply to keep the prisoner in confinement for the duration of his sentence.

Probably the most consistent adherents of this policy are those who advocate the infliction of the death penalty in a large number of cases. No punishment causes more terror than execution and nothing else gives the public greater assurance that the criminal has received his proper reward. The death penalty assumes that people are free agents who rationally weigh the consequences of their actions and may be kept to the course of virtue by the threat of severe punishment. It ignores consideration of social causation and rejects any idea that the prisoner may be rehabilitated for decent living. At the same time, it has complete confidence in the deterrent effect of savage punishment.

Actual experience has proven that results of this approach are less than might be expected. England, in the

Middle Ages, was notorious for its high crime rate although death was the penalty for relatively trivial offenses. Today, England is one of the world's most law-abiding countries although the death penalty (capital punishment) is rarely inflicted. The United States serves as an interesting laboratory for the testing of theories of punishment since some of the 48 states have the death penalty for the most serious offenses while others do not. Judging from the comparative incidence of crime, the presence or absence of the death penalty for serious offenses seems to make no difference.[7]

The current trend is to give less emphasis to the punishment of the criminal and more attention to his possible reform. In this approach, the judge is not a type of robot who looks up in the law books the proper kind of torture to fit the crime but a social engineer who decides, within wide limits of discretion, the type of treatment best designed to meet the needs of the individual offender. The policeman becomes involved in promoting boys clubs and athletic leagues while the prison personnel become practitioners of group work.

This trend has even advanced to the point where sentence to a penal institution may not automatically follow conviction if the judge feels that imprisonment would not aid the reformation of the prisoner. In this case, the judge may place the prisoner on probation which means that the individual does not go to prison as long as he maintains good conduct and reports to the probation officer at definite intervals. Or, if the individual has spent some time in confinement, he may be released on parole if the authorities consider him a good risk. Like the probationer, the parolee is under supervision for the balance of his sentence and may be returned to the penal institution if he fails to abide by parole regulations.

A distinction should be made between these methods of treatment and pardon. Parole and probation assume

---

[7] See discussion in Lewis E. Lawes, *Twenty Years in Sing Sing*, Blue Ribbon Books, New York, 1932, pp. 291 to 337.

that the prisoner is guilty but that it is undesirable to keep him in confinement. Pardon assumes that the prisoner has been punished through judicial error and is entirely innocent of criminal conduct. Actually, pardon is sometimes given as a reward for good conduct but this is a misuse of the pardoning power and parole is the proper procedure for this type of case.

The newer methods of treating crime assume the importance of both social causation and individual differences and the social worker has a vital role to play in this type of procedure. The social worker gathers data which the judge may use in making a wise disposition of the case.

The social worker, functioning as a parole or probation officer, helps the offender to develop his potentialities in a such a way that he will become a useful member of society. In the prison setting, the social worker acts as adviser to the parole board and also carries on a group work type of program. Finally, in the community itself the caseworker strives to help the actual or potential delinquent in meeting his problems while the group worker seeks to involve him in wholesome group relationships.

Some of the criticism of humanitarian treatment of criminals is based on the fact that all too often we have tried to replace punishment with a kind gesture or an eloquent lecture. This means that we have substituted sentimentality for cruelty and neither approach is adequate to the needs of the maladjusted individual who becomes a criminal. Social work has a humanitarian motivation and believes in the possibility of reformation, but it recognizes the difficulties of the process and strives to bring all the resources of scientific treatment to assist in the reformation of the offender.

In the Philippines, as elsewhere, the treatment of criminals has been a mixture of both philosophies. The idea of punishment can be seen in the narrow legalistic approach of many jurists, the crowded prisons with untrained personnel and the general lack of consideration of the prisoner's individual needs. On the other hand, the Welfareville system and the prison farms give some consideration to influences which may lead to reformation. Also a few judges strive to handle juvenile delinquents in the informal manner which characterizes a good "juvenile court."

While criminal statistics are apt to be misleading, there is a strong belief that the Philippines have suffered from increased juvenile delinquency since the time of the Japanse occupation. This is not unnatural as the destruction of the cities and the disorganization of social life furnished the type of conditions in which delinquency usually flourishes. Recognition of the seriousness of the problem has stimulated local efforts to meet the situation.

The Council for the Prevention of Juvenile Delinquency, originally "A Coordinating Council for the Prevention of Juvenile Delinquency," was created in December, 1945, to work for a more effective program for the promotion of the welfare of the youth of Manila. Boy's Home, later Boy's Town, was the council's first and foremost project.

Boy's Town is located just outside of Manila in a group of abandoned army barracks. It strives to create a "permissive" atmosphere and to develop self-respect without coercion. It has no fence and no guards and the boys are free to leave although few of them do. The priest in charge of the project wears ordinary clothes, except when conducting services, and he and the boys are on a first name basis with each other. The small size of the buildings is conducive to the development of a family type of living in which the individual is not lost in the crowd. Educational, recreational and medical facilities are provided and the boys themselves take genuine pride in the institution.

This approach to the treatment of the juvenile delinquent is an attempt to meet the real problem which produces juvenile delinquency. Facing the fact that the roots and causes are laid in the psychological and physical environment of the child, we realize that delinquent behavior is a reaction against authority. Delinquent children have been called "rebels against authority." With such knowledge, verified by numerous studies of delinquent behavior throughout the world, we should not attempt to treat delinquency by punishment and the use of discipline and authority alone. The primary concept that we must always keep in mind in dealing with the delinquent child is that there is a reason for his behavior; he is a victim of his family and environmental life, he is perhaps unhappy, neglected, confused, more "sick" than guilty. The first job that the social worker has in dealing with the delinquent is to get at the cause of the delinquent or deviant behavior that the child shows. To get at the cause, one must let the child feel that he is loved, understood, trusted, and wanted; this can only be done in homelike, secure, friendly atmosphere. This is the "permissive approach" which is the philosophy of Boys' Town.

Training for Social Work

Recognizing the increasing importance and need of expanded and more adequate and effective social welfare service, one is immediately faced with the fact that there are insufficient trained social workers to carry out the task. Only since 1950, has professional training for social work been available in the Philippines; in 1954, three universities were offering graduate and undergraduate training in Social Work and several private colleges offered undergraduate courses.

Social workers should have a good understanding of sociology, but specific social work training usually begins at the graduate level and assumes that the student already has a good background in a liberal arts curriculum. Social work training is related to many other subjects but still has a distinctive curriculum which has been found to be the type of study most directly helpful to potential social workers. As in the case of medicine and teaching, a good part of the preparation consists of supervised experience in various agencies.

Social Work seldom offers a high income although outstanding social workers will probably receive fairly adequate compensation. Whether or not one should consider social work as a career depends on the degree of interest of the individual and his personal qualifications. There are many occupations which carry greater financial rewards and there are many intelligent people whose personal traits would prevent them from being effective social workers.

What are some of the desirable qualities of a social worker? Perhaps first, the social worker should have a genuine interest in people, and a belief in the worth of the individual; he should be a warm and friendly person who has been able to make a good adjustment in his own personal life. Intelligence, flexibility, understanding, objectivity, maturity, and and an ability to use good judgment without prejudice are further characteristics which social work requires.

The Philippines is now experiencing an increased awareness and recognition of the need for social workers. Following are some of the settings where social workers are needed: public welfare programs, family agencies, child caring agencies and institutions, social group work and settlement house, community centers, youth agencies and institutions, child guidance clinics, public schools, community chests, councils of social agencies, juvenile and adult courts, prisons and parole or detention programs, rehabilitation of delinquents, prevention of delinquency, health centers, public health programs, industry, unemployment centers, and perhaps most urgently, in hospitals and other medical facilities.

While there is a great need for social workers in the Philippines, the profession is still not fully accepted. The various schools of social work are trying to turn out students who will be of service to their country. As these students demonstrate their usefulness, we may expect to see a constantly increasing demand for the services which trained social workers can provide.

Summary

Social work began in the religiously sponsored effort to meet desperate human distress. It has developed to the point where the social worker strives not only to prevent distress but to deal with the basic causes of human maladjustment. Welfare activities in earlier years involved a paternalistic process fostering pride in the givers and lack of self-respect in the recipients. It has changed to an emphasis on the dignity of the individual and demands that the social worker respect the right of the economically dependent to make their own decisions and to utilize social work assistance as a step toward independence. Much of the welfare load in the Philippines has been carried by the family but this procedure does not appear to be a satisfactory answer to all welfare needs.

Social work contributes to many fields including public relief, child welfare, recreational organization and the treatment of juvenile delinquents and adult criminals. It applies the best available scientific knowledge to social problems through the techniques of case-work, group work and community organization. The social worker requires definite professional training and this is now being offered by various schools in the Philippines. Social work has a vital role to play in the effort of democracies to extend the good life to all their citizens. With so great a responsibility, the carrying out of welfare plans cannot be left to persons who acquire positions by political pull or a sentimental interest in human welfare. Social work requires much more than a good heart and common sense, and it is dangerous for persons to take over the administration of social welfare functions without previous training and experience. Methods used by an untrained group are often ineffective and the entire social welfare program may be discredited by the acceptance of individuals as social workers who are not properly trained for their responsibilities. An effective social welfare program requires not only professional personnel but also the support of the community as a whole. Thus, some degree of social work education must be extended to the entire community so that citizens will realize the importance of social work services and their responsibility to the less fortunate of the nation.

QUESTIONS

1. What organizations in your vicinity carry on social welfare work? Explain the manner in which they function and whether or not their operation is in line with principles of social work described in this chapter.

2. Interview one of the beggars in your locality. Find out the nature of his disability and why he seeks alms rather than relying on family or institutional care.

3. To what extent has your own family operated as a social welfare agency? Describe the circumstances and decide whether or not the family adequately meets the needs of these dependents.

4. Find out what is being done about juvenile delinquents in your locality. What do the local authorities feel are main problems in this respect?

5. Read and report on one of the books or two of the magazine articles listed in the bibliography.

PROJECTS

1. Distinguish between pardon, probation and parole.

2. Explain the importance of a "permissive" atmosphere in the treatment of juvenile delinquents.

3. Distinguish between casework, group work and community organization.

4. Describe and evaluate the role of the family group in social welfare.

5. How does social work differ from sociology and other descriptive social sciences?

6. How did social work begin in the Philippines?

7. Through what stages has social work developed in the last 100 years.

SUGGESTED READINGS

de Jongh, Jan F.: "A European View of American Social Work," *Social Casework*, Vol. XXXI, No. (1950).
Analysis of American Social Work practices by one from another culture.

Ellingston, John R.: *Protecting Our Children From Criminal Careers* Prentice-Hall, New York, 1948.
Treats prevention of juvenile delinquency.

Fink, Arthur E.: *The Field of Social Work*, Henry Holt and Co. New York, 1942.
A survey of the major types of social work.

Chapter XVI. SOCIAL WORK 435

Fulgencio, E.: "Not Enough Medical Social Workers," *The Philippines Free Press*, March 14, 1953.
Analysis of the role of the medical social worker.

Gillin, John Lewis: *Taming the Criminal*, Macmillan, New York, 1931.
A survey of prison systems in Japan, Philippines, Switzerland, Belgium and the southern portions of the United Stases. Although written several years ago much of the material is still pertinent.

Katigbak, Maria Kalaw: *A Survey of Four Major Catholic Social Welfare Agencies in Manila and Suburbs*. Unpublished Master's Thesis, University of the Philippines, 1953.

Lee, Dorothy: "Some Implications of Culture for Interpersonal Relations," *Social Casework*, Vol. XXXI, No. 9, November, 1950.
Effect of cultural background on social work treatment.

Mass, Henry: "Collaboration Between Social Work and the Social Sciences," *Social Work Journal*, Vol. XXX, No. 3, July, 1950.
Respective roles of social work and related social sciences.

Paraiso, Virginia A.: "Social Welfare in the Philippines," *The Survey*, Vol. LXXX, No. 4, April, 1952.
Description and short history of organized social welfare in the Philippines.

Philippine Social Trends, Bureau of Printing, Manila, 1950.
Readable, graphic analysis of social problems and the role of welfare agencies.

Santiago, Cayetano: *"Welfare Functions of the Family in a Low Cost Housing Community in Quezon City."* Unpublished Master's Thesis, University of the Philippines, 1953.

Slade, Caroline: *Lily Crackel*, World Publishing Co., 2231 West 110 Street, Cleveland, Ohio.
A novel in a social work setting based on the story of a caseworker in a rural area in the United States. Interesting presentation of community forces which effect a sound welfare program.

Social Work Year Book, Russell Sage Foundation, New York.
Current developments are treated in the annual yearbooks.

Standar, Golda: "Social Work and Social Action in the Philippines," *The Philippine Educational Forum*, Vol. III, No. 3, 1952.
Good discussion of problems of social welfare organization.

Witmer, Helen Leland: *Social Work*, Farrar and Rinchart, New York, 1942.
A readable introductory text.

CHAPTER SEVENTEEN

THE ROLE AND SCOPE OF SOCIOLOGY

...The scientist advances knowledge; his interpreter advances the world... the theory of social and political operation is today in the hands of men who have knowledge but no power; the practice of society and politics is in the hands of of men who have knowledge but no power; the practice of society and politics is in the hands of men who have power but no knowledge. It is for you to set up a true osmosis between knowledge and power, between social action and scientific discovery.
— Albert Edward Wiggam, from his *New Decalogue of Science.*

The dropping of the atomic bomb in Hiroshima in 1945 marked the ushering in of the atomic age. This historic event in, significant both to the physical and social scientists because it made men of science more aware of the need for a social order which would bring peace and goodwill to all of humanity. Sociology is providing knowledge which men of goodwill may use to construct a better world.

Sociology is a science in itself.

Many writers of introductory sociology books commence their texts with the first chapter dealing with the nature of science in general and the special place of sociology in particular. In this text, we have intentionally placed in the last chapter the discussion on the role and scope of sociology. The chapters which have been presented previously represent but a few of the many fields of sociological knowledge, yet are representative enough to give some idea of the topics which interest sociologists. The inductive method has been used in the writing of this elementary text—from the particular to the general—to the

Chapter XVII. ROLE AND SCOPE OF SOCIOLOGY

end that students will acquire the type of social undersanding which makes them ready for a thoretical discussion.

Sociology is the science devoted to the study of man in his interaction as a member of human groups. It includes as a unified process the effect of the group on the individual of the individual on the group.

Social problems have been observed and discussed since the dawn of history, but sociology as a scientific discipline is only a little over a hundred years old. The earlier students of society were usually social philosophers who sought to understand human behavior through theological and philosophical reasoning. This meant that men started with certain basic ideas about human nature and interpreted everything they saw in the light of these basic ideas. For example, the notion was common for a long while that a man's character was due to physical heredity. Thus if a man was a successful citizen, it was because of hereditary traits; conversely, the criminal was one who had inherited vicious habits.

The early social thinkers, whom we might term social philosophers, argued about various notions concerning social life, but did not bother to test their ideas in a scientific manner. To the social philosopher, ideas were true or false either because of their logical consistency or because of the authority on which they relied. To the sociologists, the significance of ideas must be tested by the systematic observation of social life. Thus the influence of heredity would not be determined either by logical arguments or by respect for the state, church or other institutions which supported particular theories. Instead, the sociologist studies the individual and finds out the extent to which his actions may be explained by heredity and the extent to which they may be controlled by other factors. This approach may seem simple, but its application requires a highly developed methodology and it is only in fairly recent years that humanity has turned to scientific inquiry as a source of knowledge about social behavior.

Sociology first gained recognition as an independent science about 1838, when Auguste Comte, a French philosopher, publshed his *Cours de philosophic positive* (Positive Philosophy). "He did not create sociology, but he gave it a name, a program, and a place among the sciences."[1] The new disicpline was coined from the Greek word, *logos*, meaning science, and the Latin word, *socious*, or associate. Thus sociology is the science of associates or association and its scientific impetus we owe to Comte.

Comte's first name for sociology was *social physics*, The word "sociological" is used for the first time in the first volume of his *Positive Philosophy*. Positivism referred to an emphasis on scientific methods of investigation rather than reliance on the traditional assertions which had been accepted because they were based on theological or philosophical authority and elaborated in logical syllogisms. Comte felt that sociology could apply some of the methods of physical science to the investigation of social relationships. He was actually an advocate rather than a practitioner of the scientific method and sociology remained a speculation type of inquiring until the beginning of the twentieth century. Most contemporary sociologists recognize Emile Durkheim, another French thinker, as the real "Father" of modern sociology.

While some development has taken place throughout the world the greatest strides in sociological theory have been made in Europe, (particularly in France and Germany). The greatest development in methodology has occurred in the United States. Shortly before the start of the twentieth century Albion W. Small esablished a department of Sociology at Chicago University. This department concentrated on the type of empirical investigation which has now become accepted practice in sociological circles. At the present time, most American universities have strong departments of sociology and governmental and industrial research units have utilized the services of sociologists.

---

[1] Robert E. Park and Ernest W. Burgess, *Introduction to the Science of Sociology*, Chicago, University of Chicago Press, 1921, p. 34.

In the Philippines Macaraig traced the development of Sociology as follows: [2]

> The first teaching of sociology was conducted in the University of Santo Tomas when Father Valentin Marin introduced the study of social sciences in 1896. In 1900 courses in penology and criminology were added and at the present time (1938) there are more than ten courses—the great majority of which are in social philosophy. In the University of the Philippines, sociology as a study was introduced in 1911 by Professor A. E. W. Salt and President Murray Bartlett. The first gave a course in the Principles of Sociology and the second taught Social Ethics. Since then sociology has been a regular part of the university curriculum, Professor Conrado Benitez was the first Filipino to teach the subject and was succeeded by the late Professor Luis Rivera. In Siliman Institute, it was introduced by Mr. Heflin in 1919.

Professor John de Young made a study of the teaching of Sociology in 1952 which disclosed that the majority of Colleges and Universities were offering at least one or two courses and that a few had a more elaborate curriculum.[3] One should also add that the teaching of Philippine Social Life as a high school subject has carried the sociological emphasis into secondary education.

Methods used by sociologists.

Since sociologists are interested in generalizations, they study particular situations in order to discover uniformities which appear repeatedly in different contexts. A sociologist may study several political parties, not because he is interested in these specific parties, but in order to find factors which operate in different types of groups. To do this he must *classify* human behavior under head-

---

[2] Serafin E. Mamaraig, *Introduction to Sociology*, Educational Supply Co., Manila, 1938, p. 25.
[3] John de Young, *Sociological Teaching in the Philippines*, Unpublished manuscript in the files of the Department of Sociology in the University of the Philippines.

ings which may be used in a variety of situations. Thus he will speak of stages, cycles, trends and other terms which he can use in describing human conduct. He needs *concepts* which will convey his generatizations. In studying the effects of wealth and poverty, for instance, he notices that certain general attitudes are common in groups of high and low income and he develops the concept *social class*. On an even broader basis, he notices certain uniformities in all types of society and calls these *folkways and mores*. When he has classified and conceptualized a given area, he may develop principles (theories of social relationships) which can be applied in a number of situations. Human behavior is then studied to find out the extent to which it conforms to the theories and the theories are altered in the light of the information obtained. This is a continuous process which leads to a constant refinement of our knowledge about social life.

To understand the present procedures of sociologists, one must have some appreciation of the scientific method. Roucek and Warren mention eight steps which characterize scientific inquiry:

1. Careful stating of assumptions.
2. Careful definition of terms.
3. Employment of objective methods of observation.
4. Classification of phenomena observed.
5. Suggesting and testing of new hypotheses.
6. Expression of uniformities in quantitative terms wherever possible.
7. Development of a body of theory which relates different aspects of the findings in meaningful ways but which is subject to modification in the light of newer findings.
8. Continuous criticism and re-examination of generalization, which however well established they seem to be, are constantly open to critical re-examination in the light of new findings.[4]

---

[4] Joseph S. Roucek and Roland L. Warren, *Sociology*, (Ames, Iowa: Littlefield, Adams and Co., 1951, p. 6.

Chapter XVII. Role and Scope of Sociology

What is the task of Sociology as a Science?

Science, as we generally understand it, is an accumulated and accepted body of knowledge, systematized and formulated into an ordered and interrelated system with reference to the discovery of general truth.[5]

This poses a question, what then is a sociologist? Albion W. Small, one of America's pioneer sociologists, describes him as "a man who is studying the facts of society in a certain way."[6]

The term *sociologist* as a new appellation, belongs to all students of society who think of human life, past, present, and future, as somehow bound together, and who try to understand any particular fragment of human life which they may study by making out its bearing upon and its being borne upon by all the rest of human life. The sociologist then is the man who tries to fill the place in our scientific age which the old fashioned philosopher occupied in the ages of metaphysical speculation.[7]

The gaining of the elementary facts, usually termed "data," which furnish the basis for sociological thinking is a major task by itself. Through the use of logic, we may interpret the meaning of these data, but this is futile unless the data themselves are actually valid. In reality, we have very little reliable information about human life. Most people have some notions about human behavior, but usually these are only reliable in a very small group and even here may be distorted by prejudice or ignored because the value of certain data is not realized. The census is a gigantic attempt to gain social facts, but there are many types of information which the census cannot secure and there are other areas where its data may not be reliable. The family, for instance, is the major social institution, yet we know very little about

---
[5] E. B. Reuter, "The Problem of Sociology," *Sociology and Social Research*, XIII: p. 119.
[6] Albion W. Small, "What is a Sociologist?", *American Journal of Sociology*, VIII: p. 468.
[7] *Ibid.*, p. 469.

how families actually live. We may know how many families exist in a given place, but their methods of child rearing, division of authority, expenditure of money, relationships with relatives—on these and similar questions, we have only a few observations of doubtful value. To use another example, we talk a great deal about educating children in such a way that they will have strong character, but we have practically no information the effect of various types of character education on the children who have received this training. To list some other areas in which data are incomplete: we do not have reliable information on the number of people who are born and the number who die in a given year, we do not really know the income of the country or the amount of its agricultural production. For these items we have only estimates which, for many reasons, are not altogether reliable.

The first task of the sociologist is to gather the data required to begin an analysis of social life. The gathering of data, however, is only a start; for the sociologist is really interested in the relationships which are found between various types of social phenomena. He may, for instance, obtain data about the amount of juvenile delinquency (although this is difficult) and the availability of playgrounds, but this does not prove the extent to which playgrounds influence the conduct of children who are equal in other respects. When he attempts this type of study, he may find out that playgrounds are a major antidote for crime, but it is more likely that he will simply gain some insight into the role of recreation as one of the many factors which influence social behavior. In earlier days, sociologists were often intrigued with the idea that one or two factors played a major role in forming personality; now they are inclined to think that every part of social life must be analyzed in relation to man's total activities.

The task of gathering data and determining relationships has led to the development of several techniques which are classified by Hornell Hart as follows:

CHAPTER XVII. ROLE AND SCOPE OF SOCIOLOGY 443

1. The common-sense method—consisting in generalizing from data which chance to come to hand. This has been the most prominent.
2. The historical method—uses documents as its data.
3. The museum surveys and government investigations.
4. The laboratory or the experimental method—restricted in sociological research by the length of time required for social experiments, by the number and complexity of the variables involved, and by the difficulty of controlling human variables.
5. Superiority of the statistical method—this method consists in applying rigidly objective methods, aided by mathematics, to the interpretation of social phenomena which spontaneously occur.[8]

Is common sense enough?

Since sociology deals with topics which are a familiar part of our daily living, the accusation is sometimes made that the sociologist is simply one who uses tortuous language to discuss subjects which could be handled by a simple, common sense approach. Undoubtedly, common sense is required of the sociologist as well as others, but by itself, it does not give us reliable knowledge about social life. Roucek and Warren indicate some of the shortcomings of the exclusive reliance on a common sense approach:

"Everyone knows" that immigrants contribute more than their share of crime, but it just happens not to be true. "Everyone knows" that hereditary traits are transmitted from mother to child through the blood stream, but it just isn't true. Common sense is *often mistaken,* and the only way of determining when it is and when it isn't is through rigorous scientific investigation.

But even when common sense knowledge is essentially true, it is most often stated in such

---
[8] Hornell Hart, "Science and Sociology," *The American Journal of Sociology*, XXVII: pp. 365-383.

vague form that it is practically useless, if not misleading. Such statements as "You can't change human nature" can be true or false, according to what is meant by human nature. The sociologist's use of obscure terms is not usually an attempt to impress. It is rather the use of precise concepts whose meaning is agreed upon by specialists, in order that precision of meaning may be communicated.[9]

Sociology and group values.

Both fears and hopes are often expressed about the effect which the study of sociology may have on the values cherished by certain institutions. Actually, sociology is a science which, like physics or chemistry, may be used for purposes which are either good or evil. The study of group organization, for example, is important for any group and would be equally useful to Christians or Moslems, democrats or fascists, capitalists or communists. The principles of public opinion formation may be used to convert the heathen, promote foreign policy, conduct a political campaign, sell soap, or promote any other activities in which men are interested. The sociologist as an individual will probably prefer some groups to others, but sociology as a science is neutral. This is brought out clearly in a recent discussion of the relation of Catholicism to sociology. The opinions stated here would apply equally to other social groups which may be concerned about the effects of sociology on their beliefs and institutions:

> Observation, description, and classification of social facts do not depend on faith and morals; sociology is concerned with things as they are and not as they ought to be; the supernatural is of no concern except as it appears in the natural order and becomes observable to the scientist. The same applies to the theory of sociology; being scientific, this must be formulated so that its truth can be demonstrated, not directly, but indirectly, and the facts apprehended must be guaranteed by the postulates. There does not and

---

[9] Roucek and Warren, *Op. Cit.*, pp. 6-7.

cannot exist a Catholic theory of sociology; there can only be sociological theories.[10]

Pure and applied science.

Much scientific inquiry is directed toward the discovery of general principles without any particular concern for their application in specific situations. This is known as pure science and is justified on the basis that all knowledge is ultimately useful and its accumulation is worthwhile even though we may not see its utility at the present time. On the other hand, much, probably most, scientific inquiry is directed toward the solution of specific problems and is known as applied science.

Perhaps the most famous example of this distinction is found by comparing the work of Alfred Einstein and the scientists who developed the atomic bomb. Einstein was only concerned with understanding the nature of atomic structure and was not concerned about developing explosives. His research, however, proved invaluable to other scientists who were assigned the specific task of developing a powerful weapon. In sociology, we have men studying acculturation who might be termed pure scientists, while others, trying to discover ways to improve relationships between two specific ethnic groups, would be classified as applied scientists.

The two classifications indicate a difference of emphasis, but are not absolutely rigid. Pure science is ultimately useful to the man seeking a solution to specific problems and applied science may contribute information which leads to improvements in the theoretical approach of the pure scientist. A truly progressive society will encourage both types of scientific research.

Sociology and the social sciences.

We now consider the place of sociology among the social sciences. With the knowledge that the superorganic

---

[10] E. K. Francis and Jean Labbens, "Suggestions to American Catholic Sociologists for Scheme of Research," *Lumen Vitae,*, Vol. VI, pp. 160-165. Cited in *Philippine Sociological Review*, August, 1953.

or socio-cultural universe is the concern of all the social and humanistic disciplines, we must bear in mind that all scientific disciplines make one indivisible science; but for practical purposes, a division of labor requires specialization in each discipline. Sociology occupies a midway position between the disciplines which seek to describe the past and those which are devoted to analyzing a specific segment of human life which is of current concern.

Park and Burgess indicate in a general and schematic way the position of sociology among the other social sciences, as shown below:[11]

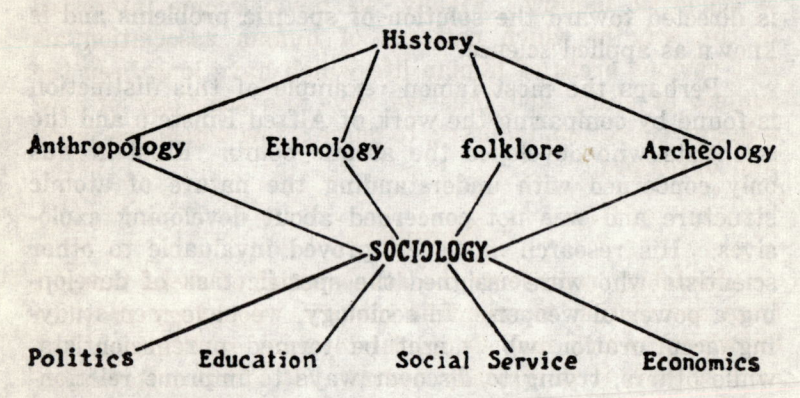

```
                    History
Anthropology    Ethnology    folklore    Archeology
                   SOCIOLOGY
Politics    Education    Social Service    Economics
```

The technical or applied social sciences such as politics, education, social service, and economics are related to sociology in a different way. "They are, to a greater or lesser extent, applications of principles which it is the business of sociology and psychology to deal with explicitly."[12] Hence, sociology may be regarded as fundamental to the other social sciences.

The economist, for example, is interested in the factors which influence business activity. He soon learns that to understand business activity he must know something about the manner in which people usually operate in human groups. The sociologist is not interested in business as such, but he is interested in the social patterns which

---
[11] Park and Burgess, *Op. Cit.*, p. 43.
[12] *Ibid.*, p. 45.

CHAPTER XVII. ROLE AND SCOPE OF SOCIOLOGY

govern the actions of labor leaders, business promoters, consumers and workers. The same type of analysis could be made of political science, social welfare and education. The major task of the sociologist is to study human groups and by so doing, he helps the specialized sciences in their tasks and from them obtains more data which may be used in the analysis of group conduct. There are also some specific fields such as criminology, the family, population, race relations, etc. which did not receive much academic consideration until the sociologists made them the object of scientific inquiry. Finally, we have become interested in the way in which patterns of human association affect various areas of human life which have long been the subject of study and thus we have the sociology of law, religion, education, industry, to name a few which are fairly well developed.

Summary

Sociology represents the development of social thought from speculation to scientific inquiry. Sociology provides knowledge which may be useful to many institutions, but as a science, it is ethically neutral. It offers information which may illuminate our understanding of society, but the use of this information depends upon the goals of the individuals concerned. Sociology directed attention to hitherto neglected fields of study such as the family, criminology, race relations, population, public opinion analysis and many others. It also offers a new approach to older subjects such as the study of law, religious institutions, education, industry, and political science. Sociologists helped to introduce professional training for social workers and sociology is still closely linked to educational preparation for welfare work. As a method of gaining a better understanding of society, sociology is an essential part of a general education. Vocational opportunities exist mainly in research and teaching.

QUESTIONS

1. What is science?
2. What are the characteristic steps common to all sciences?
3. In what way is sociology becoming scientific?
4. What is sociology? Who is a sociologist?
5. What is the position of sociology among the social sciences?
6. What methods are used in sociology?
7. How does sociology become an applied science?
8. Name some of the areas in which sociological knowledge is useful.
9. Is sociology for or against democracy? Explain your answer.

SUGGESTED READINGS

Rogardus, Emory S., *Sociology, Third Edition* (New York: The Macmillan Company, 1949), pp. 543-582. Discusses the research aspects of sociology, the methods used, and also the current sociological developments. The necessity of group research is emphasized.

Gittler, Joseph B., *Social Dynamics* (New York: McGraw-Hill Book Company, Inc., 1952), pp. 1-19. This patterns to the nature of the social and the meaning of sociology. The scientific objective is illustrated vividly with a crisis situation.

Lundberg, George A., *Social Research*, New York: Longmans, Green and Co., 1946. Sociology to be really called a science must have characteristics similar to the physical sciences. This book is an attempt to furnish the sociologist a methodological approach to the sudy of social phenomena.

Park, Robert E. and Ernest W. Burgess, *Introduction to the Science of Sociology*, Chicago: The University of Chicago Press, 1921. This book is now regarded as a classic and may be considered as the sociologist's bible in the sense that it accorded sociology its scientific prestige.

Sorokin, Pitirin A., *Society, Culture, and Dynamics*, (New York: Harper and Brothers, 1947), pp. 3-18. Discusses sociology as a science, and delineates both the organic, inorganic, and the superorganic realm—the latter being the main concern of sociology.

GLOSSARY OF SOCIOLOGICAL TERMS

Most of the definitions in this glossary are taken from *Sociology* by Joseph S. Roucek and Roland L. Warren, published by Littlefield, Adams & Co. Ames Iowa in 1951. These definitions are used by special permission of the publisher.

Accommodation. A temporary adjustment of differences between hostile parties so as to terminate conflict. The parties maintain their hostile attitudes, but modify their behaviour so that conflict will not be continued.

Acculturation. The process by which individuals or groups from one culture come to acquire the behaviour and thought patterns of a different culture. It is usually a reciprocal process.

Amalgamation. Fusing of two different ethnic groups through intermarriage.

Animism. Regarding material objects as having a life or soul.

Anthropology. The study of the human species, its origins, its varieties, and its cultures.

Arbitration. In arbitration, the terms of a compromise are arrived at by a third party, and both contending parties agree in advance to abide by the decision.

Aristocracy. In an aristocracy, whatever the governmental structure, the basic decisions are made by a relatively small, elite class, usually, though not always hereditary in nature.

Assimilation. The process by which two or more groups who have different attitudes, mores and cultural practices become alike in these things.

Attitude. A learned tendency to respond in some characteristic way toward an object, idea, situation, or value.

Autocracy. In an autocracy, government is exercised by a supreme power who is responsible to no one and against whom there can be no redress.

Average. The sum of the numerical values of all the items, divided by the number of items. This is the most widely used measure of central tendency more precisely called the mean.

Capitalism. An inclusive economic institution which provides for performance of economic functions under conditions of private property, freedom of contract, private profit, capital accumulation and investment, an extensive credit system, a free labor market, a wage system, and a commodity market in which prices are determined chiefly by supply, demand and competition.

Case study method. A method that involves intensive study of a particular instance of some social phenomenon, with great care being given to the interaction of the many factors at work, and of its development through time.

Castes. Social classes whose membership is determined solely by birth and between which there is no vertical social mobility.

Centralization (ecological). Organization of institutional functions in close proximity to each other in a limited area.

Class (social). An unorganized group of people who become members by birth or by later entry into the group, who treat each other as approximate equals, who associate with each other more intimately than with other persons, and who have approximately the same relationship of superordination or subordination to persons from other groups within the society.

Class conflict. The struggle between social classes for access to wealth, power and prestige.

Class consciousness. Awareness by the members of a particular social classes of themselves as an in-group.

Clique. A relatively small group without any formal structure, often occurring within a larger formal group, and characterized by reciprocal relationships of confidence and cooperation.

Communication. The process of transmitting facts, beliefs, attitudes, emotional reactions, or any other content of awareness between human beings.

Community. A group of people who have a certain sense of belonging together and who reside in a given geographic area in which most or all of the basic institutional activities are present.

Community organization. The term is used to describe both the institutional structure of communities and also the process by which the functions of various aspects of community living are continuously brought into closer integration with each other.

Companionate family. One in which a major value is the sharing of interests between members of the family group with a trend away from dominance by any one member of the family.

Competition. Individualized struggle for scarce goals.

Compromise. The process of mutual concessions by hostile parties in order to cease conflict.

Concentration. Clustering of large numbers of people in a comparatively small area.

GLOSSARY

Conciliation. The process by which hostile parties recognize common interests and reach a working agreement, lessening hostile attitudes but not removing them completely.

Conflict. An attempt to eliminate a rival from the competitive process.

Consciousness of kind. An awareness by members of a group of what they have in common as opposed to other people.

Contraception. Prevention of conception by avoiding the union of the sperms and the ovum. Not the same as abortion which refers to the elimination of the foetus.

Convention. A regularized form of behavior which has general support, but to which little moral importance is attached.

Conventionalization. Process by which an action that is usually forbidden becomes socially acceptable on specific occasions. An example is the act of sprinkling people with water on the feast day of John the Baptist.

Conversion. The process by which an individual is comparatively suddenly won over to a different philosophy of life, or way of viewing things, such as to a different religion or political conviction.

Cooperation. The process of working together for common goals.

Correlation. The degree to which measurements from two sets of variables correspond to each other.

Craze. A relatively short-lived behaviour pattern which is usually more novel and bizarre than the ordinary fad and which is frequently associated with a sense of deliberate variation from customary fashions.

Criminology. The study of the development of criminal behavior, the organization of criminal activities in their relation to the functioning of the institutional structure, and of the methods of dealing with the criminal in his apprehension, trial and subsequent treatment.

Crisis. Any major interruption in the usual routine of need fulfillment.

Crowd. A temporary group interacting in physical proximity with relation to some common interest or focus of attention.

Cultural monism. The doctrine that conflict involving different nationality, ethnic, or minority groups can best be resolved by the groups giving up their group differences and assuming uniform characteristics.

Cultural pluralism. The doctrine that different nationality, ethnic or minority groups should maintain their differences and consider each other with sympathetic understanding plus mutual respect.

Culture. The way of living which any society develops to meet its fundamental needs for survival, perpetuation of the species, and the ordering of social experience. It is the accumulation of material objects, patterns of social organization, learned modes of behavior, knowledge, beliefs and all other activities which are developed in human association.

Culture area. A geographical area within which the various cultures show significant similarities in important characteristics.

Culture complex. A group of traits organized around some basic activity.

Culture pattern. Organization of a culture around some characteristic theme or value.

Culture trait. The simplest unit of a culture, whether material or non-material.

Custom. An established way of doing something which is recognized by society.

Cynicism. An attitude which doubts the truth of current beliefs.

Damay. (Tagalog). A type of community life in which intimate, sympathetic and neighborly relationships prevail. Primary group contacts predominate. The rural village is the classic example of a damay community. (An equivalent to *Gemeinschaft* as defined by Ferdinand Tonnies).

Decentralization. Moving functions away from center of institutional activity, the opposite of centralization.

Deductive method. The deductive method of gaining knowlege is that of applying general principles to specific cases. Modern science uses this method in formulating from what is already known, certain hypotheses which seem to be plausible. It then employs the inductive method to test these hypotheses.

Democracy. In a democracy, whatever the structure, the ultimate authority over the state is considered to reside with the people, and so the slogan "government by consent of the governed" is perhaps the easiest way to describe it.

Denomination. A sect which has passed the conflict stage and has become accommodated as an established part of the institutional structure.

Diffusion. Spreading of cultural traits or complexes from one society to another. This is the way in which most societies acquire most of their new traits.

Discrimination. Unequal treatment of different people according to the group to which they belong.

GLOSSARY

Dispersion. The opposite of concentration; the spreading out of a few people over a relatively large area. Both processes are, of course, different aspects of the same phenomenon.

Drive. A recurrent stimulus produced within the organism such as the hunger, thirst, or sex drive.

Ecclesia. Religious group including the majority of the population with harmony between religious ideals and the secular practices of society. Concept developed by Troeltsch in *The Social Teachings of Christianity*.

Endogamy. Marriage within one's own group.

Ethnocentrism. The tendency of a society to consider its own culture the best and others inferior.

Eugenics. The study of methods of improving the quality of the population through applying knowledge of hereditary differences in reproduction.

Euthenics. The study of methods of improving the quality of the population through altering the environment.

Exogamy. Marriage outside of one's group.

Experimental method. In the experimental method, the scientist holds all other factors constant except the one whose effect he is attempting to measure. Since this is easier to do with chemical compounds or even with white mice than with human beings, the sociologist attempts to achieve similar precision through controlled observation rather than controlled experiment.

Fads. Extremely short-lived behavior patterns whose attraction is often in their novelty, and which involve minor variations in manner of speaking, eccentricities of dress or other personal adornment, or preoccupation with certain expressions or transistory ideas.

Fashions. Relatively short-time modes of action involving personal adornment, manner of speech, and many other types of patterned behavior. The compulsion which it exerts derives from its acceptance by many people as the thing to do.

Feral man. A human individual who has been reared apart from human society and hence has not been socialized. Various accounts of alleged feral men describe such individuals as more animallike in behavior than human, but the authenticity of some accounts has been questioned.

Fetish. A material object given reverence and imbued with magical characteristics.

Field study. Field study involves the investigator's actually going out and gathering data among the people he is studying although these data may then be combined with data already available from other sources.

Folkways. Sanctioned forms of behavior practiced within a society and considered to be the proper way of doing things by that society. In general usage, folkways are considered to involve less compulsion than the mores.

Gang. A primary group resembling a clique, but one which is in conflict with other groups and secures much of its cohesion from this conflict.

Gemeinschaft. See *Damay*.

Gentile. A word with strong cultural overtones. Among Jews it is applied to all non-Jewish groups. Among Christians it is applied to all non-Jews and non-Christians. Among Moslems it is applied to all who are not Jewish, Christian or Moslem.

Geographic determinism. The theory that cultural forms and social processes are determined by the geographical environment.

Gesellschaft. A type of community life in which impersonal, superficial, and business-like relationships prevail. Secondary group contacts of a transitory sort predominate. The large urban centers are the prime example of a *gesellschaft* community. (originally defined by Ferdinand Tonnies).

Group. Two or more people between whom there is some ascertainable pattern of interaction thus constituting a unit which can be thought of, by its members and by others, as a whole.

Group marriage. Marriage of several males to several females. It is unknown in its pure form, although an approximation to it is allegedly found in the Marquesas, a Pacific island group.

Historical method. Use of an analysis of past events to formulate general principles.

Human ecology. The study of the spatial arrangements of human beings in relation to their environment.

Ideology. A system of reasoning and beliefs which purports to describe the true nature of man and to derive therefrom the "right" type of socio-economic structure for his true nature.

Individual. In strict sociological terminology, the individual is simply the human organism, independent of its contact with other people. At birth, the infant is merely an individual in this sense. (This term is also often used by sociologists in the ordinary, dictionary meaning of the word.)

Inductive method. Method of arriving at general principles from actual observation of the behavior of what is being studied.

Industrial sociology. In its purely scientific aspects, industrial sociology is concerned with gaining knowledge about the social processes involved in industrial activity, and with industrial organizations as social systems. As an applied science, it applies sociological knowledge and method to problems of human relation in industry.

In-group. Any group considered by its members in distinction from other groups.

Inhibition. A self-imposed restraint on the individual's overt behavior.

Institution. Well-established patterns for meeting various human needs, which grow out of the folkways as these take on the sanction of established usage and concepts of social welfare, and develop some type of structure.

Interaction. A process in which the responses of each party become successively, stimuli for the responses of the other.

Interest. A relationship between an object and one or more persons in which the object becomes a focus for the orientation of attitudes. Much social behavior takes place in relation to such interests.

Intergroup relations. Broadly conceived, the field of intergroup relations comprises a study of the nature and principles of relations between various groups of people, whatever the basis of the grouping.

Invasion. The process by which institutions and/or members of a particular group gradually come to occupy some of the territory formerly occupied by a different group and/or institutions.

Invention. A new combination of known elements.

Kinship systems. Coordinated systems of status and role of people who are considered to be related either by heredity, marriage or adoption.

Lobbying. Attempt to influence legislation through personal contract by a representative pressure group with legislators and those who propose legislation.

Marginal man. A person who is in contact with two cultures, participating in parts of each of them but belonging fully to neither.

Mass Man. A member of a human grouping which cuts across the usual social bonds of vocation, education, wealth, etc. One who is exposed to crowd stimuli but who lacks strong primary group ties.

Material culture. Physical objects of the culture, along with the way in which they are used.

Maternal family. One in which the wife's role is predominant.

Matriarchal family. A consaguine family usually matrilineal and matrilocal, in which an older woman is the functional head.

Matrilocal residence. The condition in which a married couple live in the family home or locality of the wife.

Maturation. A biological process through which, at appropriate times in the organism's development, internal changes occur such as those associated with the onset of puberty.

Mean. The sum of the numerical values of all the items, divided by the number of items. More correctly called the arithmetic mean, it is often referred to as the average.

Median. The median score is the middle score in a distribution of items arranged according to size.

Mediation. In mediation, a third party attempts to effect a compromise between two conflicting parties through bringing them together. Neither party is committed in advance to accepting the result.

Milling. Restless, uncoordinated behavior expressed by a group of people in physical proximity as the result of a crisis or excitement.

Minority problems. Problems of intergroup relations in which each minority is the subject of prejudice and discrimination by the majority.

Mob. A crowd which is taking some form of concerted action.

Mode. That value or measure which appears most frequently in a given population or distribution.

Monogamy. Marriage of one male to one female.

Mores. Folkways which have come to be considered by a society as vital to its welfare.

Neighborhood. Within urban communities are small areas, frequently with a name, called neighborhoods. These neighborhoods show a certain degree of visiting and common participation in social life among those who live close to each other. A rural neighborhood consists of a group of families living on contiguous land who generally think of themselves as living in the same locality, to which they often give a name, and who interact with each other through visiting, borrowing, lending tools, exchanging services or participating in social activities.

Norm. See Social norm.

Objective method. A method of investigation which in so far as possible eliminates the personal bias of the observer and is available to others who would check his findings.

Out-group. Any other group than the one from whose viewpoint it is being considered.

GLOSSARY

Parole. A release from imprisonment under specific stipulations regarding one's conduct. The parolee is placed under the supervision of a parole officer, and must report frequently to him.

Paternal family. One in which the husband's role is predominant.

Patriarchal family. A consanguine family, usually patrilineal and patrilocal, in which an older man is the functional head.

Patrilocal residence. The condition in which married couple live in the family home, or locality, of the husband.

Penology. The study of penology deals with the treatment of criminals by society.

Person. In strict sociological terminology, the person is an individual who has status in one or more groups. (This term is also often used by sociologists in the ordinary, dictionary term or meaning of the word.)

Personality. The organization of biological, psychological, and sociological factors which underlie the individual's behavior.

Personality disorganization. A condition in which because of lack of internal integration or because of the development of behavior patterns at great variance with the standards of his society, the personality is unable to participate effectively in his society.

Pluralism. A situation in which groups with different cultures live in the same geographic area without either conflict or assimilation.

Polyandry. Marriage of one female to two or more males.

Polygamy. Polygamy means many wives, or husbands, and includes polyandry and polygyny.

Polygyny. Marriage of one male to several females.

Population. Population refers to the number of people in a geographic area. The study of population involves not only their numbers, but also their age, sex, and other important characteristics which differentiate one population from another.

Prejudice. An attitude arrived at without sufficient exploration of the facts. It is prejudging, in the sense of making a judgment before, or independent of, the relevant facts in the matter.

Pressure group. Publics, or parts of publics, which have organized in order to influence social events and processes in a manner favorable to their interests.

Primary (group) contact. Contact between members of a primary group. The term is often used to denote contacts between other persons where these contacts have one or more of the characteristics of the primary group.

Primary group. A group characterized by intimacy, face-to-face contact, and a relative degree of permanence.

Probation. A procedure according to which convicted criminals are permitted to live in society without being imprisoned but under the supervision of a probation worker.

Propaganda. The attempt to promote emotional attitudes on controversial issues in order to favor one side of the controversy.

Psychology. The study of the basic factors of human behavior. As such, it is rooted firmly in human physiology, but goes on to investigate such factors as temperament, abilities, motivation, learning, emotion, attitudes, and so forth.

Psychosis. A major personality disorder involving a definite break with reality, in which the personality is so warped that ordinary types of social participation may, at least at times, be practically impossible.

Public. A group of people who share similar interests but not necessarily similar opinions.

Questionnaire. A series of carefully worded questions written down on paper with provision for the informant to answer either by writing in his reply or by checking from a series of possible answers which are listed for him.

Rationalization. Process of finding a socially acceptable excuse for questionable actions.

Reincarnation. Theory that the soul is reborn after death in some other human or animal form.

Religious Institution. An established pattern of belief and behavior having to do with man's relationship to the supernatural.

Ritual. A highly stylized and carefully prescribed set of gestures and words performed by persons who are especially selected to engage in it. The ritual is usually fraught with symbolic meaning and used as a dramatization of thing which are considered sufficiently important to be considered with deference and awe.

Rivalry. A form of competition in which the parties involved are keenly aware of each other as competitors.

Rule. See Social Role.

Rural Referring to the country or farmlands as distinguished from towns and cities. However, this is an arbitrary distinction, for rural conditions of living often gradually merge into urban conditions without any sharp break.

Sacred (culture)—a society in which the culture has a unified set of folkways and mores and hence a homogeneous set of moral values. The members of such a culture thus usually acquire a consistent, traditional viewpoint which is a powerful agent of social control. Social interaction in such a society is of the "damay" (*gemeinschaft*) type.

Scapegoat. A group or individual who is blamed for social ills actually caused by others.

Secondary (group) contacts. Contacts between members of a secondary group (political association, large church organization, etc.). The term is often used to denote contacts between other persons which have one or more of the characteristics of the secondary group.

Secondary groups. Groups which show little intimacy, are relatively temporary, and involve less continuous face-to-face contact.

Sect. Religious group including only a small proportion of the population. Frequently there is a marked contrast between the ethical ideals of the sect and the ethical ideals dominant in the total culture.

Secular (culture)—a society in which there is contact between and often intermingling of varied sets of folkways and mores. In such a culture the moral values presented to the individual are thus neither consistent nor effective in social control. The values of practical necessity and expediency tend to displace the unified tradition viewpoint of the sacred society. Social interaction in such a society is of the *gesellschaft* type.

Secularization. The process of transition from a concern with theology, religious commandments, and the world to come, to an emphasis upon secular or wordly values, ethical and ideological norms, and the importance of this world.

Segregation. The process by which persons or facilities of real or assumed similar characteristics cluster together in space, either voluntarily or through various forms of compulsion.

Sex ratio. The number of males per 100 females.

Social change. Change in social processes or in the structure of society.

Social class. See Class.

Social contagion. The spread of ideas, attitudes, or behavior patterns to relatively large numbers of people through social interaction and without much rational reflection.

Social control. All processes by which society and its component groups come to influence the behavior of individual members toward conformity with group norms.

Social differentiation. The process by which members of various groups come to participate in specific parts of the culture through occupying different positions in society.

Social distance. Degree of social acceptance between individuals and groups in terms of the activities the one is willing to share with members of other groups.

Social expectations. The generalized conceptions held by various groups in society as to what type of behavior is appropriate to any given situation. They include group norms, folkways, mores, socially prescribed role behavior, and so on.

Social heritage. See Culture.

Social Interaction. See Interaction.

Social mobility. Change of social position. Simple movement in space is called geographic mobility. Change of position on the same status level is called horizontal mobility. Movement up or down from one status level to another is called vertical social mobility.

Social movement. A social movement usually emerges out of a condition of social unrest concerning certain aspects of the institutional structure which are experienced as problems. A group organizes to further a suggested method of reform, expands, and acts to further its purposes by indoctrinating the public with the desirability of its program, and, where appropriate, agitating for legislation to convert this program into law.

Social norm. Any socially accepted standard of behavior.

Social organization. Both a process and a condition. As a condition, it is the structure of the various units in society in their inter-relationship with each other. As a process, it is the development of coordination among the various units of society.

Social pathology. This is a term often used interchangeably with social disorganization or social problems. It is based on the analogy between society and a biological organism. In current usage, the organismic analogy is frankly disowned, and it has come to mean any social condition indicative of maladjustment between the felt need of a considerable number of individuals and the socially approved methods of satisfying such needs, or a maladjustment between a society's goals or expressed values and its structure.

Social planning. Social planning is the effort to direct social change through some type of coordinated program of control.

Social psychology. The study of the psychological aspects of behavior as these are modified in social interaction.

Social psychiatry. The study of the social aspects of mental disorders.

Social role. A social role is the pattern of behavior which the individual assumes in social interaction, based on his own previous experience and his degree of conformity to what he considers to be the expectation of others. Most, if not all, social behavior is carried on within such social roles.

Social status. See Status.

Social stratification. The vertical division of society into different social status levels.

Social theory. The discipline which seeks to coordinate factual knowledge about man and society. It attempts to organize the varied findings from the different branches of social science and their subdivision into a coherent framework of knowledge.

Social unrest. A widespread condition of discontent with regard to some event, process, or situation. It is often characterized by minor flare-ups of resentful behavior.

Social value. See value.

Social work. The systematic effort to alleviate maladjustments between the individual and society. It is differentiated from philanthropy, charity, and other good works in general by its deliberate orientation of helping people not only with their current problems but helping them to develop techniques of problem solving and self-help.

Socialization. The process begun in infancy, by which the human organism, learning socially approved attitudes, ideas, and behavior patterns from contact with other persons, comes to assume the roles which pattern his social behavior and which correspond to his status in various social groups. Personality is acquired in the process of socialization.

Society. A group of people in more or less permanent association who are organized for their collective activities and who feel that they belong together.

Sociological theory. That branch of social theory which coordinates and integrates the findings from the various branches of sociology. As a necessary preliminary to such systematic formulation, it examines the assumptions on which the science of sociology is based.

Sociology. The study of human beings in their group relationships. As such, it studies interaction within and between groups of people. Like any science, it attempts to describe its subject matter and to point out such uniformities of occurrence as are found to exist.

Sociology of education. That branch of sociology which studies educational institutions and educational processes. While it is recognized that the principal purpose of educational institutions is that of cultural transmission and acculturation of the young, attention is given to aspects of this process which are not customarily thought of in terms of formal education.

Sociology of religion. The sociology of religion involves systematic analysis of religious phenomena employing sociological concepts and methods.

Sociometry. A special set of concepts and methods devised to describe and measure various interpersonal relationships, chiefly those of attraction and repulsion, in quantitative and diagrammatic terms.

Sovereignty. The doctrine of national sovereignty contends that each state is completely autonomous within its own jurisdiction and interests, and answerable to no higher authority.

State. An established organization which exercises coercive authority over all the members of the society.

Statistics. A method of dealing with mass data to show their quantitative relationships.

Status. A person's position in a group with relation to other members of the group, or the position of a group with reference to other groups in some larger totality, particularly in terms of greater or less prestige, super-ordination-subordination, and such relationships.

Stereotype. A false idea or belief which regards all members of a group as having identical traits.

Stratification. A system in which economic and social privileges are distributed on a group basis. The caste system is one example of stratification.

Subsistence economy. A type of production in which the individual raises his own food and provides his own clothes and living quarters with little use of cash. Products are raised for home consumption rather than for sale.

Suburban. A term employed to describe a community or neighborhood on the periphery of a city, with peculiar characteristics which distinguish it both from rural and from urban localities.

Succession. Complete displacement of one group by another in a particular spatial area. It represents the process of invasion continued to a full turnover of the people and/or institutions in the area.

Suggestibility. The tendency to respond uncritically to a stimulus, without conscious control by the individual over the nature of the response.

Symbiosis. The process according to which two or more persons or groups live together in close physical proximity in some type of reciprocal, functional relationship. In human ecology it most frequently involves a relationship of mutual advantage.

Sympathetic contact. A contact between two or more persons characterized by a certain degree of mutual understanding and interest in the whole personality of the other.

Tecnicway. Social adjustment to technological change. In contrast to folkways and mores such adjustment occurs by deliberate rational choice within a short period of time and may be in contrast to customary behavior.

Technology. The sum total of knowledge skills and implements with which societies pattern their survival in the physical environment. The term is often extended to include techniques of organizing human relations as well.

Tolerance. An attitude of sympathetic acceptance of differences.

Toleration. A process in which parties to a conflict fail to reach a new level of agreement, but cease their conflict and maintain their unresolved differences.

Totalitarianism. An extreme degree of regulation of all types of institutional activity by certain modern states.

Urban. Referring to the town or city as distinguished from the farmlands or country area. In general, the larger a city is, the stronger are such urban characteristics as secondary group contacts, anonymity, heterogenous population, high social mobility, and specialization.

Urban ecology. The study of the spatial arrangements of people in urban areas, in relation to their environment.

Urban sociology. The study of urban people in their group relationships. It studies the characteristics of city people, their social organization and institutional activities, the basic interaction processes as they occur in urban life, the impact of social change on the city, and the various problems which confront urban society.

Value. The capacity to satisfy a human desire which is attributed to any object, idea, or content of experience.

Vested interests. In any particular social system characterized by stratification, there are always groups of people who are in positions of particular advantage which would be threatened by change. These groups are called vested interests.

Vice. Satisfaction of a biological or socially conditioned need of the organism in such a way as to do injury to the organism or to violate the mores of the society. Such patterns of satisfaction are usually cumulative, and often lead to the progressive disorganization of the personality.

Appendix A

THE HARDIE REPORT

Scope of Reform.

Except when a larger area is deemed absolutely essential for efficient production it is proposed that all land be redistributed which is beyond the capacity of one family to farm. This means that all farms owned by absentee proprietors would be subject to purchase and resale even though only a few hectares in size. Owners living on the land would be allowed to keep only the land they could care for with their own labor. The size of such farm units would vary in different regions from three to thirteen hectares with a Tenancy Commission empowered to make exceptions when these appeared to be vital for productive efficiency. Through these measures it is estimated that approximately 400,000 tenants (about 69% of the present number of tenant farmers) could acquire farms of their own.

This proposal is a sharp break from the previous emphasis on the very large estate. The report maintains that if land redistribution were restricted to very large estates, it would touch only a fraction of the total cultivated land and leave the problem largely unsolved. Also, it is felt that the tenant who rents from a small landlord may actually be in worse straits than one who lives in a large *hacienda*. In other words, tenancy is undesirable whether the landlord is a big hacendero with a large estate or a professional man in the city who owns only a few hectares.

Method of Payment.

In announcing a temporary slowing down in the purchase of large estates; President Quirino stressed the difficulty of getting government revenues sufficient to make such purchases. The Hardie report admit that current revenues are inadequate for large scale land purchases and suggests that landowners be paid in long term government bonds which would eventually be retired by the payment which former tenants make for the land.

Price Determination.

In the past, government land purchases have resulted in long negotiations between owners and government agencies which have required years to settle. Besides the time element, it is doubtful whether tenants could actually pay for land on the basis of existing prices. To meet these problems, it is suggested that a "price formula" be substituted for individual negotiations. This formula would be based on the fertility of the farm and the average level of farm prices over a period of years. It would also consider the ability of the tenant to pay and would be so designed that payments did not exceed thirty percent of the normal value of the farm production over a thirty year period.

Such a "price formula" would allow the landlords some compensation for their land, but the actual price would probably be somewhat less than they could get on the open market at the present time.

Method of Administration.

It is proposed that national, regional and local land commissions be established and empowered to administer the proposed reforms. Based on the Japanese experience with a similar project, it is expected that these commissions could accomplish the actual transfer of land ownership in two years time.

Other Proposals.

While the report advocates a drastic reduction in the amount of tenancy it does not envision its complete elimination, and a number of proposals are made for the regulation of land-lord-tenant relationships. It further recognizes that the tenant who becomes a farm owner still faces many problems and it makes a number of suggestions similar to those discussed under the heading of General Rural Improvement. Land redistribution is not regarded as a simple solution to agrarian troubles, but as a necessary part of the total program for rural reconstruction. (This summary is not taken verbatim from the report and represents only the text's appraisal of its most important features. The student should also read the report itself.)*

---

* Philippine Land Tenure Reform Analysis and Recommendations, Special Technical and Economic Mission, U.S. Mutual Security Agency, Manila, 1952.

Appendix B

NOTE ON MINORITY PEOPLES IN THE PHILIPPINES

The most distinct cultural differences between the majority of the populace and other groups are noticeable between the mountain tribes, the Moros and the rest of the population. The mountain tribes number about a half million people and the greatest concentration is found in the Mountain Province in central and northern Luzon, although scattered groups are found in other parts of the Philippines. The Moros number about three quarters of a million and are found mostly in Mindanao and Sulu. The most conspicuous type of difference from the majority group is found in religion since most of the mountain tribes follow an animistic type of worship while the Moros are Moslem. This religious difference is a manifestation of the fact that these peoples had resisted Spanish culture and hence are further removed from a western orientation than is true of the rest of the Philippines. The mountain tribesmen often prove amenable to missionary efforts and a considerable number have accepted Christianity. The Moros are deeply rooted in the Moslem faith and Christian missions have made few converts.

Offer differences from majority practices include the persistence of strong tribal governments (usually covering only a very small area) which control the lives of the people more than does the official governmental authority. Polygamy and divorce are usually tolerated although outlawed in the rest of the Philippines. Land titles are almost unknown and land ownership is based on oral tradition. A distinctive style of dress identifies the inhabitants. The Moros wear a style of flowing garment familiar in Moslem countries while the mountain tribesmen wear a scanty G string in the case of the men and a simple tapis (skirt) for the women. Styles are changing rapidly particularly in the case of the Moro men who now can often only be identified by a distinctive headgear.

Formal schooling is very popular in the rest of the country but is looked upon with suspicion by these groups and only a minority of their children attend school for an appreciable period of time. The elders fear, with some justification, that children attending school may be unfitted for tribal life since they sometimes lose their respect for their elders and become ashamed of the traditional types of work. Parents are particularly hostile to the education of girls and their attendance is much less than that of the boys.

The American regime feared that the minority groups might be exploited by the dominant part of the population and formed a Bureau of Non-Christian Tribes to safeguard minority interests. The general theory of the American regime was to maintain peace and order but to follow a policy of "attraction" rather than coercion. The policy of "attraction" was to gradually persuade the minority groups to follow western practices but to avoid a direct attack on native institutions and to work through local leaders and utilize local customs. While the Bureau hoped to lower the death rate and accelerate education and economic development, it tried to accomplish these aims without destroying the local culture.

The Commonwealth regime abolished the Bureau of Non-Christian Tribes but attempted no basic alterations in policy. In general, Filipino officials have sought to expand social services and education while refraining from drastic attempts to force assimilation. A high degree of tolerance for cultural differences is found in the provision exempting these groups from the operation of the Civil code. They are allowed to follow their own customary law and are exempted from the general prohibition of divorce and polygamy. This exemption from the general law is for a limited period but presumably will be renewed as long as sharp cultural differences persist.

The minorities do not live in isolation since the Ilocanos have penetrated many of the mountain areas while Visayan farmers and Chinese traders have entered Mindanao in large numbers. Law and order is not perfectly maintained since quarrels often break out between feuding groups of natives and also result from conflict between the natives and Christian settlers over land ownership. On the other hand, an increasing number of the native groups are being educated and a small middle class is developing which is assuming a political leadership. Villages in the mountain areas are usually governed by a council of the elders while the Moros follow the leadership of Datus (chiefs) who may have considerable authority over local areas. Several of the Moro datus have sent their sons to college and a considerable number of them have married Christian girls, although usually without making a break with Islam.

At the present time, the older patterns persist to a great extent among both the Moros and the mountain tribes although a process of change is discernible. Some evidence of strain appears in the mountain tribes between those who would conform to western culture and those who cling to the ancient ways; in the case of the Moros, the leadership of the educated group is dependent upon their maintaining the loyalty of the masses and this produces a closer degree of cooperation. The Moro datus are also finding an outlet as political leaders which tends to tie them into the greater Filipino community.

APPENDIX B 469

While most of the Christian Filipinos (term used here as a cultural rather than a spiritual label) disparage minority cultures, the government policy has been one of restraint and tolerance which should enable the minorities to develop along modern lines while still retaining a large part of their traditional cultures.

Appendix C

THE SCOPE OF SOCIOLOGY AND FIELDS OF SPECULATION

Comparatively speaking, sociology as a scientific discipline is rather young, but it has already attained the maturity of a full-grown life, considering the magnitude of its achievement and the vista of its future. An evidence of this may be shown in the following list which was developed by the American Sociological Society and presented to the Humanities and the Social Sciences sections of the American Councils of Learned Societies.[13] This list serves as a blue print regarding the scope of sociology and fields of specialization.

SOCIAL ORGANIZATION
    Community
    Social Stratification
    Institutions
    Social Structure
    Industrial
    Occupations
    Military
    Comparative
    Primitive

INTERPERSONAL RELATIONS
    Group Dynamics
    Small group analysis
    Leadership
    Sociometry
    Socialization

INTERGROUP RELATIONS
    Race and ethnic
    Labor-management
    International
    Religious

SOCIAL DISORGANIZATION
    Criminology
    Juvenile delinquency
    Drug addiction
    Prostitution
    Alcoholism
    Poverty and dependency

SOCIAL CHANGE
    Social control
    Social process
    Social movements
    Technological changes
    Social mobility

FAMILY
    Marriage and marital relations
    Parent-child relations
    Child development
    Consumer problems

RURAL-URBAN
    Rural
    Urban
    Community analysis
    Human ecology
    Regional studies

SOCIAL PSYCHOLOGY
    Personality development
    Personality and culture

---

[13] The office of the American Council of Learned Societies is located at 1219 Sixteenth Street, N. W., Washington 6, D.C.

Social psychiatry
Mental health
Collective behavior

PUBLIC OPINION AND COMMUNICATION
Public opinion measurement
Propaganda analysis
Market research
Mass communications
Attitude studies
Morale studies

APPLIED SOCIOLOGY
Penology and corrections
Regional and community planning
Marriage and family counseling
Human relations in industry
Personnel selection and training
Housing
Social legislation
Health and welfare
Problems of the aged
Recreation
Sociodrama and psychodrama
Youth and child welfare

AREA STUDIES
Latin America, Eastern Europe and USSR, Central Europe, Africa, Near East, Far East, Southeast Asia, Underdeveloped areas

POPULATION
Vital statistics
Internal migration
International migration
Labor force
Population characteristics
Population trends
Social biology

RESEARCH METHODOLOGY
Social Statistics

Survey methods
Experimental design
Research administration
Tests and measurements
Case study of life history
Content analysis

THEORY
Systematic
Comparative
History of theory
Social thought

INTERDISCIPLINARY SPECIALTIES
Educational sociology
Political sociology
Sociology of religion
Sociology of law
Sociology of knowledge
Sociology of science
Sociology of war
Sociology of art and literature
Sociology of medicine

RELATED SPECIALIZATIONS
Anthropology
Aesthetics
Archaelogy
Economics
Education
Fine Arts
Geography
History
Linguistics and Literature
Musicology
Political Science
Psychiatry
Psychology
Philosophy
Social Work
Statistics

Appendix D

TYPES OF AGENCIES WHICH EMPLOY SOCIOLOGY AND SOCIAL WORK MAJORS

It must be noted that the types of agencies listed below are more common in the United States, although their Philippine counterparts are steadily becoming more numerous.[14]

ADMINISTRATIVE AND FUND RAISING
  Council of Social Agencies
  Community Chests
  Social Service Exchange
  Welfare Council
  Minority Welfare Association Group

EMPLOYMENT PROBLEMS AGENCIES
  Workmen's Compensation Bureau
  Unemployment Works Relief Bureau
  Vocational Rehabilitation Bureau
  State Unemployment Bureau
  Unemployment Compensation Bureau
  Personnel Department
  Employment Office

PUBLIC ASSISTANCE AND PRIVATE ASSISTANCE AGENCIES
  County or City Home
  Department of Public Welfare
  Philippine Red Cross
  Salvation Army
  Shelters for Homeless
  Women's Bureau
  Homefinding Agency

DENOMINATIONAL SOCIAL SERVICES
  Catholic Charities
  Church Social Service Departments
  Protestant Charities, Missions

SOCIAL RESEARCH AGENCIES
  Intergroup Council
  Mayor's Committee on Intergroup Unity
  Public Opinion Research
  Educational Research
  Human Relations Studies
  Army Research Projects
  Morale Divisions
  Statistical and Research Divisions
  Research Councils
  Government Research Divisions

OLD AGE
  Pension Bureau
  Old Age and Survivor's Insurance Bureau
  Old People's Home
  Private Agencies Working with the Aged

GROUP WORK WITH YOUTH
  Boy and Girl Scouts
  Boy's and Girl's Clubs

---

[14] The next two lists are taken from Roucek and Warren, *op. cit.*, pp. 238-240.

APPENDIX D

Camp Fire Girls
Community and Neighborhood Center
Group Work Agencies
Department of Public Recreation, Parks and Playgrounds
Leisure Time Agencies
Y.M.C.A. and Y.W.C.A.
Youth Council, Nursery School
Settlement House

GROUP WORK WITH ADULTS
Department of Public Recreation
Leisure Time Agencies
Social Center
Parent Education Association
Settlement House

CHILD CARE AND PLACEMENT
Foster Home Placement or Adoption Agency
Aid to Dependent Children
Child Labor Bureau
Children's Agency
Children's Aid Societies
Day Nurseries
Health Association
School Social Service Departments

PHYSICALLY AND MENTALLY HANDICAPPED CHILDREN
Children with Retarded Mental Development
Crippled Children's Societies
Blind, Partially Seeing, Deaf, and Hard-to-Hearing Children
Children's Institutions

MENTAL HEALTH SERVICES FOR CHILDREN AND ADULTS
Children with Retarded Mental Development
Child Guidance Clinics
Diagnostic Clinics
Mental Hospitals
Mental Hygiene Clinics

Psychiatric Clinics
Veterans Administration
School Social Service Departments

JUVENILE DELINQUENCY AND CRIME
Prevention
Delinquency Prevention Association
Police Athletic Leagues
Children's Aid Socieities
Community Center
Juvenile Court
Juvenile Protective Association
Settlement House
Police Department
Probation Department

INSTITUTIONAL CARE OF DELINQUENTS
Juvenile Courts
Institutional and Reform Schools for Delinquent Children
Detention Homes, Reformatories
Other Correctional Institution

ADULT CRIMINAL OFFENDERS
Criminal Court
Parole Department
Parole Board
Penal Institutions
Police Department
Prisoner's Aid Society
Probation Department

MEDICAL CARE AGENCIES
Social Hygiene Clinic
Tuberculosis and Health Association
Disabled Veterans
Maternity Homes
Medical Social Service
Hospital Social Service

MISCELLANEOUS
Vocational Counseling and Rehabilitation
Marriage Counseling

Family Counseling
Goodwill Industries
Salvation Army
Teaching
Foreign Relief
Refugee Service
Immigration Aid
International Reconstruction Agencies
Public Housing Authority
Housing Projects
Financing Agencies and Poundations

INDUSTRIAL
Market Surveys
Advertising Research
Industrial Sociology
Industrial Social Welfare Workers

JOB TITLES FOR WHICH SOCIOLOGY IS AN APPROPRIATE UNDERGRADUATE MAJOR

Each occupational item in this list is followed with one or more numbers. These are code numbers and their corresponding meanings are stated in the footnote. These job titles, it will be noted, are definitive and specific so the student may be guided to make his choice for a particular position and the amount of training pertaining thereunto.

Employment Manager [2, 4]
Employment Interviewer [2]
Employment Clerk
Personnel Clerk
School Principal [2, 3]
Psychologist [1]
Vocational Examiner [2]
Personnel Counselor [2]
Mental Tester [1]
Welfare Director [3]
Manager, Personnel [4]
Manager, Floor [4]
Manager, Office [3]
Social Worker [2]
Social Group Worker [2]
Home Visitor [2]
Juvenile Court Worker [2]
Medical Social Worker [2]
Psychiatric Social Worker [1]
Traveller's Aid Worker
Welfare Investigator
Dean [1, 3]
College or University Teacher [1]
Grade or Grammar School Teacher [2]
Teacher Mentally Deficient [1]
Educational Supervisor, Penal Institution [2]
Educational Director [2, 4]
Registrar, College or University [2, 4]
Neighborhood Organizer [2]
Playground Director
Camp Director [4]
Recreation Director
Community Center Worker [2]
Camp Counselor
Occupational Therapist [2]
Community Service Worker [2]
School or College Director of Admissions [2]
Social Case Worker, Child Placement or Family [2]
Family Counselor [1]
Parole Officer [2]
Probation Officer [2]
Social Worker:
　Medical [1]
　Psychiatric [1]
　School [2]

APPENDIX D

Home Visitor [2]
Visting Teacher [2]
Case Work Supervisor [1, 3]
Research Supervisor [1, 3]

Research Assistant [2]
Community Research Organizer [1, 3]

---

[1] Requires extensive postgraduate study.
[2] Often requires some postgraduate study.
[3] Requires extensive working experience.
[4] Often requires some working experience.

NAME INDEX

Aguinaldo, L. R., 333, 349
Alip, Eufronio M., 69
Alzona, Encarnacion, 72
Bazaco, E., 207
Benedict, Ruth, 56, 57, 61
Benitez, Conrado, 224, 439
Beyer, H. Otley, 171, 192
Blair, Emma H., 210
Blumer, Herbert, 96, 117
Bodenhafer, W. B., 19
Bogardus, Emory S., 20, 178
Bowring, John, 163
Brayne, F. L., 234
Berry, Brewton, 170
Britt, Stewart H., 120
Burgess, Ernest W., 95, 107
Burma, John H., 188
Burnham, Daniel H., 283, 284
Castillo, Andres, 252
Castrence, Pura Santillan, 212
Catapusan, Benecio T., 187
Chase, Stuart, 5
Cheng, K'un Cheng, 187
Cole, Mabel, 51
Coller, Richard W., 243
Collier, John, 196
Comte, August, 437, 438
Colley, C. H., 21
Corpus, Severino F., 191
Costa, Horacio de la, 375, 376
Davis, Allison, 152
Davis, Kingsley, 82
de Young, John, 439
Du Bois, Cora, 154
Durkheim, Emile, 438
Eels, Kenneth, 130, 140
Eggan Fred, 197
Ellinger, Tage, U. H., 197
Ellwood, C. A., 22
Earnsworth, Paul R.,
Fauconnier, Henry, 211
Fonacier, Tomas S., 316
Folsom, Joseph K., 77
Francis, E. K., 444
Gillen, J. L. and Gillen J. P., 10, 15
Gist, Noel P., 268
Goldman, Irving, 50
Guazon, Mendoza, Maria Paz, 40
Halbert, L. A., 268
Halili, Fortunato, 333
Harper, E. B., 19
Hart, Hornell, 442, 443
Hauserman, John W., 347, 449
Hawely, Amos, 293, 295, 297, 301, 304, 319
Hayden, Joseph Ralsten, 145, 147, 148, 160, 219, 359
Hartshorne, Hugh, 226
Hayner, Norman S., 280
Heiser, Victor, 144
Hertskovitz, M. J., 15
Hertzler, Joyce O., 379
Hunt, Chester L., 191
Isidro, Antonio, 357, 395, 404
Jacoby, Erich H., 181, 393
Jimenez, Max., 332
Kalaw, Maximo M., 47
Katigbak, Maria, 421
Kennedy, Raymond, 386
Kinsey, Alfred, 152
Kpineburg, Otto, 39
Labens, Jean, 444
Landis, Paul H., 290, 299, 301, 319
La Piere, Richard T., 36
Lasker, Bruno, 331
Laubach, Franck Charles, 184, 210
Lawes, Lewis E., 428
Laya, J. C., 46, 212, 393, 394, 409
Leclerq, Jacques, 79
LeRoy, James A., 140, 211, 219
Linton, Ralph, 11
Locsin, Teodoro, 399
Lubin, Isador, 353

Macaraig, Serafin E., 97, 98, 133, 140, 145, 296, 300, 301, 438
Manuel, Arsenio E., 192
Marx, Karl., 158, 150
Masa, J. O., 250
Matela, Arcadio G., 396, 397
Mayo, Elton, 334
Mayo, Katherine, 212
McHale, Thomas R., 183, 329
McKenzie, R. D., 281
Mead, Margaret, 40
Meeker, Marcia, 130, 140
Mendoza, M. G., 402
McMillan, Robert T., 239
Miller, Nathan, 383
Moore. Wilbert E., 339
Murdock, Geo P. ,41
Nakpil, Carmen Guerrero, 53-56
Nimkoff, Meyer F., 104, 136, 299, 305
Ogburn, William, 3, 104, 136, 305
Orata, Pedro, 396
Osias, Camilo, 46, 204
Panlasigui, Isidoro, 398
Paraiso, Virginia, 421, 424
Park, Robert E., 13, 95, 107, 438, 446
Pelzer, Karl J., 143, 359, 360, 362
Perez, Asuncion, 424
Prator, Clifford H., 177, 405, 407
Purcell, Victor, 192
Puyat, Gonzalo, 333, 344
Queen, Stuart A., 19
Quezon, Manuel, 147, 219
Reuter, E. B., 441
Rivera, Generoso F., 239
Rivera, Vicente, Jr., 261
Rizal, Jose, 44-47

Robertson, James A., 210
Rodriguez, Fe, 194
Rose, Arnold, 178
Roucek, Joseph S., 440, 443, 444
Rotz, H. Wilton, 255, 256
Santiago, Cayetano, 421
Serquina, Conrado A., 343
Singer, H. W., 326
Small, Albion W., 438, 441
Soriano, Andres, 349
Stander, Golda, 424
Sumner, William Graham, 384, 412
Sutherland, R. L., 100, 114
Sycip, Albino, 349
Taeuber, Irene, 295
Tangco, Marcelo, 172, 192
Tan, V. A., 24
Tawney, R. H., 207
Teodoro, Toribio, 332, 349
Tolentino, Arturo M., 239
Tonnies, F., 25
Thomas, William I., 251
Thompson, Warren, 293, 294, 297, 304
Troeltsch, Ernest, 207
Tylor, E. B., 2
Veblen, 272
Warner, W. Lloyd, 130, 140,
Warren, Roland L., 440, 443, 444
Weightman, George, 194, 310
Weber, Max, 207
Wiggam, Albert Edward, 436
Woodbury, Robert, 148
Woodward, J. L., 100, 114
Woody, Thomas, 382, 411
Yorro, Dionisio K., 136
Young, Kimball, 111, 117
Znaniecki, Florian, 251

SUBJECT INDEX

Aglipayan, Social Distance, 159, 160; Origin, 215, 216
American Class System, 133, 134, 138, 139
American and Filipino Contacts, 184-189
American-Philippine Guardian Association, 186
Applied Science, 445
Augustine, Statement on Prostitution, 79
Beggars, as Social Work Problem, 414
Boys Town, 430, 431
Baclaran Church, 119
Barong Tagalog, 52
Bontoc Family, 62, 63
Case Work, 416, 417
Catholicism and Sociology, 444
City Planning, 283, 284
Class, Nature of Social Class, 130, 131; Varieties of Class Structure by National areas, 132-134; Philippine Class Structure, 134-137; Class and Caste, 137-140; Categories of Social Class in Philippines, 140-142; Cacique System, 142, 144; Class Structiore of Minorities, 145, 146; Behavior and Class Status, 146-153, Dynamics of Class structure, 153-158; Class Struggle, 158-160; Development of Filipino Middle Class, 144, 145, 330, 331
Chinese, Family, 89; As a Commercial Middle Class, 157, 158; Social Distance, 174, 175; Intermarriage, 182, 183, 192, 193; Immigration, 308, 310; Economic Role, 310, 311

Collective Bargaining. See Labor Unions
Community Schools, 243
Communism and Agrarian Revolt, 372-376
Colorum Uprising, 160
Community Chest, 424-426
Cottage Industries, 253
Community Organization, 417, 418
Court of Industrial Relations, 344
Chicago Family, 64-66
Civil Code and Family Roles, 72
Crowd, Crowds and Culture, 101, 102; Circular Interaction and milling, 99, 100; Conventional Crowd, 97; Acting Crowd, 97, 98; Expressive Crowd, 98, 99; Casual, 96, 97; Conventional, 97
Craze, 120
Cultural Pluralism, 170; Future of Cultural Pluralism in Philippines, 193-199
Culture, patterns, 12; culture change, 14, 15, 16; culture and individual differences, 44, 46; culture area, 13, 14
Cycle of group relation, 170, 171
Death Penalty, 427, 428
Drinking in rural areas, 251
Deviant Behavior, 28, 29
Divorce, 80
Ecclesia, 208, 209
EDCOR, 366
Education, sociological viewpoint, 379-382; primitive education, 385-387; American policies, 387-389; appraisal of Filipino education, 392-394; professional emphasis, 394-398; diploma mills, 398-404, language problems,

479

404-408; Community schools 408, 409
Ethnocentrism, 27
English Language as Communication Media, 124, 125
Ethnic, distinguished from Racial, 165-167; ethnic conflict, 167, 168; segregation, 168, 160; assimilation and amalgamation, 169, 190-193; ethnic composition of Philippines, 171, 172; economic basis of ethnic pattern 178, 179
Fad, 120
Fashions, 120, 121
Filipino Family, courtship, 69-71; 90, 91; authority, 71-74; size of family 74, 75; religion 75-77, conflict, 82-85; security, 85, conservatism, 86, 87; civic participation, 87, 88; economic influence, 88-90; rural family, 240, 241; Urban family, 268-270; welfare function, 419, 420, 421
Fiestas, 250
Folkways, 5, 6
Fortune magazine, 134
Group Work, 417
Geographic Factors in Social Life, 39-44
Hardie Report, 371, 372
Health and Medical Care, in rural area, 246-248
Herbolario, 248
Hilot, 248
Hindu Caste System, 137, 138
Hukbalahap, 160, 356, 357
Ifugao, struggle for status, 49, 50; caste system, 138, 139
Iglesia Ni Kristo, social distance, position, 174, 175; description, 216, conflict, 223.
Identification, 33
Industrial Sociology, 334, 335
Illegitimacy, 79, 80
Ilocanos, family cooperation, 89
Inquilino, 363

Imitation, 31
Jews, social distance, position, 176
Jungle Philosopher on Mechanization, 367, 368
Kasama, 363
Landlord-tenant Relationships, Pre-Spanish Pattern, 359, 360; Proportion of tenancy, 362; Land titles, 361; Current tenancy practices, 363-365; Tenancy Legislation, 365, 366
Labor Unions, 339-345
Language Differences, 172, 173, 404-408
Land Settlement, 367
Literacy, Southeast Asian Countries, 386; Philippines, 403
Lipa City, 119
Manila, Family, 63, 64; City Planning, 283, 284
Malayan Religion, 211
Marginal man, 53-56, 254
Marital Adjustment, 80, 81
Mass Interaction, 117, 118; Example of Mass interaction at Lipa City and Baclaran Church, 119, 120
Medical Training, 402
Mestiza Dress, 52
Methodist Social Creed, 229
Mores and Law, 7, 8, 9
Moslem, law, 207; Philippine origin 218
Motion Picture Coverage, 125; in rural areas, 249
Magsaysay, as defense secretary, 365
Masons, 65, 224
Mechanization of Agriculture, 367-369
Medical Social Work, 415, 416
Middle Class Development in Philippines, 144, 145; 330, 331
Mindanao, Migration from other areas, 317
Moros, 146
NAMFREL, 257
Negritos, 51

SUBJECT INDEX 481

National Economic Council, 126
Negro and White, Comparison by intelligence, 29; Social Distance, Position, 174, 175
Newspaper and Magazine Circulation, 122, 125; In the rural areas, 249
Parole, 428, 429
Paternalism in Industries, 336-338
Philippine Rural Community Improvement Society, 257
Philippine Rural Reconstruction Movement, 257
Population, Philippine, birth rate, 296-300; death rate, 300-302; life expectancy, 302-304; population distribution, 305-307; population movement, 308-318; age composition, 318, 319; population pressure, 320
Pure Science, 445
Protestants, Social Distance Position, 175; Philippine Development, 217
Pre-Christian Survivals, 210-213; 244, 245
Paganism. See Pre-Christian Survivals
Philippine traits, 46-47
Polo, Bulacan, 26
Prejudice and its cultural setting, 176, 177
Probation, 428, 429
Propaganda, origin of term, 111; devices, 111, 113; limitations of propaganda, 114, 115
Prostitution, 78, 79
Public, defined, 102, 103; and communication, 104
Public Opinion, and social interaction, 107, 108; and research, 108, 109
Public School Enrollment, 122
Purok, 239
Querida System, 79
Resistance to change in rural areas, 255, 256

Red Cross, 416, 422
Roman Catholic, Social Distance Position, 174, 175; Community Cooperation, 222-224; Foreign Influence, 216, 217; Social Teachings, 229
Religion and Social Life, 204, 208; Effects of Urbanization, 213-215, Philippine Church Membership, 215, 216; Religious Pluralism 218-220, 226-227; Religion and education, 220, 226-228; Legislation and Religion, 221; social policies, 229-231; rural religion, 244-246
Radion Stations, 126, radion coverage in rural areas, 249
Roads, 125
Rural Government, 238, 29
Rural Schools, 241-243
Schurman Commission, 38
Social Legislation, 338-339
Sect, 208, 209
Sakdals, 160, 358, 359
Social Welfare Administration, 424
Sympathy, 32
Suggestion, 32
Sacred and Secular Societies, 25, 26
Sexual Division of Labor, 39-42
Social Distance, 173-176
Southeast Asia, Ethnic Stratification, 179-182; Changes in Agriculture, 354-355; Population Changes, 294-296
Spanish, class system, 133; social position, 136; intermarriage with Filipinos, 182, 183
Stereotype, 115-117
Shipping in Philippines, 126
Stratification by Ethnic Groups in Philippines, 182-184, 189, 190
Switzerland, Ethnic Relations, 152, 153, 193
Tayug outbreak, 160
Telegraph Stations, 126

Telephones, 126
Urban, Growth in Philippines, 263, 264; Social Relationships, 264, 268; Family Life, 268-270; Birth Rate, 272, 273; Ecology, 276-282
Welfareville, 422, 423
Wood, Gov. General Leonard W., Interest in Social Welfare, 186